PUBLIC SPEAKING

JOHN K. BRILHART
Southwest Missouri State University

JOHN S. BOURHIS
Southwest Missouri State University

BONNIE R. MILEY
Iowa Western Community College

CHARLENE A. BERQUIST
Southwest Missouri State University

■ HarperCollins*Publishers*

Sponsoring Editor: Melissa A. Rosati
Development Editor: Anne Boynton-Trigg
Project Editor: Melonie Parnes
Design Supervisor: Jaye Zimet
Text and Cover Design: Circa 86
Photo Researcher: Carol Parden
Production Manager/Assistant: Willie Lane/Sunaina Sehwani
Compositor: Ruttle, Shaw & Wetherill, Inc.
Printer and Binder: R. R. Donnelley and Sons Company
Cover Printer: New England Book Components, Inc.

For permission to use copyrighted material, grateful acknowledgment is made to the copyright holders on p. 393, which is hereby made part of this copyright page.

Practical Public Speaking

Library of Congress Cataloging-in-Publication Data

Practical public speaking / John K. Brilhart . . . [et al.].
    p. cm.
  Includes index.
  ISBN 0-06-040995-9
  1. Public speaking.   I. Brilhart, John K.
PN4121.P68   1991
808.5′1—dc20   91-21479
                                                            CIP

    92 93 94   9 8 7 6 5 4 3 2

CONTENTS

PREFACE

Practical Public Speaking began several years ago during a conversation between two of the authors who were dissatisfied with what they found in pubic-speaking textbooks: a high degree of dependence on tradition; inadequate use of rhetorical principles emerging from social, cognitive, and educational psychology; the idea that the purpose of speaking should be described as what the speaker would do rather than as response behaviors of listeners; and the concept that a speech is "delivered" (like a letter or package) rather than being created while engaging in a transactional process with listeners. We had spent many years clarifying our beliefs and practices, both as teachers and in extensive speaking outside the classroom. The authors collectively have approximately 75 years experience teaching basic public-speaking courses in high schools, community colleges, four-year colleges, and universities. We wanted to share with other teachers of public speaking what we had found to be valid and practical in our experience and observations as public speakers, teachers, and consultants. From this background, *Practical Public Speaking* was conceived.

▶ Distinguishing Characteristics

(1) We have applied the accepted belief that public speaking should be audience centered rather than just speaker or message centered more consistently than most textbooks. We believe that the purpose of speaking should be stated as an observable response from specific listeners, not in terms of what the speaker intends to do.

(2) We wanted to emphasize the sequential procedure required in preparing to speak extemporaneously in a way that encourages freedom from other than the briefest of notes for short speeches.

(3) Throughout we have depended heavily on examples from the students we have known. The best of these examples are realistic *models* with which we think students can identify more readily than with such great public

figures as Dr. Martin Luther King, Jr., President Kennedy, Prime Minister Churchill, or Citizen Demosthenes.

(4) We think no other book has made adequate use of research and theory in disciplines other than rhetoric. We are not acquainted with all such writing, but we have drawn heavily on cognitive and educational psychology. For example, no other public-speaking text has tapped Bloom's seminal work in developing a taxonomy of objectives for instructing (of which public speaking is often a major part) or much of the extensive research in perception and memory.

(5) Like most instructors of public speaking, we no longer accept the dictum that we are "just teachers of rhetoric and not responsible for what our students do with the principles of this amoral art." Insofar as possible, we feel it our duty to produce good citizens who can speak well, not just good speakers. Teachers of how to exert power through speech should be known for teaching ethical behavior. So we have included a chapter about the morality essential for a democratic community to exist (Chapter 2). *Practical Public Speaking* is one of the very few public-speaking textbooks with a chapter devoted entirely to the ethics of public speaking. The source of this morality is distinctly humanistic, yet it is congruent with teachings of the major religions with which we are familiar.

(6) We felt that there was a need to clarify what audience analysis involves. While other books emphasize demographic analysis, they do not explain how to use it to make inferences about listeners' knowledge, beliefs, attitudes, and perspectives toward the speaker and subject.

(7) Outlining requires a high level of cognitive development, a major challenge for some of our students. We provide a clear introduction, without oversimplifying, by using analogies to computer programs and other precise analytic and synthetic procedures.

(8) Speakers frequently need and use a variety of types of sensory aids to complement and give meaning to their words. However, most public-speaking textbooks are limited almost entirely to *visual* aids. We have placed more emphasis on the idea of inputs through any or all sensory organs, not just the eyes, as supplements to speaking. To do this, we have provided examples of speakers using sound, taste, texture, activity (kinesthesia), smell, and other sensory aids.

(9) Although many books about public speaking stress both speaking to inform and to persuade, several colleagues have argued that such a distinction is artificial and unrealistic. We agree that responses of different listeners may be classifiable as changes in belief or as being limited to demonstrated understanding of the same speech. We think the distinction between speaking to inform and to persuade is useful, as explained in Chapters 4 and 14.

(10) Our chapter devoted to speaking to persuade, Chapter 15, is long on "theory" and endnotes. Why? A book with the term *practical* in its title should stress practical applications, should it not? We do not expect many students to use all of the theory we have included in their classroom speeches. However, we think good theory is highly practical, in this case as intellectual

armor or a set of templates with which to judge what people who try to influence are doing. We want to inoculate students against would be persuaders whose arguments and tactics cannot stand the scrutiny of critical thinking. Also, we should not oversimplify what is known today about how to persuade. We hope you and your students will stick with this chapter because of its special importance in a world where *caveat emptor* is a motto listeners forget at great risk. In a recent article in *Communication Education,*[1] Mike Allen and Raymond W. Preiss pointed out that there are differences among public-speaking textbooks that many teachers do not recognize. Using meta-analysis to evaluate the congruence of chapters about speaking to persuade with research findings, they found major differences among the books, differences that many instructors were apparently unaware of. We are pleased that a draft of Chapter 15 from this book was included in their analysis and stood up to the test of that analysis better than any text in print.

(11) We believe that speaking impromptu should be a component of a basic public-speaking course. Every person needs the freedom gained by knowing how to rise in a public gathering to speak with confidence, clarity, and conciseness about some unanticipated issue of personal concern. We have made a direct adaptation of the procedure for preparing to speak extemporaneously to speaking impromptu.

(12) We do not usually include anything about small-group communication in the public-speaking courses we teach, but we know that many colleagues do. We've intentionally focused on speaking and listening in small groups rather than trying to give a watered-down version of a course in small-group communication. If you include a unit about communicating as a group member, we think our Chapter 17 has a focus you will find much more appropriate and manageable than most.

▶ Structure of the Book

Part I, "Orientation to Practical Public Speaking," is planned to orient the student to a collegiate-level study of public speaking. After showing the practicality of the course, public speaking is explained as purposeful communicating rather than display or an art form. The student is given an overview of a procedure for speaking extemporaneously both to preview detailed study of method and principles and to guide preparation of early speeches. Speaker responsibility (ethics) is addressed next, followed by listening to public speeches. After these basic foundations, the process of preparing to speak extemporaneously is taken up in detail in the next two parts: "Analysis of the Elements of the Speech Event" and "Creating the Message." Part IV is devoted

---

[1] Mike Allen and Raymond W. Preiss, "Using Meta-Analysis to Evaluate Curriculum: An Examination of Selected College Textbooks," *Communication Education* 38 (April 1990):103–115.

to a more intensive study of "Common Types of Speech Situations," including speaking to inform, to persuade, impromptu, and in more specialized situations. Instructors can assign chapters in other sequences without serious loss of understanding by readers.

▶ Pedagogical Aids

Practical Public Speaking incorporates numerous aids for the student, many of which can be used in the classroom.

1. Each chapter begins with a content outline, a set of study and review questions (written to fit into the familiar SQ3R technique of study), and a list of key terms that the students should be able to define and use when study has been completed.

2. Line art has been employed to illustrate concepts and processes throughout the book.

3. The importance of extemporaneous speaking in the professional world is highlighted with boxed quotations from public figures.

4. Emphasis on the research base for rhetorical principles is achieved with research notes.

5. Each chapter ends with a variety of learning activities, from which instructor and student can select to develop and test understandings and skills.

6. Numerous examples from student speeches and some from other sources are given to help relate abstract principles to the ongoing world.

7. Speech transcriptions and outlines are provided for study and analysis, both within selected chapters and in the appendix.

8. Also included is a comprehensive glossary to which the student can refer for help when some key term has been momentarily forgotten.

Supplements

The book is accompanied by an *Instructor's Manual* providing samples of syllabi (including schedules and attendance and grading policies), instructional objectives, lists of supplementary bibliographic and instructional media sources, transparency masters, additional learning activities, forms for responding to student speeches, and a bank of test questions from which the instructor can draw. Videos are available from HarperCollins.

► Acknowledgments

The authors accept responsibility for the published manuscript of *Practical Public Speaking*. However, we cannot accept credit for all that it represents. We are indebted to many persons for the completed form of this work.

First, we express appreciation to family members and friends who accepted our apparent addictions to desks, typewriters, and computers and in many ways supported our efforts.

Second, we thank the numerous reviewers who have so conscientiously studied, evaluated, and proposed improvements in the manuscripts: John K. Heavilin, Indiana Wesleyan University; Roger Dale Smitter, North Central College; Samuel P. Wallace, University of Dayton; John Lucaites, Indiana University; Gwenn Schultze, Portland Community College, Rock Creek Campus; Lois J. Eihorn, State University of New York, University Center at Binghamton; James J. Jones, Villanova University; Dan B. Curtis, Central Missouri State University; Jeffrey C. Hahner, Pace University; Lawrence J. Rifkind, Georgia State University; David Ballard, Miami University, Middletown Campus; Richard P. Haven, University of Wisconsin, Whitewater; Mark Schaefermeyer, Virginia Polytechnic Institute and State University; Benjamin Sevitch, Central Connecticut State University; Jeanne Dunphy, Los Angeles City College; Jerry Ferguson, South Dakota State University; Ralph Dowling, Ball State University; Jerry Goldberg, Pace University; Jerry L. Winsor, Central Missouri State University; E. Sam Cox, Central Missouri State University; John P. Hart, Northeast Missouri State University; Karen Foss, Humboldt State University; Donald Williams, University of Florida; Jon Winterton, University of Colorado at Denver; E. Joseph Lamp, Anne Arundel Community College; Sujanet Mason, Luzerne County Community College; David Lawless, Tulsa Junior College; Jerry Agent, Hinds Community College; Theresa Rogers, New Community College of Baltimore; Marvin Lowery, Daytona Beach Community College; Steven Grant, Florida Community College; Carol Wallace, University of Scranton.

One reviewer was extraordinarily helpful—Professor John K. Heavilin of Indiana Wesleyan University. We were impressed with the thoroughness of his criticisms of an intermediate draft and asked that he continue to work with us. John consented and helped us make many improvements in the manuscript.

Third, we acknowledge a great debt to the instructors, mentors, colleagues, and students who have provoked the thinking that led to this book. We could not name all we remember without greatly extending this preface, and we would almost certainly forget to mention some people from whom we benefitted greatly.

We very much appreciate the professional assistance provided by personnel of HarperCollins. We are especially grateful for the clarity and thoroughness of the developmental editing supplied by Anne Boynton-Trigg and for her support when our spirits were down.

Finally, we are grateful to the numerous students and publishers who gave permission to use speeches and excerpts. Without them, this book would be vague indeed.

Jack Brilhart
John Bourhis
Bonnie Miley
Charlene Berquist

PART 1

Orientation to Practical Public Speaking

Public Speaking in Human Affairs

Questions to Guide Reading and Review

1. Why is it important for you to become an effective public speaker?
2. What are the seven major components of a public-speaking event? What are the characteristics of each component?
3. How do these components function together during the transactional process called *communication*?
4. What are some of the reasons why students fear public speaking? What can you do to help minimize this common fear?
5. What are the four methods commonly used for preparing and speaking in public? How do these methods differ from one another? What are the advantages and disadvantages of each method?
6. What is the purpose of each of the three major phases in the procedure for preparing yourself to speak? What is accomplished during each phase?
7. What are the nine steps in preparing to speak? What is accomplished during each step?

Key Terms

Audience
  Captive
  Voluntary
Channel
Extemporaneous

Feedback
Impromptu
Listener
Message

Noise
Signal
Situation
Transactional process

▶ Why Study Public Speaking?

"Why should I study public speaking?" Perhaps you are studying public speaking by choice because you realize how important it will be to your personal and professional life. You might be required to demonstrate proficiency in public speaking in order to complete a degree at your university. Maybe an advisor recommended public speaking because it will make you more market-able as a college graduate. Whatever your reason for studying public speaking, you have made an excellent choice. The study of public speaking is one of the best investments you can make in your future.

The ability to communicate your thoughts and feelings effectively to others is the single most important skill you can learn. This ability will directly affect your success in everything you pursue: school, career, and family. Because you will be asked to make speeches throughout your career, no other skill is more practical or important than public speaking. Consider the following examples:

John Crabin, DDS, was invited to speak to an organization of parents on the subject of hypnosis in dentistry. John's reaction: "I turned them down. I'm no public speaker. I couldn't face all those folks." John had decided early, "I'm going to be a dentist. I don't need to study public speaking while I am a student." By choosing not to speak, Dr. Crabin missed a wonderful opportunity to allay superstitions about hypnosis. He might also have gained patients who could have benefited from his use of hypnosis.

Tom Walman, a carpenter, belongs to several dog clubs. He frequently has to report at gatherings of from 12 to 50 or more people. Often his listeners are confused, alienated, or bored. In the past, Tom had thought, "I'm a carpenter—I don't need to study public speaking!" However, on several occasions Tom has asked one of the authors of this book, "How do I get them to understand me?"

Brenda Wilson found that much of her time as a nurse was spent explaining and soothing. When Brenda realized that she wanted to communicate her beliefs about her work, she found herself hesitant to face any group. So she studied public speaking and enrolled in an assertiveness training course. Twice she has served as president of her national nursing association, has taught numerous workshops on communicating as a nurse, and has even taught surgeons about communicating with patients and other medical personnel.

One of your goals in attending college is to secure an enjoyable and rewarding job. A survey of members of the American Institute of Plant Engineers found that "the art of effective communication" was the highest ranked professional interest item, followed closely by "effective presentation techniques."[1] A number of national surveys have consistently demonstrated that communication skills, in particular, public speaking, are the most important skills necessary for obtaining employment and successful job performance.[2] Public-speaking skills are essential to securing a desirable position and succeeding in it.

▶ **The Ten Most Important Factors in Helping Graduating College Students Obtain Employment**

1. Oral (speaking) communication skills.
2. Listening ability.
3. Enthusiasm.
4. Written communication skills.
5. Technical competence.
6. Appearance.
7. Poise.
8. Work experience.
9. Resume.
10. Specific degree held.

Source: Dan Curtis, Jerry Winsor, and Ronald Stephens, "National Preferences in Business and Communication Education," *Communication Education* 38 (January 1989): 11.

Kathleen Kendall asked people residing in predominantly blue-collar neighborhoods the following question: "In the past two years how many times have you spoken to a group of ten or more people at once?" About half the respondents had made such speeches, and nearly a third had spoken four or more times to public audiences in the preceding two years. In addition, Kendall found a strong association between level of educational attainment and the frequency of speech making. The more education one has, the more likely that person will be asked to speak.[3] Your study of public speaking will prepare you to speak with poise, confidence, and effectiveness.

More and more universities are requiring graduates to demonstrate proficiency in oral communication. This requirement is based on the philosophy that well-educated people can effectively communicate their thoughts and feelings to others. College graduates should be able to share knowledge and to lead fellow citizens toward responsible goals. Doing so requires effectiveness as a public speaker.

Oral communication proficiency will also enable you to evaluate the persuasive attempts of others. You constantly receive messages from sources wanting you to buy, donate, cooperate, give, endorse, sign, or boycott. "Vote for me," urges one politician, "I'm the candidate who will lower your taxes." The opponent claims "A vote for my opponent is a vote for higher taxes." "Our organization needs your support." "Stop studying for that test and come to the game with me." People are constantly trying to get you to believe and act in their best interests, not necessarily yours. As intelligent and concerned members of society, we must be able to detect fraud, unmask the unsubstantiated claim, see past sensationalism, and point out the lie. Your study of public speaking will enable you to be an effective advocate in your own right. More importantly, you will learn how to evaluate the persuasive efforts of others who attempt to manipulate you to act or think in a certain way.

▶ Public Speaking as Communication

To understand what happens when you speak in public, you first need a model of the process of human communication. One way to begin the study of a complex phenomenon such as public speaking is to name and describe its component parts, then to consider how these parts influence each other. Figure 1.1 represents both the components and the process in which they interact.

The Components of Public-Speaking Events

Seven major components can be identified in any public speaking event: (1) speaker, (2) message, (3) channels, (4) listeners, (5) response signals, (6) noise, and (7) situation.

SPEAKER   During public speaking a speaker creates a primary message called a *speech*. The speaker has information, attitudes, experiences, and activities that he or she wants to share with others. The speaker's message begins as an idea or mental image of reality, a personal perception existing in his or her mind. This image is the result of the speaker's interaction with the world of experiences and with other people. Personal awareness cannot be shared directly with another person. The speaker must translate personal experience into signals that can be carried through available channels to the intended listener of the message. This process of translation is called *encoding*.

MESSAGE   The *message* includes both the speaker's planned verbal and non-verbal symbols and unplanned, uncontrolled *signals*. The speaker's outline, note cards, or manuscript contain elements of the intended verbal message.

7

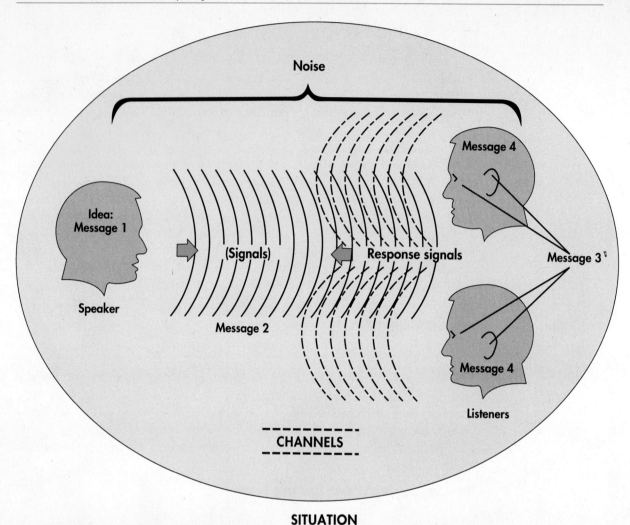

SITUATION

Figure 1.1   A model of the communication process during a public-speaking event.

The speaker also consciously attempts to send nonverbal signals such as facial expressions and hand gestures to enhance the verbal message being shared with the listeners. These nonverbal signals are at least equal in importance to the verbal signals in determining the impact of the message upon any listener. Nonverbal signals include posture, dress, gestures, facial expressions, voice cues, and personal grooming. How could a speaker send the following messages nonverbally?

"I am sincere in my concern for this issue."
"There is no time to waste; we must act now!"
"Trust me; I know what I am talking about."

Sometimes unintentional, nonverbal signals are transmitted that are coun-

> *A great deal of the ability to project the proper business image depends on a person's skill at speaking effectively. When I say effectively I mean speaking in such a manner as to achieve clear, crisp, relaxed, and thoughtful verbal communication.*
>
> *To effectuate such successful verbal communication it is necessary not only to be able to control exactly what you say, but how you say it.*
>
> Source: Norman King, *The First Five Minutes* (New York: Prentice–Hall, 1987). (Mr. King is chairman of the board of American Marketing Complex, Inc. He is one of the foremost media and marketing consultants.)

terproductive to the goals of the speaker. For instance, consider how a speaker might unintentionally send each of the following messages:

"I am really nervous about being poorly prepared."
"I really do not care about my topic."
"I don't know what I'm talking about. You'd be foolish to trust me."

When messages like these are perceived by listeners, whether intentional or unintentional, they can minimize everything else the speaker does to achieve a stated goal.

"Message" is not a simple, unitary concept. In any public speaking event there are at least four messages:

1. The message in the mind of the speaker.
2. The message consisting of all the signals shared by the speaker with the listeners.
3. The message consisting of the signals actually perceived by the listeners.
4. The message consisting of the meanings given to those perceived signals by a specific listener.

Each listener will assign a somewhat different meaning to each message. The successful speaker recognizes how complex messages can be and learns how to adapt to this complexity.

CHANNELS *Channel* refers to the medium or media in which signals are transferred from speaker to listeners. As authors, we are creating signals in written form for a print channel of communication. Print relies on light as a channel for transmitting messages. As a speaker, you rely on air waves as a channel to convey signals from your speech apparatus (lungs, larynx, mouth, tongue, lips, etc.) and on light waves to carry signals from your body as you move, gesture, and display visual aids. Other channels you might rely on for communication include those used by mass media (e.g., radio, television, newspapers, film), touch (e.g., a pat on the back, a gentle brush of shoulders, a handshake), and radiation (heat energy).

How a message comes to us is an important component of the message. A proposal of marriage sent in a letter would be perceived and responded to differently than an oral marriage proposal. A story read in a newspaper may be given more credibility than if told to us by an acquaintance. Visual images of the Persian Gulf War broadcast on the evening news had a greater impact on the American public than stories that appeared in leading newspapers. Each channel has advantages and limitations. The effective speaker takes the available channels into account when planning messages.

Face-to-face public speaking is the most personal and direct way to communicate with an audience. A speaker on radio or television encounters channel limitations not imposed on a speaker before a live audience. Only the public speaker has the advantage of immediate responses of listeners when presenting a carefully planned message. Effective speakers exploit the intimacy and immediacy of this face-to-face contact to enhance their messages.

LISTENERS   *Listeners* who receive and respond to a speaker's signals form the audience. Each listener comes to the speech event with somewhat different knowledge and experience, beliefs, ways of thinking, interests, and needs relevant to the speaker's message. Even though an audience may appear to be homogeneous, differences among the listeners always affect how they participate in the public-speaking event.

Audiences may be either *captive* or *voluntary*. Captive audience members have little choice but to be present. However, they may choose not to listen to the spoken message. For example, employees are sometimes compelled to attend a company safety or product demonstration. The students in your public-speaking class are a captive audience. Your classmates did not come to class because they are interested in the topic you are speaking about; they are probably required to attend on days when others are speaking. Voluntary audiences are composed of persons who choose to attend and are predisposed to listen carefully. Knowing that an audience is captive or voluntary should be taken into account when planning a message.

RESPONSE SIGNALS   Audience members are constantly doing something, if only sitting quietly, smiling, or taking notes during someone's speech. Some audience member behaviors, especially movements and sounds, become signals in the channels of communication. When these behaviors are reactions to what a speaker has done they constitute response signals. Listeners might scratch their heads or make confused facial expressions while a speaker is explaining the process of nuclear fusion. They might lean forward, rise from their seats, or squint their eyes as the speaker displays a particular visual aid. They might frown, shake their heads "no," or mumble something under their breath when the speaker proposes a solution to increasing tuition costs. These response signals can be perceived and adjusted to by the speaker. The speaker can reexplain a point that is confusing, adjust a visual aid so it can be seen more easily, or modify a position. These response signals can also be perceived and responded to by other listeners in the audience. For example, one listener applauds loudly at the end of a speech and is joined by the rest of the audience.

NOISE *Noise* refers to signals in a communication circuit that interfere with the signals sent intentionally by the speaker. Noise signals are like weeds that rob nourishment from desired plants. Similarly, noise interferes with the effectiveness of intentionally produced signals.

Interfering signals can produce noise anywhere in a communication circuit. A speaker who stutters excessively, wears a T-shirt with a verbal message irrelevant to the topic, or speaks in accents unfamiliar to listeners is creating noise that may interfere with the impact of the intentionally created signals. Other examples of noise include the siren on a passing police car, loud laughter in the hallway outside the classroom, flickering of lights, the annoying odor of fresh paint, hard seats, or extreme heat in the room. Noise can also originate within the listener from aching back muscles, concern about an upcoming test, hunger, exhaustion, or concern about a personal problem.

It is important to anticipate potential sources of noise before you speak. You can then plan how to eliminate or reduce sources of noise you can control and how to overcome those you cannot. For example, a speaker might rearrange furniture in a room, remove distracting pictures from the walls, erase a chalkboard, speak loudly enough to overcome noise in the background, and verbally emphasize the benefits to be gained from listening to the speech.

SITUATION *Situation* refers to the entire context in which speaker and listeners join in a communication circuit. All communication occurs within a specific situation. The situation has a tremendous impact upon the form and content of our speaking. Contextual components include the room, the reason for meeting, listener expectations about the occasion, events happening in the immediate past or foreseeable future, cultural norms, social values, time of day, and many other factors. Think of what you consider appropriate for a speaker to say and do at a memorial service for a close friend. This situation will affect both what the speaker says (content) and how he or she says it (form). It would be inappropriate to criticize the deceased, tell jokes, or use profanity (content). The speaker should talk quietly and express sincere emotion in the voice (form). In contrast, how would the situation affect a coach's speech at a pep rally before a big football game? Every public speech occurs in some situation with physical, cultural, historical, and social characteristics that affect outcomes. The speaker must consider and adapt to them while planning a message.

The Transactional Process

These seven components interact in the process of communication during public speaking. Speaker and listeners are engaged in the dynamic transactional process called *communication*. As communication theorist David Berlo described it, a process "does not have a beginning, an end, a fixed sequence of events. It is not static, at rest. It is moving. The ingredients within a process interact; each affects all the others."[4] Berlo would say there is no precise moment at which a public speech event begins; the factors shaping the speaker, events leading up to the meeting between speaker and listeners, and other components of the situation have no precise beginning point. For convenience, however, we start at the moment a speaker rises, walks to the front of a group, and begins to utter words. The speaker's thoughts exist as patterns of electrical signals in the brain, which sends nerve signals that produce muscle actions resulting in sounds and gestures. However, communication has not occurred yet, only the creation of message signals. These message signals are carried in the air and light to listeners, where they are converted back into electrochemical nerve signals that are fed into the brain. Despite the incoming signals, if an audience member is focusing attention elsewhere, he or she may never be aware of the speaker's message. When a listener is aware of the signals, he or she will interpret them. That interpretation is the listener's meaning of the message, created in the mind of the listener. When such a meaning has been evoked by signals, communication has taken place.

Put another way, communication is a listener phenomenon; without a responding listener, communication has not occurred. A listener does not just recreate a message. Instead, the listener creates a new message, different to some degree from the one that is in the mind of the speaker.

Listeners also *react* to messages they perceive. Even the absence of an overt change is a listener response. Most of us respond overtly: We smile, nod, twist in our seats, take notes, roll our eyes, frown, and perhaps raise a hand. We may even speak a word of agreement or disagreement. Public speaking is not a one-way flow of signals from speaker to listener, but a multidirectional process of signals passing simultaneously from speaker to listener, listener to speaker, and among listeners. That is what we mean by *transactional process*.

The alert public speaker is constantly trying to perceive, interpret, and adjust to responses rather than plowing ahead without regard for listener reactions. When a speaker adjusts to responses, *feedback* has occurred. In the feedback process, responses from the listeners influence the speaker's future behavior. Skilled speakers seek listener responses to help them achieve the purpose for making the speech. A speaker's reaction to response signals is like driving: You press harder on the accelerator when the engine slows down or brake when you feel centrifugal force from a curve.

During a public-speaking event each listener can be receiving signals from many others. Listeners not only respond to the speaker, but also to other audience members. A laugh can spread from a few persons to many. Respected listeners are often observed by others for clues about how to respond. A few buzzing persons can sometimes start so much interlistener conversation that the speaker cannot be heard.

Increasing the complexity of what happens during a speech is the fact that human communication is a symbolic process. Humans depend on symbols, which have no intrinsic meaning, for their communicating. Words are symbols.

Because we are symbol users, we gain great flexibility and thinking ability. However, as we explain in Chapter 12, we also suffer confusion and misunderstanding when symbols are unfamiliar or used differently by other people. For example, the words *freedom, equality, justice,* and *democracy* are usually interpreted differently by each listener.

Early in a public-speaking course many students express anxiety about making speeches. For that reason we turn next to some practical actions you can take to increase your confidence as a public speaker. After that we explain how to prepare for speaking in a way that will allow you the flexibility to adjust to listener responses during the process of transactional exchange with an audience.

▶ Building Confidence as a Public Speaker

Some students approach public speaking with a high level of anxiety, even debilitating fear. National surveys have found that Americans rank fear of speaking before a group even higher than fear of heights, death, snakes, flying, illness, and disease. Some people even talk of public speaking as a "fate worse than death."[5] It is important to understand that public-speaking anxiety is a learned fear and that it can therefore be unlearned or at least minimized.

If you fear making public speeches, perhaps you can recall an event that had a formative impact on your attitude toward speaking. Try to go as far back in memory as possible. Most of us had a role in an elementary school pageant, singing or dancing our way on stage to entertain Mom and Dad. Do you recall anyone saying "Aren't you nervous?" "What if you forget your lines?" or "I'd probably faint from sheer fright if I had to give a speech!" Perhaps as you grew older you were given bad advice such as "Look above the heads of the audience and you won't get so nervous." Many students describe experiences when they forgot lines of a memorized recitation, became tongue-tied, or were embarrassed by an adult in front of an audience. These experiences seemed unbearable. After that, even the prospect of facing an audience produced anxiety. The individual had been taught to experience public-speaking anxiety.

Most of us have watched speakers who floundered and failed to interest us. The discomfort we experience as we try to listen to such speakers comes in part from empathy with them and in part from fear. The fear stems from projection—we see ourselves in the situation and become convinced that we would react similarly.

Some apprehension about public speaking comes from the desire to excel. We aspire to succeed, but fear not meeting our own high standards or the standards of significant other persons. Such anxiety can motivate us to do our best, or it may become great enough to be harmful. Many professional performers and speakers report "butterflies"—increased heart rate, dry mouth, loss of appetite, and nausea before a performance—but like athletes, they use

Many well-known entertainers report experiencing anxiety about performing before an audience.

this surge of energy to heighten their performance. The more experience a person has in speaking the more beneficial such "anxiety" can be. An increased level of arousal before speaking in public is desirable, so long as we do not turn it into fear.

Your public-speaking course will provide you with the guidance and practice you need to become a more confident speaker. The classroom will provide a laboratory in which you can safely practice skills while gaining confidence and insight from the support and feedback of your peers and instructor. Your instructor and classmates will act like the training wheels on a bicycle to support you. The following advice will also help you develop confidence when speaking to an audience.

Be committed to your topic. One of the biggest mistakes of beginning speech students is selecting topics that do not interest them personally. Speakers who are deeply concerned about their topics demonstrate much more enthusiasm and confidence than those who try to please someone else by choosing a "good" topic. Consider that in a nonclassroom speaking situation you will be asked to speak because you are recognized as an expert on an issue, or you will choose to speak on some issue of vital importance to you personally. It is essential that you perceive yourself as a person with important information to offer listeners based on your background, experience, and study. You have hobbies and job skills; you have investigated topics of special interest; you have been places not familiar to your audience; you have strong personal concerns and convictions. These are the topics about which you should speak. Confidence begins with a topic that you care about deeply, not from talking about what you think your instructor or classmates want to hear.

Prepare thoroughly. Sufficient time to rehearse and revise leads to a sense of eager anticipation before the speech and an increase in energy while speaking. An effective means for developing your confidence as a speaker and minimizing anxiety is thorough preparation. Your instructor will guide you in preparation so that you need not worry about forgetting major points.

Remember that listeners are not likely to notice your anxiety. If you worry about appearing nervous to listeners, you have greatly exaggerated the ability of most listeners to perceive speaker discomfort. Numerous studies have concluded that fear of appearing nervous is unjustified.[6] When listeners were asked to rate the degree of anxiety they believed the speaker experienced, even veteran speech instructors underrated the amount in comparison to the speaker's self-rating. In other words, you may feel that your knees are knocking visibly, but listeners report not seeing such reactions. If someone sees your hands shake, so what? Most people react with something like "She is just nervous like me."

Focus on audience responses. This advice is similar to that given batters and golfers to "keep your eye on the ball." In any skill, the best performers are those who concentrate on the objective. To do so requires thorough preparation and extensive practice. The objective of public speaking is a speaker-defined listener response, not the presentation of a speech. The speech is a means to an end, not an end in itself. Keeping your attention on listener responses to your ideas will help you to avoid the self-defeating cycle of thinking about yourself while speaking. Audiences respond favorably to speakers who are attentive to them, but unfavorably to speakers who appear to be thinking about how they are doing as speakers. Be sure that you are observing and responding naturally to listeners' smiles, nods, moves, facial expressions, laughter, and note taking.

Create positive self-messages. Many speakers who experience severe apprehension about public speaking give themselves negative messages before, during, and after speaking. What they anticipate tends to happen. If a speaker thinks "I will probably forget what I want to say," the chances will be increased that such forgetting will occur, if only because energy was spent in worrying that could have been used to think of ideas and to note how listeners were responding. The following examples illustrate the difference between negative and positive self-messages:

NEGATIVE SELF-MESSAGES	POSITIVE SELF-MESSAGES
I will probably fall apart and forget everything I planned to say.	I will probably be nervous, but that's normal, and I am so well prepared that I won't forget anything important.
Everyone will laugh and make fun of me if I make a mistake.	Everyone in this class wants everyone else to do well. My friends are pulling for me. Anyone who would laugh at me is sadistic—who cares what such a person thinks!
Nobody will be interested in what I have to say.	Nobody may be aware of how important this is to them, so I will point out how it affects their lives. What I have to say can really help them.
My knees may knock and my hands shake. Everybody will see how nervous I am.	Listeners really don't watch hands and knees very much, and if they do they can't notice much. Even experts can't tell! My listeners are more interested in my ideas than my movements.

▶ Four Methods of Preparing and Speaking

The following example illustrates what can happen when a student has prepared properly for a public-speaking assignment:

> Craig looked at us with a warm, confident smile, then told a dramatic story about a Mafia execution and a statistic describing the billions of dollars this organization costs us each year. The only notes Craig referred to were two charts he fastened to the chalkboard while describing the organization of the Mafia and the sources of its income. When he finished, applause from classmates was very loud.

Good preparation will help you speak with confidence. No speaker can predict exactly how an audience will react to a message or what distractions may develop while speaking. The well-prepared speaker can adjust to almost any contingency that may arise while trying to achieve a desired response from listeners. This chapter provides guidance for early speeches given before you have studied all the details of preparing and describing how each step in preparation fits into the whole procedure.

The four methods for preparing and speaking in public are (1) writing and reading a manuscript, (2) writing and memorizing a manuscript, (3) extemporaneous speaking and (4) impromptu speaking. The first three methods all require extensive advance preparation. Impromptu speaking occurs when a speaker has little if any time to prepare in advance of the speech, although he or she may be very knowledgeable about the subject. Each method of preparation and delivery can be effective depending on the context and demands of the speech event.

Reading from a Manuscript

When a speaker writes the complete text of the speech, then reads it word-for-word to the audience, the speaker is using the manuscript method of preparation and delivery. There are two advantages to using this method. First, the manuscript method ensures precise wording without the danger of forgetting or stumbling over words. In some situations accurate wording is vital. Precision matters to the president when giving major policy speeches, to ambassadors, to an attorney presenting a legal brief, to State Department spokespersons responding to an international crisis, to Peter Jennings as he presents the evening news, and in similar public situations. If accurate wording is critical and/or the speaker anticipates being quoted by others, the manuscript method is an appropriate choice.

A second advantage of reading from manuscript is that this enables a public speaker to present numerous messages without investing the time necessary to become very familiar with any one speech. The speaker can give numerous speeches in less time than would be required if he or she relied upon the memorized or extemporaneous methods. For instance, the president of the United States relies on this method because it is time efficient. The manuscript method is an appropriate choice for a few speakers who must deliver many speeches written by other persons.

Unfortunately, the disadvantages of this method for the average speaker far outweigh these two advantages. First, most speakers have not had the training that is required to use the manuscript method effectively, or they fail to rehearse sufficiently to read fluently while maintaining acceptable eye contact. When reading, the speaker's voice often contradicts the verbal message. Trained oral readers such as Presidents Roosevelt, Kennedy, and Reagan could read so that their voices supported their words. The average speaker reads aloud with little emphasis or feeling. Eye contact is minimal as the speaker stares at the manuscript, and the ability to move while speaking is limited because the speaker is dependent on the manuscript. You can easily lose your place in a manuscript, making you appear incompetent to an audience. While reading a speech manuscript, you can do very little to adjust to listener response signals or unanticipated happenings. Listeners frequently resent it when a speaker does not adapt to their responses.

Second, written and oral composition are very different. Most speakers do not know how to write a manuscript using an oral style. The language of an essay does not sound right to listeners. Researchers have confirmed that the styles of speaking and writing are noticeably different.[7] Speaking vocabularies are simpler and sentences tend to be both shorter and more direct. Unless listeners accept the manuscript as a necessity, they may resent the speaker for appearing not to be interested in their responses.

Because the disadvantages of speaking from a complete manuscript outweigh the advantages, avoid this method. If your job requires great precision in wording, get special training in oral reading so you use a manuscript effectively. At this point in your development as a speaker, the most you should read aloud is a short quotation, brief story, or short poem. Practice reading even such short passages until you can do so fluently and with feeling.

Memorization of a Manuscript

In this method the speaker writes a manuscript, then memorizes it word-for-word. The speaker usually rehearses aloud until the speech can be delivered without errors or referring to notes. Even gestures and movements may be memorized. This is the method of preparation and delivery that actors use. Memorization of a manuscript is the most difficult and demanding method a public speaker can choose.

Memorization of a manuscript, like reading a manuscript, ensures precision. If done effectively, this method also enhances delivery characteristics that are vital to a speaker's effectiveness. Memorization of a manuscript enables the speaker to have maximum eye contact with listeners and flexibility of movement. Such delivery can convey confidence, expertise, and thorough preparation to listeners.

The disadvantages of this method are obvious. Memorization of a manuscript is extremely difficult. Imagine how difficult it would be to memorize a ten-minute speech! This method requires more time and effort than most speakers have available. Like manuscript speaking, the speaker must know how to write in an oral style; otherwise the language of a written speech committed to memory is likely to sound unnatural to listeners. It is also virtually impossible for a speaker to make adaptations if he or she has memorized a manuscript. Finally, it is very easy to forget a word, a phrase, or large sections of a memorized speech. If that happens the speaker is usually lost completely, unable to pick up the thread of language and continue. The anxiety a public speaker normally experiences increases the likelihood of a memory loss. In only a few rare circumstances (such as an oratory contest or special toast) is speaking from memorization of a manuscript appropriate. Avoid this method!

> *I never liked speaking from a piece of paper. A text is sometimes necessary for precise meaning, but to this day I'm not comfortable with one. It always seemed more natural to me to share my immediate feelings with the people sitting nearby.*

> *An unwritten speech based on a clear outline is usually much closer to an individual's true convictions.*
>
> Source: Barry M. Goldwater, *Goldwater* (New York: Doubleday, 1988), p. 125. (Now retired, Goldwater is a former U.S. senator, presidential candidate, Air Force general, business executive, and author.)

Extemporaneous Speaking

Extemporaneous speaking means that a speaker has prepared thoroughly for a specific speech event, including careful outlining. However, actual word-for-word composition of the speech is done while speaking. Although the Latin root of *extemporaneous* indicates something done right at the time without advance planning, only the actual wording of the speech and minor adjustments are left to the moment of speaking.

The extemporaneous method has one great advantage over other methods of delivery. It allows the speaker to anticipate listeners' reactions and plan appropriate adaptations while retaining the spontaneity, emphasis, and directness audiences prefer. Senator John Danforth (R-Mo.) explained the advantages of this method:

> The vast majority of my speeches are extemporaneous . . . . When my notes are too elaborate, I tend to rely too much on deciphering what I have jotted down, and too little on putting my message across to the audience. . . . The more I rely on thinking on my feet, the more power is in the message. . . . One reason I like giving extemporaneous speeches is that, in looking at the audience, I can judge whether my remarks are understood, and restate ideas which, I feel, are not clear.[8]

Extemporaneous speaking combines the best of planning with the best of spontaneity and flexibility. This method lends itself to a conversational speaking style and allows for appropriate amounts of eye contact and a reasonable degree of speaker mobility. The extemporaneous method should be the preferred choice for almost all of your public speaking. That is why *Practical Public Speaking* is devoted to this style of speaking. An overview of the steps involved in preparing and speaking extemporaneously is provided later in this chapter.

Impromptu Speaking

Impromptu, from the Latin meaning "in readiness" or "at hand," refers to speaking without specific advance preparation. The person who speaks impromptu has prepared for speaking only in the sense of having studied and worked with a particular subject. If you answer a question from your audience following your speech, you are speaking impromptu. Conversation is impromptu. When your instructor asks you to respond to a specific question in class, your answer is impromptu. There are numerous situations that require us to speak impromptu. The ability to speak effectively using this method requires extensive practice and a thorough knowledge of the fundamentals of public speaking. Because of its importance, Chapter 16 has been exclusively devoted to this method of preparation and delivery.

▶ Preparing to Speak Extemporaneously

In most public-speaking courses you will present an extemporaneous speech within the first two weeks of the class. These speeches are usually informal and last for only a few minutes. They are an important diagnostic tool used by your instructor, and they help to establish a supportive classroom environment. An Extemporaneous Speaker's Record of Preparation is a checklist to help you prepare to speak. At this point you may not be able to do all that the record of preparation calls for, but at least you can follow the general procedure and do as much of what it says as you now understand. In the second part of the book we take up each of these steps in detail. After studying Parts II and III you will be able to complete all parts of the record. The three major phases in preparing to speak are (1) analyzing, (2) organizing, and (3) rehearsing.

Phase I: Analyzing

Many beginning speakers plunge into planning a speech without adequate investigation of the major components of the speech event. The speaker as a source, the audience members as receivers, the situation, the available information relevant to the topic, and relationships among these components must all be analyzed.

STEP A: SELECT A TOPIC AND GOAL　The first thing to do when you have been assigned to speak in class is to decide what you want to speak about. The topic will be a function of your expertise and the situation in which the speech occurs.

　　Sometimes you will be assigned a general purpose, usually to inform or to persuade. Which type of general purpose is primarily a matter of whether you want listeners to understand new information (inform), or to agree with some proposition about which reasonable people disagree or take some specific action (persuade).

　　Next you will need to write two carefully formulated sentences, a tentative central idea and a tentative desired response. The central idea sentence narrows your general topic down to a specific generalization about some aspect of the topic. For instance, the topic might be the Vietnam War, and the central idea

(*Text continued on p. 24.*)

▶ **Record of Preparation for Speaking Extemporaneously**

NAME _____ DATE SCHEDULED TO SPEAK _____

Instructions: Use this guide as a checklist and record of your preparation so you do not overlook an important step in preparing to speak extemporaneously. If you fill out the form in pencil, you can easily erase and make changes when you need to revise. In the left-hand column record the date when you complete each step. Be sure to answer each question as concisely and completely as possible. If you need more room for an answer, attach a supplementary page. If you are uncertain about how to answer a question, consult the pages indicated in parentheses.

(Date)

Phase I: ANALYZING

_____ A. Select the topic and tentative goal (pp. 64–70)

1. Topic: _____

2. General purpose: _____

3. Central idea (tentative): _____

_____

4. Desired response (tentative): _____

_____

_____ B. Analyze the audience (pp. 81–94)

1. What do my listeners already know about my topic?

2. What beliefs and attitudes do listeners have about my topic?

3. How does my topic relate to listener needs and interests?

4. How are listeners likely to perceive me as a source of information about my topic?

5. *In light of the answers to the above questions, what adaptations should I make to help me achieve my desired response?*

_____ C. Analyze the speaking situation (pp. 94–98)

1. What brings these people together as an audience?

2. What is expected of me as a speaker in this situation?

3. What else is occurring or has occurred that may affect my listeners' responses to my topic, central idea, and desired response?

4. To what features of the physical setting will I need to adjust?

5. *In light of the answers to the above questions, what adaptations should I make to the speaking situation?*

_____ D. Gather information on the topic (pp. 103–116)

1. How adequate is my present knowledge of the topic?

2. What sources should I consult? (Compile bibliography.)
   (a) Books.

(b) Articles.

(c) People.

(d) Other sources.

Phase II: ORGANIZING

_____ E. Organize the body of the speech (pp. 148–159) (Check each item when you complete it.)

    _____ 1. Central idea and desired response statements, confirmed or revised.

    _____ 2. Sequence (schema) selected for main points: _____

    _____ 3. A clear, direct sentence composed for each main point.

    _____ 4. Appropriate developmental materials indicated on outline as support for each main point or subpoint.

_____ F. Organize the introduction for the speech (pp. 166–175)

    _____ 1. Statement to focus listener attention on topic. Type of attention

    getter chosen: _____

    _____ 2. Statement to motivate listener interest.

    _____ 3. Statements to establish my credibility with listeners (if needed).

    _____ 4. Statement to preview organization of the body of the speech.

    _____ 5. Any other background needed by listeners:

_____ G. Organize the conclusion (pp. 176–180)

    _____ 1. A synthesis of main points (usually a summary) to reemphasize the central idea.

    _____ 2. Concluding application or appeal.

_____ H. Finish the outline (pp. 185–197)

   _____ 1. Transitions to connect all main points and major sections of the speech, written in parentheses.
   _____ 2. Title written at top of outline.
   _____ 3. List of references (if called for) with full details of all sources actually used.

Phase III: REHEARSING

_____ I. Visual and other sensory aids prepared (pp. 205–225).

_____ J. Silent rehearsals, including wording and possibly preparation of a speaking outline.

_____ K. Oral rehearsals.

   1. First oral rehearsal: Date_____; length_____

   2. Subsequent oral rehearsals.

DATE	CHANGES MADE
_____	_____
_____	_____
_____	_____
_____	_____

List below any characteristics of delivery to which you gave special attention during rehearsals and about which you would especially like to receive comments from your instructor:

might be that "The Vietnam War left thousands of Amerasians who are rejected in both Vietnam and the United States." The desired response sentence is a description of what you want the listeners to do as a direct response to your speech. It will describe observable behaviors of listeners, something you could see or measure as a way of determining the effect of your speech. For example, "After hearing my speech, I want listeners to vote for legislation that makes it easier for Americans to adopt Amerasian children." Both these sentences are still tentative unless you have already done extensive study (research) on your topic.

STEP B: ANALYZE THE AUDIENCE   The primary purpose of audience analysis is to give the speaker a view of the topic from the perspectives of the listeners. How you understand your listeners in relation to your subject and desired response is critical to what you do as a speaker. Even though you might speak to dozens of audiences on the same topic, some adjustment would be made each time on the basis of what the analysis of that specific group revealed. Most of the analysis is done in advance of the speech, but in a sense it continues as you speak. You receive feedback from listeners and adjust to that feedback while speaking. It is important to determine what the listeners know and believe about your central idea and how it relates to their interests and lives.

STEP C: ANALYZE THE SITUATION   You need a good understanding of the situation in which you will be speaking. Your speech occurs in a context of other events in the personal histories of the listeners. This includes events in the news, social norms and expectations, a shared culture, and the specific occasion and location of your speech. You can plan adaptations to these and other situational characteristics once you understand them. For instance, you may connect your topic to some project of the organization to which you are speaking or refer to a forthcoming campus event that relates to your topic.

STEP D: GATHER INFORMATION   As a speaker you must be current in knowledge and attitudes about the topic. In many cases you will need to do research to examine information and opinions available from experts. You might also do some interviewing, observing, and searching for information in print. When you are confident that you know your subject thoroughly, you are ready to proceed with the detailed organizing and outlining that produces a plan for your speech.

Phase II: Organizing

The end product of Phase II is an outline of what you will probably say in order to achieve the desired response to your central idea. Several steps are involved, beginning with the confirmation or reformulation of your central idea and desired response statements. Next you will organize your information into a few main points that develop the central idea in the body of your speech. Then you will outline an introduction to prepare the listeners for the body of the speech and a conclusion to reemphasize the central idea and urge listeners to make an appropriate response to it. Finishing touches on the outline include writing connective statements to link major sections together and help emphasize key thoughts.

STEP E: ORGANIZE THE BODY   In this step you first divide the central idea into major components, called *main points*, then decide how to develop each of these main points with relevant developmental materials. Main points should follow one type of sequence, such as time, space, problem and solution, cause and effect, or major characteristics of the topic. In a longer speech it may be necessary to divide main points into subpoints. The main points become landmarks that structure recall by both speaker and listeners.

Each point needs to be made concrete and believable with developmental materials. You may use examples of what you are talking about including detailed descriptions, statistics, testimony of experts, and comparisons to things with which listeners are already familiar. All these components of the body are written down in outline form to show how each statement is related to others, thus providing clarity, emphasis, and unity to the body of the speech.

STEP F: ORGANIZE THE INTRODUCTION   With a first draft of the outline of the body of your speech completed, you are ready to outline introductory remarks to prepare your listeners for the body of the speech. The introduction must focus attention on your topic, arouse a desire to hear you talk about it, establish you as a credible source on the subject, and focus attention of listeners on your main points. Each of these major purposes of the introduction will be a main point in the outline of the introduction. With the introduction planned, you are ready to organize the conclusion.

STEP G: ORGANIZE THE CONCLUSION   The final section of a speech is called the *conclusion*. You will summarize the main points, then suggest how listeners can use the information or urge them to take some definite action as a direct result of listening to your speech. This part of the overall speech outline should be quite brief, often limited to two points, with no new information or supporting materials.

STEP H: FINISH THE OUTLINE   Final details of the outline for your speech are now put into place: transition statements to connect the introduction to the body, the main points to each other, and the body to the conclusion; title; and reference list (if needed). The entire outline is now assembled into one whole unit, somewhat like the set of drawings that collectively make up the plans for a house yet to be built.

Phase III: Rehearsing

Both silent and oral rehearsals may be needed to develop the confidence and fluency that will allow you to focus attention alternately on what you are saying and on your listeners' reactions. Then you will be ready to actually compose the speech as you participate in the public-speaking event for which all this detailed preparation has been made. Strive to speak in a semiformal conversational style, establish eye contact with listeners, and be as animated as possible when speaking.

In review, you will notice that the three phases of preparation include a total of nine steps you must complete in specific order while preparing yourself to speak:

A.   Select a topic based on your interests from which you tentatively develop a general purpose, central idea, and desired response.

B.   Analyze the audience.

    C.   Analyze the situation.

    D.   Gather information.

    E.   Organize the body.

    F.   Organize the introduction.

    G.   Organize the conclusion.

    H.   Finish the outline.

    I.   Rehearse.

Effective public speaking is not something done easily or quickly. It can be done confidently and comfortably and with predictable outcomes. As Lee Iacocca, chief executive officer (CEO) of Chrysler Corporation, wrote in his autobiography:

> Public speaking, which is the best way to motivate a large group, is entirely different from private conversation. For one thing, it requires a lot of preparation. There's just no way around it. You have to do your homework. A speaker may be very well informed but if he hasn't thought out exactly what he wants to say, *today, to this audience*, he has no business taking up other people's valuable time.[9]

▶ Summary

In Chapter 1 we have explained several reasons why studying public speaking means developing proficiency in a highly practical art, essential in the process of becoming educated. You will need public-speaking skills to share knowledge with others, exert influence in both work and social situations, and protect yourself from those who would attempt to deceive you.

Public speaking is a dynamic transactional symbolic process, requiring listener perception and response for communication to occur. The major components of a public-speaking event are a speaker, message, channels, listeners, response signals, noise, and situation. During public speaking, signals flow in all directions between speaker and listeners, requiring flexibility in planning and presentation by the speaker.

Fear of public speaking is a learned response to an essential skill. Because the fear is learned, it can be unlearned or at least minimized. The classroom provides a laboratory in which you can learn effective speaking skills and practice those skills in an environment that is supportive. You can develop greater confidence as a speaker by speaking only on those topics in which you are personally interested, making the commitment to prepare thoroughly and early, reminding yourself that listeners are unlikely to see most signs of your anxiety, keeping attention focused on the response of the audience members, and replacing negative self-messages with positive ones.

Four major methods of preparing and speaking in public are reading from a manuscript, memorizing a manuscript, speaking extemporaneously, and speaking impromptu. Extemporaneous preparation and delivery is most practical in most speaking situations because it combines thorough preparation with flexibility. By following a three-phase, nine-step procedure, you can speak extemporaneously with competence and confidence. Beginning with a topic of importance to you, you will analyze all components of the speech event and plan appropriate adaptations to both audience and situation. You will create a detailed preparation outline to guide your remarks so that you can develop your central idea and gain the desired response from listeners. You will rehearse, without depending on a manuscript or memorizing word-for-word, until you are confident of fluency while presenting the speech.

▶ Learning Activities

1. Make a list of information that members of your class would like to know about each other, such as name, major, home town, high school attended, hobbies, major activities, job, etc. Each person in turn writes his or her name on the chalkboard in front of the room, then faces the class and describes these features of self. Be sure you try to see each classmate, one at a time, while you are speaking.

2. Attend a public-speaking event with at least one classmate. In a brief essay identify and describe each of the major components of the event. Then describe how the transactional process actually seemed to occur. How flexible, direct, and responsive to the listeners was the speaker? Share your essay with the other person who attended with you, and read that person's description. Together, write a joint report of your findings and any recommendations you would make to the speaker.

3. Interview two professionals in your chosen career field. Ask each how important public speaking is in the type of work she or he does. Ask for examples of presentations made by the person. Report your findings in a brief speech to your class or a small group of classmates.

4. Select a general topic of major importance to you. Your instructor may assign a type of topic, such as "learned skill." If so, you will explain to your classmates either how to do this action or how a skilled person does it (e.g., how a clerk does a credit check on a customer). Do not try to teach your classmates to do something unless they can realistically be expected to actually do it in the foreseeable future. For example, a speech on how to fuel a hydrogen-powered car would not be of practical interest to your listeners. Work your way through the steps of the procedure for preparing yourself to speak extemporaneously as best you can at this stage in the course. Keep a detailed record of all you do and plan on a record form following exactly the sequence outlined in the Record of Preparation for Speaking Extemporaneously. Submit the final draft of your preparation outline to your instructor.

a. As you listen to your classmates speak, note what techniques work best to capture your attention and hold your interest throughout the speech. After all the speeches have been given, discuss what to do or not do in opening remarks.

b. Did anyone appear to be reading from a manuscript or speaking from memory? If so, how could you tell? What effect did such delivery have on your responses?

c. Did anyone seem to have shortchanged the effort and time needed to prepare to speak extemporaneously? Why do you think that? How did you respond to such evidence of apparent inadequate preparation for speaking?

5. Make a list of all the negative and positive self-messages you have given yourself about making public speeches. Second, assess the degree of validity of each statement on your list. A statement may be completely valid, partly valid but exaggerated, or a myth with no basis in fact. Negative messages can be changed by analyzing the assumptions that underlie them, then giving yourself counterarguments or helpful positive guidelines.

Notes

1. Robert VanBranken, president of American Association of Plant and Industrial Engineers, personal interview, February 26, 1985.

2. See Dan B. Curtis, Jerry L. Winsor, and Ronald D. Stephens, "National Preferences in Business and Communication Education," *Communication Education* 38 (January 1989):6–14.

3. Kathleen E. Kendall, "Do Real People Ever Give Speeches?" *Central States Speech Journal* 25 (Fall, 1974):235.

4. David K. Berlo, *The Process of Communication* (New York: Holt, Rinehart & Winston, 1960), p. 24.

5. "What Are Americans Afraid of?" *The Bruskin Report* 53 (July 1973); Robert J. Doolittle, *Professionally Speaking* (Glenview, IL: Scott, Foresman, 1984), p. 6.

6. Susan R. Glasser, "Oral Communication Apprehension and Avoidance: The Current Status of Treatment and Research," *Communication Education* (October 1981):321–341; Theodore Clevenger, Jr., "A Synthesis of Experimental Research in Stage Fright," *Quarterly Journal of Speech* 45 (April 1959):134–145.

7. James W. Gibson, Charles R. Gruning, Robert J. Kibler, and Francis J. Kelly, "A Quantitative Examination of Differences and Similarities in Written and Spoken Messages," *Speech Monographs* 33 (November 1966):444–451; Milton Horowitz and John B. Newman, "Spoken and Written Expression: An Experimental Analysis," *Journal of Abnormal and Social Psychology* 68 (1964):640–647; Joseph A. DeVito, *The Psychology of Speech and Language* (New York: Random House, 1970), pp. 10–12.

8. John C. Danforth, personal letter, cited in Michael S. Hanna and James W. Gibson, *Public Speaking for Personal Success*, 2nd ed. (Dubuque, IA: Wm. C. Brown, 1989), p. 126.

9. Lee Iacocca and William Novak, *Iacocca: An Autobiography* (New York: Bantam Books, 1984), p. 55.

Ethics in Public Speaking

Questions to Guide Reading and Review

1. When we discuss ethics in regard to public speaking, what are we talking about? Why is this an important issue in the United States?
2. What are the ethical implications and requirements of political democracy and social responsibility?
3. Why is each of the following issues considered when thinking about ethical behavior as a public speaker: the nature of rhetoric, consequences versus intentions, sources, emotional appeals, nonverbal deception, speaking as a representative, ends versus means, and changes in personal speaking style?

Key Terms

Communication ethics   Rhetoric   Social reciprocity

Communication, as a primary instrument of human behavior, pervasively touches and affects the lives of others. Therefore, the argument goes, communication if it is to contribute to the growth of society, must be associated with and governed by ethics. If such is not the case, the power of communication will be used by self-seeking and self-serving individuals and groups for essentially destructive ends.[1]

We cannot open a newspaper, turn on the television, or listen to the radio without reading, seeing, or hearing another example of unethical behavior. What did then Vice President Bush know about the arms-for-hostages deal and when did he know it? The speaker of the House of Representatives was censured for unethical behavior by his colleagues. A Marine "hero" was convicted of diverting funds for personal advantage and of lying to the Congress of the United States.

A 1987 poll by *U.S. News and World Report* indicated that 71 percent of respondents were dissatisfied with current standards for honesty. The majority believed that people were less honest than they had been ten years before.[2] *Time* observed: "Ethics, often dismissed as a prissy Sunday School word, is now the center of a new national debate."[3]

In 1984 the Speech Communication Association, an organization of communication scholars and professionals, established a commission on ethics. This commission reflects the concern among communication scholars for the communicative ethics of students, business leaders, and public officials. In 1988 the Central States Speech Association made "responsible communicators" the theme of its convention, further reflecting the interest of communication teachers in ethics. Today, most teachers of public speaking feel responsible for encouraging their students to act according to a strict code of ethics when speaking in public.

> *The speech itself is important, but it is the speaker that makes it happen. If you want to deliver a message, you must have a dependable messenger. . . . A speech is one of the most effective forms of communication, and the character of the speaker determines whether real communication happens or not.*
>
> Source: Rex Kelly, "Speakers and the Bottom Line," *Vital Speeches of the Day* (November 1, 1987):48. (Mr. Kelly is general manager of Corporate Communications, Mississippi Power Company.)

Communication *ethics* involve intentional choices about what one ought to do when communicating in relation to such values as "justice," "goodness," and "truthfulness."[4] Nilsen, in *Ethics of Speech Communication*, wrote that speaking is ethical only if it meets two criteria: (1) it contributes to the overall well-being of others and (2) that was the intent of the speaker.[5] In other words, the speaker *wanted* to benefit the listeners and did so. Because public speakers can profoundly influence beliefs and actions of listeners, they are morally obligated to evaluate choices they make when planning and speaking.

Being a responsible public speaker is not required by law. Short of advocating the overthrow of the U.S. government, shouting "fire" in a crowded theater, or slandering other persons, there are few things you could say in public that are "illegal." Responsible communicating is a matter of personal morality, dependent upon the extent to which your conduct is governed by a self-imposed code of right and wrong, good and evil, or "I will" and "I won't."

The decade of the eighties has often been called the "Me" decade. Best-selling books like *Looking Out for Number One* encouraged self-centered, self-serving behavior. Many people lived by the philosophy of "If it feels good, do it." Believing that everything is relative led to rationalizing a host of unethical behaviors. In the short run the self-centered and socially irresponsible may reap riches. In the long run, however, those not governed by a social conscience lose. We hope you never speak by the ethic of "I'll do whatever it takes to gain my immediate goal."

How can you decide on the ethical standards that will guide you? The following guidelines are intended to help you answer this question.

▶ Guidelines to Developing Personal Ethics as a Public Speaker

We must all confront our personal beliefs about ethics in speaking. Not to develop a standard of ethics to guide your preparation and practice as a public speaker is to be unethical. You cannot take moral refuge in the cliche "Everyone is doing it" or "He told me to say that." *You* choose how you will act when speaking in public. Your choices have implications for your listeners, your organization, your community, your nation, and your self-concept and self-esteem. The following two ethical perspectives are choices we encourage each of you to make as public speakers.[6]

Political Democracy

In developing a basis for ethical public speaking, Karl Wallace, a distinguished historian and critic of American public address, concluded that four values are central to political democracy of the type created by the Constitution of the United States.

1. The dignity and rights of the individual must have priority over the state and other values. This idea was presented in the Declaration of

Independence, and was expressed by President Lincoln in his Gettysburg address as "government . . . for the people."

2. Each person must have equal opportunity under law to make informed choices, aim for a higher standard of living, and otherwise secure the benefits of liberty.

3. So long as the rights of other persons are respected, each individual should be free to make personal choices about what to eat, where to live, which job to take, for whom to vote, and so on.

4. Each individual should have a chance to develop to the limits of his or her full capacity.[7]

From these four values Wallace established four ethical guidelines to govern communicative behavior in the American democracy. These guidelines are an excellent basis for your personal code of ethics as a public speaker.

1. During public speaking events one person is often the sole source of information and argument, so the speaker is obligated to have a thorough knowledge of the subject. The speaker should be able to answer any question relevant to the central idea of the speech.

2. Only by presenting a representative sample of facts and opinions on a given topic can a speaker make it possible for listeners to make informed judgments about what is said.

3. In order to allow listeners to evaluate bias, prejudice, or self-serving behaviors that might have influenced the selection of supporting materials, speakers must always report the sources of information and opinions included in a speech.

4. The speaker is obligated to display a "tolerance for dissent," shown by respecting opposing arguments in any controversy and encouraging opposing arguments by other speakers. Any effort to conceal arguments by opponents would be unethical. Ridicule, sarcasm, and distorting or ignoring arguments advanced by opponents are all unethical. Treating a multisided issue as if there were only one position worth considering would be unethical by this standard.[8]

Social Reciprocity

In addition to being knowledgeable, fair in the presentation of information, providing sources, and tolerating dissent, the ethical public speaker demonstrates social reciprocity. *Social reciprocity* can be illustrated by asking yourself the question, "How shall I treat my fellow human beings?" Several major religions have given the same general answer to this question, an answer grounded in a sense of social reciprocity, otherwise called *fair play*. The answer is, "Treat others as you want to be treated by them." This is a universal value that can be referred to as a guide for conduct in every public-speaking situation.

Deceptive speaking by government officials, advertisers, religious leaders, professionals, and others who exercise public influence affects each of us and threatens the core values on which our political democracy depends. If we copy the ethics of the unethical leader on the grounds that everyone is doing it, the fabric of freedom is destroyed. The most central guideline for ethics in your speaking is to treat your listeners the way you want to be treated as a listener.

▶ Some Issues to Consider When Developing a Personal Code

How to apply the social reciprocity guideline raises a number of issues speakers face while preparing and speaking in public.

The Amorality of Rhetoric

Collectively called *rhetoric*, the principles and techniques of effective public speaking are only tools. Like the martial arts of judo and Tae Kwan Do, rhetoric is neutral and can be used for good or evil. A knife can be used to perform many beneficial tasks or it can be used to murder. Public speaking techniques can be used to serve self at the expense of others or to serve self and others at the same time. As a speaker, you can choose to use rhetorical tools to make lies appear true, subvert critical thinking, or make the worst choice appear the best. The responsibility for such acts is yours. Rhetoric per se is amoral.

Consequences versus Intentions

If you kill a person with your car, whether as premeditated murder, negligence, or drunk driving, the result is the same—the person is dead. The same is true of public speaking. You do not have to intentionally deceive or mislead for your words to have harmful consequences for listeners. Inadequate preparation and careless use of language can have the same harmful effect as intentional deception. If your research is inadequate and you do not discover that a particular charity you persuade others to support is really a front for organized crime, you deceive your listeners despite good intentions. Taking a public stand on controversial issues like abortion or capital punishment is a great responsibility. To speak publicly without thoroughly considering the possible consequences of your speech is questionable. To speak carelessly in public without adequate information is like shooting a rifle without considering where the bullet may strike.

▶ **Eight Issues to Consider When Developing a Personal Code of Ethics**

1. The amorality of rhetoric.
2. Consequences versus intentions.
3. Sources of information and opinions.
4. Emotional appeals.
5. Nonverbal deception.
6. Speaking as a representative.
7. Ends versus means.
8. Changes in personal speaking style.

All public speaking requires listener time and energy. If you speak to 25 classmates for only five minutes, that is over two hours of other people's time and energy. Do any of us have a right to waste the time of people who are virtual captives in a classroom audience? Imagine that you are a professional speaking to 300 people at a training conference. They have taken a day from work to attend at their own expense. You are scheduled to speak for 45 minutes. That means you are responsible for 225 hours of collective time. At only $15.00 per hour you would be using over $3000 worth of work time. Was your preparation adequate to merit such an investment? Did you adapt as well as you could have to the needs and concerns of your listeners? Both the consequences of your speaking and your intentions determine the ethics of your speaking.

Sources of Information and Opinions

In a very real sense, no information used in a speech is better than its source. Robert and Dale Newman, scholars of public debate, summarized dozens of critiques of "news" stories and editorials in publications such as the *New York Times, Newsweek, U.S. News and World Report,* and the *Washington Post.* They also evaluated press releases from academic scholars, the Department of State, and the White House. They found inaccuracies, bias, unsubstantiated information reported as fact, and erroneous conclusions. One conclusion is clear: It is unethical to use evidence in a speech without checking the source and the information carefully.[9] To pass on as true or valid what one writer or agency has said without cross-checking the information may put you in a position of passing on lies, omissions, and half-truths. Such behavior is a failure to take personal responsibility for what you say that may have significant consequences for listeners.

A speaker must also decide when to give credit to sources of information and ideas. Not doing so restricts the ability of the listener to evaluate the speech

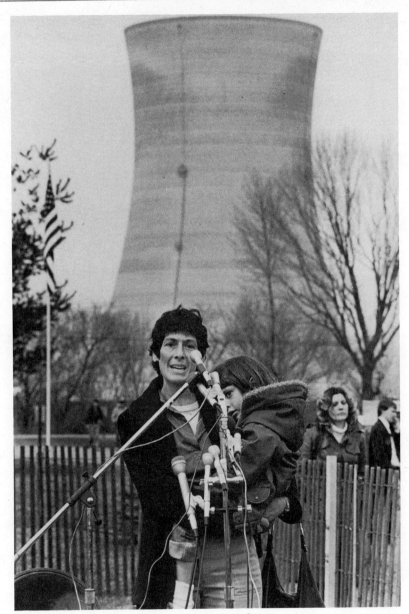

Speaker at an outdoor protest against nuclear power plants.

and sometimes takes credit for work done by other people. Failing to give credit when information is not generally known by people familiar with an issue or when an idea originated with someone else is to be guilty of plagiarism. Senator Joseph Biden was forced to withdraw from his presidential campaign after he was found to have plagiarized. Most colleges and universities punish students proven to have plagiarized on papers or speeches, usually with a grade of F and/or expulsion. Scholars who plagiarize are considered unethical by colleagues and are usually barred from professional organizations, fired by their universities, and/or ostracized. In an academic environment plagiarism is a very serious ethical violation. The principle of treating other people as you want them to treat you applies to crediting sources of ideas and information. Just as you like to be given credit for work you do, give credit to others on whose thinking and ideas you depend.

Emotional Appeals

Sometimes speakers use testimony, statistics, and examples irrelevant to an argument to distract, subvert rational criticism, or cover up a lack of substantive evidence and reasoning. Emotional appeals are one such strategy. If you know how, it may be possible to use music, visual aids, or atypical or irrelevant stories to evoke strong emotions such as pity, sympathy, or fear, then transfer the feelings of your listeners to your central idea. For example, in order to arouse hatred and violence, bigots used to claim that Jews sacrificed babies during the celebration of Passover. Hitler used martial music, signs, and other techniques to arouse an audience before he began to speak. Both Khomeini and Saddam Hussein call the United States "The Great Satan" in order to arouse hatred from Muslims. To arouse strong emotions by appeals to listeners' drives, needs, hopes, prejudices, and fears when there is no logical connection between these feelings and the facts is unethical.

Some writers have questioned whether it is ever ethical to evoke powerful emotions to influence listener responses. They ask if emotional stories of suffering, disaster, or even joy are ethical in speaking. The answer depends on how, when, and why the speaker attempts to evoke powerful emotions. Even the most objective statistics about the increased probability of dying of cancer if one is exposed to radon gas in one's home, of getting acquired immunodeficiency syndrome (AIDS) if one is sexually promiscuous, or of painful tooth decay if one is careless about dental hygiene will have a highly emotional impact on listeners when used as evidence for the logical proof of a claim. Listeners often do not have time or resources to determine whether materials used to develop ideas are either logical or emotional. There is nothing unethical about the use of such materials if they are used accurately to create a valid image and they are not intended to subvert listeners' critical thinking skills. The challenge to the public speaker is one of arousing appropriate emotion and integrating it with reasoned critical thought. If emotion-evoking materials are used as a substitute for valid evidence and to deflect critical evaluation of a speaker's ideas, they are used in a deceptive, unethical manner.

Sincerity of emotion on the part of a speaker is not sufficient warrant for using materials. The speaker's claim must always be well grounded in careful observation. A conclusion must be logically valid, not just what the speaker wants us to believe regardless of evidence and logic. Personal feelings can be presented ethically if clearly stated as the personal feelings of the speaker. Anything done by a speaker to lead listeners to do less than make critical choices about what to accept as information, what to believe, and what to do is ethically suspect.

Nonverbal Deception

Nonverbal signs can be used in many ways to deceive listeners. One common technique is to wear signs of group membership when the speaker is not a member of the group represented. For instance, actors dressed as physicians recite claims for nonprescription drugs. Slogans and mottos can be displayed; parts of uniforms, insignia, pictures, false diplomas, identifying jewelry such as a star of David or a cross, or clothing that is associated with special expertise or affiliations can be displayed without comment. If the speaker has no personal membership in the group or organization suggested, the speaker may be attempting to deceive listeners.

Speaking as a Representative

It is unethical to conceal or misrepresent the fact that you speak as a representative of or advocate for another individual or organization. For instance, it would be unethical for a person on the payroll of the National Education Association to speak in support of a bill to increase federal support for public schools without acknowledging being a representative of the National Education Association (NEA). A physician paid by the American Tobacco Institute would be acting unethically if in speaking about the relationship between using tobacco and diseases he or she did not state clearly that the Tobacco Institute was his or her employer. Not to acknowledge membership in such organizations as Right to Life, National Rifle Association, Friends of Animals, or a nuclear power lobby when speaking on controversial issues that these groups have taken a strong public stand on reduces the opportunity for listeners to judge your possible bias. We are not urging you to emphasize differences from your listeners, but to reveal information they need in order to evaluate what you say.

Ends versus Means

Sometimes you may be tempted to use deception, hide a vital fact from listeners, or otherwise distort because you think the cause you represent is so important it justifies an exception to the standard of truth. For example, Colonel Oliver North lied to Congress about his violation of the law in diverting funds to support the military efforts of the Nicaraguan Contras. North claimed that the defeat of a Communist government in Central America justified breaking the law and lying. Lying, distortion, exaggeration, and manipulation in public speeches are never justified. We agree with the statement often repeated by Mahatma Gandhi: "Evil means, even for a good end, produce evil results." Lying, murder, and taking credit for deeds of others are never justifiable as ethical behavior, regardless of the result.

Changes in Personal Speaking Style

Students sometimes ask if it is ethical to develop two or more different styles of speaking and more than one spoken vocabulary. "Shouldn't I be true to the way I grew up?" For instance, if you grew up in a rural area of eastern Kentucky or a barrio of Los Angeles, would it be ethical for you to learn general American dialect and use it as a public speaker in college, then again use your original speech patterns when back home? If you come from New Jersey, would it be right to take on the accent of a midwesterner while attending college at the University of Illinois? Is it ethical to practice being more flexible and forceful in voice and gestures? The answer is "Of course!" Virtually every person living in our media-connected world develops several dialects and unconsciously shifts from one to the other in different social contexts. There is nothing unethical about consciously and intentionally learning the special jargon of a trade or profession or the vocal characteristics of a particular group. Your speech patterns will shift naturally if you move into a geographic area or social class of people you like. It is ethical to choose words your listeners are most likely to understand and to develop new-to-you speaking techniques to help your listeners understand as you intend. Learning to speak in new ways is as ethical as any other learning so long as it is not done to deceive.

▶ Summary

In recent years concern for the ethics of people in a position to influence the beliefs and actions of others has become a major subject of public discussion in the United States. No public speaker can avoid responsibility for developing a personal code of ethics. Following orders or doing as unethical people do is no defense. This is not primarily a matter of law, but of personal choice.

Maintenance of freedoms in the United States depends on following a value requiring that public speakers must serve the best interests of listeners, as they see those interests, rather than seeking to exploit them. Socially, the most important parts of preparation are the moral choices you make in deciding what to accomplish and what materials and rhetorical strategies to use. To be an ethical public speaker who emphasizes democracy and freedom, you must acquire a thorough knowledge of your topic, be fair when presenting information, help listeners make informed choices, and be willing to live with dissent from other equally ethical speakers.

Basic to being ethical is preparing and speaking as one would want other speakers (to whom one listens) to prepare and speak. At a minimum this means employing rhetorical tactics only for socially defensible ends, finding and using the best available sources of information, giving credit to sources for information and ideas, attempting to arouse only emotions that are appropriate to the facts of the matter, and avoiding all forms of deception. It means never rationalizing the use of unethical tactics because the objective is noble and important. Being socially responsible when many speakers around are self-serving, deceptive, and exploitive will be difficult and may even seem impractical at times. In the long run, however, your credibility with others and your own peace of mind will be your reward.

▶ Learning Activities

1. Following are questions for class discussion.
   a. What ethical guidelines shall we expect of each other when speaking to this class?
   b. What standards of ethics do we use to evaluate speaking by such leaders as politicians, government officials, scientists, teachers, and preachers?
   c. What are the implications of this ethical imperative for public speaking: "No one has a right to engage in any activity that if engaged in by all would be disastrous"?
2. Locate an historical account of unethical public speaking. Briefly describe the event to your classmates, including what was done and said that was unethical, and both the short- and long-term effects on both speaker and listeners. Some examples can be found in the lives of Adolph Hitler, Senator Joseph McCarthy, Vice President Spiro Agnew, President Richard Nixon, the Reverend Jim Jones, Colonel Oliver North, and Senator Joseph Biden.
3. Under what conditions might intentional deception be justifiable as moral and ethical? Consider government coercion of religious practice and personal beliefs, being a prisoner of war, threats of torture by kidnappers, terrorism, failing businesses, losing an election, and hurting another person by telling the truth.

Notes

1. Russel B. Windes, "Preface," in Thomas R. Nilsen, *Ethics of Speech Communication*, 2nd ed. (Indianapolis, IN: Bobbs-Merrill, 1974), p. v.
2. Merrill McLoughlin, Jeffrey L. Sheler, and Gordon Witkin, "A Nation of Liars," *U.S. News and World Report* (February 23, 1987):54–60.
3. "What Ever Happened to Ethics?" *Time* (May 25, 1987): 14–29.
4. Vernon Jensen, "Teaching Ethics in Speech Communication," *Communication Education* 34 (October, 1985):324–330.

5. Thomas R. Nilsen, *Ethics of Speech Communication*, 2nd ed. (Indianapolis, IN: Bobbs-Merrill, 1974), pp. 16–18.

6. Richard Johannesen, *Ethics in Human Communication*, 2nd ed. (Prospect Heights, IL: Waveland Press, 1983). Johannesen also presented several other perspectives from which the ethical guidelines proposed in this chapter can be deduced.

7. Karl Wallace, "An Ethical Basis of Communication," *Speech Teacher* 4 (1955):1–9.

8. Wallace, "An Ethical Basis of Communication," pp. 1–9.

9. Robert P. Newman and Dale R. Newman, *Evidence* (Boston: Houghton Mifflin, 1969), pp. 91–225.

CHAPTER 3

Listening to Understand and Evaluate Speeches

Questions to Guide Reading and Review

1. What is the best indication that a person has listened well?
2. What is untrue about each of the three common misconceptions about listening?
3. What are the unavoidable problems one faces when trying to listen well, and what can one do to offset them?
4. What can one do to correct avoidable problems contributing to ineffective listening?
5. As a listener, what are eight steps you can take to improve your understanding, evaluation, and recall of a speaker's ideas?

Key Terms

Active listening	Evaluating	Listening
Attention	Hearing	Paraphrase
Egocentrism	Information overload	Passive listening

In Chapter 1 communication was defined as a process requiring the response of a receiver to perceived signals. *How* we perceive and respond to signals from other persons determines much of our success in interpersonal and professional relationships. Listening well to others' statements is not something we do naturally. Humans are born with an ability to hear; *listening* is a skill that must be learned. How many people have you known whom you thought listened really well to you? Who listened poorly? Most of us take it for granted that we listen well; most of us are incorrect in this assumption.

▶ The Importance of Listening Well

Studying principles of listening can help you become a better listener. It can also help you understand how to speak in ways that enhance listening. Productive listening is not just a listener activity; it is equally a result of an audience-centered speaker. The speaker who is aware of the psychology of listening behavior can adapt a message in order to improve the chance of gaining listener understanding and support.

There are two standards for evaluating how well you have listened:

1. How well you understood the message intended by the speaker.
2. The validity of your evaluation of the message you received.

In other words, the ultimate test of how well you have listened to a public speech is to attempt to *paraphrase*, or restate in your own words the central idea and main points of, the speaker's message, then express a judgment about the probable validity of the message based on information and reasoning provided by the speaker and your prior knowledge.

Listening, the most frequent communication activity, comprises half of our communication behavior. Early research showed that the average person spends about 70 percent of his or her waking day communicating with other persons. In studies reported in 1929 and 1975,[1] this time was found to be divided among four major types of communicative activity:

1929	1975
9% writing	8.4% writing
16% reading	13.3% reading
30% talking	23.2% talking
45% listening	54.5% listening

As you can see from these data, listening is even more important now than in the early twentieth century. Another study of college students found that they spend over 50 percent of their communication time listening (14 percent writing, 16 percent speaking, 17 percent reading, and 53 percent listening).[2] Members of the Academy of Certified Administrative Managers were asked to indicate the communication skills most critical for successful management. These managers ranked listening as the most important communication skill.[3]

Because most of the information we receive comes through listening, it is important that we become proficient as listeners, evaluators, and retainers of this material.

- What you get out of college depends greatly on how well you listen. Ralph Nichols, father of modern listening research, found that without prior listening training, college students answered correctly only 50 percent of items on immediate recall tests and only 25 percent on delayed recall tests.[4]
- Ineffective listening by employees is costly to both them and their corporations.[5] Numerous CEOs have complained that educational institutions are not doing enough to teach graduates to listen well.
- As a consumer, you need to protect yourself from misinformation, exaggeration, and deception in advertising. Americans make major political, ethical, and financial decisions based on messages received through the mass media.
- Finally, as a public speaker you need to prepare yourself based on how people listen. Understanding how we listen and remember can greatly improve the effects of your speaking on listeners.

In this chapter we identify some common misconceptions about listening, causes of poor listening, avoidable and unavoidable difficulties encountered while listening, and what you can do to improve your ability to listen effectively.

▶ Misconceptions about Listening

Listening and Hearing Are the Same

Passively hearing a speaker and actively listening are completely different. *Hearing* is a sensory process of converting air waves into nerve signals. During the hearing stage of listening, no mental interpretation or evaluation of ideas is involved. *Listening* involves decoding, interpretation, and assimilation. Another way to explain this is to say that "we create meaning for ourselves in response to what we perceive as we listen." Figure 3.1 illustrates the relationship between hearing and listening.

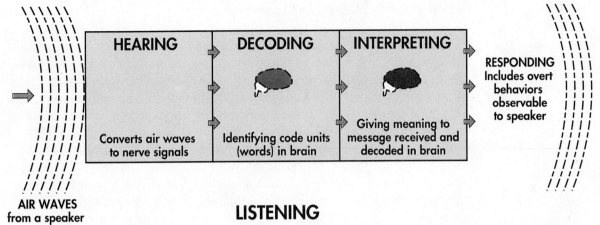

Figure 3.1 Listening and hearing are not the same; listening includes hearing and other processes.

It is critical for speakers to remember that meanings are created by people as they listen. Meanings are not inherent in messages. Speakers who assume they can transmit their meanings directly to an audience do not understand the listening phase of the communication process. Meaning is created by the listener based on past experiences, expectations, needs, goals, biases, and education. At best, understanding is partial. Consequently, a speaker must constantly check for and adapt to responses in order to ensure that listeners understand the message as intended.

After hearing and interpreting a speaker's message, listening involves evaluative activity during which the listener makes decisions about the credibility of the speaker, the validity of the arguments, and the usefulness of the information. That is one reason why early in the speech the speaker must create an interest in the topic and establish credibility as a source of information on that topic.

Listening Is Passive

Both speaker and listener share responsibility for effective listening. Listening is not simple behavior; it is often difficult work. Listening effectively is especially hard if the speaker has failed to take responsibility for motivating the listener or for presenting information in an interesting, organized manner. Some members of an audience sit back, cross their arms, and nonverbally indicate they do not plan to expend any effort to listen to your speech. The speaker has a tough job to overcome such passive listening, but careful audience analysis can help with creating motivation and adapting the speech to a need felt by the audience. Audience members will not be passive listeners if they feel a need for the information. If the speaking occasion is one where the need was predetermined by the group, the speaker has less of a problem than when the program is open to any topic, as it is in most public speaking classes.

Forgetting Results from a Poor Memory

Have you ever asked for directions, only to say "I forgot, do I turn left or right at this corner?" Have you forgotten someone's name immediately after being introduced? These apparent memory losses are more likely products of inefficient listening. Assignments are late, appointments broken, calls unreturned, and important information lost all as a consequence of hearing without listening well. It is often difficult to convince people that they were not listening; they know they "heard you say something, but just can't quite remember what." The problem is that the person heard, but did not listen actively. Instead, the focus of attention was something the person was thinking, some aspect of delivery, or some other noise in the communication process. More often than not when we forget something of importance the problem is not one of memory but of inattentive or passive listening.

▶ Why Don't We Listen Better?

If listening is so important, why aren't we better at it? In addition to misconceptions that affect how we listen, there are many reasons we do not listen effectively. The speaker needs to be aware of these recurring problems in order to reduce their impact on audience members.

Unavoidable Listening Problems

Some listening problems cannot be totally eliminated for they are inherent in human nature. However, we can reduce their undesirable effects if we understand how they work and how best to respond.

INFORMATION OVERLOAD   We are continuously bombarded with information and cannot attend to it all. If we do not screen out much of the information arriving at our senses we suffer a confused state called *information overload*. To combat information overload we block out what we perceive to be unimportant, irrelevant, and meaningless information. This explains why you can carry on a conversation with a friend in a crowded room and not be distracted by other conversations around you. You hear other sounds, but you have mentally tuned them out until something stimulates your interest.

Think of how distracting 100 percent listening would be in a classroom situation. You would not only be aware of the instructor and relevant student discussions, but would also be acutely aware of other sounds such as

Your own heart beat; a heating or air conditioner fan; scratching pencils; papers and books being shuffled; coughing, yawning, and sighing; feet scraping along the floor; chalk sliding on the board; buzzing fluorescent lights; birds chirping outside; fingers tapping; classmates whispering; footsteps outside the door; traffic and construction noises; someone scratching; people talking in the hall, and the rain falling outside!

We are necessarily selective in our listening. The danger is that we may inadvertently block out important messages. When sounds become meaningless background noise to our thoughts, we miss important messages such as assignments, explanations, and warnings.

EGOCENTRISM It is difficult to listen effectively to another when personal problems or interests are preoccupying our attention. The preoccupied listener may say "uh-huh," "that's right," "really?" and "I see," but rarely has any interest in or understanding of the ideas being expressed by the speaker.

To say that listeners are ego centered is not to imply that they are rude, don't care about, or are unfriendly toward the speaker. A common problem arising from *egocentrism* occurs when someone hears a speaker mention a familiar topic and then begins to daydream about that topic. Realistically, we are all ego-centered. We act on the basis of what appears in the long run to be in our own best interest, and we interpret everything from a personal perspective.

THOUGHT-SPEECH TIME DIFFERENTIAL One of the reasons we often find ourselves focusing on our own thoughts while another person speaks is that we are able to think at a much faster rate than anyone speaks. Humans think at about 600 words per minute, while the average speaker utters only about 150 words per minute. In the absence of verbal stimulation sufficient to occupy our brain, we may shift attention to other matters than the speech. The disciplined listener has learned to use this extra word-processing capacity to reword, review, evaluate, and think of personal uses for the information provided by the speaker. Thus attention remains on the speaker's message. The undisciplined listener uses this time for mental vacations from the speaker's message. The problem is that such vacations often turn out to be one-way tickets; the listener never returns to the speaker or does so only after missing important information.

LACK OF HEARING ACUITY Not all poor listening is a result of information overload, egocentrism, or unproductive use of mental verbal capacity. Sometimes physiological limitations affect reception of sound. Deafness is an obvious example of a physiological barrier to listening. Even a slight hearing loss resulting from a cold can impair a listener's reception and interpretations. Although the speaker cannot eliminate the impact of hearing loss, a sensitive speaker and motivated listener can minimize the problem. A public address system can help eliminate reception problems that are not severe. People with reduced hearing can help themselves by choosing front seats or avoiding parts of a room with background noise. Skilled speakers watch for signs that any listener is having trouble hearing and adapt appropriately.

Avoidable Listening Problems

LACK OF TRAINING   An often overlooked reason for listening ineffectiveness is lack of training in listening skills. Listening is thought by many to be a natural ability. Although students spend much of their classroom day listening, often little or no formal training is offered to improve listening skills. As illustrated in Figure 3.2, an inverse relationship exists between the amount we depend on a communication skill and how much attention is given in schools to increase that skill. Think for a moment of how much listening skill training you have received in your education. Even without extensive training in listening, being aware of how one listens, being motivated to listen more effectively, and knowing how to listen well can do much to overcome avoidable listening problems. You may want to enroll in a course or other special instruction devoted to listening.

INSENSITIVITY   The nonverbally insensitive listener attends only to the verbal message of the speaker. Neither the emotional tone of voice nor the physical actions of the speaker are used in interpreting the speaker's meaning. The insensitive listener fails to recognize changes in voice inflection, posture, and facial expression that imply significantly different meanings for the same words. According to psychologist Albert Mehrabian, 93 percent of the emotional meaning of a message comes from these nonverbal cues, whereas only 7 percent of such meaning is communicated verbally.[6] The source of meaning has been broken down further to illustrate the impact of voice and bodily activity on communicated messages:

> 7 percent words.
> 38 percent vocal cues: pitch, tone, rate, volume.
> 55 percent facial expression and bodily activity.

Has anyone ever asked "What is wrong?" to which you answered "Noth-

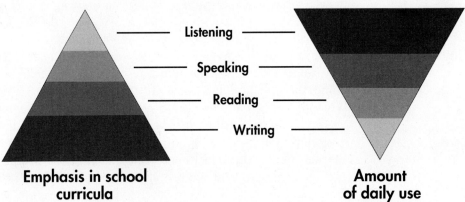

Figure 3.2   The inverse relationship between how much we use a communication skill and the amount of training given for the skill in school.

ing." If so, recall how you felt and whether you really meant "nothing." Now try saying "nothing" using appropriate nonverbal behavior to communicate anger, dissatisfaction with the other person, annoyance, and a feeling of satisfaction. Were there noticeable differences in voice, facial expression, gestures, and other body cues? For a brief period of time pay special attention to the nonverbal cues provided by speakers and how these imply different meanings for words. Doing so can increase your sensitivity and consequently improve your listening skill.

MISPLACED FOCUS   Another cause of poor listening is misplacement of the focus of *attention*. The misfocused listener attends to details, but misses the important ideas and issues and often fails to identify and recall the central idea or purpose of a speaker. This listener needs to recognize the interrelatedness of the speaker's ideas. Four common areas of misplaced focus are (1) the speaker's appearance, (2) the speaker's style of delivery, (3) emotion-laden words, and (4) physical surroundings. We are not suggesting you should be insensitive to these signals, but that they should not be the focus of your attention.

Overattention to the speaker's appearance can detract from understanding the intended message. A listener who is unable to disregard most details of dress, hairstyle, or physical appearance of the speaker soon loses track of what is being discussed. For example, one student wrote the following about how he benefitted from learning to overlook such details.

> In college I took a composition class from a professor who not only dressed in wrinkled, mismatched clothes, but whose hair and skin seemed unclean. . . . I felt he could not possibly have anything worthwhile to say, so I tuned him out. After nearly failing the first exam I tried unsuccessfully to transfer. I had to have this class! I had to learn the material from this professor! I had to refocus on the content and avoid being distracted by his appearance. I was amazed! Not only was he a very good instructor, but a talented writer with several publications to his credit. I finished the course with a new focus on the subject and a new appreciation for the instructor and earned an A.

Focusing on the speaker's delivery style results in poor listening. Listeners may be distracted either by what they label "poor" or "excellent" speech delivery. Although an effective speaker's delivery should not call attention to itself, many listeners act as if hypnotized by enthusiastic bodily activity of a speaker. They cease to focus on the message. If you pride yourself on being very aware of all the details of a speaker's delivery, you probably aren't listening to his or her ideas very carefully.

Listeners with poor understanding and recall of what a speaker said often report focusing on an unusual dialect or vocal characteristic.

You cannot focus attention on the speaker's delivery and understand the message well.

> Julie was from South Carolina. When she finished her speech, Mark said he did not understand her central idea: "I was so intrigued with your accent I forgot to listen to what you meant," he said. "Listen to me! I have something to say. I can't help how I learned to talk. I'm trying as hard as I can to change that," Julie shouted at her Midwest classmate.

Unusual speaking habits and mannerisms are understandably hard to disregard. However, the listener must consciously and quickly tune these out in order to focus on the speaker's ideas.

Overreacting to emotion-laden words leads to misunderstanding. Sometimes a word or phrase used by a speaker triggers a highly emotional reaction from a listener, blocking that person's ability to listen effectively. Many people respond to words with highly positive or negative feelings regardless of how the speaker is using the word. This is particularly common when listening to a controversial speech with which the listener initially disagrees. Most listeners in such circumstances become annoyed or angry and stop listening, often carrying on an internal argument against the speaker. Skilled listeners try to understand the speaker's feelings and intentions, often mentally paraphrasing the speaker's ideas. Words and phrases to which many listeners have especially strong reactions are likely to be associated with religion, government, race, and sex. Which of the following words triggers an emotional reaction in you: chick, boy, dumb jock, evolution, honky, coon, dago, kike, dike, nigger, abortion, right-to-life, socialism, communism, redneck, hick, egghead, nerd, and fundamentalism? We are not saying that you should overlook name-calling, just that you should try to understand the speaker's meaning before you agree or disagree.

Details of physical surroundings provide innumerable distractions to listeners who focus attention on the speech situation. Any feature of the setting can become noise for a listener who allows it to be a distractor: decor, paintings, music in the background, how other audience members are dressed, or objects lying on a table. The most effective listener very briefly notes environmental cues if they are relevant to him or her personally. Then the listener consciously refocuses attention on the message of the speaker. Poor listeners continue to think about the object on the table, the music, or other contextual details. Focusing on irrelevant signals from the environment often results in failing to comprehend or retain important ideas and information provided by a speaker.

AVOIDING DIFFICULT MESSAGES   Many persons develop a habit of shifting attention away from a speaker's message when the content is difficult to understand. It takes concerted effort to follow an explanation of a complicated multistage process, such as the geological cycle of rock formation, nuclear fusion, or gene splicing. Even when the speaker designs simple visuals and uses them well, makes frequent comparisons to the familiar, and uses shared language to define new terms, the listener still must work very hard to comprehend the complex components and interaction involved. To listen well in such situations calls for personal discipline and attention of the kind required to master any complex skill or art.

▶ Guides to Listening Well

Listening is an active process involving intentionally focused attention, perception, and interpretation. *Active listening* is required to overcome both the avoidable and unavoidable problems that interfere with listening well. Using these principles as a foundation, we next offer guidelines to help you become an effective listener. Many of these guidelines have direct implications for speaking to achieve desired responses.

Correct Faulty Conditions

In order to keep your attention focused on the speaker's ideas, do whatever you can to remove distracting environmental noise. For instance, some environmental distractions can be eliminated quickly by closing a door or window. Sitting in the front of a room or moving to a chair with a better view can help.

If you can't hear adequately and can't move to a better seat, politely let the speaker know your problem. Chances are that other audience members have the same difficulty. You can try to get the speaker's attention by cupping your hands behind your ears or waving a hand in the air. If you aren't noticed or responded to with an increase in volume, it is sometimes appropriate to call out "Can't hear" or "Louder, please."

Listen with a Definite Purpose in Mind

Research in understanding and recall indicates that you will give much better attention if you have a definite purpose for listening. Listen carefully to the introduction for a statement revealing the speaker's purpose. If you don't detect such a statement, try to estimate the speaker's probable objective from the situation and the content of the introduction. Decide if that objective could in any way help you understand the world and people around you, solve problems

Skilled speakers watch for signs that any listener is having trouble hearing and adapt appropriately.

you might encounter, or enrich your life in some way. If nothing else, your objective might be just to understand the beliefs, thinking, and motives of the speaker.

Focus on Ideas and Key Terms

Keep in mind that you will probably remember only a small portion of all the speaker says that is new to you. It becomes important, then, to be able to recall what is most important. What you focus on is what you are most likely to remember.

A skilled speaker will provide guideposts to help the listener follow the organization of a speech. Listen for signposts, sudden changes in volume or intensity of the voice, and transitions that indicate a new idea is about to be introduced. While you listen to details such as statistics or examples, keep looking for the point or idea that the detail is supposed to develop or support. If you focus on the detailed supporting materials, you will likely recall less of them than will listeners who focus on the main points. Details will then be associated in memory with main points.

Ignore Trivial Details

Do not allow the speaker's dress, dialect, or delivery style to absorb your attention. Avoid overreacting to words that evoke a strong emotional response. Even if a speaker is foolish enough to violate social norms by using profanity or sexist or racist language, he or she might have something worth understanding and sharing if you keep listening for it. Watch out for a tendency to give unwarranted attention to humorous stories or vivid personalized examples.

Use Your Extra Thought Capacity to Review

Because we think about four times faster than the average person speaks, as listeners we can use this extra time to review the speaker's ideas. If you use key words or phrases to represent each main point, you can quickly review them. This use of time while listening will help keep you focused on the goal of understanding and recalling.

Listen to Paraphrase

Set yourself a goal of understanding the speaker's meaning and intentions. This requires that as listeners you avoid disagreeing mentally before you have understood the speaker's viewpoint fully. Be especially careful about a tendency to ambush. Your first goal as listener should be the ability to paraphrase the main points to the speaker's satisfaction. Only when you can do so are you in a position to evaluate responsibly the merits of a speaker's ideas.

Assess the Meanings Beyond the Words

Use nonverbal signals such as changes in pitch and tone, gestures, facial expressions, posture, and movements to help you understand the meaning of the speaker. Nonverbal signals are especially revealing of feelings of the speaker toward whatever is being discussed and of attitudes toward listeners. Try to listen empathically, putting yourself in the position of the speaker. The point here is not to agree or disagree, only to understand the speaker as fully as possible.

Listen to Evaluate the Merits of the Speaker's Evidence and Claims

We put this piece of advice last because it should only be followed when you are certain that you have understood the speaker as the speaker intended. To focus on *evaluating* too early will often lead to misunderstanding. If you are listening actively and empathically, you will be in a position to use some of your spare mental time to make brief judgments about the following questions:

1. What is the basis for statements the speaker presents as information?
2. How adequately does the speaker support any controversial claims or interpretations of fact?

3. How dependable and current are the sources of evidence cited by the speaker, or is there a lack of citation?

4. How were statistics used to support arguments? Are they from scientific samples or possibly misleading?

5. How valid are conclusions drawn from the evidence provided? Are there obvious instances of exaggeration or overgeneralizing?

You are responsible for what you choose to believe and do in response to a speaker's appeal. The more you know about evidence, logic, and psychology the better equipped you will be to do so.

▶ Summary

Most of us received little or no formal training in listening, even though this is our most frequent and important communicative activity. Even a brief study of the process, problems, and psychology of listening can help when listening and speaking. What we learn as students, how well we function as employees, and our security as citizens and consumers all depend on how well we listen. The purpose of listening to public discourse is to understand what the speaker means and to make valid judgments about what we have understood.

Three major misconceptions contribute to poor listening: (1) listening and hearing are synonymous; (2) listening is a passive process; and (3) forgetfulness, rather than improper focusing of attention, is the major cause of not remembering what we have been told. Also contributing to poor listening are information overload, egocentrism, misuse of the thought–speech differential, insensitivity, improper focus of attention, and avoidance of difficult messages.

Listeners can do a lot to help themselves listen better by correcting faults in the listening environment, establishing a personal objective for listening, keeping the focus of attention on ideas and off of trivial details, reviewing a speaker's main points, trying to paraphrase them accurately, using both verbal and nonverbal signals to interpret, and listening to evaluate only after being confident of a speaker's meaning.

▶ Learning Activities

1. Attend a public speech to observe listening behaviors and speaker responses to listener reactions. Sit where you can unobtrusively observe most of the audience members as well as the speaker.

   What kinds of listening behavior do audience members seem to be engaging in? Who would you judge to be listening especially well? Why do you make this judgment? Who seems to be listening poorly? What behaviors indicate poor listening to you? Are these conspicuous?

Does the speaker in any way seem to acknowledge and respond to listener feedback? How? What adjustments does the speaker seem to make as a response to listener behaviors? If the speaker did not respond to listener behaviors, did this lack of response seem to affect the outcome of the speech?

2. After listening to a classmate's speech, write out what you think are the central idea of the speech and the main points of the body. Read aloud what you have written, then ask if the speaker can confirm that you understood what was intended. If the speaker makes some corrections, again paraphrase what you understood to be the central idea and main points. Continue until the speaker confirms that you have understood the speech as intended.

If you did not initially understand as the speaker intended you to, what might have been the reasons for this misunderstanding? What can you do to be a more effective listener? What might the speaker do to make your job of listening easier?

3. Interview a person whom you believe to be a very good listener (this may be a personal friend, teacher, counselor, family member, work associate—anyone you believe listens exceptionally well). Ask the person the following questions and make brief notes about the answers so you can share them with classmates:
   a. How important are listening skills in your life?
   b. Why do you think you are perceived as a good listener?
   Make a list of behaviors that you think good listeners display that help communicate interest and empathy. Compare your answers with those of your classmates. What answers are most common and seem to be most important?

4. Interview a successful specialist in your major field. Ask that person how important effective listening is to job success. What different types of listening skills are needed for the job? What are some obstacles to listening well that are common to this job? Your instructor may want to have the class tabulate the answers and discuss what they mean.

5. Practice giving and receiving instructions.
   a. Explain to a classmate a step-by-step procedure or a geometric drawing provided by your instructor. Try to anticipate problems the listener will have in understanding, following, and remembering your instructions. As soon as you finish, your classmate should do his or her best to follow your instructions. Watch carefully to see how well your partner can do what you intended. If the outcome is different from what you intended, to what degree is that a result of how you gave instructions, and to what degree to faulty listening behavior by your partner? See if the two of you can agree on this question.
   b. Now exchange roles: Your partner becomes the instructor while you

listen and then try to do what the partner explained. As in step a, discuss the outcome and probable reasons for it.

6. List three topics about which you become highly emotional. How well do you listen when others disagree with you on these topics? Can you listen adequately to restate the belief of a person who disagrees with you on one of these topics to the satisfaction of that other person? Try doing this the next time these subjects come up in conversation or for discussion. Remember, listening well does not mean agreeing, but being able to paraphrase another speaker's ideas to that person's satisfaction.

7. As your instructor reads aloud passages from speeches, try to summarize the main points of each in clear, concise declarative sentences. Several people may be asked to read aloud what they have written after listening to each passage. If you are having trouble doing this correctly and consistently, identify what you are doing that is ineffective.

   a. Are you focusing on the wrong stimuli?
   b. Are you engaging in some form of egocentric divergence from what was said in the speech?
   c. How are you using the thought–speech time differential?
   d. If you are having trouble hearing, what have you done to compensate for that problem?
   e. Are you listening insensitively to nonverbal cues?
   f. Are you overreacting to words that are emotion laden?
   g. Are you tuning out when the message seems difficult?
   h. What else might you be doing that is unproductive?

Notes

1. Paul Rankin, "Listening Ability," in *Proceedings of the Ohio State Educational Conference's Ninth Annual Session*, 1929; E.K. Warner, "A Study of Communication Time," M.A. thesis, University of Maryland, 1975, p. 26, reported in A.D. Wolvin and C.G. Coakley, *Listening* (Dubuque, IA: Wm. C. Brown, 1982), p. 5.

2. Larry L. Barker et al., "An Investigation of Communication Activities by College Students," *Journal of Applied Communication Research* 8 (1980):101–109.

3. Samuel L. Becker and L. R. V. Ekdom, "That Forgotten Basic Skill: Oral Communication," *Association for Communication Administration Bulletin* 23 (1980):12–25.

4. Ralph G. Nichols, "Do We Know How to Listen? Practical Helps in a Modern Age," *Speech Teacher* 10 (March 1961):119–120.

5. Lyman K. Steil, "Secrets of Being a Better Listener," *U.S. News and World Report* 88 (May 26, 1980):65.

6. Albert Mehrabian, "Communication Without Words," *Psychology Today* 2 (September 1968):53–55.

PART II

Analysis of the Elements of the Speech Event:

THE BASIS FOR PLANNING A MESSAGE

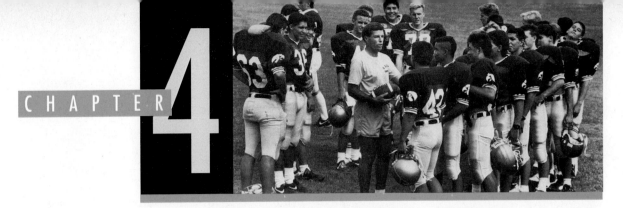

CHAPTER 4

Formulating a Central Idea and Desired Response

Questions to Guide Reading and Review

1. What should be the primary source of your speech topics? Why?
2. What are the major general purposes of public speakers?
3. How does the response desired by a person speaking to inform differ from that of a person speaking to persuade?
4. How is a central idea sentence related to the topic and general purpose of a speech?
5. What are the characteristics of a carefully stated central idea?
6. What are five guidelines for composing a desired response statement? Why is each important?

Key Terms

Behavioral objective

Central idea

Desired response

General purpose

To inform

To persuade

To entertain

To commemorate

In Chapter 1 we introduced a three-stage, nine-step procedure for preparing yourself to speak to an audience. The following true story illustrates how knowing and following this procedure can increase your confidence as a speaker.

Sue walked to the lectern, feeling nervous about the challenge of speaking before her class. She had recently told her instructor that her greatest worry was that she would "go to pieces" in front of her classmates. Her palms and face were moist with perspiration, and her heart was racing. As Sue walked to the front of the class she was thinking: "Knowing the truth about mental retardation is important. Most of my classmates believe prejudices and myths about mental retardation, myths that hurt me as the mother of Tony, my mentally retarded 6-year-old son. I want to set them straight, and I can. I really know my stuff, having studied and lived with mental retardation for so long. I have a simple outline of ideas to follow and good visuals to help me remember them. I can do it!" Then she was looking out at her audience and began to speak: "I'd like you to meet Tony, my son, my blessing and my curse. He is severely retarded. Someday odds are that some of you will have a retarded child and that all of you will have family or friends blessed and cursed with a retarded child."

Sue ended her talk six minutes later to the sound of loud, prolonged applause from her classmates. Several listeners raised their hands to ask for more information on her topic. Sue had succeeded. Believing in the importance of what she had to say gave Sue the confidence to reach her goal.

Preparing to speak in the way Sue did yields the feeling of confidence that comes from believing you have an important goal in speaking and knowing you are well prepared to achieve it. In this chapter we consider the first major step in preparing to speak in public: selecting a topic and general purpose, tentatively phrasing a central idea, and phrasing a desired response from listeners. We said "the first major step" because topic, general purpose, central idea, and desired response are inseparably interrelated. Sometimes you can do them in a 1, 2, 3, 4 order, step by step. More often, however, narrowing the topic to a central idea statement and specifying an observable desired response happen at the same time.

As you proceed with your analysis, changes may become necessary. Even the general purpose may have to be changed (if it was not assigned) before you can proceed with planning. Sometimes your investigation of the topic will lead you to change the wording of your tentative central idea. Many times a student begins audience analysis and research with a tentative central idea, then discovers this idea is unsound, inappropriate for the audience, or much too broad to develop within the time allotted for the speech. More infrequently you may change the topic and start all over.

In Chapter 5 we describe how to analyze the audience and speaking situation so you can make appropriate adaptations. Then in Chapter 6 we discuss how to gather information for developing an up-to-date, accurate message. Only through analysis of each major component of a forthcoming speech event can you discover and plan the adaptations necessary to bring listeners together with your central idea. We begin this chapter by helping you analyze yourself as a source of speech topics.

▶ Selecting a Topic

"What should I talk about? I want my speech to be interesting, but I don't know what to talk about." Sound familiar? Many conferences between a public-speaking student and his or her teacher begin with such a question, often asked in a tone of despair close to the day on which the student is scheduled to speak. Although the teacher can help, only the speaker can answer this question. What to talk about must initially be determined by self-analysis.

Outside of the public-speaking classroom, topic selection is seldom a problem. Most speeches are given as part of your work, your interest in some subject under discussion, your concern for a cause, or as a result of being recognized as an authority on some subject. Put another way, what we speak about should be a reflection of who we are. If you are not motivated as a speaker on the topic you have chosen, it is extremely difficult to motivate your audience.

One of the surest ways to develop a lack of confidence and suffer speech anxiety is to begin the search for a topic on the basis of probable interest of listeners. Never begin with the question "What would my audience be interested in?" Rather, begin with the questions "What am I interested in? What do I care deeply about? What would I like to learn more about, study, think about, discuss, and do?"

A good way to begin your preparation for speaking in class is to write down a list of possible topics suitable for you as a speaker. Just jot down a word or phrase for each; there is no need to elaborate at this point. How many did you discover? Most students come up with from six to ten, some even more. If you wrote "sports," name the specific sports. If "reading," list the kinds of reading or books you most enjoy. Your topic list is a good start at self-analysis as a public speaker. As you take on new roles and interests, some topics may be dropped from your list, others added.

Deciding on a topic, general purpose, tentative central idea, and tentative desired response is like taking aim.

Next, rank the topics according to how much you are interested in and enjoy them. Put them on clean sheets of paper, with about three inches of blank space between topics. Under each topic write more narrowed, specific topics on which you might speak in your class. Your final list of topics should resemble the examples below:

HOUSE PLANTS
Repotting a plant.
Rubber trees as house plants.
Growing a pineapple in your dorm room.
Small-scale hydroponic tomato culture.
Starting your own cacti.

EARTH SCIENCE

How caves are formed.

Tectonic plate theory.

Predicting earthquakes.

Radon gas.

Geyser action.

BEVERAGE ALCOHOL

Effects of alcohol on the brain.

Development of an alcohol dependency.

Four stages in making wine.

The credo of Alcoholics Anonymous.

COMPUTERS

The benefits of owning your own microcomputer.

How to clean a microcomputer.

How to get the best bargain in a personal computer.

How to select the best word-processing program.

DOGS

The world of dog shows.

Characteristics of the pug.

Dog intelligence testing.

Housebreaking a puppy with a cage and consistency.

Congratulations! You have taken the first step toward being a successful speaker. By systematic self-analysis you have discovered topics on which you might speak.

Even a somewhat narrowed topic like those in the previous examples deals with a broad area of human knowledge and behavior. A topic may have to be narrowed further to fit an assigned general purpose, the audience, and the situation in which your speech will occur. Before you can analyze your audience and situation, you must at least partly narrow the topic by tentatively deciding on a central idea and the response you want listeners to make to it. These statements must also be adapted to the situation in which the speech will occur. The situation always involves some time frame. For example, lectures are prepared to fit into all or part of a class period. Every congregation has expectations about the length of a sermon. Speakers are given specific time slots in dinner, convention, and training programs.

How you narrow a general topic is dependent on the situation in which speaker and listeners come together in the communication process. The situation may be a special occasion on which certain topics are appropriate and others taboo. Audience needs, interests, and expectations are other factors to consider while narrowing your topic to the central idea of your speech, and deciding on the response you will seek. Some topics may not be adaptable to some audiences, such as speaking on the design of surfboards for an audience of nursing home residents in western Kansas.

▶ General Purpose

Having selected a topic, you need to consider the type of *general purpose* you were assigned or want to accomplish. Many writers in the field of public address classify public-speaking objectives into broad categories: *to inform, to persuade,* and *to entertain.* These are not exclusive categories. While a speech might be primarily informative, new information will often persuade some listeners to do something they would not have done if they had not heard the speech. Persuading listeners to change a belief or take some action requires giving them information about the topic. Information can also be highly entertaining.

Public-speaking instructors sometimes assign the general purpose of a classroom speech, but give students complete freedom in selecting topics, writing central ideas, and desired responses. We next explain the two most common categories of general purposes, then briefly describe others.

To Inform

The central idea of a speech to inform is accepted as true or correct by people knowledgeable on the subject. It is not controversial. In contrast, the central idea of a speech to persuade is usually controversial among people informed on the subject. For example, an informative speaker might describe one way of writing a resume. If the speaker argues that this is the best way to write a resume, the purpose would be to persuade, not to inform. A speaker might describe how an abortion is performed, but if the speaker claims abortion is immoral, the speech is to persuade. A speech to inform might describe the content, requirements, and grading of a psychology course (information), but urging listeners to take the course would turn it into a speech to persuade. The central idea has become "You should take Psychology XYZ because. . . ." You might inform an audience about the political beliefs of a candidate, but if you urge listeners to vote for the candidate, your general purpose is persuasive, not informative.

Speaking to inform is both common and important. In addition to informative speaking in nearly all classrooms from preschool through graduate study, such speaking is done in a wide variety of work settings. Neighbors often instruct each other about how to perform some maintenance or lawn chore. Skilled craftspeople explain to tourists how they make lye soap, weave cloth, tan leather, mill grain, carve wood, build barrels, or rifle a gun barrel. Coaches inform athletes about how to perform. Building supply stores provide workshops for customers. Rangers explain flora, fauna, and geological features of the parks in which they work.

As a result of informative speakers, each of us is able to understand, enjoy, and function more safely and effectively than otherwise. We are at ease with things that might otherwise frighten us. We can begin where others have left off without having to reinvent for ourselves all the wondrous devices created by our predecesors. As an informative speaker, you pass on some part of the accumulated knowledge and wisdom of humankind, making a personal contribution that enriches the lives of others. Principles of informative speaking are explained in detail in Chapter 14.

To Persuade

We are constantly subjected to attempts to persuade us and in turn attempt to persuade others. Perhaps this morning your mother, spouse, or roommate tried to persuade you to eat breakfast before leaving for school or work. If you listened to the radio this morning you heard numerous commercials designed to persuade you to do something. A friend may have attempted to get you to go to the theatre, movie, or out to dinner. Perhaps you tried to get another friend to study with you for an exam. A classmate may have asked you to sign a petition and presented several persuasive arguments for signing.

If for no other reason, you need to understand the process of persuasion to protect yourself from speakers who try to engage you in dubious causes, convince you of false ideas, or get your money for shoddy goods. On the other hand, as a concerned and involved citizen you will want to contribute to worthwhile causes and efforts by persuading other people to support them.

Democracies can function because people, responding to persuasive messages, voluntarily agree to cooperate. Actions are taken in clubs and other volunteer organizations to which you belong on the basis of a majority vote, not which member is the strongest or has the most cash or a weapon. A majority usually means that members have succeeded, through persuasive speaking, in convincing others to accept a particular point of view or action.

The general response desired by a persuasive speaker is a change of listeners' beliefs or behaviors. The central idea in a persuasive speech will often be controversial: Some knowledgeable people will agree with it, some will be neutral, and others will disagree. The target audience of the speaker either will not agree with the central idea or will not have been acting in some way desired by the speaker. A persuasive speaker might simply try to convince listeners that their taxes for national defense should be raised, caffeine is addictive and dangerous, or a bond issue should be passed in order to rebuild city sewers. The speaker might ask listeners to take a specific action, such as to call senators and urge them to vote for increased military spending, quit drinking all beverages containing caffeine, or vote for a bond issue on a city ballot.

Speakers frequently seek to arouse listeners who agree with the central idea, but who have very little personal involvement or commitment to it. For instance, a person might agree that we ought to conserve oil for the sake of future generations, but act as if this is entirely a matter for others to be concerned about. You might generally agree that Martin Luther King was a courageous leader, but have no strong urge to adopt any of his political philosophy. The speaker then would try to involve your self-concept with the belief to such an extent that you would find it almost impossible not to act in ways that seem congruent with the belief. As a result, you might decide to drive a fuel-conserving car, avoid plastics and fertilizers made from crude oil when suitable alternatives are available, and stand up at personal risk against laws you deemed unfair. Listeners have to believe and feel that such actions are more desirable than the alternatives or they will not respond as desired. Persuasive speaking is explained in detail in Chapter 15.

Other General Purposes for Speaking in Public

On some occasions, the primary purpose for speaking in public may be neither to inform nor to persuade. For example, speakers may be asked to entertain or *to commemorate.*

If the primary purpose is to entertain, the speaker is concerned that the listeners enjoy themselves in response to the speech, not that they demonstrate the retention of new information or skills, or make some change in belief or action. Entertaining speaking is often a part of a dinner or banquet program or included with music, magic, dancing, and other programming presented either live or through electronic media. Frequently the overt response desired of listeners is laughter. A person speaking to entertain may want us to enjoy vicariously an adventure or trip of some sort or an extended dramatic story. In such a speech the primary desired response would be involuntary attention and vivid images in the perceptions of the listeners. Of course many an entertaining speech has a serious point underlying it, which the speaker wants listeners to accept as a secondary purpose. Some excellent speeches that are primarily to inform or persuade are also entertaining. Abraham Lincoln, for instance, was famous for using humorous stories to make a point.

On many special occasions speakers primarily commemorate ideals or traditions, often as part of a ceremony. Anniversary celebrations, birthdays, commencements, completion of successful fund-raising campaigns, holidays, the dedication of a new building, and funerals are examples of occasions when groups of people gather to reaffirm shared values and beliefs. Unwritten rules for behavior are a major factor in such ceremonial occasions. The speaker needs to be aware of and adhere to these special social expectations. A speech is planned into the program in order to emphasize the symbolic meaning of the occasion to the people gathered. The broader general purpose of speeches on such occasions is usually to persuade, often to strengthen beliefs or secure a greater sense of personal involvement by each listener with values emphasized in the ceremony. Speaking on special occasions is described in greater detail in Chapter 17.

Now that we have explained the major types of general purposes for speaking, we next consider how to formulate the central idea.

▶ Creating a Central Idea

The *central idea* is a single declarative sentence that gives the speech focus and unity. It summarizes what you will say about the topic in a single sentence that makes some point about the topic. Some writers call the central idea a *thesis sentence, theme,* or *proposition.* At this stage in preparing to speak, you may be able to express this sentence only tentatively, even somewhat vaguely. You will need to formulate it clearly and precisely after doing a detailed analysis of the audience and situation and conducting any research needed on your topic. However, those steps can be taken efficiently only if you have first formulated a tentative central idea.

Everything in a speech should be clearly related to the central idea: no story, example, joke, fact, or question belongs unless it advances the listener's interest in, understanding of, and commitment to that central idea. When written in final form, the central idea is a standard against which you judge every bit of information and everything you might say to decide whether or not it belongs in your speech. Without the focus of a central idea you are likely to wander around the landscape of a broad topic arriving nowhere in particular, leaving listeners confused about your point. They do not know what to focus on, what to remember, what is major and minor. Each listener is likely to have a very different idea of what your speech meant. For effective speaking, the central idea statement should be a full sentence that clearly expresses one major idea.

Clarity: The Central Idea Is Written as a Complete Declarative Sentence

A central idea sentence includes the topic, but is not the same as the topic. It contains both the topic (subject) and what you have to say about the topic (predicate). The contrast between a topic in the form of a word or phrase and a central idea sentence is illustrated in the following examples:

> *Broad topic:*   Crime
> *Narrowed topic:*   Organization of the Mafia
> *Central idea:*   The Mafia in the United States is organized into 24 families, each of which is further organized into four levels of responsibilities.

> *Broad topic:*   Baseball
> *Narrowed topic:*   The role of a second baseman in making a short-second-first double play.

Central idea:	The second baseman must move rapidly and efficiently to cover the base, receive from shortstop, pivot, and throw to first when making a short-second-first double play.

Broad topic:	Litter
Narrowed topic:	Beverage-container return laws
Central idea:	A beverage-container return law would greatly reduce the ugliness, waste, and danger from litter in our state.

A question is not a central idea statement even though it is a complete sentence. A question can raise curiosity about a topic or a policy issue, but it does not present an idea or point. A central idea is an answer to some question, whether that question has been stated or only implied. The following question was initially proposed as a central idea statement by a student, then reformulated so it became a declarative central idea sentence.

Topic question:	How does pornography affect society? (From this question we can infer that the speaker will say that pornography has some effect, but we do not have any idea what effect(s) he or she will claim.)
Central idea:	Pornography depicting crimes of child abuse, rape, and murder stimulates some persons to commit such violent acts. (Notice how the central idea statement has answered the question, narrowed the topic, and specified the effects the speaker will claim during the speech.)

From the above examples you should now be able to distinguish between a topic and a central idea. As you can see, you could write many central idea statements about any broad topic. For instance, consider the topic "the English language":

English is the language of the world of science.
English is a highly flexible language.
English has origins in several other languages.
English reflects our gender prejudices.

Unity: The Central Idea Makes One Major Point about the Topic

A central idea sentence should express one idea about the topic. Marlene's central idea read "Walnut trees grow differently in different locations, and their wood is valuable for making furniture." Which idea did she want the listeners to remember as the *central* idea: that the quality of walnut lumber is affected by where a tree grows or that walnut is an excellent furniture wood? This statement could be revised in several ways to give unity to the speech:

> The quality of walnut lumber is affected by soil composition, amount of sunlight, and rainfall.
>
> Appearance, stability, and workability make walnut a superior furniture wood.
>
> The suitability of walnut for building furniture is influenced by such variables as soil composition, amount of sunlight, and rainfall.

As his central idea, David wrote that "Abortion is okay in certain situations and should be legal." David's wording is vague. What does "okay" mean? What does the speaker mean by "certain situations"? The central idea also sounds like two different theses: "Abortion is acceptable on some grounds" and "Abortion should be legal." After considerable rethinking David was able to produce a unified statement of his central idea: "Abortion should be legal in instances of rape or pregnancy of an unmarried juvenile."

Coherence: The Central Idea Suggests the Organization of the Body of the Speech

You may have noticed in the preceding examples that a clearly worded, unified central idea suggests the organization of the body of the speech. The sequence of main points discussed in a speech comes directly from the way a central idea is stated. Thus, a well-worded central idea contributes to coherence among the points of a speech so that each idea flows logically into the next one. We explain this principle in detail in Chapter 8.

The central idea composed for a particular speech will be determined by the speaker's purpose in relation to listeners' concerns, interests, and needs. Next we consider how to formulate the purpose you seek to achieve as a listener response to your central idea.

▶ Formulating the Purpose as a Desired Response

A speaker may have several purposes in making a speech. For instance, while seeking to have listeners understand his or her latest research finding, a scientist might also hope to win their support for an award. One of these purposes is the *primary* desired response, sought from the listeners as their immediate reaction to the speech. The primary desired response is directly related to the general purpose. The scientist in our example has a primary general purpose of "to inform"; "to persuade" is a secondary general purpose. The formulation of a tentative desired response statement should begin as you are considering various topics. The relationship among the selection of a particular topic, central idea about that topic, and possible *desired responses* is dynamic: your central idea will shape your desired response just as your desired response will influence the topic and central idea you select. Thinking about and writing the central idea and desired response statements must be done concurrently, not as sequential steps.

▶ Three Guidelines for Composing Central Idea Statements

1. The central idea is written as a complete declarative sentence.
2. The central idea makes one major point about the topic of the speech, giving unity to everything the speaker says.
3. The central idea suggests the organization of the body of the speech.

To maximize your effectiveness as a speaker, it is essential for you to think of and state the desired response as some observable or measurable behavior(s) of the listeners. Although you may not actually observe whether or not the listeners respond as you have specified, it should be possible to do so. Such a statement is sometimes called a *behavioral objective*.

Comparisons with other activities may help you to understand why the desired response statement should describe a specific behavior of the listener. If you are fishing, the purpose of casting and working your lure is to have a fish bite. If you are shooting baskets, the goal is for the ball to pass through the hoop. The purpose of a drop shot that barely makes it over the net is for your tennis opponent to be unable to return the ball. In speaking you will be much more successful if you learn to think of your purpose as being the precise action you want from listeners as a response to your speech. The desired response statement describes specific behavior you are seeking as a response to your speech.

As a practical matter, you should always limit the desired response statement to something that is realistically achievable. This principle is a corollary of the principle that the topic must be focused into a central idea. In a seven-minute classroom speech you cannot expect to get skeptics to believe that the Bible is the literal word of God, that socialism distributes wealth more fairly than capitalism, or to recall the major steps in the rise and fall of the Roman Empire. However, they probably could learn three reasons why fundamentalists believe the Bible is the literal word of God, four major differences between socialism and capitalism, or how the practice of slavery contributed to the decline of the Roman Empire.

The following examples contrast descriptions of observable behaviors as desired responses with statements that fail to specify observable responses.

Ineffectual examples describe what the speaker will do rather than what the speaker wants listeners to do.

Ineffective: To persuade my listeners about the benefits of reading as a pastime. (Speaker centered, fails to specify listener behavior.)

Effective: As a response to my speech I want my listeners to plan a reading program for free-choice time as an alternative to watching whatever is available on television. (Listener centered, describing observable behavior as a response.)

Ineffective: To inform about the ingredients of a martini.

Effective: As a response to my speech, I want my listeners to be able to ask three questions of a guest in order to determine what combination of the two major ingredients and garnish would make the most pleasing martini for the person.

Ineffective: To persuade my listeners that our state needs a beverage-container return law. (This purpose statement provides no basis in listener responses for judging how well the speaker has achieved the aim of the speech. No observable behavior has been specified.)

Effective: As a response to my speech I want my listeners to agree with me that our state should enact a beverage-container return law.

or

As a response to my speech, I want my listeners to phone their local state legislators, urging them to vote for LB 783, the beverage-container return bill. (These improved versions of the purpose statement provide for a specific response on an opinion ballot if the speaker gives a questionnaire to the listeners.)

▶ Summary

The first major step in preparing to speak in public is to decide on a topic. Outside of the public-speaking classroom, most topics are determined by your work, the occasion, or the organization that invites you to speak. For classroom speeches, always choose your topic based on what interests, excites, and motivates you. Avoid the common mistake of choosing a topic based on what you think the members of your audience want to listen to. As you are selecting a topic, begin thinking about the goal of the speech. Although you may have secondary purposes for speaking, there should always be one primary type of general purpose. From the speaker's perspective, almost all public speaking can be classified as primarily to inform, to persuade, to entertain, or to commemorate. You should be able to write two types of statements needed to define your goal: a central idea sentence in which you affirm one idea about the topic of your speech and a sentence describing the desired response of listeners to that idea. Having formulated these two statements in tentative form, you are in a position to analyze the audience and speaking situation as the next steps in preparation.

▶ Guidelines for Composing Desired Response Statements

1. Write the statement as a descriptive sentence focusing on what the listeners can or will do if you achieve your speaking objective.
2. Describe the response behavior in such a way that it can be observed or measured.
3. Be sure the goal is a response you can realistically hope to achieve within the limits of your resources and the time available.
4. Be sure the behavior is not something the listener could or would have done if you had not spoken.
5. Begin with the phrase "As a response to my speech . . ." in order to emphasize the idea that the listeners' behaviors are a response to a message created by you. As an alternative wording, you may begin with "To have my listeners. . . ."

▶ Learning Activities

1. Each of the following items has some deficiency as a central idea. For each item first identify the deficiency, then revise the statement as a possible central idea for a five- to ten-minute speech to be given in your class. Be sure to follow all the guidelines for writing central idea statements!
   a. Advantages of belonging to a sorority or fraternity.
   b. What is likely to be the effect of genetic engineering on our society?
   c. The U.S. constitution—its strengths and limitations.
   d. College versus high school.
   e. How fuel injectors and antiskid brakes work.
2. What is the type of primary purpose for each of the following central idea statements? Indicate your response with one of the following letters: I, informative; P, persuasive; E, entertaining.
   a. A blind date is like fishing with a tennis racquet.

b. Before being permitted to possess and/or carry a handgun, a U.S. citizen should have to demonstrate a felony-free record, knowledge about handguns, and proficiency in safe handgun usage.

c. Both selective- and clear-cutting are practiced in national forests.

d. Persons convicted of a capital crime should be permitted no more than three appeals within one year of original conviction before being executed.

e. Most advanced nations have much more stringent driving while intoxicated (DWI) laws than does the United States.

f. When a person is convicted of DWI, the vehicle used (unless stolen) should be confiscated, sold at public auction, and the money used to reimburse victims or the state.

3. Identify the type of primary purpose for each of the following desired response statements: I, informative; P, persuasive; E, entertaining.

a. As a response to my speech, I want my listeners to be able to describe the effects of genetic heterosis on the growth, size, and health of offspring.

b. As a response to my speech, I want my listeners to be able to construct a paper jumping frog.

c. As a response to my speech, I want my listeners to agree that we should tax heavily enough to pay all federal expenditures in any peacetime year.

d. As a response to my speech, I want my listeners to vicariously participate in my ski trip to Steamboat Springs.

e. As a response to my speech, I want at least three of my classmates to make a deposit for the next United Students charter trip to Steamboat Springs.

4. Each of the following items was written as a desired response statement, but does not measure up to one or more of the five guidelines for writing such statements explained in Chapter 5. First, identify what is inadequate about each item, then revise the item to correct all deficiencies.

a. I want to inform my classmates about the two major types of Portland cement.

b. To convince my classmates that possession of any fully automatic weapon by a private citizen should be a felony.

c. As a response to my speech, listeners will understand how gene swapping occurs spontaneously in nature.

d. As a response to my speech, my classmates will want to take a public-speaking class.

e. I want to tell my listeners about the stupidity of using credit cards.

5. Below are two sets of main points for the body of speeches. For each set of main points write a central idea and desired response.

BODY

I. Food habits of eastern bluebirds are highly beneficial to humans.

II. Eastern bluebirds depend on humans for nesting boxes.

Central idea:
Desired response:

BODY

I. Many major universities lack the resources needed to conduct research into the causes of acquired immunodeficiency syndrome (AIDS).
II. The lack of funding for AIDS research will have a devastating impact on the world's population.

Central idea:
Desired response:

6. Select three topics appropriate for you as a public speaker and your speech class as an audience. For each of these topics write four different central idea statements. Then for each central idea statement write a desired response statement. You will now have 12 central idea and matching desired response statements that are potential topics for your public-speaking class. All of these should be feasible in speeches of five to ten minutes in length.

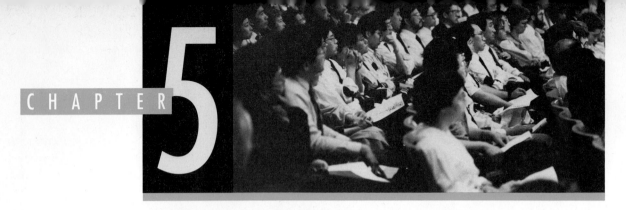

CHAPTER 5

Analyzing and Adapting to Audience and Situation

Questions to Guide Reading and Review

1. Why is it necessary to do an analysis of the audience early in your preparation for speaking?
2. Why is it important to make specific adaptations to an audience based on answers you generate to each of four questions about the audience presented in the first part of this chapter?
3. Why is it important to estimate the strength and consistency of listener beliefs and attitudes toward your topic and central idea?
4. How might you gather the information needed to perform an adequate audience analysis?
5. For what kinds of information would you use fixed-answer, scale, and open-ended questions on a listener survey questionnaire?
6. In order to plan appropriate adaptations, what four questions do you need to answer about the situation in which you will be speaking? Why is each question important?

Key Terms

Adaptation	Credibility	Questionnaire
Attitude	Demographic data	Scale question
Audience analysis	Fixed-answer question	Situation analysis
Belief	Open-ended question	Value

Beth Kearney was enthusiastic about returning to school after her children had grown and left home. For her first persuasive speech, she decided to convince the class that a mother should be at home when children are small. She selected many quotations from authorities advocating full-time parenting and denouncing working mothers for neglecting the duties of child rearing. Beth was well prepared, enthusiastic about her central idea, and confident that the class would accept her arguments. She was surprised to observe disapproving and hostile responses. The longer she spoke, the more restless and even rude the class became. Although Beth began with confidence and poise, she finished weakly.

What went wrong with Beth's speech? She failed to analyze and adapt to the beliefs and attitudes of her listeners. She did not realize that most women in her class were young mothers, attending college while their children were at day-care centers. Some class members came from families in which both parents had worked while they were small children.

As this story indicates, you must adapt your speech to the audience and situation. Otherwise, you will not achieve your desired response. Appropriate *adaptation* can be made only after careful analysis of these components of a speech event. In this chapter we present questions about the audience and situation that you must answer if you are to plan effective adaptations. We also

Adapt your speech to both the audience and the situation.

suggest several ways to get such answers. In this and following chapters we explain how to use your answers to make needed adaptations.

> *Yet time after time I've seen speakers give the wrong speech for an audience. . . . The speech may have been patronizing, offensive, or worse, irrelevant to the audience. And it's usually because the speaker and writer just don't do their homework.*
>
> *Along that line, I've heard speeches which didn't fit the occasion. I've heard speakers deliver a speech that belonged in a lecture hall, rather than a union hall—or deliver a tedious, solemn policy address at graduation ceremonies in which graduates and families just want to hit the exits and have a good time.*

Source: Robert B. Rackleff, *Vital Speeches of the Day*, March 1, 1988, p. 311. (Mr. Rackleff is a free-lance speech writer. This speech was delivered to the National Association of Bar Executives, Charleston, SC, September 26, 1987.)

▶ Audience Analysis

Adapting well to audience members depends on how adequately a speaker can answer four questions:

1. What do my listeners already know about my topic?
2. What beliefs and attitudes do they hold toward my topic?
3. How does this topic relate to listener needs and interests?
4. How will listeners initially react to me as a source of information on this topic?

The speaker who answers these questions carefully will be ready to plan how to capture audience interest and gain acceptance of the central idea.

Question 1: What Do My Listeners Already Know about My Topic?

To plan appropriately for speaking you must determine what the audience members already know about the topic. Adaptations can then be made to listener's backgrounds. Two common errors result when speakers fail to discover and adjust to what listeners already know.

First, speakers commonly assume listeners know too little about the topic. If a speaker fails to discover what listeners already know about the topic, the speech may be too elementary to sustain attention. Listeners will resent the speaker for wasting their time. For example, Sandra described how to use the

"Infotrac" program in the university library to locate articles on a topic. She failed to discover that all but two of her classmates had already completed an English course in which they were taught how to use Infotrac. Audience members gave signs of being bored and irritated at Sandra.

The second type of error results from assuming that listeners know far more than they do. Listeners will be confused and feel annoyed at the speaker who does not address their level of knowledge. For example, students often complain about math instructors who assume their listeners understand some mathematical operation when in fact they do not. "I can't keep up" is a common complaint. Older speakers often forget that younger listeners did not experience such events as the Korean War or the resignation of President Richard Nixon. We are not saying one should not speak on a topic outside the experience or education of listeners. We mean that special adaptations must be made when doing so. Techniques for this are explained in chapters devoted to developing ideas (Chapter 7) and informative speaking (Chapter 14). A desired response will not be achieved unless the listeners perceive how the ideas of the speaker are related to them personally. The speaker must adapt the message to the level of knowledge of listeners without either oversimplification or unnecessary complication.

When performing an *audience analysis*, you will want to learn as much as you can about the personal experience listeners have had with your subject. Firsthand experience is reality for them, influencing their interest in a topic and greatly affecting how they respond to your information and ideas. For example, people who have lived with a chemically dependent person are likely to react more emotionally to examples, statistics, and expert opinions on this subject than people who have not. Also, you will want to know what language the listeners use to refer to concepts you plan to talk about so you can literally speak their language. You can learn about such matters by listening sensitively to what they say and through interviews or questionnaires, as explained later in this chapter.

Question 2: What Beliefs and Attitudes Do Listeners Hold Toward My Topic?

Knowing how listeners are likely to react to a central idea and information you might use to develop it is crucial to convincing an audience. Only a speaker who is rhetorically insensitive ignores the combination of beliefs and attitudes listeners have toward a speech subject. Belief, attitude, and value are concepts that refer to opinions, feelings, and tendencies to react toward things we encounter.

Beliefs are ideas or conclusions a person accepts as true about other people, objects, or ideas. For instance, you may believe that the president of the United States should be elected by a direct vote of citizens instead of by the Electoral College or that the earth was created by a Big Bang.

Values are beliefs that are judgmental. People, objects, or issues are evaluated as good/bad, right/wrong, just/unjust, or moral/immoral. Many values are about how people should behave (called *norms*), such as "People should not assault each other" and "Be kind and courteous to classmates when they speak." Other values refer to judgments about the worth of ideas and organizations. Examples include: "Democracy is the best form of government"; "The Ku Klux Klan is a racist organization"; and "Student government is important." Values serve as standards for our judgments of many central ideas and as guides to our responses to attempts to persuade.

Attitude refers to an enduring tendency to act positively or negatively toward a type of object, person, or idea. Attitudes are based on beliefs and values. For example, because one of the authors thinks Honda cars are reliable (belief), and reliability is important to her, she is inclined to buy a new Honda (attitude) when she goes car shopping. You probably have a positive attitude toward items marked "100% cotton" and a negative one toward DWI.

Beliefs, values, and attitudes may be inconsistent or even contradictory to each other. For instance, someone might think we should increase the penalty for DWI, yet agree with a friend who says "You cannot legislate morality." Such contradictions and inconsistencies make this a difficult area of audience analysis. However, discovering the strength and consistency of a listener's beliefs, values, and attitudes related to the central idea is necessary if a speaker is going to adapt to listeners. This is especially important when listeners strongly disagree with your central idea.[1]

The source of information on which a belief or attitude is based can influence the strength of the belief. Personal experiences usually produce stronger beliefs and attitudes than those produced by what we read or are told.[2] For example, a listener who had recently been the victim of an armed robbery would have a stronger attitude toward gun control than a listener who had viewed a report about gun control on "60 Minutes." Also, the more a listener knows about a subject, the more difficult it tends to be to change beliefs and attitudes toward that subject.[3] For instance, you probably need more evidence to change a dietician's attitude toward drinking milk than to change the attitude of a computer programmer. In addition to source and amount of knowledge, the more central a belief is to a listener's self-concept, the more difficult it will be to change.[4] For instance, opposition to abortion is central to the self-concepts of many people who believe that a human individual exists at conception. It will be difficult or impossible to convince such a listener to favor legalized abortion.

Question 3: How Does My Topic Relate to Listener Needs and Interests?

People are egocentric: We listen best to information we perceive to be of personal value. When a speaker begins the introduction to a speech, the listener is usually wondering "How does this apply to me?" If the speaker does not answer this question quickly and to the satisfaction of the listener, she or he may cease listening. For example, a speaker might begin by telling fellow students how they can save $1200.00 a year on school costs. Saying "I'm going to talk about the costs of higher education" is not as likely to motivate class-mates to listen.

People have both needs that must be met and interests that motivate attentive listening and recall. People need to feel secure, affiliate with and love others, have a sense of self-worth, understand the world as they experience it, and be creative. How to analyze and adapt to these needs is discussed in detail in the chapter on persuasion (Chapter 15).

Interests are more subject specific than are needs. Football, ballet, French history, growing tomatoes, classical music, and politics are examples of interests. A topic can suddenly become interesting if it is related to previously established interests or if it is a striking part of a new experience. For instance, someone might notice some elaborate behavior of a strange bird, then get interested enough to look up the bird in a reference book and supply nesting boxes and food for it. When analyzing an audience, think about needs and interests your listeners already have that are related to your topic and tentative desired response. For example, a campuswide interest in the environment might be used to arouse listener interest in how local sewage is polluting a river, or a need for security could motivate listening to a speech about stopping date rape. Likewise, you might think of some way to provide your listeners with an experience that would arouse their interest in the topic. For example, one student played a recording from the band Mannheim Steamroller to classmates unfamiliar with this music. After hearing the music, several listeners ordered tapes from the speaker, who worked in a music store.

How can you get information to help you answer questions 2 and 3? One way is by listening carefully to what your fellow students say in their speeches and conversations. You will hear many expressions of beliefs and values. You might interview a few classmates, asking them what they believe about your tentative topic and how much it matters to them. You may be able to do a brief survey of your class, as described later in this chapter, or find a survey of people like your listeners. Sensitive listeners can answer such questions. People who perceive others only as stereotypes, projecting how they think, feel, and believe on others, cannot answer such questions well or adapt effectively as speakers.

While assessing listener needs and interests, be sure to consider the following questions:

1. What needs related to my topic are felt strongly by my listeners at this time?
2. In what topics and activities do they express interest through conversations, attention, special efforts, spending time, and money?
3. What have other speakers in the class said or done that has received attention?
4. If there is no preexistent sense of need or interest in my topic, to what long range concerns of the listeners is it related (e.g., being a parent, paying off college loans, getting a good job, etc.)?

5. How did I initially become interested in this subject? What developed my interest? Would this be an approach that might capture interest of my listeners?

6. If experienced, what specific details of my subject are likely to be stimulating and exciting in themselves?

After you have thought through answers to such questions, you can plan what to do and say to focus attention. It is important to be very specific when linking your topic to the needs and interests of listeners. If you don't, most listeners will respond politely without believing, remembering, or applying what you say. The following example illustrates the process of analysis and adaptation:

> Luann had spent most of her life on a ranch, helping her father raise beef cattle. She anticipated becoming a rancher in her own right. To her, scientific cattle breeding was a fascinating subject. However, her class-mates were all from the city; few could tell a Simmental or Angus from a horse. How could she make a connection between their lives and her fascination with beef cattle? Well, they all said they enjoyed steak and hamburgers. She had heard classmates complain about the cost of food. Two classmates had discussed health in relation to nutrition, stressing the need for keeping cholesterol intake low. To most people, beef means cholesterol. That's it! They are interested in good-tasting food, good health, and keeping costs down. She would explain how breeding with the "black factor" in cattle genes lowered cholesterol while improving protein quality at low cost. She could do it as a detective story or riddle to arouse curiosity. With this lead, Luann went on to focus attention so well that after class her listeners were talking about how beef was being improved nutritionally without costing more!

Question 4: How Will Listeners Initially React to Me as a Source of Information on My Topic?

The common saying "Who does he think he is?" indicates the importance of considering how listeners initially perceive you in relationship to your topic. You know that parents may tell children things that are not valid and that authorities do not always know what they are talking about. As a listener, we urged you *always* to wonder "How does this speaker know this? How dependable is his or her developmental material?" Critical listeners will be quite skeptical when *you* speak, asking themselves "How does she know that?" and "Why should I accept his opinion?"

Question 4 reminds you to think about how listeners perceive you *before* you begin to speak. If needed, you can then plan how to enhance the *credibility* or trust listeners will place in what you say. Ken failed to realize the importance of such adaptations.

Ken had barely finished describing the preparation of a body for viewing at a funeral home when a member of his class blurted out: "How do you know about embalming?" "Oh, I didn't tell you, did I, that I'm a licensed mortician." Although Ken seemed to know his topic well, curiosity about how a fellow student would know so much about mortuary practice had been a serious distraction to the listeners.

This example illustrates the need to answer question 4 and plan appropriate adaptations so listeners will perceive your statements as credible. Chapter 9 on organization and Chapter 15 on persuasive speaking will further assist you in accomplishing this goal.

Finding Information about Audiences

You can gather information needed to make educated inferences about knowledge, interests, and beliefs of listeners from demographic data, interviews, and surveys.

▷ Four Key Questions for Audience Analysis

> 1. What do my listeners already know about my topic?
> 2. What beliefs and attitudes do listeners hold toward my topic?
> 3. How does my topic relate to listener needs and interests?
> 4. How will listeners initially react to me as a source of information on my topic?

DEMOGRAPHIC DATA   *Demographic data* refers to the statistical description and analysis of characteristics of a group of people. Although demographic data can provide a lot of detail, it is wise to proceed cautiously when using such facts to make inferences about interests, beliefs, and attitudes. People do not always practice what their churches or unions urge, vote a party ticket, act like others their own age, or choose what other members of their socioeconomic class choose.

Information about the characteristics of members of an audience can be obtained in a number of ways. For speeches outside the classroom, you can often ask questions of the person who invites you to speak and/or other members of the organization whom you know. Some organizations have done extensive surveys of member characteristics and will provide such information if you request it. Sometimes you can distribute a questionnaire asking for demographic information. Visual observation of your class can tell you a lot about age, sex, and other observable attributes.

The number of potentially important demographic characteristics is virtually limitless. You will have to ask yourself "What characteristics of my audience are likely to be related to their knowledge, beliefs, and current interests in my topic?" Then your survey or interview questions can focus on those characteristics. The following seven demographic variables are likely to be helpful in predicting responses to a variety of topics: social context, age, sex, education level, occupational background, religion, and ethnic background.

(1) **Social context.** Social context refers to the people with whom the individual has regular contact and groups in which one is a member that influence beliefs and attitudes. Many of your attitudes, beliefs, and values were learned from members of your family, friends, and neighbors. Whether people live in a ghetto, urban development, suburb, or rural area indicates the probability that they have certain beliefs, values, and interests. Membership information is useful to the degree that members of a culture or group share norms, motives, needs, and interests.[5] For example, if your topic was loss of top soil through erosion, it would be helpful to know whether audience members have rural or urban backgrounds.

(2) **Age.** Knowledge, beliefs, and interest in topics can be predicted from a listener's age. To illustrate, consider the age group(s) to which each of the following topics would be of greatest interest:

Adjusting to dorm life.
Planning for a secure retirement.
Insurance—whole life or term?
How to survive the empty-nest syndrome.
Planting a vegetable garden.
Buying a new home.
Using social security benefits.
Hearing loss and rock music.

Although some topics are obviously directed to a specific age group, almost any topic can be made interesting if the speaker relates the topic to needs of the listener. For example, a speech about retirement planning could be made engrossing to 20-year-old college students by stressing the accumulation of interest paid on savings over a period of 30 to 40 years.

Each stage of life is associated with concerns that can be helpful in selecting focal points of interest. Young adults tend to be idealistic, receptive to new ideas and methods, impatient, strongly influenced by peers, and responsive to rapid delivery. On the other hand, older persons are more responsive to appeals to tradition, reluctant to risk major changes, patient, and favor highly structured organization and slow delivery. Social scientists have demonstrated a clear link between age and persuasability, with preteens being most persuadable, followed by a steady rise in resistance as age increases.[6]

However, speakers must be cautious when applying demographic stereotypes. The idea that people over 70 are decrepit, poverty stricken, and uninterested in learning does not accurately describe this group. Many retired persons have more discretionary income, are more active in hobbies and physical sports, and join more community groups than younger people. Information about age of listeners must be used cautiously in conjunction with other demographic information when planning how to adapt to an audience.

(3) **Sex.** Differences in experiences and interests between men and women are indicated by the content of magazines published primarily for women and those primarily published for men. Consider, for example, such magazines as *Ms., Family Circle*, and *Working Woman* in comparison to *Esquire, Gentleman's Quarterly*, and *Popular Mechanics*. As with age, be cautious when relying on sex stereotypes. Jobs, activities, and interests once treated by society as the domain of men *or* women now involve both. The only universal rule is to avoid all sexist language and stereotypes. Anything interpreted as indicating a sex bias on your part is likely to arouse defensiveness or even hostility. How do you react to the sexist biases shown in the following statements heard by the authors?

> Mr. Jones was assisted on this project by his charming young assistant, Connie. Give the little lady a round of applause.

> Mrs. Smith has put a lot of time and effort into this project. We thank her husband for letting us have so many of her Saturdays. With the project completed I am sure Doug will be eating better.

> John has been such a good father you would think he was their mother.

> I can't expect you men to understand how sensitive an issue this is, but you women can relate to the importance of bonding in the early years of child development.

Comments like these will identify you as an insensitive sexist. For example, at the annual banquet for personnel of a college, the vice president offered a toast to the assembled faculty, staff, and spouses: "I want to salute the men of this college and thank them for their dedication and service to this institution. I also salute our wives for their loving inspiration and support." Many of the faculty members were women, as were most of the staff members. It was weeks before people stopped talking about such offensive sexist remarks from an educated man.

(4) **Education.** Determining the educational levels of members of an audience will help the speaker select appropriate material and language. Specific adjustments must be made by speakers who address audiences of different educational levels about the same topic. For example, you would use a different vocabulary when speaking to high school students than when addressing graduate students. If the audience is not informed about the area of discussion, no matter what their general educational level they will not understand technical jargon or slang used by people who are familiar with the subject. Oversimpli-

fication of a concept or elaboration of a point already understood can annoy listeners; at best it will bore them. It is important both to avoid talking over the heads of the audience and to avoid patronizing by speaking below their vocabulary level.

(5) **Occupational background.** Closely related to educational level is job experience. With people spending much of their time at work, it is not surprising that work is central to self-image. Even at social gatherings people talk more about work-related topics than anything else. Speakers can relate to these interests and use them to estimate knowledge and experience developed on the job. Usually a person who invites you to speak can tell you a lot about the training and experience audience members will have that are related to your topic.

(6) **Religion.** Knowing the religious affiliations of listeners might be useful, depending on the topic, the nature of the speaking situation, and the relationship of the desired response to religious belief and practice. Many values are established during formal and informal religious training, often with lasting results. If your topic concerns such values or issues, you should at least consider religious affiliation when planning what you will say.

(7) **Ethnic and racial background.** Most differences among ethnic and racial groups are learned rather than innate. In the United States minority citizens often face discrimination and oppression, resulting in heightened sensitivity to stereotyped language and prejudices. A public speaker needs to avoid any statement, no matter how innocently expressed, which might be interpreted as condoning or encouraging any form of racial or ethnic discrimination. Abused ethnic group members and supporters of social justice who are not members of the ethnic group will be offended by such statements.

The attitudes, beliefs, and values a listener holds may be directly related to his or her ethnic background. Knowing that your audience consists of immigrants or descendants of immigrants from a particular country or culture might provide clues to their attitudes toward work, family, government, money, and other important concepts. For example, most people from China place very high value on family traditions and formal education.

In addition to the seven major demographic characteristics discussed, there are others to which you may need to adapt, such as hobbies, marital status, economic status, military service, political affiliation, union membership, and other group affiliations that people use to define themselves. The basic question to ask is "What other characteristics of audience members might affect their knowledge, beliefs, attitudes, and interests related to my central idea and desired response?"

INTERVIEWS   Interviews with contact persons, such as the program chairperson who arranged for you to speak, group members you know, or past speakers to the group, can provide you with specific information and suggestions to guide your speech preparation. These people can usually supply demographic information and insights that cannot be acquired through your own limited observations. Ask people who have firsthand experience with the audience such questions as

1. Why was I selected to speak on this topic?
2. How many people are likely to attend?
3. What percentage are males? Females?
4. What are the approximate ages of group members?
5. What are the educational and experiential backgrounds of listeners on this subject?
6. If appropriate to the topic, what are the religious, political, or ethnic backgrounds of the group's members?
7. Is there something I could read to learn more about your organization?

SURVEYS   Findings from published surveys can sometimes help a speaker analyze knowledge, interests, and attitudes of prospective listeners. For example, the newspaper *USA Today* publishes surveys on a wide variety of topics in each issue. When using published survey results such as a Gallup poll, you will need to evaluate the relevance of the findings to your intended listeners. The survey sample may have been very different from the people in a specific audience. For instance, it is likely that a New York City resident would have stronger feelings about issues such as air pollution and gun control than a person living in Springfield, Missouri, where the air is much cleaner and the murder rate is low. You can sometimes check to see if the survey findings are consistent with other similar surveys. The following are important questions to consider in evaluating survey results:

What is the date of the survey? (Beliefs do change through time.)
What organization or person conducted the survey? (It or they could be biased.)
Are the demographic characteristics of the people surveyed like those of your audience in ways related to your topic?

If you need more specific information, it may sometimes be feasible to gather it with a *questionnaire* you develop and administer. For example, a survey might help in adapting a series of speeches about participative management to members of a corporation. You may be able to do a simple survey of your speech class if your purpose requires it.

The kind and quality of questions you ask will determine the validity and usefulness of the responses. Referring to your initial audience analysis will help you decide exactly what additional information you need and guide the construction of your questionnaire.

Fixed-answer questions give the respondent a choice among alternative answers provided with the questions. The familiar true–false and multiple-choice questions are fixed-answer items. Such questions are very good for finding information about listeners' knowledge and experience. Although these responses are easy to tabulate, they do not allow flexibility if a respondent wants to give a different answer from those supplied. Figure 5.1 shows some examples of fixed-answer questions from an audience analysis questionnaire.

Scale questions are used to measure the strength of beliefs and attitudes or the frequency of some sort of behavior. By checking a position along a

```
3. If a friend told you he or she was tired of
   living, would you know how to respond?
   (   ) Yes
   (   ) No
   (   ) Uncertain

4. Has a member of your family or a close friend
   ever committed suicide?
   (   ) Yes
   (   ) No
```

```
2. Which of the following state parks have you
   visited one or more times? (check all that
   apply)
   ____Ash Hollow
   ____Chadron
   ____Fort Robinson
   ____Indian Cave
   ____Niobrara
   ____Platte River
   ____Ponca

3. How many times have you stayed in a state-owned
   cabin in one of the state parks you checked
   above?
   ____0
   ____1-3
   ____4-6
   ____7 or more
```

Figure 5.1 Fixed-answer questions provide several optional answers for respondents.

91

continuum, respondents indicate the strength of their positions. The following is a very common scale:

Strongly agree	Agree	Neutral	Disagree	Strongly disagree
+2	+1	0	−1	−2

The closer an opinion is to a +2 or a −2 the more consistency can be predicted between opinion and behavior. If the respondent holds a position of +1 or −1, the speaker can predict with confidence that sufficient relevant information could move the listener in the desired direction. A summary of such responses can be used by the speaker in selecting materials and reasoning to convince and motivate a specific target audience. The answers provide a basis for estimating the degree to which listeners are self-involved with an issue. Figure 5.2 shows additional examples of scale questions.

Open-ended questions encourage respondents to answer in their own unique ways. Such questions are especially useful for discovering unanticipated beliefs, personal reasons, and values. The answers may be difficult to interpret and tabulate, but sometimes they provide unanticipated information vital to making appropriate adaptations to listeners. For example, a specific question such as "How do you feel about eating veal?" could reveal information you might not obtain using a different question format.

Open-ended questions seem easy to write, but exactly how such a question is worded greatly influences the responses it receives. It is very easy to end up with biased answers to open-ended questions by suggesting socially desirable responses. For example, "In what ways has the company treated you unfairly?" suggests that the respondents *have* been treated unfairly. The question may lead respondents to recall negative experiences even if these were insignificant.

Answers to open-ended questions can be very hard to interpret. People are not equal in their ability to respond to such questions. One might answer briefly or not at all, yet be far more involved with the question than a fluent person who writes a lengthy response. Because such questions take more time to answer than do specific-answer or scale questions, some will not be answered, which could yield a distorted picture of the audience. The box on p. 94 contains open-ended questions typical of those used in conducting an audience analysis. Many of the problems associated with open-ended questions can be corrected by trying out the questions on a few people before administering the questionnaire to potential listeners.

Four general guidelines will help you prepare questionnaires that will yield information useful for adapting a speech to listeners:

1. *Keep it brief.* Ask only questions to get information you need to do your audience analysis. If you can get the needed information elsewhere, do so. The length of a questionnaire will affect the quality and quantity of responses. The rule of thumb is: Shorter is better.

2. *Ask questions in clear and concise language.* Make your questions as

simple as possible. Before you distribute questionnaires, ask a few people what they think you mean by each question. Revise any questions that produce uncertainty.

3. *Use a variety of types of questions.* The best questionnaires employ a combination of fixed-answer, scale, and open-ended questions. Each type of question will provide you with a different kind of response about the same issue.

---

4. Eaten in moderate quantities, chocolate is nutritious and healthful.
___Strongly agree
___Agree
___Uncertain
___Disagree
___Strongly disagree

5. How often do you feel guilty after eating chocolate?
___Never
___Rarely
___Occasionally
___Frequently
___Always

6. Chocolate is (check space on line that best reflects your opinion):

```
   :     :     :     :     :     :     :     :
_____
Delicious                                Repulsive
```

---

7. What is your position on smoking?
___Anyone should be allowed to smoke anywhere.
___Anyone should be allowed to smoke if no one else in a room objects.
___No one should be allowed to smoke in any public room occupied by other persons.
___No smoking should be allowed in any building.
___No smoking should be allowed anywhere.

Figure 5.2 Scale questions measure strength of opinions and feelings, as well as frequencies of behaviors.

93

What do you most enjoy doing while on vacation?

What is your opinion of chocolate as a food?

Please describe any training or teaching you have had about how to recognize suicide hints and how to respond to them.

Open-ended questions provide respondents with a lot of latitude in answering, so be sure to provide plenty of space for answers.

4. *Ask how important an issue, concept, or behavior is to the respondent.* Answers to many questions will not reveal the degree of self involvement the respondent has with the topic. For issues vital to your desired response, it is best to ask how important the issue is to the respondent with one or more scale questions.

In summary, gathering information to answer four major questions is the beginning of audience analysis. The answers you receive are then used to make inferences about listener knowledge, interests, beliefs, and attitudes toward your tentative central idea and desired response statements. These answers will help you to select materials, language, and rhetorical techniques to meet the needs and concerns of your audience.

No matter how thorough your analysis and prespeech adaptations, you still need to be prepared to encounter unexpected responses from some listeners. There is always a good chance that something you failed to learn about the audience will affect the response, an inference you made was erroneous, or some planned adaptation will fail. You must respond on the spot to the best of your ability rather than ignoring unanticipated responses.

▶ Speaking Situation Analysis

You will also need to analyze and adapt to the situation in which you will meet with the audience. Communication always occurs within a specific context to which the form and content of a message should be adapted. The following four questions will help you analyze characteristics of the speaking situation so that you can plan adaptations:

1. What brings these people together as an audience?
2. What is expected of a speaker in this situation?
3. What else is occurring or has recently occurred that could affect my listeners' responses?
4. To what characteristics of the physical setting for the speech will I need to adapt?

Question 1: What Brings These People Together as an Audience?

First, you must find the purpose for which the audience will assemble. If they are gathered for the express purpose of learning more about your subject or out of enthusiasm for you, you have a voluntary audience; audience members are already motivated to listen and your credibility is probably high before you speak. More often, however, your central idea may be peripheral or irrelevant to the reason for assembling, producing a captive audience of people who did not come to hear what you have to say. Many organizations invite guest speakers to add to their programs, but the speaker is almost incidental to the purpose of the gathering. Many groups meet for purposes such as fellowship, to fulfill requirements for periodic meetings, to plan group activities, to raise funds for community service, and to gain professional or business contacts. In many cases the speaker must find some common interest on which to establish a sense of unity with the listeners. Often the speaker is invited because of position or reputation rather than to speak on some specific subject.

The person who invites you to speak is an excellent source of information about the speaking situation. Asking the following questions will help in analyzing the speaking situation:

1. What is the purpose of this meeting?
2. Why was this topic chosen at this time?
3. What else is on the program?
4. What will members be doing before and after I speak?
5. What are the current projects of the organization?
6. What have members been discussing at recent meetings?
7. When was the last time you had a guest speaker? What did he or she speak about? How was the topic received?

Answers to these questions will help you select developmental materials and otherwise adapt to the occasion as perceived by the listeners.

Question 2: What Is Expected of Me in This Situation?

After finding out what you can about the purpose of the meeting at which you will speak, you need to know exactly what is *expected* of you in the situation. Norms for different types of situations determine the appropriateness of humor, length of the speech, and whether or not audience participation is desirable. To be effective, the speaker must understand and adapt to these rules of behavior. For example, you would expect a commencement speaker at a college or university to speak much differently than an after-dinner speaker at the annual sports award banquet. Both speakers should be well prepared, but the style of delivery, language, and content of the speeches would be expected to reflect very different situational requirements. Sometimes a speaker can break such conventions with good effect, but the speaker must understand the norm, have a good reason for breaking it, and believe that breaking it will increase the degree to which listeners will respond as desired.

Although public-speaking classes may not be very formal or restrictive about topics and content, you should consider the norms governing speaking behavior in this type of situation. Are there expectations regarding dress, use of humor, or profanity? Your teacher will be evaluating your performance based on a set of standards that indicate what you must accomplish and how you must accomplish it. You have a captive audience who came to study public speaking, not to hear about your favorite topics. You are probably only one of several speakers that day, each with an interesting topic. You will be expected to stay within assigned time limits out of fairness to other speakers, but if your speech is shorter than expected, listeners may feel cheated or suspect that you know little. Some college students fail to think of situational expectations when planning and so alienate their listeners. Thinking about the following questions can help you discover what is expected of you when speaking:

1. What are the time limits or expectations regarding my speech?
2. Are there any special expectations regarding my personal appearance and behavior?
3. Are there any special expectations regarding topic selection, developmental materials, and use of language?

Question 3: What Else Is Occurring or Has Recently Occurred That Could Affect My Listeners' Responses?

In addition to the expectations listeners have for the occasion or assignment, the speaker must also consider other events going on at the time of the speech that are related to the subject and/or interests of the audience. A speaker can thus capitalize on events in recent news, other speeches on the program, and special occasions such as holidays to gain interest and attention. Timeliness is an important attention device.

Be sure you are up on recent news about your topic, or you may lose credibility with listeners who are. For instance, a speaker who urged listeners not to smoke in public buildings lost all credibility because he was not aware that a law had recently been passed banning smoking in such buildings. If crime is your topic, you might use a report on a campus robbery from the morning news.

One way of creating a sense of timeliness is to find out what else is on the program, then refer to those events early in the speech. In a classroom, referring to a previous speech or speaker will help gain interest. For example, when Joella spoke about access for the handicapped to public buildings she began with a reference to what two previous speakers had said:

> Remember the heated discussion we had last week following John's speech encouraging us not to use the restricted parking stalls designed for the handicapped? I had never paid much attention to it before, but I do now. . . . After trudging up the stairs to the front door of the Council Bluffs library it occurred to me that a person in a wheelchair couldn't get up those stairs. I looked for a ramp or another entrance, but there was none. I couldn't believe it. . . . The only public library in our town and it had not been remodeled for access by wheelchair!
>
> I wanted to know why. That is when I found out how right Nancy was when she said that our city councils are too busy with government regulations to get things done for the people who need them. . . . Today I will discuss with you three ways you can actively participate to effect change in public access for handicapped persons.

Student speakers often fail to determine what other speakers will discuss to their dismay. In one class three students had identical desired responses. They could easily have determined in advance what other speakers were planning to talk about and adapted accordingly. It pays to determine what else will occur in the situation that may require you to adapt your speech.

Many students have used their listeners' eagerness for a coming holiday to help arouse interest. For example, just before Thanksgiving Rachelle used the long drives home and back to campus to involve her classmates in the subject of defensive driving.

Question 4: To What Characteristics of the Physical Setting Will I Need to Adapt?

How will the physical setting enhance or constrain your ability to speak effectively? Temperature, atmosphere, size, and arrangement of a room can all influence listeners. Audible noises, visual distractions, poor sight lines, or bad acoustics can significantly decrease the speaker's effectiveness unless anticipated and compensated for in planning. Rearranging desks in a classroom might be necessary if you plan to teach classmates to do the polka. You may need to come to class early so you can clean the chalkboard or remove distracting objects. Sometimes a speaker cannot change conditions, but can reduce their negative impact on the audience. For example, the speaker might have to move around the room, make large transparencies from small posters, or ask people scattered around a large auditorium to move closer together.

How audio, video, or other aids will work must be thought out. If you are planning to use an overhead projector in front of the room, you need to be sure there is an outlet nearby or an extension cord to reach one and a place to put the projector at a sufficient distance from the screen. If you plan to use a film you want to be sure the room can be darkened. Never assume the room comes equipped with a slide projector, chalkboard, easel, lectern, and so on. More specific guidelines for the use of sensory aids are presented in Chapter 11.

▶ The Continuous Process of Analysis and Adaptation

Audience and situation analysis do not end when rehearsal of a speech begins, but should continue until you finish speaking. A speaker must be sensitive to nonverbal feedback of listeners and adapt accordingly. Nonverbal signs of confusion, disapproval, disinterest, or enthusiastic support tell the speaker when to explain, emphasize, use more evidence, or continue as planned. A speaker who ignores such reactions runs the risk of losing attention and even of alienating the audience. However, if your analysis of the audience and situation were thorough you should encounter few surprises. If you have prepared to speak extemporaneously, you will be able to make impromptu adaptations.

▶ Summary

Adaptation to listeners requires that you first do a competent audience analysis. The analysis provides answers to four important questions concerning what the listeners already know about the topic, the beliefs and attitudes they have related to the topic, the relationship of the topic to listeners' needs and interests, and how listeners are likely to perceive you as a source before you begin to speak. Data from which to infer answers to these questions can come from demographic descriptions of audience members, interviews, and personal surveys. Preparation should allow for adaptations while speaking when unanticipated listener responses occur.

Analysis of the context in which you will be speaking provides the basis for planning adaptations to the situational component of the forthcoming public-speaking event. You need to determine what will bring people together in an audience, what will be expected of you as a speaker in the situation, how other recent and future events or parts of the program might affect listener responses, and how to adapt to the physical setting of the speech.

In public speaking, as in most complex activities, to fail to prepare is to prepare to fail. The speaker who has prepared adequately is free to attend to unexpected responses, adapting as necessary in order to succeed in achieving the desired response.

▶ Learning Activities

1. Select one item from your list of topics, preferably the one on which you are currently most knowledgeable. Write tentative central idea and desired response statements that you think appropriate for your public-speaking classmates at this time. Next, write a brief questionnaire to gather information needed for audience analysis in regard to your tentative central idea and desired response statements. This questionnaire will be duplicated and distributed to each classmate. The questionnaire should include at least two specific-answer questions, two scale questions, and one open-ended question. Administer and collect the completed questionnaires, and tabulate the responses. Using the tabulated responses and any other available information, write answers to the four major audience analysis questions. Finally, based on these answers, write out specific plans for adapting to the audience.

2. Prepare a brief questionnaire to be administered during interviews with a sample of at least five classmates. Tabulate and interpret the results.

3. Do an estimate of your credibility with your classmates on any two of the topics appropriate for you as a public speaker. On a scale of 5 to 1 (5 = high credibility to 1 = no credibility), rate yourself as you think classmates who are *skeptical* would rate you on each topic. Be sure you can explain the basis for your self-rating.

4. Using the topic you have chosen for your next speech, analyze the two public-speaking situations that follow. For each analysis, write your best-guess answers to questions 1 through 4 of a situation analysis.
   a. For situation 1, the audience is your public-speaking class.
   b. For situation 2, describe a group of people other than college students for whom you might speak on this subject on a specific date as part of a regular meeting of the group at their regular meeting place. This should be a real group with which you are familiar.
   c. Plan appropriate adaptations of your speech for both situations.

Notes

1. Charles U. Larson, *Persuasion: Reception and Responsibility*, 4th ed. (Belmont, CA: Wadsworth, 1986), pp. 45–46; Milton Rokeach, *Belief, Attitudes, and Values: A Theory of Cognition and Change* (San Francisco: Josey Bass, 1968).

2. Larson, *Persuasion*, p. 46.

3. Daniel J. O'Keefe, *Persuasion: Theory and Research* (Newbury Park, CA: Sage, 1990), pp. 45–59; Martin Fishbein (ed.), *Readings in Attitude Theory and Measurement* (New York: Wiley, 1967), pp. 257–266, 389–400.

4. Muzafer Sherif, Carolyn Sherif, and Roger E. Nebergall, *Attitude and Attitude Change* (Philadelphia: Saunders, 1965).

5. Larry Samovar and Jack Mills, *Oral Communication: Message and Response*, 6th ed. (Dubuque, IA: Wm. C. Brown, 1986), p. 221.

6. William J. McGuire, "Attitude and Attitude Change," in Gardner Lindzey and Elliot Aronson (eds.), *Handbook of Social Psychology*, II (New York: Random House, 1985), pp. 287–288.

CHAPTER 6

Gathering Information

Questions to Guide Reading and Review

1. Why is doing research before speaking on many topics a matter of ethics?
2. What is an efficient way to review previously acquired knowledge and experience of a topic?
3. How do you locate books, articles, and other print materials relevant to your topic?
4. How might you use an on-line data base to speed up your search for bibliographic items?
5. How do you prepare for, conduct, and follow up an interview with a person who has specialized information on your topic?
6. Why is it important to begin research with an open mind and as far in advance of your speech as possible?
7. What are efficient, effective ways to read and keep notes while you do research?

Key Terms

Bibliography
Card catalog

Dewey decimal system
Library of Congress
    classification system

On-line data base
Periodical

As a public speaker you have an ethical responsibility to be knowledgeable and current on the topics you have selected. Ethical speakers make sure that what they say is congruent with the relevant knowledge available to them. With the constantly accelerating rate of knowledge growth, it is a challenge to be sure you are current on your subject. For example, think of the amount of knowledge that has been accumulated about the cosmos, propulsion, automotive design, medicine, and computers in just the last five years.

Start your research early, keep an open mind about your central idea while doing it, and keep detailed notes of what you discover and where you find it. The following procedure will help you to gather efficiently the information available on your topic:

1. Review what you already know about a subject.
2. Compare what you know with experts on the subject.
   a. Through research in the library.
   b. Through interviews.

This chapter explains how to follow this procedure so you can locate, select, and use the best available information to illustrate and support your topic.

▶ Review What You Already Know

You began your preparation for speaking by selecting a topic on which you already have considerable knowledge. You need to be deeply interested in the topic to take the time required to become thoroughly prepared before speaking. If you are enthusiastic, research will be an enjoyable process of discovery.

To start the compilation of information about your topic, ask yourself questions to stimulate recall of what you know. Jot down notes about the answers you come up with. These notes will help you narrow your topic and direct your research for more specific information. Here are some examples of the kinds of questions that will help you recall what you already know about a particular topic:

Why is this subject so important to me?
How and when did I first get interested in this topic?
What personal experiences have I had with the topic?
What have I read about the topic?

Has anything related been in the news recently?

What have I heard in discussions about my topic?

What have I heard on radio and/or television?

Blank sheets of paper, the first of which has the tentative central idea and desired response written on it, can be used to make notes of what you remember. Use key words and phrases to represent information you recall while answering questions like those above. When you finish, a review of your notes will help you decide what you most want to share with listeners and indicate subtopics you need to learn more about or confirm through research. Then you will be ready to begin an efficient search for additional material. The following story illustrates how to proceed.

Tim decided on this tentative central idea: "Skydiving can bring excitement into your life at a reasonable cost." After a review of what he knew about his favorite hobby, Tim developed the following questions to guide his research:

How did skydiving become a sport?

What leads people to want to jump out of a plane?

How dangerous is skydiving in comparison to other sports?

How is the experience similar to and different from what most people expect?

What does skydiving cost?

Are there physical limitations on participation?

Tim could answer some of these questions from his experiences as an amateur skydiver. But he wanted to know how others felt about the sport, and he realized he could not adequately describe the dangers and limitations. Tim began his research in the library, then interviewed his diving instructor and several skydivers he had met at scheduled meets.

▶ Compare What You Know with Experts

This step in preparing to speak can be done through library research and interviews with knowledgeable persons. These sources can provide the speaker with information needed to speak responsibly.

The Library

Although they realize that the library would provide supporting material for a speech, many students fail to gather information they need. They do not know how to use the research tools libraries have that can simplify the job of compiling a *bibliography*, which is a list of possible sources of information and ideas, related to a topic. Research tools can help you find available information and examine all sides of a controversial issue. In recent years, computers have expanded the services a library can provide, making research easier for the student who learns how to use them. To learn more about using library tools, you may be able to take an orientation tour or a computer-assisted program offered by the library at your school. If you did not take a library tour as part of your student orientation program or in conjunction with one of your classes, ask a librarian when you can schedule a personal tour. Library staff members are eager to help students. Don't hesitate to take advantage of their expertise.

Most colleges and many universities have one central library serving the entire campus. In addition to the central library, many universities have satellite libraries serving special areas of study. Regardless of the physical location where a work is shelved, all of the holdings will be catalogued in the central library. To locate materials there are many research tools with which every speaker needs to be familiar, including the card catalog, reference works, periodical indexes, catalogs of government documents, on-line data bases, and lists of nonprint resources.

THE CARD CATALOG   The *card catalog* has a complete list of all books held in the library or system of university libraries. Many card catalogs also list records, tape recordings, slides, pamphlets, computer software, films, and other resources. Each holding of the library has three different listing cards in the catalog: title, subject, and author cards. By using any of these three alphabetical listings, the researcher can find the location of a particular item (see Figure 6.1).

Although many libraries still have card catalogs housed in numerous small file drawers, most now store the same information on microfiche, magnetic tape, or computer disks. The computer-output microfiche (COM) is computer produced and updated frequently. Special reader machines used to access information on fiche may be available in several locations on campus. Holdings on magnetic tapes or disks are retrieved at special computer terminals.

Both the COM and a computer terminal are used in the same basic way as the traditional card catalog drawers. This involves looking up the source by subject, title, or author in an alphabetical list. If you know the specific title of a book that you want to use for your research or you know of a specific author who has published works on the subject of your speech, you can use the title or author card to locate the materials.

Early in your research it is often helpful to look for books on your topic by using the subject headings of the card catalog. If one subject listing does not lead you to needed information, try others. Subject listings can help you find the subject headings used by most libraries. Knowing these will speed up your work. The most comprehensive of these reference books is the *Library of Congress Subject Headings*. Most libraries consider this two-volume set to be the "rule book" on subject classification. Every library will have either this or a similar reference work that you can use. You may have to ask for these

```
                    CONSUMERS
   658.834 Engel, James F
   E57c       Consumer behavior / James F. Engel,
   1986       Roger D. Blackwell, Paul W. Miniard.—
              5th ed. — Chicago: Dryden Press,
              1986.
                  xvii, 633 p. : ill. ; 25 cm.
                  ISBN 0-03-001892-7 : $33.95

              1.Consumers.  2.Marketing research.
              I.Blackwell, Roger D.
              III.Title.
   HF5415.3.E53 1986        658.8'342
                            dc19
                                       85-16139
           CATALOG CARD CORPORATION OF AMERICA·   AACR2       MARC
```

```
                 MARKETING RESEARCH
   658.834 Engel, James F
   E57c       Consumer behavior / James F. Engel,
   1986       Roger D. Blackwell, Paul W. Miniard.—
              5th ed. — Chicago: Dryden Press,
              1986.
                  xvii, 633 p. : ill. ; 25 cm.
                  ISBN 0-03-001892-7 : $33.95

              1.Consumers.  2.Marketing research.
              I.Blackwell, Roger D.
              III.Title.
   HF5415.3.E53 1986        658.8'342
                            dc19
                                       85-16139
           CATALOG CARD CORPORATION OF AMERICA·   AACR2       MARC
```

Figure 6.1 Subject, title, and author cards from the card catalog.

volumes because they are often kept behind the circulation or reference desk.

Whether you are looking at a subject, title, or author card you will find most of the following information:

1. Call number.
2. Author's name.
3. Birth and death dates.

```
658.834  Engel, James F
E57c          Consumer behavior / James F. Engel,
1986      Roger D. Blackwell, Paul W. Miniard.—
          5th ed. — Chicago: Dryden Press,
          1986.
              xvii, 633 p. : ill. ; 25 cm.
              ISBN 0-03-001892-7 : $33.95

          1.Consumers. 2.Marketing research.
          I.Blackwell, Roger D.
          III.Title.
HF5415.3.E53 1986        658.8'342
                         dc19
                                       85-16139
         《《 CATALOG CARD CORPORATION OF AMERICA·   AACR2      MARC
```

```
              Blackwell, Roger D.
658.834  Engel, James F
E57c          Consumer behavior / James F. Engel,
1986      Roger D. Blackwell, Paul W. Miniard.—
          5th ed. — Chicago: Dryden Press,
          1986.
              xvii, 633 p. : ill. ; 25 cm.
              ISBN 0-03-001892-7 : $33.95

          1.Consumers. 2.Marketing research.
          I.Blackwell, Roger D.
          III.Title.
HF5415.3.E53 1986        658.8'342
                         dc19
                                       85-16139
         《《 CATALOG CARD CORPORATION OF AMERICA·   AACR2      MARC
```

Figure 6.1   *(continued)*

4. Title of work.
5. Subtitles.
6. Coauthor's name.
7. Notes on editor, compiler, and illustrator.
8. Edition number.
9. Place of publication.
10. Publishing company.
11. Date of publication.

```
                    Consumer behavior
       658.834  Engel, James F
       E57c         Consumer behavior / James F. Engel,
       1986      Roger D. Blackwell, Paul W. Miniard.—
                 5th ed. — Chicago: Dryden Press,
                 1986.
                    xvii, 633 p. : ill. ; 25 cm.
                    ISBN 0-03-001892-7 : $33.95

                 1.Consumers. 2.Marketing research.
                 I.Blackwell, Roger D.
                 III.Title.
       HF5415.3.E53 1986        658.8'342
                                dc19
                                          85-16139
          ◀◀◀ CATALOG CARD CORPORATION OF AMERICA·   AACR2          MARC
```

Figure 6.1

In addition, the card will indicate the physical location of the item.

The call number on the upper left-hand corner of the card is the key to locating an item. Libraries use two different systems to classify materials, the *Dewey decimal system* and the *Library of Congress classification system*. If the call number begins with a number, the book is classified by the Dewey decimal system. If the call number begins with a letter, the library uses the Library of Congress classification system.

Whether your library uses the Dewey system or the Library of Congress classifications to catalog holdings, you will find the same numbers on the spines of the books as on the catalog cards. By using shelf guides you can find the location in the library for any holding for which you have the call number.

REFERENCE WORKS   Although the card catalog is an excellent tool for finding books, to support an idea you will often need to locate some specific fact such as a supporting statistic. It would be very inefficient for you to read numerous books and magazine articles in hope of finding a fact such as the number of people killed in highway accidents in Missouri in 1991, the number of foreign automobiles imported during the last five years, the rate of population growth in Dallas, or the origin of the word *leotard*. The resources that supply such information are called *reference works*. You have used many reference works such as encyclopedias, dictionaries, and atlases. However, you may not be aware of many specialized reference works that can help you with narrowed topics. The following commonly held reference works are classified by the type of information they contain.

1. **General encyclopedias.** General encyclopedias provide concise summaries and histories on a wide range of subjects. They are good for getting an overview of a subject. Examples include the *Encyclopedia Britannica, Encyclopedia Americana,* and *World Book.*

2. **Subject encyclopedias.** Some encyclopedias are limited to specific fields of knowledge. These encyclopedias are likely to be better sources of developmental materials for a central idea then are general encyclopedias. For example, there is an *Encyclopedia of Education, Encyclopedia of Philosophy,* and *Encyclopedia of Psychology.* Your library is likely to have many more special encyclopedias.

3. **Special dictionaries.** You are familiar with general dictionaries that help you with definitions and the pronunciation of a word. There are also dictionaries that provide the terminology of specialized fields of study. These are helpful in reading articles by specialists or clarifying technical jargon. Among these are *Black's Law Dictionary, Communication Handbook: A Dictionary, Dictionary of Word and Phrase Origins,* and *Safire's Political Dictionary.*

4. **Biographical reference.** Biographical reference books provide specific information about people. They are an excellent source of information on credentials of persons whose testimony you are considering using in a speech. Some of the major biographical reference works are: *Who's Who, Who's Who in America, Who's Who of American Women, Who's Who of American Education,* and *Who Was Who in America.* There is even a *Biography Index* to help you locate biographies.

5. **Yearbooks.** Yearbooks (annual publications) and handbooks provide annual reviews, statistics, and other specific facts that can be very useful for developing statements on public issues. Among these reference works are *Annual Review of Psychology, Facts on File Yearbook, Guiness Book of World Records, Information Please Almanac, Statistical Abstract of the United States,* and *World Almanac.*

6. **Atlases.** Atlases and gazetteers provide tables of geographical, social, and political data, as well as maps that can be used to help create visual aids. Among the more helpful are *Rand McNally Cosmopolitan World Atlas* and *Time Atlas of the World, Comprehensive Edition.*

7. **Books of quotations.** These books provide quotations on various topics, usually listed by subject area. They can help you find testimony to support an idea or quotations that dramatize and emphasize. Among these are *Bartlett's Familiar Quotations, The Home Book of Quotations, The Oxford Dictionary of Quotations,* and *Quotable Women.*

Reference books of the types listed above can help you locate specific information. Most are updated regularly. Often it is important, however, to find more recent information than such works provide, particularly about topics currently in the news. Periodicals and newspapers provide the most current information in print.

PERIODICALS   Publications issued at regular intervals of less than a year and more than a day are called *periodicals*. Most are aimed at specific audiences. You may have a personal subscription to a periodical such as *Psychology Today, Business Week, Forbes, Time, U.S. News and World Report*, or *Popular Mechanics*. Periodicals aimed at a general readership often contain simple, clear summaries of information on topics of current public interest in areas such as health and medical care, environmental concerns, child care, the economy, popular psychology, international relations, defense, crime, automobiles, home maintenance, family problems, and travel. *Time, U.S. News and World Report*, and *Newsweek* are particularly helpful to the student speaker.

Finding the information you need is tedious and unlikely if you merely browse through stacks of back-issue periodicals. An index enables you to locate quickly articles on any subject. The index for locating specific articles in popular periodicals is *The Reader's Guide to Periodical Literature*. It is easy to use, with entries from more than 150 general-interest periodicals alphabetized by subject headings and author names (see Figure 6.2). When listing bibliographic items from an index, be sure to copy down enough of the publication information about an article to enable you to locate it (see Figure 6.3). You will need to know the name of the magazine, the date of the issue, the volume number, the author, the title of the article, and page numbers. Some libraries have back issues of the most used magazines on microfiche or in a computer data base;

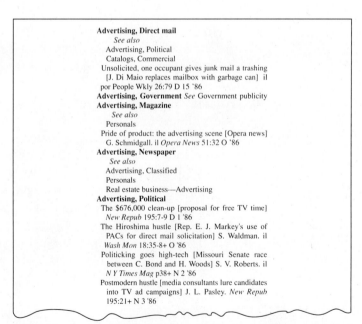

Figure 6.2   Part of a page from an issue of *The Reader's Guide to Periodical Literature.*

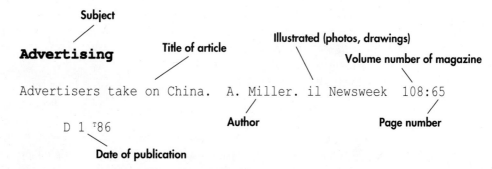

Figure 6.3 How to interpret an entry in *The Reader's Guide.*

if so, you will need to learn how to access information using the equipment the library provides.

Besides *The Reader's Guide to Periodical Literature,* there are several specific subject indexes that can direct you to more specialized journals and periodicals. For example, the *Business Periodicals Index* includes entries from over 250 journals in the fields of business and economics. Some of the indexes held by many college and university libraries include *Applied Science and Technology Index, Biological and Agricultural Index, Education Index, Social Science Index, Congressional Record Index,* and *Public Affairs Information Service Bulletin.*

NEWSPAPERS Newspapers provide even more current information than do magazines. Most libraries subscribe to local papers and leading papers from other cities. Like magazines, some major newspapers are indexed for quick retrieval of specific articles on subjects being researched. The index listing includes the month and day, section number, page, and column number. Among the newspapers indexed are the *New York Times (New York Times Index),* the *Christian Science Monitor,* the *Wall Street Journal,* the *Chicago Tribune,* and the *Washington Post.* Most libraries carry back issues of major newspapers on microfilm. By using an index you can find a list of articles on your subject printed in the newspaper during the year of the index. Again, you will need to learn how to request back issues of newspapers and how to use microfilm equipment for viewing and copying materials.

GOVERNMENT DOCUMENTS Many college libraries are depositories for government documents. Publications are frequently received at no cost from municipal, county, state, and federal government agencies. The federal government is the largest publisher in America, producing information on an almost endless variety of topics, some of which is not available elsewhere. Usually government documents are kept in a designated area of the library, where a special librarian may be available to help students locate documents.

From 1895 to the present, federal documents have been indexed in the *Monthly Catalog of Government Publications.* From 1881 to 1894 they can be located with the *Comprehensive Index of the Publications of the United States.* Federal documents published from 1774 to 1881 are indexed in the *Descriptive Catalog of Government Publications.* In addition to these comprehensive indexes, lists and catalogs of federal documents are published on various topics such as forestry, agriculture, and congressional hearings.

Federal documents are listed alphabetically by issuing agency and assigned a number. This number appears at the beginning of each entry, either in the margin or centered in boldface type. Referred to as the SuDoc number, this combination of numbers and letters is used like a call number to locate the document in the library's collection. Because indexes have changed formats over the years, read the instructions located in the front of each monthly volume.

In addition to federal documents, state governments publish many things about such topics as agriculture, industry, and people of the state. These state documents are also indexed. A reference librarian can tell you what is available and how to locate it in your library.

ON-LINE DATA BASES   A growing number of libraries have been equipped to access *on-line data bases,* which are computerized indexes and collections that can be searched by using a computer terminal. In order to locate the information you need, you must use key words to call up the list of materials held in a data base. The key words you use should be as specific as possible. There is a cost for data base searches, so the researcher needs to narrow the subject as much as possible. On-line data base searches by a computer can save hours of tedious searching for references on a topic, often for only a few dollars.

After you find the entries you need, it is possible to read the article on a library computer terminal or have a copy printed out for you. If your college or university does not have on-line data base access, check with other academic libraries in your area. Until you are confident in conducting such a search, a librarian can help you.

NONPRINT RESOURCES   In addition to print resources, most libraries house many nonprint sources of information such as records, slides, audio and video tapes, and films. Nonprint resources can often provide the researcher with useful information. Some recordings, charts, maps, slides, or even films may be appropriate for use as sensory aids during a speech. Many libraries include nonprint resources in the general card catalog; others have special audiovisual catalog files for nonprint materials. Your library will also have equipment that will enable you to examine any of the nonprint materials it holds.

The library is the place to initiate research for your speech. The reference tools, books, periodicals, and nonprint resources will provide information to illustrate and support the main points of your speech. Although the library is the most common place to start research, do not overlook other sources of information such as personal observations, materials you might acquire through the mail, and interviews.

An on-line data base of references can save hours of manual bibliographic searching.

The Interview

An excellent way to increase your own knowledge about a subject is to interview people who have direct personal experience with it. Many times an interview can uncover specific information that might take hours to find in a library. Experts can provide the most current information on topics too specialized for general-interest periodicals. For example, the question of whether part-time students at your college should pay student activity fees would not be covered in most periodicals. The best sources of information on this topic would be individuals on your campus who are actively involved with the issue, such as student leaders and the Dean of Student Affairs. Your campus has numerous resident experts on a wide range of topics on which you might speak. Not only are faculty members experts on a variety of subjects, your classmates and professional staff bring with them a wide range of experiences that can be tapped. Everyone is a potential resource for an interview on the right topic.

Before you can decide whether an interview would be of value, you must identify what you need to learn more about. Only then can you select the best person(s) to contact for the information. One student who wanted to know more about a controversial project being planned by the city council decided to interview two members of the council, as well as the attorney representing an opposing citizens group. The information received from these interviews was much more detailed than articles in the local newspaper. Quotations added authority and interest to the speech. In order to be useful, interviews must be well planned, and responses must be recorded accurately. There are several things you should do before, during, and after an interview in order to get the best possible results.

BEFORE THE INTERVIEW   After you have decided whom you need to interview, make an appointment for a time and place convenient for the interviewee. Describe the reason for the interview and the nature of the questions you will be asking. It is rude to barge in on someone without warning in hopes of catching the person off guard. The person may refuse to see you. You will get the most valuable information if the person has had time to think about the kind of information you are seeking. Students have reported that when they followed this advice, the interviewees not only gave them productive interviews, but prior to the interview had pulled information from files and made copies for them.

Make a tentative list of questions to ask during the interview to get the information you need. Review your list of questions and eliminate any that could easily be answered through available print materials. Screen the remaining questions to be sure they are phrased clearly in a nonleading, nonhostile way. Avoid asking questions that betray a bias or suggest answers to the interviewee, such as "Why should the city council waste the taxpayers money on such a useless project?" "Don't you think that the majority of citizens will be opposed to this project?" "How can you be against such an important project?" These questions argue more than seek information and may produce less than candid answers. You are there to learn what the person knows and believes, not to argue.

Knowing something about the expertise of the person you will interview and background information about the subject will help you generate good questions. This will also increase your credibility with the interviewee. Most people are pleased that you have learned something about them and will be more likely to respond positively during the interview. You can demonstrate this knowledge by asking questions like "Yesterday's *World-Herald* stated that you had previously been in favor of the project. What led you to change your position?" "Since your landslide election to the City Council you have voted affirmatively on every proposal to improve public education. How do the circumstances of this project, which you oppose, differ from those you supported?" "Three years ago when this project was brought before the City Council it was defeated unanimously. What has changed since then to influence the council's decision to begin discussion on the project now?"

After you have polished your list of questions, you need to plan how you will record the answers during the interview. No matter how good your memory, it is not a good idea to rely on it alone. Note taking during interviews is not easy, so you will need to develop your own abbreviation system. Often you will have time to record only key phrases. Many interviewers prefer to record interviews on audio tape, eliminating the difficulties of note taking. The major disadvantage of tape recording an interview is that some people become nervous or uncomfortable when being recorded. It is essential, therefore, to ask permission before recording.

If you decide to use a tape recorder, practice using it in a nondistracting way. Use a battery-powered recorder that has a built-in microphone.

Having defined a goal, identified a resource person, made an appointment, developed a list of clear, direct questions, and decided on a note-taking plan, you are ready to conduct the research interview. Your behavior during the interview will greatly influence the responses you receive.

DURING THE INTERVIEW Always be on time for an appointment and never overstay your welcome. After a greeting, state the purpose of your interview. Many students have found that saying they are students in a speech class seeking background information for a speech seems to relax the interviewee. If you have permission to use a recorder, set it up and leave it alone until the end of the interview.

As you ask your planned questions, always listen actively to the answers in order to decide what to say next. You may find that some of your questions are answered before you ask them. Asking a question that the interviewee has already answered will reveal that you are not paying attention. When you have any doubt that you understand fully, paraphrase statements of the interviewee and ask for clarification. For example, "You have stated that you are concerned about the burden this project will put on taxpayers, but you feel it is important enough to override any temporary taxpayer protests. Is that correct?" "You seem really angry because you feel that city government is not being responsive to the concerns of the citizens. Is this the reason you are organizing a mass demonstration at the City–County Building on Thursday?" Restatement and paraphrasing allows the other person to correct you if you have misinterpreted his or her comments and often evokes further explanation.

When concluding, be sure to thank the interviewee for taking time to answer your questions. Allow the respondent to ask you questions about how you intend to use the information. This informal exchange will leave the door open if you need to telephone at a later date to clarify some note made during the interview.

AFTER THE INTERVIEW Review and clarify your notes as soon as possible after the interview. If you wait several days you will forget many details, and your notes may not make much sense to you. Even a tape-recorded interview will not be as meaningful as it would be if played back while you still can recall nonverbal behavior of the interviewee.

Be sure to date your notes or transcriptions of a recording, including the name, title, and phone number of the person interviewed. Interviews should be included in a bibliography or reference list on your preparation outline and cited appropriately during the speech. For example,

> Sam Walton, founder and chair of the Board of Wal-Mart Corporation; private interview in Bentonville, Arkansas; June 3, 1989.

▶ Start Your Research Early with an Open Mind

One of Murphy's laws states: "Everything takes longer than you planned." Preparing a speech is no exception to this rule. We cannot stress too strongly the importance of beginning preparation as early as possible. Even the most experienced speakers attest to the importance of getting started early to cope with unexpected delays. The book or magazine article you want is checked out of the library. The resident expert you need to interview cannot see you until next week. The audiovisual department has a backlog of work. These are very common hazards of late planning that have happened to many speakers. By giving yourself plenty of lead time, you can cope more easily with temporary setbacks. You can put a hold on the book you need and wait for its return. You will more likely be able to arrange an interview with your key expert.

An additional advantage of early research is that you give yourself more opportunity to think about your topic in light of the information you have gathered. Many students have come into our offices stating that they have changed position on a topic after completing research. If you have not given yourself ample time it will be difficult to reorganize your thinking and change your central idea to reflect new information you have uncovered.

A final advantage of early research is that it allows you time to polish the organization of your speech and to rehearse. Early preparation will help you avoid what happened to Margaret:

> Margaret received a low grade on her speech. She lost points due to an obvious lack of familiarity with her information and outline. She read most of it from a manuscript, and she failed to prepare an adequate introduction and conclusion. Although the developmental materials were excellent, the overall impact of her presentation was minimal due to poor adaptation and delivery. She explained that she had been researching until the night before the speech was to be given and did not have time to rehearse.

Try to complete your preparation outline at least one week before you are scheduled to speak. This will give you ample time to become completely familiar with your organization and supporting materials and to revise if necessary.

▶ Read Efficiently

With bibliography in hand, you are ready to begin gathering books, periodicals, newspapers, pamphlets, and so on, and reading them. Few college students can afford to spend time reading thoroughly all the books and articles that might be listed in an initial bibliography. Nor would they want to do a shoddy job of investigating a complex issue. It is important that you learn to read efficiently. If you do not have practice in reading efficiently, here is one way that works well.

You need to locate the most promising passages in a print item quickly. If you find an abstract (summary) of an article, read it first to see if the contents seem appropriate enough to merit taking time to read the whole article. If a book has an index, use it to locate pages on which your topic (or subtopics) are discussed, then turn directly to those pages. If there is no index, use the table of contents to locate the most promising chapters or sections. For any article, chapter, pamphlet, or essay, you may find it efficient to read the introductory section and summary first in order to determine whether or not the entire work should be read.

You can also practice skim reading, in which you scan a page very rapidly while looking for key terms, mention of your topic, or specific kinds of information. When you spot something promising, slow down and read carefully.

Of course you will test all information you find in print for recency, expertise of source, validity of conclusions drawn from data, possible bias or prejudice on the part of the writer, and whether the writer is a firsthand observer or presents information originally generated by others. It will be especially important to compare statements from authorities who disagree on a subject or have approached it from different perspectives. When you read something you think might be useful in your speech, you will need to take detailed notes about that part of your reading.

▶ Keep Detailed Notes

If you followed all the previous guidelines for research, but failed to keep clear, accurate notes, you may have spent a great deal of time with very little to show for it. All of us have read an article and thought that we would never forget a shocking statistic or vivid example, only to find ourselves embarrassed as we stumbled while mentally searching for a piece of information. The result was that we appeared to be either absentminded or fabricating support. Here is an example from a student speech:

> I read this article once about this guy who lost lots of money by investing in some type of stock. It probably wasn't one of the big companies like those we hear about on TV, but it shows how dangerous the stock market

can be for the investor who is not informed about the correct way to invest.

The previous passage did not help the speaker support his idea. Keeping good notes would have enabled him to add important details to the example and thus appear credible to the listeners.

Keeping good research notes is not difficult, but it does require a system for recording, storing, and retrieving information. The main criteria of any note-taking system must be accuracy and usefulness. The following suggestions should help you develop note-taking skills that will ensure accuracy and flexibility in using your research findings.

(1) **Keep all notes for your speech preparation in one place.** Avoid jotting notes down on whatever you happen to have handy. Some speakers choose to take all notes on cards that they keep in a small envelope or bind with a rubber band. Others use a special notebook for all speech preparation information. Each system has advantages and disadvantages. Both will ensure the speaker a minimal chance of losing information.

The note card system has flexibility as its main advantage. The researcher records only one idea or supporting statistic, example, or quotation per card (see Figure 6.4). Later, as the speaker is organizing an outline, it is easy to sort through the cards and select materials to develop each point in the outline. The cards allow the speaker to organize information with little effort.

The main disadvantage to the card system is the possibility of using information out of context. Information recorded while reading an article two weeks ago may be misinterpreted without the context of the article. It is important, therefore, to record reference information on the card.

The notebook system has consistency as its major advantage. When using this method the researcher records all the notes from any one source on one or more pages. Each source of information is recorded on a separate sheet. With this technique the researcher can reduce the risk of taking a quotation or statistic out of context. The obvious disadvantages to this note-taking system are that it is not flexible, a specific fact may be hard to locate, and information must be recopied while the speech plan is being organized.

(2) **Record complete bibliographic information for all sources.** Include this information on all note cards or pages you use. These data are essential if you need to relocate a source in order to check for accuracy, reread for greater depth, describe sources to enhance credibility, prepare the bibliography to accompany the outline, or answer specific questions from a listener.

Bibliographic information gathered from print sources should include (1) author's full name; (2) author's qualifications if provided; (3) title of book or article; (4) title of periodical; (5) volume or edition; (6) date; (7) name of publisher and place of publication of a book; (8) page number where the item was found; and (9) call number if material is housed in the library. For nonprint library materials, record the source, author or producer, title, address, date, and any other production details provided on the label or package. Information needed on other nonprint sources includes name of source and qualifications,

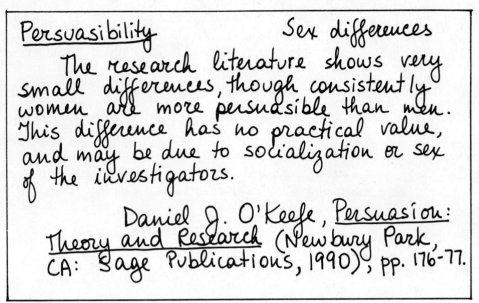

Figure 6.4 A typical note card with general heading, subject heading, information, and source.

occasion (interview, press conference, etc.), date and place, and how to contact the person if further information is needed.

Clearly indicate whether the information recorded is an exact quotation, paraphrase, or summary. If the source you are using is an abstract of an original source, record the location of the original document as well as the abstract. You may need to refer to it if you find the secondary source information to be inconsistent with other sources on the topic.

(3) **Never knowingly take any information out of context.** The temptation may be great to use a quotation or statistic out of context, thus cutting down your research time and making your point sound impressive, but the consequences can be severe. Such behavior is always deceptive, hence unethical. A speaker who is confronted by an audience member who can expose mishandled information looks incompetent and/or dishonest and loses credibility. Such behavior is grounds for an F in most public-speaking classes and for disqualification in speech contests.

(4) **Record all resources consulted, even if you did not directly use any specific information from them.** You may want to reread a source at a later time for information you previously thought was unimportant. Also, you might want to use these sources in a bibliography for a future research paper.

▶ Summary

By following the procedures outlined in this chapter you will be able to gather and record information efficiently. Always begin with an assessment to review and evaluate information you already have in memory. Comparing what you know with the knowledge and opinions of experts will assure you of being thorough and current. The library is an excellent source of both general and specific references, but a speaker should also consider whether to use interviews and other available sources of information.

By beginning early and taking good notes the speaker will have time to analyze the information collected, confirm or revise the tentative central idea and desired response statements, organize the speech, and rehearse. Time and effort taken during the research phase of speech preparation will simplify and enhance the subsequent steps in the process of preparing to speak. Too little effort during this stage or a willingness to settle for less than the best information will result in an ineffective speech.

▶ Learning Activities

1. Do a review of what you already know about a topic you have chosen for a forthcoming speech assignment. To be sure you are up-to-date and accurate in what you might say, list the types of sources and reference tools you will need to consult as you do research for your speech.

2. Participate in an orientation to your college or university library. With the help of a librarian, answer the following questions about your library:
    a. Does the library participate in interlibrary loan programs? If so, with what libraries? Is there a cost for this service? How long will it take to get information on loan, and how long can you keep it?
    b. What is the library's loan policy for general collection books, reference books, magazines, professional journals, and recordings?
    c. Which of the following does your library have available for student use: typewriters, word processors, computers, calculators, video cassette recorders, and conference rooms?
    d. To which newspapers does the library subscribe?
    e. What are the library hours?
    f. What classification system does the library use for general works?

3. Identify two specific reference works in which you would expect to find each of the following types of materials:
    a. Basic facts and statistics.
    b. Dates of specific events.
    c. Quotations.
    d. Information about living leaders.
    e. Brief, authoritative background articles.

4. Using appropriate reference sources, identify the following people:
    a. Jerry Brown.
    b. Paul Harvey.
    c. Phyllis Schlafly.
    d. Lee DeForest.

    e. Lee Harvey Oswald.

    f. George Lincoln Rockwell.

    g. Sam Walton.

5. Select two topics on which you might speak in the future. For each topic compile a list of available print sources, including

    a. Three or more books.

    b. Four to six magazine articles.

    c. Two recent newspaper articles.

    Next, list names and positions of persons you might interview to enhance your knowledge of the topic. On which topic do you feel you could speak with more authority?

6. After reading up on a topic you have selected for a speech, arrange an interview with a local authority on the subject. Following the advice in this chapter, prepare for the interview, conduct it, and follow through. The questionnaire you take to the interview should have room to write summaries of the interviewee's answers to each question.

7. Using one or more of the books listed in this chapter, find two quotations you might use to introduce a forthcoming speech or to make one of your points more dramatic. Copy each quotation on a separate note card; with the quotation record the original source of the quotation and the exact place where you found it.

P A R T

Creating the Message

CHAPTER 7

Developing Ideas to Make Them Concrete and Convincing

Questions to Guide Reading and Review

1. Why is it important to develop every main point or subpoint in the body of a speech?
2. What are the two primary functions of developmental materials?
3. What are the four major types of developmental materials? How is each defined, and how do they differ?
4. On what bases would you decide whether or not to use a specific example, statistic, testimony, and/or comparison to develop an idea?
5. Why are examples so useful for developing ideas in speeches?
6. What is the major characteristic of each of the major forms of comparison: metaphor, simile, analogy, anecdote, parable, and fable?
7. Why are comparisons often useful for illustrating to evoke listener understanding?

Key Terms

Analogy

Anecdote

Brief example

Comparison

Correlation

Developmental materials

Example

Extended example

Fable

Hypothetical example

Idea

Illustrate

Metaphor

Parable

Simile

Statistic

Testimony

"What do you mean?"

"Can you give me a for instance?"

"What's it like?"

"How do you know?"

"Where did you hear that?"

"Why do you say that? Can you prove it?"

Such requests are made when a speaker fails to develop an idea to the satisfaction of listeners. In public-speaking situations there is often little or no opportunity for the listener to ask the speaker to develop an assertion that the listener finds confusing or unconvincing. Yet many speakers do not explain or give evidence to support their ideas. The following statements are examples of speakers *failing* to develop assertions:

Abortion is murder, and murder is a crime. So abortion should be treated as a crime. It must be illegal and punishable. All of us who are civilized, moral people will be against crime. So I want you to sign my petition asking the state legislature to make it illegal to request or provide an abortion.

Only superstitious people don't believe that humans evolved from simpler forms of life. Such people are against what we know from science.

Evolution is a false theory because the Bible says God created all the creatures of earth, including humans. The Bible says that it's true, so evolution is a false theory.

The limbic system controls the smooth muscle and hormonal systems in which stress is produced, leading to negative emotions. So you can reduce stress and negative feelings by controlling the limbic system.

Speakers want listeners to understand, accept, and act upon *ideas*, which were previously explained as generalizations about things, classes of things, relationships, and processes. In this chapter we consider how to select and use information to clarify and support ideas. First, we explain the two functions of developmental materials. Second, we describe the four types of developmental materials and their uses. Third, we provide some general guidelines for selecting and using materials you collect while investigating your topics.

▶ Functions of Developmental Materials

Public speakers express ideas as statements about topics, from very general to very specific. As with central idea statements, the sentence expressing an idea includes both a *subject* (topic) and a *predicate* (what is said about the subject). Idea statements *generalize* or make affirmations about objects, classes of objects, or experiences. In contrast, descriptive sentences report the sensory experience of a particular observer at a particular time and place. Idea statements are about whole classes of such experiences and concepts based on them. Thus, I can record in sentence form my *observation* of a traffic accident or a history book, or I can express a general *idea* about traffic accidents or history books.

Idea statements are valid only to the extent they are based on careful observation. Some ideas are based on hearsay, such as myths handed down from generation to generation, rumors, and superstitions. Inferences, estimates, conjectures, and projections are all ideas based on guessing. Many people once believed the idea that cigarette smoking was a harmless and desirable social practice. From observations we now believe cigarette smoking is dangerous and often socially irresponsible. Our point is that *ideas should not be included in a speech unless they rest on careful observations*. A speaker has an ethical responsibility to distinguish between reports of observations and inferences drawn from those observations.

Figure 7.1 visualizes how *developmental materials* can both connect an idea statement to experience and provide listeners with a basis for believing it. If a listener lacks firsthand experience with an idea, the speaker can substitute for experience with descriptions and comparisons to experiences of the listener. Such materials *illustrate* what the speaker is talking about. *Illustrate* comes from the Latin word *illustrare*, "to illuminate," or "to make bright." If the speaker is successful, the result is called a *vicarious experience* for the listener.

Intense experiences are more likely to be recalled than those that are less vivid. The sharper an image, the better we can recall it and an idea with which it is associated. For example, you probably remember best those experiences that were so vivid they seemed to reach out and grab your attention, rather than ideas to which you had to force yourself to pay attention. Such peak experiences can be recalled clearly after many years, although other events at the same time are forgotten. Dramatic developmental materials can be used by a speaker to focus listener attention, evoke vivid images, arouse strong feelings, and thus make an idea almost impossible to ignore or forget.

In addition to relating what a speaker says to observation or experience, developmental materials also function as evidence to *support* an idea. Before a critical listener will accept a speaker's general idea, the speaker must provide developmental materials as evidence. The same developmental item can sometimes both illustrate and support an idea. Developmental materials selected as evidence should meet such critical-thinking tests as validity, relevance, and representativeness. These criteria are developed in Chapter 15, which is about speaking to persuade.

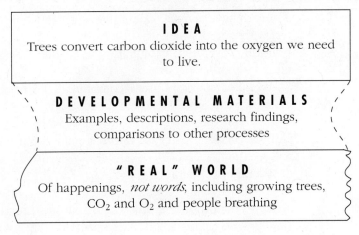

Figure 7.1 Developmental materials connect ideas to observations (reality).

▶ Types of Developmental Materials

For the sake of clarity and recall we have classified all developmental materials into four broad categories: examples, statistics, testimony, and comparisons and contrasts.

Examples

Example refers to "a particular single item, fact, incident or aspect that may be taken as typical or representative of all of a group or type" or as "an instance . . . serving to illustrate a rule or precept."[1] Synonyms for *example* include *instance* and *case in point*. Each member of your public-speaking class is an example of a student of public speaking. Former President Nixon and Senator Gary Hart are examples of speakers whose credibility was reduced when they were proven to have lied.

Research into how people form and defend their opinions has demonstrated that concrete examples have more effect in establishing and changing beliefs than any other type of supporting material.[2] Like anything that will affect another's welfare, examples should be used correctly. When used as evidence to support a generalization, an example should be shown to be typical of the class of objects named in the generalization. An example of a 4.0 grade point average (GPA) student in an appeal for more funding for college education may be misleading. Perfect GPAs are the exception, not the rule. An example of either an exceptionally well cared for or a severely abused animal would be deceptive if the speaker intended to create an image of how most research animals are treated. When used as evidence of a controversial point, examples should be instances that actually happened or exist. For instance, in a speech to convince, one student argued that some heavy metal music and lyrics are socially beneficial by using examples of lyrics attacking air pollution, political corruption, exploitation of workers, and knowingly passing the AIDS virus to another person.

Skilled speakers use a combination of brief, extended, and hypothetical examples extensively in their speeches.

BRIEF EXAMPLES   A *brief example* is named but not described. Often a speaker will mention several brief examples to clarify or define an idea. An accumulation of several brief examples may be used as evidence to show that some condition or problem is quite common. Such a list will often stimulate listeners to think of similar additional examples. Below are samples of brief examples from a variety of speeches. Each brief example is in **boldface.**

> Several of us in this room have studied cardiopulmonary resuscitation and might save lives in an emergency: **John, Ed,** and **Karen.**

> Rude drivers are dangerous. Just this morning as I drove to school **a rude driver trying to beat a yellow light almost hit my car as I started into an intersection.**

> **Beth** is a typical Iowa State student: used to hard work and very conscientious.

> This suitcase contains typical travel items: **underwear, socks, camera and film, shirts, extra shoes, a belt, and a book.**

President Reagan was a master at using brief examples. In a televised speech to the nation in March of 1986 supporting military aid to the Contras, President Reagan claimed that the Sandinistas were persecuting ethnic and religious groups. He effectively used a series of brief examples to illustrate his claim:

> Like Communist governments everywhere, the Sandinistas have launched assaults against ethnic and religious groups. **The capital's only synagogue was desecrated and firebombed. Protestant Bible meetings have been broken up by raids, by mob violence, by machine guns. The Catholic Church has been singled out— priests have been expelled from the country, Catholics beaten in the streets after attending mass.**[3]

You can see how brief examples that name or list items can evoke images and make ideas clearer and/or more convincing to listeners.

EXTENDED EXAMPLES   When a speaker wants to evoke a particularly vivid image in the minds of listeners, arouse feelings, or dramatize an idea, an *extended example* with detailed description should be used. Extended examples include detailed descriptions of instances and stories. They are especially useful for clarifying when listeners are unfamiliar with a class of items or for dramatizing ideas with which the speaker wants listeners to identify and empathize. Listeners can get deeply involved with the subject of a detailed story. For instance, in order to evoke an emotional response from his national audience, President Reagan used the following extended example to support his claim of religious persecution by the Sandinista regime of Nicaragua:

> Evangelical pastor Prudencio Baltodano found out he was on the Sandinista hit list when an army patrol asked his name. "You don't know what we do to the evangelical pastors. We don't believe in God," they told him. Pastor Baltodano was tied to a tree, struck in the forehead with a rifle butt, stabbed in the neck with a bayonet—finally his ears were cut off, and he was left for dead. "See if your God will save you," they mocked. Well, God did have other plans for Pastor Baltodano. He lived to tell the world his story—to tell it, among other places, right here in the White House.[4]

Regardless of political view, the listener had a strong sympathetic reaction to the story told by the president. Extended examples enable the speaker to paint vivid word pictures. Here is an extended example used both to illustrate and support an idea:

> But retarded people do fit in and do lead useful and rewarding lives. A few years ago, I worked with a girl who is educably mentally retarded. Mary went to my high school and attended two normal classes—home economics and physical education. She had a burning desire to become a waitress. Her determination was evident as I tutored her in addition, subtraction, making change, and figuring sales tax. She is working today in a small restaurant—happy and self-supporting.[5]

The previous examples illustrate the detailed description characteristic of effective extended examples. The effectiveness of an extended example depends on how well the speaker uses words to refer to specific sensations, images, and impressions. Describing well evokes memories of similar sensory experiences in your listeners, anchoring the idea in experience. An abstract idea thus becomes real to the listeners. Speakers need to describe because they can provide few direct sensory experiences for audience members. All the senses can be stimulated through description: vision, hearing, smell, taste, touch, and others. Speakers cannot bring a jungle, prairie, battle, or herd of elephants to listeners, so they try to evoke sensations by using descriptive words. We will say more about developing abstractions with descriptive language in Chapter 14 on informative speaking.

HYPOTHETICAL EXAMPLES Sometimes no example of an idea you want to explain can be located to illustrate a complex idea. Then a rhetorical device called a *hypothetical example* can be invented to do so. A hypothetical example contains details typical of actual cases even though it is not a report of any actual event. Following is a hypothetical example typical of those created by speakers to clarify abstract ideas:

Ignorance can be deadly to one of our natural allies in the war against rodents and insects in the garden. That ally is the common garter snake, which eats small rodents and insects. But what happens when Jane Gardener spots a garter snake trying to hide in her garden? No doubt the little snake is greatly frightened by this human towering above it. Jane screams, grabs her hoe, and chops the helpless reptile to bits. Then she rushes to tell her neighbor about the horrible snake that actually struck back when she hit it with her hoe! That snake, which only wanted to be left alone, would have eaten hundreds of voracious grasshoppers, sowbugs, Japanese beetles, and other plant-consuming pests if Jane had spared it. In her ignorance she saw danger instead of help. Out of ignorance she destroyed a gardener's friend.

Jane Gardener and the events described are fictional, designed by the speaker to represent how many gardeners behave when they see a beneficial snake.

In the introduction of a speech, hypothetical examples can be used to direct attention to the topic. For example, Randy asked a question in order to focus listeners on the need for his speech:

Imagine you are on a hike with your father when he suddenly grasps his chest, utters a moan, and slumps to the ground. He has suffered a serious, but not necessarily fatal heart attack. What would be the next part of the scene? His funeral? Or would you know what to do to save his life? If you learn what I can teach you about cardiopulmonary resuscitation, you could keep him alive until medical help arrives.

Another student used this hypothetical example to begin her speech on the need for increased campus security:

Picture a young woman—let's call her Katie—heading toward her car after a late evening speech class. Because Katie is so tired, she does not hear the footsteps behind her until she is in complete darkness some distance from the building. Katie quickens her pace. . . .

The second hypothetical example dramatizes the general problem in human dimensions of the hypothetical woman, Katie, with whom listeners could feel empathy. You can invent such hypothetical examples to clarify and emphasize when an appropriate real example is not available to you, so long as the example you create represents what could really happen and you state that the story is hypothetical. Hypothetical examples should never be passed off as evidence.

Statistics

The words *statistics* ("a collection of quantitative data") and *statistic* ("a single term or datum in a collection of statistics") refer to numbers that may be used to develop and support ideas.[6] A single statistic may be used to describe some measurable characteristic of an object or members of a population of objects. For instance, the power of atomic bombs is measured in megatons, weight of people in kilograms or pounds, the population of a city in number of residents, and distance in miles or light years. Descriptive statistics can also be used to demonstrate trends and probabilities as evidence of a claim.

DESCRIPTIVE STATISTICS   These are numbers that represent counts or measurements listeners need to form sharp images. For example, you might describe the length and weight of your prize bass, not just say "It was a whopper." Instead of the vague statement "A lot of codfish were used in making fish and chips last year," you could report the number of tons of cod and make that even more vivid by describing it as a certain number of boxcars of cod making up a train so many miles in length. The following examples indicate how speakers use descriptive numbers:

> Each year more than a million teenagers become pregnant. Four out of five of them are unmarried; there are some 30,000 of them that are age 14 or younger. State officials of Illinois estimate that overall the U.S. spends 8.6 billion dollars each year for income support for teenagers who have become pregnant or who have already given birth.[7]

> From 1960 until 1973, the United States had a capital investment rate of 13.6 percent of our Gross National Product. During that same period, the Japanese had a rate of 29 percent. You take a look at the years 1965 to 1975 to see the results of these capital investments.

> The United States had an increase in output per man hour in manufacturing of 2 percent, while the Japanese, riding on the benefits of their increased capital investments, had an increase of 9.5 percent.[8]

AVERAGES   Statistics often summarize a lot of examples into one number. *Averages* are compiled from numerous examples of some class of objects. Used properly, they can give listeners a valid picture. Used carelessly or inappropriately, averages will mislead as badly as any lie. There are two major types of averages: the *mean*, or arithmetic average, and the *median*, or middle score in a set of scores. You should always make sure you are using the appropriate average. Each is calculated to represent a typical score or measurement, but if improperly used can create a false picture.

A *mean* average is calculated by adding together a set of scores, then dividing their sum by the number of scores. The mean is seriously biased by exceptionally high or low scores, especially if the total number of scores is small. On the other hand, if it presents a fair picture, the mean is more precise and easier to calculate than the *median*. The median is the central point in a set of scores, a sort of balance point. Consider the impression given by the mean and median population numbers for the largest five cities in two different states:

STATE A		STATE B	
8,700,000		1,200,000	
640,000		487,000	
325,000	median	335,000	median
241,000		233,000	
137,000		138,000	
10,043,000/5 =		2,393,000/5 =	
2,008,600 mean		478,600 mean	

The medians suggest similarity in the size of cities in these two states, whereas the means suggest a great difference. In this example the medians are far less influenced by very large numbers, and thus give a more accurate impression of the size of typical cities than do the mean averages.

TRENDS AND PROBABILITIES   Numbers can describe a change through time or the probability that a predicted event will occur. For example, a recent report from the National Center for Health Statistics showed that the number of years a person in the United States can expect to live after age 40 has increased steadily since 1940, with gains of from 0.8 to 2.1 years for each decade. This statistical trend could be used to support the prediction that Americans will live still longer in 2000 and the claim that we are a healthier people now than at any point in history. The *Statistical Abstract of the United States* reported attendance at dog-racing tracks in 1970 was 12.7 million, climbing to 21.4 million by 1981; symphony orchestra attendance climbed from 12.7 million to 22.8 million in the same period of time. These trends could be used to support the arguments that Americans had much more discretionary money in 1981 than in 1970 and that Americans enjoy dog racing as much as they do symphonies.

CORRELATIONS   Relationships between two sets of measurements or scores are indicated with statistics called *correlations*. For example, if you want to compare level of education with income or incidence of smoking with lung cancers per thousand persons, the appropriate statistic is a correlation. Correlations can range from +1.0 (positive correlation) to −1.0 (a negative correlation). A positive correlation between two measures means that as one measure increases so does the other. A negative correlation means that as one measure increases the other decreases.

When using correlations in a speech, it is easy to misinform listeners by confusing a correlation with a causal relationship between two or more events. Correlations only show that scores or measures are related, not that one *causes* the other. For instance, student GPAs are positively correlated with Scholastic Aptitude Test (SAT) scores, but not perfectly. GPA depends on work habits, desire, time available, and other variables not reflected by an SAT score. Anyone with a high GPA is likely to have at least a moderately high SAT score, but many persons with high SAT scores have low GPAs! Such correlated measures may both be effects of the same cause rather than one being the cause of the other. Because of the complexity of correlations, we urge you to use them cautiously.

USING STATISTICS AS EVIDENCE   Several guidelines should be followed when using statistics to develop ideas. These special guidelines make it easier for listeners to grasp and interpret the numbers and form valid images and ideas from them.

(1) Round off large numbers unless doing so will cause some distortion or misrepresentation. Large raw numbers are hard to understand. For example, instead of saying "The population of the earth is estimated to be 4,664,238,571," you should say "There are about 4.6 billion people living on the earth."

(2) Visualize large numbers by comparing them to concrete, readily perceived objects. For example, saying a building is 750 feet long is less meaningful than saying the building is 2.5 times as long as a football field.

(3) For concreteness and interest, translate abstract percentages and proportions into descriptive numbers appropriate to the audience. For example, one of our students said this: "One-fourth of the women on our campus have been victims of date rape by the time they graduate. That means that of the 16 women now in this room, four have been or probably will be raped by acquaintances."

(4) Cite the source and date of your statistics. Be sure your listeners know that the source is competent and unbiased. This is especially important when using results of a survey. Unless a survey is done correctly, the results may be invalid. Not all pollsters are as careful and accurate as the Gallup or Yanklevich organizations, nor as free of bias as the National Opinion Research Center. All numbers can change dramatically over time, so dating the statistic is as important as its accuracy. Failure to provide a date may cause critical listeners to disregard the statistic.

(5) Create charts to depict statistical trends. If you need numbers to show a trend or comparison, put these numbers in graphs or other charts so listeners can *see* the pattern among the numbers. Personal computers with graphic programs make this easy to do. Trying to remember a series of numbers presented by a speaker is virtually impossible. Listeners are likely to quit trying and think of something else. However, the audience will follow the same numbers visualized on a chart. Printed tables and graphs can be handed to listeners, presenting numbers in a form easy to understand.

(6) Be fair in your use of numbers. It is very easy to present a misleading picture with statistics. To say that crimes of assault increased by 15 percent

may suggest an increase in violence on the streets, yet most of the increase may have come from a redefinition of "assault" to include crimes not previously classified as assaults. Saying that 20 percent of female faculty members were promoted in 1983, whereas only 5 percent of male professors were promoted that year might be used to indicate that women were getting better treatment. In reality, most of the men were at the top academic rank already, while few women had been granted that rank.

(7) Avoid drawing incorrect conclusions from correlations. Simple correlations do not prove a casual relationship between types of phenomena (intelligence quotient scores and grades). Nor should you put much weight on low correlations (under 0.50).

(8) Always explain and stress the *idea* the statistics support. Numbers by themselves are not ideas; they must be interpreted and explained. Do the numbers show a trend through time, an exception from a rule, a drastic change, or an unusual feature? A 7-foot nose has a very different meaning when we discover that it is part of the anatomy of a whale than when it is part of the anatomy of a human!

Testimony

Testimony means using the opinions of others as evidence to support an idea. A speaker who relies upon the opinions of recognized experts on a particular topic is making use of expert testimony. In some cases, the speaker may be a recognized expert and have personal knowledge and experience on a given topic. A speaker who relies upon his or her own opinions to support an idea is making use of personal testimony.

EXPERT TESTIMONY   Testimony is only credible to the extent listeners perceive the source to be an expert on the topic. Citing the opinion of a famous National Hockey League goalie on gun control would fail to strengthen the speaker's argument and could lower the speaker's credibility with critical listeners. The same person's testimony could be very effective when used in support of a proposal to reduce violence in professional hockey.

If you quote someone directly, indicate exactly what words are quoted. As mentioned in Chapter 2, this is a matter of ethics. There are many verbal and nonverbal techniques for indicating when you are quoting someone directly that avoid the overused phrase, "And I quote," or "Quote . . . unquote." For example:

"As President John F. Kennedy **once said. . . .**"

"**Let me cite** Charles Larson, author of a best-selling book on persuasion: . . . ."

"**According to** Leonard Woodcock, president of the United Auto Workers. . . ."

"Andrei Sakharov, the noted Soviet physicist and dissident, put it bluntly in 1977 **when he said:** "The unchecked. . . .""

"**In the memorable words of** Abraham Lincoln: "You can. . . .""

"Support for my argument is provided by Liu Pao, **who wrote. . . .**"

"**Dr. Allen testified that. . . .**"

Tone of voice, reading a note, and pausing before and after the quotation nonverbally signal your use of a quotation.

All testimony, whether direct quotation or paraphrase, must explicitly support the idea for which it is used as evidence. Furthermore, an ethical speaker will never use a quotation out of context to support an idea the original speaker or writer did not intend to support. Listeners will insist that your use of testimony adheres to three additional guidelines:

(1) If the testimony is a report of some observation, the person cited should be an eyewitness to the event. In courtrooms, secondhand testimony about an event is not allowed; such "hearsay" evidence is notoriously unreliable.

(2) Unless already known to the audience, the credentials of the source should be described. People earn their credibility as experts by holding specific credentials such as a doctorate, a law degree, certification, national reputation, title, ability, or a record of outstanding success. Your personal opinion about the effects of overpopulation is less persuasive than the opinion of Dr. Paul Ehrlich, Nobel Prize-winning ecologist from Stanford University. Unless listeners know of Dr. Ehrlich and his credentials, the *speaker* has an obligation to provide the audience with information that implies "This person is an expert on my subject and I am a credible speaker for choosing only the best sources for this speech." When in doubt about listeners' knowledge of your source, *always* provide the relevant source qualifications.

(3) The authority should either have no vested interest in the issue or have spoken against what appears to be his or her best interest. People are prone to interpret facts to fit their personal interests, wants, and needs. Thus the expert should be demonstrated to your audience to be free from self-serving bias. In a series of tobacco advertisements the president of a large tobacco company was quoted as saying that there had been no direct proof that smoking caused lung cancer and heart disease in humans. On the other hand, a very large number of medical researchers have concluded from statistical trends that smoking does contribute to these diseases. Which of these sources is more believable to you? Why? Why would citing the opinion of the president of American Airlines that unions are often beneficial to both employees and industry be more convincing than quoting the president of the AFL–CIO?

Using the quotation of an expert does not absolve you of the responsibility for using the testimony. You are still personally responsible for promoting the idea such testimony supports and for having selected the testimony as evidence.

So critically evaluate testimony before using it; not to do so is to be ethically irresponsible. Noted persons can and do say false, faulty, and stupid things!

Sometimes speakers use short, vivid quotations to make ideas clear and memorable rather than as evidence of the validity of an idea. Such quotations can be used to add humor, grace, or flair to your words, but never as evidence or proof of a controversial point. They are not testimony. For example:

> "We have met the enemy and he is us!" (Pogo, the cartoon possum created by Walt Kelley)

> "A rose by any other name would smell as sweet." (Shakespeare)

> "A fool and his money are soon parted." (Benjamin Franklin)

PERSONAL TESTIMONY One effective technique for increasing the audience's perception of your credibility as a speaker is to demonstrate your knowledge or expertise on the topic of your speech. In some cases speakers are experts in their own right. *Personal testimony* refers to the opinion(s) of a speaker who is an expert on the topic. If you are speaking against rising tuition costs at your university and its effects on students, your opinion would be more credible than that of a professor. If you worked in the university's financial aid office your credibility would be even greater. If you were an elected student representative on a university committee to study the problem, your credibility would be greater still. The following are examples from speeches of students who made use of personal testimony:

> Raising horses has been a passion for me all my life. I learned to ride a horse with my father before I could even walk. I owned my first horse at age eight; worked on a horse ranch since I was nine; participated in 4H programs since grade school and won a state championship in riding last year. Today, I want to convince you to treat your horse with kindness.

> Mental retardation is no laughing matter. I know, my little brother was born mildly retarded. I have spent my entire life defending him against those who find his inability to perform simple tasks amusing. I die a little bit inside each time I hear someone laugh at Tommy.

Like expert testimony, the persuasiveness of personal testimony depends on *the listener perceiving the speaker as an expert*. The speaker must provide the listeners with enough information for them to form a judgment of speaker expertise. Personal testimony should be used sparingly and with the knowledge that it is not a substitute for other evidence. Where appropriate and used correctly, personal testimony can have a dramatic effect on an audience.

Comparisons and Contrasts

Comparisons and contrasts are used primarily to illustrate and clarify. Only occasionally is a comparison used as evidence in support of an argument. Much of our learning occurs from comparing new experiences and information to what we have previously experienced. From bits of past experiences we assemble new images and new ideas that, although similar in some details to previous perceptions, are different. We learn by comparing and contrasting with what we previously knew. I may understand that a new-to-me synthetic fabric is similar in strength to nylon, but in contrast to nylon is warm to the touch, like cotton. I can understand a nuclear chain reaction by comparing it to how one kernel of popcorn causes many others to jump in the pan when it pops. I can understand the complex idea that too many stresses can lead to a personal breakdown by comparing that to the much simpler break I've seen in a steel spring when it is flexed too far too often.

A *literal comparison* is used to explain a new concept by comparing it to something with which a listener is familiar. If you were a resident of a large city, and I wanted you to have an idea of the appearance of a grain elevator, I could compare the grain elevator to a skyscraper. In contrast, if you were a farmer who had never seen a skyscraper, I might compare skyscrapers to the grain elevators you were familiar with in order to help you form some image of their height and size. I could help you understand the size of an acre by comparing it to a football field.

Speakers can use a figure of speech called *metaphor* to make a *figurative comparison. Metaphor* means that the speaker calls something by the name of the item to which it is being compared: "Crime is a **cancer** in the body social"; "The future is **covered by a veil** through which we see dimly"; "Life is a **narrow valley** between the cold and barren peaks of two eternities"; "My car is a **lemon**." Metaphors evoke vivid images. Like all comparisons, metaphors are effective only if audience members have some image of the item with which the comparison is made.

A simple one-point figurative comparison in which the comparison is stated with the word "like," "as," or "resembles" is called a *simile*. Similes are used extensively by speakers to illustrate. For example, "An earth-sheltered house resembles a cave with its mouth facing south"; "The professor roared like a lion"; "A word processor is like a typewriter with a memory and a brain"; "The dulcimer sounds like a cross between a bagpipe and a violin." One type of simile to avoid is the overworked cliché: "hungry as a horse," "sick as a dog," and "like greased lightning." When used too frequently, a simile loses its power to evoke vivid images.

A more complex type of comparison is the *analogy*, in which several features of two things, situations, or other phenomena are compared. *Literal analogies* are used both to illustrate and as evidence. *Figurative analogies* are used primarily to explain ideas; they do not constitute evidence, although they may be convincing to some uncritical listeners. For example, information retrieval from the memory unit of a computer has frequently been compared in detail to the locating of a stock item in a well-organized warehouse. Although computers and warehouses have some similarities, they are literally very different things. A figurative analogy to the pecking order in a flock of chickens has been used to explain how people in groups establish status relationships among themselves. This sort of comparison can be useful for explaining complex behavior of people, but it proves nothing about human nature. Chickens are not people.

When using a literal analogy as evidence, a speaker argues that because two situations resemble each other in several important characteristics they will be alike in some other characteristic. For example, one might support the claim that socialized medicine would be beneficial to citizens of the United States on the grounds that it has been beneficial to citizens of Canada. The assumption underlying the analogy is that the United States and Canada are so similar that what works in Canada will work in the United States. However, a counterargument might be that because socialized medical programs in Britain have been costly and provided relatively poor service, they would be disadvantageous for U.S. citizens. So before you use an analogy as evidence, be sure the two situations or items being compared are alike in all characteristics relevant to your conclusion. Otherwise, your causal reasoning may be faulty.

Imaginative stories use comparisons to dramatize or clarify abstract ideas. When humorous, these imaginative stories are called *anecdotes*. In the following example, a speaker used an anecdote to clarify the abstract concept *projection*:

> A story of a city slicker with a rented car illustrates projection. It seems that this dude had rented a car at the airport in Cheyenne in order to drive to a ranch about 150 miles north where he was to try to close a land deal for his client. About 50 miles from Cheyenne, where houses are miles apart and only four or five cars a day go down the road, he had a flat. Looking in the trunk, he discovered the rental car had no jack. So our dude began hiking down the road looking for a house. Finally he saw a house sitting a quarter mile from the road. As he turned in the lane he got to thinking: "These ranchers have a reputation for not liking city folks. He may not be willing to lend me a jack. In fact, I better be careful or he might sic his dog on me or take a potshot at me." Just then a man in blue jeans and boots stepped around a low shed and said "Hi, stranger. What brings you to our place?" To this the city slicker replied, "You can keep your blasted jack, you red-necked cowboy." Now that's projection.

Imaginative stories with a moral or point are often used to teach lessons in ethical, moral, or wise conduct. These we call *parables* and *fables*. *Fables* usually involve miraculous powers or acts by animals, whereas *parables* are equally fictitious, but involve human actors. You probably can think of examples of both. Can you recall the fable of the tortoise and the hare? Jesus is reputed to have used many parables to explain his teachings. In the tradition of Aesop, some modern writers use fables to illustrate and impress, especially for audiences of children. What is important is that the moral (idea you are trying to make clear and concrete) be exemplified in the imaginative story. You can find useful imaginative stories in the speaking or writing of other persons or invent your own.

In any fanciful comparison the abstract idea being explained must be compared to something with which listeners are familiar. For instance, in the famous parable of the sower, Jesus compared the reactions of four types of people to his message to how wheat grows when sown in four types of soil: thin rocky soil, hard-packed soil, good soil full of weed seeds, and good clean soil. This was appropriate because his listeners in Palestine 2000 years ago depended on wheat for their diets and were all familiar with how it was grown. The same parable would not be very meaningful to most city dwellers of the twentieth century, nor to Eskimos who herd reindeer in a climate where wheat cannot be grown. To create a fanciful comparison to clarify and dramatize an idea, first ask yourself: "What is this idea like that my listeners could visualize or understand from their past experiences?" Then, "How could I create a vivid story to illustrate my point?"

By searching for comparisons and thinking creatively, you can locate or invent literal comparisons, metaphors, similes, analogies, anecdotes, parables, and fables to make clear ideas that would otherwise elude listeners.

We next consider how to select and use all sorts of developmental materials.

▶ Selecting and Using Developmental Materials

How you select and use materials to develop your ideas is as important as their validity and relevance to your ideas. The following six guidelines can help you to select and use developmental materials effectively.

(1) *Develop every idea.* Never present a generalization, idea or point without material to explain and relate it to firsthand experience. If the idea is controversial, provide sufficient evidence for critical listeners to evaluate and accept the idea. Your speech outline should show that you have located and selected material to develop every point in the body of your speech so that it is likely to be clear and convincing.

(2) *Use a variety of types of developmental materials.* Too many statistics will overwhelm and confuse listeners. Combined with a few examples and comparisons, they will be far more meaningful. Even specific, concrete examples get boring if overused. Testimony alone may give the impression that you could find nothing but opinions to support your ideas. Comparison should be used only to the extent necessary to evoke concrete images you seek as responses. In short, use a variety of materials.

(3) *Developmental materials should refer to actual experience.* When used in this way, they evoke a valid idea or image in listeners. Sensory descriptions in extended examples may help listeners to have vicarious experiences. Even when you create a hypothetical example, figurative analogy, or fable, it should be highly plausible and comparable to actual experience. Comparisons

should only be made to experiences of listeners. So you can see that thorough audience analysis is essential before you can decide how to develop a central idea.

(4) *Personalize your materials whenever possible.*   When you can do so without danger of embarrassing someone, use examples from among your listeners. Explain statistics in terms of listeners' lives. Testimony of persons already respected by listeners as experts on your subject will be received better than testimony from experts unknown to the audience. Give names to people in your examples, even if they are pseudonyms.

(5) *Use developmental materials that are new to the audience.*   If a story or statistic was not convincing to listeners the first time they heard it used to support an argument, repeating it is unlikely to help you win agreement. To be persuaded, the listener needs to hear new evidence or new arguments from evidence he or she is familiar with. Although comparisons are made to things familiar to listeners, the comparison itself must be a new one if it is to be interesting and truly illuminating. A good comparison puts the familiar in a new setting.

(6) *Cite sources.*   Cite sources of materials, especially evidence used to support a point someone might disagree with. You will need to demonstrate or describe the competence of sources not familiar to your listeners as experts on your topic. You will frequently need to explain how statistics were created, especially those from surveys.

▶ Summary

In Chapter 7 we have urged you to develop all ideas in the body of the speech. Developmental materials perform two major functions: to illustrate or clarify ideas and as evidence to support them. As you conduct your research you will be looking for appropriate examples, statistics, testimony, and comparisons to relate your ideas to the listener's reality.

Examples can be real or hypothetical, ranging from very brief to extended narratives. Statistics may be simple descriptive numbers, averages, trends, or correlations. Most statistics need to be explained and visualized by the speaker. Comparisons to illustrate new ideas can range from simple metaphors and similes to extended analogies, parables, and fables. As evidence for an idea, testimony of experts can be presented as direct quotations or paraphrases. The following six general guidelines will help in selecting and using information you have collected:

1. Develop every idea.
2. Use a variety of types of developmental materials.
3. Be sure comparisons refer to actual experiences of your listeners and that they will evoke valid images and ideas.

4. Personalize materials to the extent feasible.
5. Select materials new to listeners.
6. Cite sources of supporting materials.

The major principle is to develop every point in your speech with sufficient material to make it clear and credible to your audience.

▶ Learning Activities

1. Plan how to describe something with which most of your classmates are not acquainted, such as the appearance of your brother, sister, or friend; your front yard following a heavy snowfall or hail storm; your favorite food or dish; your favorite restaurant; twilight at your favorite rural area; a group of your favorite animals or birds, including appearance, movements, smells, and sounds; your favorite park; a house that intrigues you; a car you would like to own. After some practice, present this description to a small group of classmates. They will ask you questions about anything they are uncertain about. One person should then describe what he or she has imagined as the object of your description. Each member of the group will describe something in turn.

2. For an audience of your classmates, make up comparisons to explain any two of the following items with which you are acquainted, but they are unfamiliar with. The comparisons may be written, or you may present them orally before either a small circle of listeners or the entire class:

   A fuel injection system in a modern automobile.
   An integrated circuit chip.
   A musical instrument.
   Any tool or implement.
   How an electronic smoke alarm functions.
   A subway train system in some city different from yours.
   Effects of a drug on the human nervous system.
   Another topic supplied by your instructor.

3. The statements that follow fail to conform to one or more of the guidelines for using developmental materials. Identify what is inadequately done in each statement, then create a revision conforming to the guideline(s) ignored in the original.
   a. "Scientists say the earth is billions of years old."
   b. "As Michael Jackson says, Imagination Motors builds cars that last."
   c. "In a recent survey it was found that college students on several campuses

favored free tuition for all serious students. Clearly this is an idea that has widespread support in America."

d. "Last year 44,261 persons were killed in auto accidents involving drinking drivers. Of these victims, 21,462 were drivers and 22,799 were passengers or pedestrians."

e. "The CEO of the Postal Service recently said that the mail service he heads is efficiently operated to keep costs minimal."

f. "Free-world petroleum production is now more than 50 million barrels per day, with a potential surplus of as much as 10 million barrels a day. In the United States natural gas production is expected to be roughly 18 trillion cubic feet. Coal consumption in 1984 is expected to rise to over 800 million tons."

g. "The ship of state is sailing smoothly along the highway of progress."

h. "May Jenkins won't talk to anyone who isn't a Greek. Annette Breeden thinks she is the most important person in the world. Cathy Jacobs is stuck up. They're all sisters of Delta Rho Sigma. As you can see, sorority women are impossible snobs."

i. "To study efficiently you need a system like that of a skilled PERT analyst. First you break down the job into all essential steps. Then the analyst lists all available resources, including personnel. . . ."

j. "According to a survey my roommate and I did of students walking along West Commons, 85 percent of students at Southern State want a better system of advising."

4. Select one simple idea that is a favorite of yours. It may be a moral, a cliché or proverb, a possible main point for a future speech, a characteristic of something in which you are interested, or a statement about how two types of events are related. For example:

"It pays to be prepared for the unexpected when camping."

"Putting off necessary tasks interferes with taking advantage of unexpected opportunities."

"Colors should be selected to complement each other."

"Habits govern the behavior of cats."

"All successful diets balance caloric input and output."

"Ballet is increasing in popularity among young people."

Next, select at least one each of the four types of developmental materials that could be used to explain and support this idea in the minds of listeners. Your goal is that your classmates could explain this idea to someone else after hearing you do so. Prepare to present and develop this idea orally to your class in a one-idea exercise taking not more than 90 seconds.

Follow this format when you speak:

1. State the idea in a simple declarative sentence (with no apology, explanation of why you chose it, or other introductory remarks).

2. Present your four developmental materials, one each of the four types (an example, a statistic, testimony, and a comparison).

3. Restate the idea, and then sit down.

5. Do the same sort of exercise as in learning activity 4, developing one idea with four types of developmental materials. However, this time the idea should be a controversial one with which some of your classmates disagree. For example:

"Inflation is beneficial to most people."

"It should be illegal for anyone except a licensed kennel or cattery owner to keep a fertile dog or cat."

"The penalty for conviction of DWI should always include confiscation of the vehicle being driven (unless it was driven without the owner's consent)."

Your goal in speaking is to have classmates who initially disagree with your idea agree with you as a result of the developmental materials you present.

Notes

1. *Webster's Third New International Dictionary of the English Language*, unabridged (Chicago: G. & C. Merriam, 1966), Vol. I, p. 790.

2. Richard Nisbett and Lee Ross, *Human Inference: Strategies and Shortcomings of Social Judgment* (Englewood Cliffs, NJ: Prentice–Hall, 1980), pp. 43–62.

3. Ronald Reagan, "Nicaragua—Address to the Nation, March 16, 1986," *Public Papers of the President* (Washington, DC: U.S. Gov. Printing Office, 1986), p. 372.

4. Reagan, "Nicaragua."

5. Kathy Weisensel, "David—and a Lot of Other Neat People," in Wil A. Linkugel, R.R. Allen, and Richard L. Johannesen (eds.), *Contemporary American Speeches*, 5th ed. (Dubuque, IA: Kendall/Hunt Publishing Co., 1982), p. 83.

6. *Webster's Third New International Dictionary of the English Language*, unabridged (Chicago: G. & C. Merriam, 1966), Vol. III, p. 2230.

7. Jennifer Adams, classroom speech, University of Nebraska at Omaha, 1986.

8. W. F. Rockwell, Jr., "The Japanese Connection," *Vital Speeches of the Day* (November 1, 1977): 61–62.

Organizing the Body of a Speech

Questions to Guide Reading and Review

1. What are the three major parts of a speech, and what is the purpose of each?
2. How are the principles of limited perception, recall by association with parts of a whole, and logical sequences applied in planning the outline of the body of a speech?
3. What are the major topical sequences for ideas to which people are accustomed through their language? Can you give an example of each being used to arrange ideas for the body of a speech?
4. What is the major difference between a coherent topical sequence and a jumble of points loosely related to a broad topic?
5. How and where do you indicate supporting materials on the outline for a speech?

Key Terms

Body of a speech	Landmark	Spatial
Causal	Main point	Subpoint
Chronological	Problem	Topical
Criterion	Schema	Whole
Gestalt	Solution	

Having completed collecting materials to develop your central idea, you are now ready to organize them into a plan to achieve the response you desire from listeners. Your organizing will produce an outline to follow while you speak. Having completed an outline as a plan for speaking extemporaneously (or for writing a manuscript), you will be ready to create any sensory aids and to rehearse your speech.

▶ Overview of Organizing/Outlining

Like central idea and desired response statements, organizing and outlining are not separable in practice. Planning any complex procedure involves organizing your efforts and always results in some sort of *outline* of the procedure. The outline may take the form of blueprints, a critical path, a game plan, a program, or a strategy involving specific tactics for a campaign of battle or advertising. In preparing for public speaking, planning involves organizing, or selecting and arranging information and ideas into a plan for the actual speaking called a *preparation outline*. The outline is undergoing development during the process of selecting and organizing information. Of course all this planning is about how the speaker will try to achieve a desired response to a central idea from a specific group of listeners in the context of a specific situation. In Chapters 8, 9, and 10, we explain this organizing/outlining process in detail, emphasizing principles for organizing the body of a speech in Chapter 8. In Chapter 9 we explain how to plan introductions and conclusions for speeches, and in Chapter 10 we give detailed instructions about writing an outline. However, organizing and outlining are not really separate; all outlining involves organizing, and organizing for speaking means creating an outline.

To get some idea of the importance of organizing the information in a speech, examine the two rectangles in Figure 8.1. How many dots are displayed in each rectangle? Most people say they can count the dots in the rectangle to the right more quickly because those dots are organized into sets. They even seem to add up to something. Similarly, materials in a speech must be organized around meaningful points or ideas that collectively comprise the central idea of the speech. Without a simple outline structure, both listeners and speaker are likely to become confused, unable to see a pattern, and therefore unable to understand your central idea.

The first step in organizing/outlining is to write your central idea and

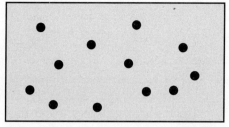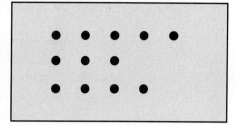

Figure 8.1 Organizing information simplifies and clarifies it.

desired response statements in *final* form in light of information you discovered while researching your topic. Now is the time to confirm what you wrote before analysis of audience and situation, to make needed revisions, or even to change your mind about the central idea and/or specific response. Write your finished central idea and desired response statements near the top of a sheet of paper on which you will begin organizing your information into the first draft of an outline of your forthcoming speech. Next comes the planning of the *body of the speech*, then the planning of an *introduction* and *conclusion*.

You may wonder, "Why outline the body before the introduction?" The answer is that introductory remarks depend on what you plan to say in the body of the speech about your central idea. The conclusion depends on what you say in both the introduction and the body of the speech.

One of the least effective ways of preparing is to write a speech manuscript before trying to write an outline. If a manuscript is needed, it should be composed *after* (and from) the outline. Writing a speech manuscript before outlining is like trying to build a skyscraper without plans, then drawing blueprints of what you have built. Both the speech and the building will be chaotic, inefficient, and unattractive. If a manuscript is required, you should always write it after the outline.

We begin this chapter by presenting some principles of perception and memory on which effective speech organization depends. Second, major sequences for organizing main points and subpoints in the body of a speech are explained and illustrated. Third, we explain how to organize your developmental materials into the outline of main points.

▶ Principles for Organizing Ideas and Information

Research in cognitive psychology has yielded principles of perception and memory important to public speaking. Three major factors are critical to the understanding and recall of information.

Perception Is Limited

Humans are deluged by sensory information, but can consciously perceive and recall only a small amount of it. Our needs, previous experiences, mental organization of those experiences (*schemas*), and characteristics of the stimuli all influence what we will be aware of and recall. We can perceive and remember only small numbers of items in groups. Estimates of how many range from as few as three to as many as eight or nine.[1] To help us remember them, telephone companies group the ten digits of each phone number into chunks of three and four. You may find it difficult to remember addresses when the street number exceeds four digits in length. We may say "thirty-six twenty-three" instead of "three thousand six hundred and twenty-three" to help us remember.

To accommodate limited perception, you must limit the number of main points into which you analyze your central idea. Usually you should organize all you will say about the topic into not more than four main points. You can then include a lot of information, but it will be organized into sets and subsets, called *main points* and *subpoints*. With information thus grouped, both you and your audience have a better chance to remember both the main points and the information that develops them.

The need to organize information into a simple sequence of not more than four main points that make a larger whole is illustrated in the following example. Stan worked in a factory where firebricks were manufactured; the other class members worked in mills where firebricks were used to line steel-making furnaces. Stan's speech topic was how firebricks are made. His seven-minute talk had 20 steps in the making of bricks:

1. Fireclay is dug from open pit mines.
2. The clay is hauled to a pug mill in trucks.
3. The clay is ground into small particles by the mill.
4. The particles are screened for size.
5. A special blend of clays and salts is mixed for firebricks.
6. Water is blended until the mixed clay resembles putty.
7. Wet clay is put into a molding machine.
8. The molding machine stamps out wet bricks.
9. The green bricks are placed on special pallets.
10. The pallets of bricks are loaded onto a conveyer.
11. The green bricks are dried by blasts of hot air.
12. The dried bricks are loaded on special buggies.
13. The buggies are loaded into a cool kiln.
14. The kiln is sealed.
15. Gas jets heat the kiln to cooking temperature.
16. The kiln is cooled very slowly to anneal the bricks.

17. The cooked bricks are removed from the kiln.
18. The cooked bricks are inspected for color and shape.
19. The bricks are cleaned and packaged on pallets for shipment.
20. Pallets of brick are loaded into box cars for shipment.

So he could remember all of these steps, Stan practically read them to the audience. When Stan finished, listeners were asked to write down the steps in making firebrick. No one could remember more than ten steps, and no two listeners had the same sequence of steps.

Together the instructor and students simplified Stan's speech by organizing the 20 detailed steps into four main points in a chronological sequence. The outline of the body of the speech then looked like this:

I. Fireclay is prepared as the raw material for bricks.
   A. The clay comes from an open pit mine.
   B. The clay is ground and screened for consistency.
   C. Clays and salts are mixed in special proportions.
   D. The mix is blended with water to putty-like consistency.
II. The clay mixture is molded into green bricks.
   A. Mixed clay is put into a molding machine.
   B. The molding machine stamps out green bricks.
   C. The green bricks are dried to keep their shape and reduce water content.
III. The green bricks are cooked in a kiln.
   A. They are loaded onto kiln buggies.
   B. The buggies are stacked in the kiln so heat can spread evenly.
   C. The kiln is heated to clay-fusing temperature.
   D. The kiln is cooled slowly.
IV. The cooked bricks are prepared for shipment to a steel mill.
   A. Buggies of bricks are removed from the cool kiln.
   B. Bricks are inspected for proper color and shape.
   C. Acceptable bricks are cleaned.
   D. Finished bricks are packaged and loaded into cars.

Later, Stan gave his reorganized speech to a different audience. When asked to write down the steps in making firebricks, all 22 of these listeners got the four main steps in order, and over half of them had all of the substeps in sequence! This was dramatic evidence of the importance of grouping information into a limited number of points.

Information Is Perceived and Recalled as Associated Parts of a Whole

Gestalt psychologists established the principle that we perceive and recall information as complete figures, or *wholes*.[2] According to the gestalt principle, a speech needs to be organized so that listeners can see a subject as a unified whole (the central idea) of interrelated parts (main points). This means that a speaker needs to create a *pattern* among the main points in a speech so they fit together as a psychological whole. Likewise, all detailed information provided with each point should be clearly related to the point, thus creating a perceptual unit. Numerous studies have shown that information not associated and grouped mentally by the listener is forgotten quickly.[3] The main points become *landmarks* of memory. Landmarks are used to recall specific details associated with them. For example, you will recall what you did on January 3 by relating that date to what you were doing on the landmark days of January 1 or New Year's Eve. A visual illustration of the importance of a unified whole and landmarks to the recall of specific information is provided in Figure 8.2. Each of the drawings in the figure contains nine lines, but the organized, patterned figures are more meaningful and memorable.

Main Points Should Follow One Schema

The ways in which we perceive and organize information are based on assumptions programmed into our brains through language.[4] For example, consider the common assumption that every event is caused by preceding events. Our language reflects this assumption in such statements as "Why did Joel commit suicide?" and "I don't understand what caused. . . ." Both speaker and listeners can follow a causal sequence outline of main points. Any speech that is easy for both speaker and listeners to follow and recall will have the topics of its main points arranged in accord with one of the basic *schemas*, structured sequences programmed into the language they share. A loose collection of topics that do not add up to a whole and fit into one of the sequence schemas of the shared language will certainly result in confusion. As Jerome Bruner, a noted educational psychologist, said, we need to consider how information "should be structured so that it can be most readily grasped by the learner."[5]

Research has consistently demonstrated the importance of organizing information into a limited number of meaningful groups that are organized in one schema. Three main advantages of such organization are increased listener

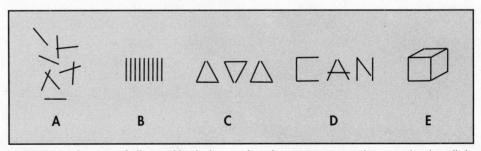

Figure 8.2   Information of all types, like the lines in these drawings, is more easily perceived and recalled when organized into meaningful groups.

comprehension and retention,[6] enhanced perception of the speaker's credibility by an audience,[7] and greater persuasive impact of messages.[8]

▶ Sequences of Main Points and Subpoints

The most important schemas for organizing information and ideas are very familiar because we use them constantly to organize our perceptions. Schemas embedded in the English language that are especially useful to public speakers include chronological, spatial, problem-solving, causal, and a number of other special sequences for topics. We say "sequences for topics" because there is a *topic* in every idea or main point sentence. So *every* sequence is topical, although many writers have used the term *topical* as if it were a schema like chronological or spatial.

The appropriate schema for ideas (topics) in a particular speech depends on what the speaker wants listeners to perceive and remember about the subject of the speech, be it an evolutionary history (chronology), visualization (spatial), observable characteristics, reasons, consequences, structure of a system and its function, or how to solve a problem. The schema and its sequence of main points is implied in a well-stated central idea.

In this section we primarily discuss main points in the body of a speech. However, it is frequently necessary to divide main points in the body of a speech into two or more subpoints. Sometimes it is even necessary to divide subpoints into sub-subpoints. As an example and model, the outline at the end of Chapter 10 shows subpoints in the body of the speech. The subpoints of a main point are related to it in exactly the same way that main points in a speech are related to the central idea. Just like main points, the topics of each set of subpoints should be arranged in one and only one schema. All the principles we explain for organizing and writing main points apply to creating and arranging subpoints. First we present four very commonly used schemas for main points, followed by a variety of other familiar schemas that are easy for both speaker and listeners to follow and recall.

Chronological

Chronological means that the events described follow a time order, usually from first to last, but sometimes a reverse order from last to first. A chronological schema is appropriate for main points when explaining a procedure, instructing how to do some task, emphasizing major turning points in the history of a person or institution, and telling a story. Stan's speech about making firebricks followed this sequence. Here is a typical example of main points from a "how-to" instructional speech:

153

Central idea: You can install ceramic tile in your own bathroom in four steps.

Desired response: As a result of hearing my speech, I want my classmates to be able to install ceramic tile in their homes.

BODY

I. Gather materials and tools needed to install tile.

II. Lay out the walls so the tile will be plumb and centered.

III. Cement the tiles in place with waterproof mastic.

IV. Grout the joints to keep out water.

The next example shows how a reverse chronology might be used to advantage:

I. We worry today about dying of cancer or heart disease before the age of 80.

II. Just 100 years ago our ancestors worried about dying of bacteria before the age of 40.

When you choose a time schema to organize information, remember that there should be only a few main time periods arranged in one direction, past to present or present to past, so listeners can follow the sequence easily.

Spatial

Spatial means that there is a space relationship among the major topics dealt with in the body of the speech. The speaker chooses a spatial schema to emphasize the arrangement among parts or sections, rather than to emphasize what will be seen first, second, and so on in time. The emphasis can be on what we *see* as we move from left to right, east to west, inside to outside, or some other continuous visual flow. As with a chronological pattern, there should be one spatial pattern among the main points; don't jump from compass points to inner–outer direction or from middle to top to bottom. In the following examples each of the central ideas indicates a spatial sequence of main points.

Nebraska's major geographic regions are the prairies of the east, sand hills of the north central region, and high plains of the far west.

Law enforcement officers have different missions at the city, county, and state levels.

A cowboy boot must have correctly designed shaft, heel, instep, and toe if it is to wear well.

For each of the above central ideas the main points should stress what is special about each part in the total space described. For example:

BODY
I. The prairies of eastern Nebraska produce outstanding grain crops.
II. The sand hills of central Nebraska nurture great herds of animals on their native grasses.
III. The high plains of western Nebraska are semidesert wheat and cattle ranches.

Notice that each main point emphasizes an important feature of the area, not just its spatial relationship to other parts of the state. Notice, also, that each states a point about the topic; a main point should not just announce its topic.

Causal

Sometimes instead of a sequence in time or space you may want to emphasize the logical relationship we call *causal*, or cause–effect. There are several possible variations of the causal schema. For instance, the main points could proceed from cause(s) to effect(s), from a cause to several effects, or from a combination of several causative forces to one major effect. We can also reverse the order, beginning with effect(s), then proceeding to cause(s). The following are examples of appropriate applications of the causal schema for main points. The first example emphasizes a simple cause–effect relationship.

Central idea: An unmanaged deer herd produces an ecological disaster.
I. Deer have a great reproductive potential.
II. Excess deer destroy habitat for themselves and other creatures.

The next example reverses the order of main points, from effect to cause.

I. Fear of public speaking is epidemic in the United States.
II. Critics of our culture say this fear results from our emphasis on competition with other people.

The third example of the causal sequence attributes several effects to one cause:

Central idea: Deficit federal spending will increase our imbalance of trade, lower our standard of living, and reduce our national security.
I. The federal government has practiced deficit spending for many years.
II. The federal deficit lowers our ability to compete in world markets.
III. The federal deficit puts a greater share of the wealth in the hands of a few persons at the expense of the many.
IV. The federal deficit threatens our ability to pay for military security.

The causal pattern may be chosen to emphasize what is producing our benefits, but it can also stress what is causing a problem. When we want to explain how to *solve*, we need the organizing sequence called *problem–solution* or *problem solving*.

Problem Solving

When the speaker's central idea concerns the solution to a problem, the appropriate sequence for organizing main points is problem solving. We have all been familiar with this schema since childhood—first a problem, then how to solve it. There are several variations of the problem-solving sequence, all beginning with a description of the problem and proceeding to a description of a way to overcome, reduce, or solve the problem. The sequence can be simple—"I. Problem. II. Solution"—or it can contain several main points, often including a discussion of causes of the problem and/or criteria for evaluating proposed solutions. Before considering actual examples of main points in problem-solving sequences you need to understand how we use the terms *problem, criteria,* and *solution.*

Problem refers to a situation or condition unsatisfactory to some person. Unless someone is dissatisfied with the way things are, no problem exists. So a problem is the difference between a present condition and a desired one. Only when two or more people agree on the existence and nature of a problem can they cooperate in working to change the unsatisfactory condition.

A *criterion* is a standard on which a judgment or decision may be based, a yardstick against which possible solutions can be measured. For example, a criterion for a truck might be that it can haul at least 10 tons. The criterion for a grade of A is often 90 percent of a possible total score. There may be several criteria for selecting among possible courses of action. The criteria you used when selecting a college probably involved location, costs, and reputation.

Solution refers to a way of changing an unsatisfactory situation to a satisfactory one. Most often a solution is a plan for removing the cause(s) of a situation not to our liking. A solution may also be an answer to an unanswered question.

We can now examine some examples of main points in a variety of problem-solving sequences. Notice that each sequence adds one new step to the sequence that preceded it.

I. Mudville floods every four or five years (**problem**).
II. A system of levees could end flooding forever (**solution**).

I. Many students and staff members cannot find parking on or near campus (**problem**).
II. Any solution to the parking shortage must be within the financial resources of students, and it must save time (**criteria**).
III. A remote lot with shuttle buses to campus best meets the criteria of cost and time (**solution**).
   A. A parking garage would require parking fees of $500 per car per year.
   B. Adjoining surface lots would cost at least $300 per car per year.
   C. Parking on city-owned vacant land with free shuttle buses would cost only $50 per car per year.
   D. Parking on the remote lot would save time over hunting for parking on or near campus.

I. Acid rain is killing lakes and forests (**problem**).
II. Most acid rain comes from burning fossil fuels (**cause**).
III. A solution must remove the causes without increasing our imbalance of trade (**criteria**).
IV. Electrostatic scrubbers will greatly reduce acid rain at a small increase in costs (**solution**).

In many speeches the overall schema is problem solving, but the problem has already been understood and accepted by listeners, so the central idea is about solving the problem. The speaker just mentions the problem briefly in the introduction. For instance, polls have shown that a large majority of Americans think that the high rate of pregnancy among teenagers is a serious problem. The main points in the body of a speech dealing with such a problem would not need to include a detailed description of the problem if listeners already perceive the problem similarly. Instead, the first main point in the body of a speech might be an analysis of the causes, with additional points presenting a solution or solutions designed to remove those causes, as in the following example:

I. The continuing federal deficit is largely the result of a living standard in excess of our productivity as a nation (**cause**).
II. To end federal deficit financing, we must increase our productivity per worker hour (**first solution**).
III. To end federal deficit financing, we must match our living standards to our productivity (**second solution**).

A speaker's central idea may emphasize that one of several possible solutions is best. For this purpose the *applied criteria* version of the problem-solving sequence is best. Again, the need for a solution is mentioned in the introduction. The first main point in the body of the speech establishes appropriate criteria by which to judge among proposed solutions. The remaining main points then compare the proposed solutions to the criteria until it is evident to listeners that one solution is superior. For example:

I. Any solution to the greatly increased cost of medical care must meet criteria of both adequacy and quality.
II. Government-managed medicine is likely to be of poor quality.
III. Private insurance does not provide adequate coverage for millions of persons.
IV. Health maintenance organizations with government subsidies for the very poor can provide adequate medical coverage of high quality.

Other variations on the problem-solving schema can be used to accommodate specific central ideas. When using any variant of the problem-solving sequence, be sure you stress the problem–solution schema by using the terms *problem* and *solution* in stating your main points.

Additional Schemas

When information about a subject is organized into categories on any basis, the resulting sequence of ideas can appropriately be called *topical*. As we said before, *all* sequences for main points are topical, for every point is about some topic. In the previous organizational patterns the topics of the main points were related to each other in a chronological, spatial, causal, or problem-solving pattern. Many other topical schemas can be used to focus attention on certain aspects of a subject. For example, topics can be selected to emphasize component parts, structure and functions, a set of reasons for supporting a course of action, a group of causes that contributed to some event, or major observable features.

Only one basis for selecting the topics should be used in a short speech. A speaker should not mix components and characteristics, or reasons and functions, in one set of main points. Such a pattern does not fit into any of the schemas with which we have been familiar since childhood and makes it very difficult for most people to remember the connections between the points. A well-stated central idea will not suggest a confusing array of topics as the basis for main points, for such an array does not make a whole, or gestalt figure.

Functions of the subject of a speech are categories into which information developing the points can be placed. For example, dogs are classified into groups on the basis of the services they provide:

Central idea: Dogs function as hunting assistants, workers, guardians, and companions.
  I. Hunting dogs assist humans in locating and securing game animals.
 II. Working dogs assist in the handling of livestock or carrying burdens.
III. Guard dogs protect people and their possessions.
IV. Companion dogs provide love and affection to their masters.

Characteristics can be the basis for main point topics. For example, cats are classified according to the length of their hair:

 I. Longhaired cats tend to be gentle and passive.
II. Shorthaired cats tend to be active hunters.

A speaker giving advice on how to evaluate used cars organized advice around three major components of a car. Because these components intertwine in space, he could not use a spatial pattern, such as from front to back.

  I. Examine the chassis for signs of a major accident.
 II. Examine the body for signs of rust from the inside.
III. Examine the engine for signs of serious wear.

A speech on dairy goats was organized around the names of the major breeds, stressing the different characteristics of Toggenbergs, Alpines, and Saanens. A student majoring in heating and air-conditioning explained the structure and functioning of a humidifier:

I. A humidifier consists of a water reservoir, a fan, and a wick or belt.
II. The humidifier adds moisture to air by blowing dry air over the wick.

A list of *reasons*, or arguments, as topical main points might look like this:

I. Helmets save motorcyclists' lives.
II. Helmets spare families from grief.
III. Helmets save society a great deal of money.

The following example illustrates how a list of *effects* can be organized as main points. A list of causes would be organized similarly.

Central idea: Economic boycotts do little good, but much harm.
I. Economic boycotts have not stopped tyrants.
II. Economic boycotts have not stopped abuses of human rights.
III. Economic boycotts have seriously damaged our farm economy.
IV. Economic boycotts have increased our imbalance of payments.

Topics in brief informative speeches are often carelessly thrown together. Do not use a topical sequence carelessly; always be certain that there is one and only one schema for selecting or creating the topics. A hodgepodge of miscellaneous points will not long be remembered, and the listener is likely to misunderstand the central idea.

▶ Organizing Developmental Materials

Regardless of which schema you select as appropriate for your central idea, the outline of the body of the speech must indicate relevant developmental materials for each main point (and/or subpoint). Each point must be followed by sufficient developmental material to make it possible for all listeners to form a clear image of what you are discussing. If the main point is controversial, there must be sufficient evidence and reasoning to lead listeners to give credence to it. These developmental materials are indicated on the outline, subordinate to the main points they develop. The developmental materials need not be written out in full sentences like main and subpoints; it is sufficient to refer to them with a word or phrase. In the following outline of the body of a speech by Bill Marx you will notice that developmental materials come immediately after the first main point. The second main point is divided into subpoints, with material developing each of them.

I. A successful student organizes time on a calendar.
  A. Two hours study/one hour lecture.
  B. Reading ahead in history.
  C. My calendar for this week.

II. A successful student realizes personal limitations.
    A. Solve a problem when you first encounter it.
       1. Tutor in math.
       2. Instructor in statistics.
    B. Set realistic goals for the future.
       1. My determination.
       2. Joanne's goals.

After you have indicated where each item belongs, check to see that every piece of developmental material is subordinate to the main point under which it is written. Delete anything that is not directly related to the point above it, no matter how witty, funny, vivid, or exciting it might be to the listeners. The criterion now is *relevance*. Consider the following example:

I. The helmet is the most important safety item for a motorcyclist.
    A. Ninety-two percent of injuries to head.
    B. Drakulich accident and death.
    C. Heavy pants and jacket.
       1. Brush burns.

Item C does not belong under I, which is about helmets. Can you spot the problem in the next outline sample? How would you revise the outline?

I. Vampire bats must feed on warm-blooded victims.
    A. Cut neck with tongue.
    B. Lap up blood.
    C. Often they leave germs in the victim.
       1. Rabies.

Item I.C. should be main point II: Vampire bats often leave germs in their victims.

The outline for the body of an upcoming speech may indicate more developmental materials than the speaker could possibly use in the time allowed for the speech. Such planning will allow the speaker to choose those materials that seem to be most effective with a particular audience, give further evidence if needed when answering listeners' questions, and adapt to nonverbal indications that some listeners do not understand or accept a point.

▶ Summary

Unorganized information is meaningless. In the body of a speech, developmental materials must be organized around main points that collectively comprise the central idea. In order to adapt to limitations of human perception and recall, information should be clustered into no more than four main points. Likewise, the number of subpoints under any main point should be limited. If subpoints and developmental materials are clearly related to main points by a speaker, the main points serve as landmarks for recall, benefitting both speaker and listeners. Main points should be arranged in a single schema. The schema should be based on one of the major topical patterns we are familiar with from the structure of our language, such as chronological, spatial, causal, problem–solution, characteristics, reasons why, and structure–function. Similarly, each group of subpoints should follow one schema.

Each and every main point should be developed with relevant materials to make it clear and/or persuasive to listeners. Developmental materials need not be written in the outline as full sentences, but can be indicated with a word or phrase. Having created a rough outline of the body of the speech, the speaker is ready to focus thought on the introduction and conclusion.

▶ Learning Activities

1. Name the schema organizing the main points in each of the following sets from the outline of the body of an actual speech.

    a. I. Many house fires are started by heating and cooking.
        II. Fire extinguishers are the best line of defense against such fires.

    b. I. Tent theatre provides amusing entertainment for a date.
        II. Tent theatre provides an inexpensive date.

    c. I. Airways in the lungs of an asthmatic narrow during an attack.
        II. Asthma attacks are responses to both internal and external forces.

    d. I. Arthritis is an inflammation of joints.
        II. Arthritis is diagnosed from symptoms and analysis of joint tissue.
        III. Treatment of arthritis involves combinations of medications, exercise, and rest.

    e. I. During the winter football players rebuild and condition their bodies.
        II. During the spring football skills are improved.
        III. During the summer football players get into peak condition mentally and physically.

    f. I. On the first floor, the Business Advisory Center helps clients with management and marketing difficulties.
        II. On the second floor, simulation labs provide students with a realistic setting for business games.

III. On the third floor, lecture halls and general classrooms provide flexible space for classes.

IV. On the fourth floor, offices provide space for administrators and faculty to work.

    g.   I. A heart attack begins with the blockage of a coronary artery.

          II. The blockage is followed by a shortage of oxygen to brain and body.

2. What's wrong with each of the following schemas for main points? How might each be improved?

    a.   I. Led by two famous pioneers, the world was led into the wireless age in the early 1900s, Marconi and Fessenden.

          II. Lee DeForest is known as "The Father of Radio."

    b.   I. Most adults dream a great deal.

          II. Dreams carry messages from you to you.

          III. Our unconscious minds create dream pictures using symbols and metaphors.

    c.   I. The first stage in a heart attack is blockage of a coronary artery.

          II. Such a blockage can stem from several causes.

          III. The second stage is a loss of oxygen to the brain and muscles.

          IV. Insufficient oxygen produces symptoms ranging from weakness to death.

3. Which schema for organizing main points is implied by each of the following central ideas?

    a. Employers should take an active role in solving child-care problems encountered by their employees.

    b. There are four major steps in refinishing a piece of furniture: stripping, sanding, staining, and sealing.

    c. Federal deficits lead to depressions.

    d. A walnut consists of a pulpy hull, a hard shell, and a living kernel.

    e. When buying a diamond, consider the color, cut, clarity, and carat weight.

    f. The culture of the Glenwood Indians was notable for substantial houses and farming for food.

Notes

1. George A. Miller, "The Magical Number of Seven, Plus or Minus Two: Some Limits on Our Capacity for Processing Information," *Psychological Review* 63 (1956):81–97; G. Mandler, "Organization and Memory," in K. W. Spence and J. T. Spence (eds.), *The Psychology of Learning and Motivation* (New York: Academic Press, 1967), Vol. I.

2. For a summary of this research, see Edwin G. Boring, *A History of Experimental Psychology*, 2nd ed. (New York: Appleton–Century–Crofts, 1950).

3. For a concise summary of research supporting these statements see Robert S. Woodworth and Harold Schlosberg, *Experimental Psychology*, revised edition (New York: Henry Holt, 1954), pp. 695–737.

4. For example, see John Carroll (ed.), *Language, Thought, and Reality: Selected Writings of Benjamin Lee Whorf* (Cambridge, MA: MIT Press, 1956); Norman Gerschwind, *The Human Brain* (San Francisco: Freeman, 1979); and Jean Piaget, *The Origins of Intelligence in Children* (New York: International Universities Press, 1952), pp. 7–8 and passim.

5. Jerome S. Bruner, *Toward a Theory of Instruction* (Cambridge, MA: Belknap Press, 1966), p. 41.

6. Ernest C. Thompson, "Some Effects of Message Structure on Listeners' Comprehension," *Speech Monographs* 34 (1967):51–57.

7. Arlee Johnson, "A Preliminary Investigation of the Relationship Between Message Organization and Listener Comprehension," *Central States Speech Journal* 21 (Summer 1970):104–107; Christopher Spicer and Ronald E. Bassett, "The Effect of Organization on Learning from an Informative Message," *The Southern Speech Communication Journal* 41 (Spring 1976):290–299.

8. Harry Sharp, Jr., and Thomas McClurg, "Effect of Organization on the Speaker's Ethos," *Speech Monographs* 33 (June 1966):182–83; James C. McCroskey and R. Samuel Mehrley, "The Effects of Disorganization and Nonfluency on Attitude Change and Source Credibility," *Speech Monographs* 36 (March 1969):13–21.

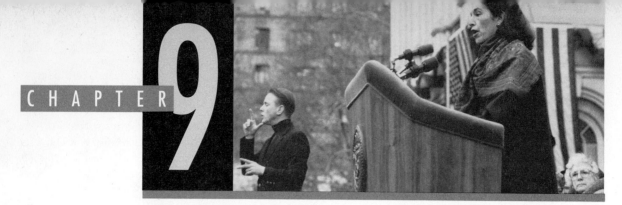

CHAPTER 9

Planning Introductions and Conclusions

6
167-172

164

Questions to Guide Reading and Review

1. What four functions need to be accomplished in the introduction to a speech and why?
2. What techniques are effective for accomplishing the functions of an introduction?
3. What are the three major functions to accomplish in the conclusion to a speech and why?
4. What techniques are useful for accomplishing the functions of a conclusion?
5. How long should an introduction and conclusion typically be, relative to the length of the body of a speech?

Key Terms

Closure
Conclusion
Introduction

Preview summary
Rhetorical question
Startling statement

Startling statistic
Summary

Once you have planned the body of a forthcoming speech into rough outline form, you are ready to plan the introduction and conclusion for your speech. Unfortunately, many speakers exert too little effort doing so. Although outlines of an introduction and conclusion are planned late in the procedure you follow to prepare yourself to speak to an audience, this is no time to let up on careful thinking—analysis and adaptation to listeners. In this chapter we discuss functions, organization, techniques, and length of both introductions and conclusions.

▶ Planning an Introduction

Like the overture before a musical and the warm-up act before Janet Jackson comes on stage, the *introduction* prepares the audience for what follows—the body of the speech. The introduction should bring the speaker, listeners, and subject of the speech together. In an effective introduction, you do or say what will be necessary for listeners to give sustained attention and follow the body of your speech. The introduction should be as short as possible while still accomplishing four essential functions.

Functions of the Introduction

Four functions must be accomplished prior to or in the introduction:

1. **Direct listeners' attention** to the topic of the speech.
2. **Interest the listeners** in the topic, purpose, and issues of the speech. *Interest* means that a listener believes that a personal need or desire can be met by attending to the speech.
3. **Establish trust in the speaker** as a credible source of information on the subject of the speech.
4. **Focus attention on the sequence of ideas or issues.** For listeners to perceive the speech as a whole of interrelated points and focus listening on the *main* points, they must know what topics the speaker will discuss and in what order.

You need to be prepared to accomplish these four functions for yourself when addressing an audience. When you speak as a guest or invited expert, a moderator or master of ceremonies may perform some of these functions while introducing you to the audience. If so, you should modify or delete parts of your preplanned introduction designed to accomplish those functions.

ATTENTION   Before audience members can listen they must have their attention focused on the speaker. Many introductions successfully gain the attention of the audience, but misdirect it to the speaker as a person or to the rhetorical device used rather than to the purpose of the speech. One speaker realized this when she dressed in a bikini to deliver a speech on waterskiing. Her attire drew the attention of audience members to *her*. When polled immediately following the speech, many listeners could not even identify her central idea, let alone recall the main points! Another student was presenting an informative speech on the use of rattlesnake venom to treat a variety of diseases. He began by opening up a canvas bag and dumping a live rattlesnake on the table! Although he gained the audience's attention, no one was concentrating on his words. Most of the listeners were absolutely terrified that the venomous snake might bite them.

Effective attention-directing techniques include using stories, reference to the audience or occasion, rhetorical questions, and startling statements and statistics. These techniques can direct the attention of the listeners to the topic of the speech. However, whatever you say to capture attention must be perceived as relevant to the subject rather than as a gimmick used to entrap the audience into listening.

Speakers very often use *stories* in order to direct attention and hold audience interest. Stories are extended examples that can be hypothetical or real. Beginning your speech by recalling a personal experience related to the topic is an example of a story. The object of the story is to direct audience attention to the central idea of the speech, not to the story used. The following example from a speech on leadership illustrates how a story can be used to focus attention:

> Many years ago my father told me a story about lemmings. He told me that in Greenland, once a year the entire population of these small rodent-like animals would dash madly, following a leader toward a cliff overhanging the North Sea. Upon reaching the edge of the cliff they would jump to their deaths. When I asked my father why the lemmings did such a thing he said they were just following their leader. Now, I do not know if the story is true, but most legends do have some basis in fact. The truth of the story is not important in this case. What is important is the concept of "follow the leader."

Gene Walker's story about lemmings directed the attention of his classmates to the topic of the speech—uncritical following of a leader. The story format used in introductions creates a point of interest and reference for the audience.

Speakers can also use *reference to the audience or occasion* in order to direct the attention of listeners. President Ronald Reagan used this technique effectively in his first inaugural address.

> To a few of us here today this is a solemn and most momentous occasion. And yet, in the history of our nation it is a commonplace occurrence. The orderly transfer of authority as called for in the constitution routinely takes place as it has for almost two centuries and few of us stop to think how unique we really are. In the eyes of many in the world, this every-four-year ceremony we accept as normal, is nothing less than a miracle. Mr. President, I want our fellow citizens to know how much you did to carry on this tradition. By your gracious cooperation in the transition process you have shown a watching world that we are a united people pledged to maintaining a political system which guarantees individual liberty to a greater degree than any other. And I thank you and your people for all your help in maintaining the continuity which is the bulwark of our republic.[1]

With his positive reference to the occasion and to retiring President Carter, newly elected President Reagan evoked a feeling of national unity and a positive audience attitude toward the speech that followed.

Rhetorical questions are used frequently to direct attention. A rhetorical question is one to which the speaker neither expects nor wants an overt response from the audience. The speaker invites the audience to participate by responding mentally, thus focusing attention on the topic of the speech or idea. In the following example the speaker used a series of rhetorical questions to direct the attention of prospective college students.

> How many of you would consider buying a car without first test-driving it? Would you purchase a home without going through it or having it inspected for termites, electrical, or construction problems? Would you invest your money with a stranger if he had no references to support his claim to be able to make wise investments for you? Would you accept a loan from your bank without knowing the terms of the loan and interest rate on the money borrowed? Your answer to each of these questions is probably "No." You would be a foolish consumer if you answered "Yes." I agree, and yet thousands of college students each year make unwise investments when they select which college they will attend without adequate preparation or knowledge.

Rhetorical questions can be used to arouse a feeling of need for information, either because a vital interest of the listener is involved or curiosity has been aroused. For example, Suzanne Bell used rhetorical questions to direct the attention of her classmates to the need for cardiopulmonary resuscitation (CPR) training:

> What would you do if you and a friend were walking out in the woods and he suddenly doubled over and stopped breathing? What would you

do if a companion fell out of your boat and by the time you could pull her out of the water she was unconscious? What would you do if your opponent on the racquetball court grabbed his chest and collapsed onto the floor?

To arouse curiosity, another student used a rhetorical question about a news story every listener had heard:

> We recently heard about the poisoning of several people by cyanide, which the murderer had put into Tylenol capsules and several other over-the-counter medicines. Did you ever wonder how a tiny amount of cyanide could kill a person or even an elephant?

By using rhetorical questions each speaker aroused a feeling of need for the information being presented.

Startling statements can be used to direct attention, but only if the speaker avoids arousing excessive psychological noise. It is ethically imperative that startling statements used for directing attention be honest representations of fact. A speaker who sensationalizes for the sake of attention soon gets the same reputation for distortion as tabloids that employ this kind of misrepresentation. The following are examples of legitimate startling statements used to direct attention.

> In 1926, Lee de Forest, the man who invented the cathode ray tube, said "While theoretically television may be feasible, commercially and financially I consider it an impossibility, a development of which we need waste little time dreaming."

> Thomas J. Watson, chairman of the Board of IBM Corporation, said in 1943: "I think there is a world market for about five computers."

> In 1945, Admiral Leahy said this about the atom bomb: "This is the biggest fool thing we've ever done . . . the bomb will never go off—and I speak as an expert on explosives."

Statistics are usually thought of as developmental material for main ideas of a speech. However, *startling statistics* can be used to direct attention, as illustrated by the following example.

> Today, I shall address, "Health care in the 80s: Changes, Consequences, and Choices." Last year the health care industry had total expenditures of $384 billion. This is three times the revenue of the American auto industry. Think of it, $1 billion in the last 24 hours. . . . That is $1 of every $9 worth of goods and services produced in the entire economy.[2]

Jennifer Adams used the following statistics on teenage pregnancy to arouse the concern and attention of her classmates:

Each year more than a million teenagers become pregnant. Four out of five of them are unmarried. There are some 30,000 of them that are age 14 or younger. State officials of Illinois estimate that overall the United States spends $8.6 billion each year for income support for teenagers who are pregnant or who have already given birth.

INTEREST Interest is aroused when the listener feels that a personal need can be satisfied by attending to and remembering the speaker's message. Unless interest is gained the speaker will be wasting time and energy on speech preparation and delivery. If done well, the audience will be committed to listening until the felt need has been satisfied. If interest has been aroused, attention is not fleeting, but sustained throughout the speech.

In his speech "Drugs in America" John C. Lawn, head of the Drug Enforcement Administration, established interest in his topic by demonstrating that drugs are everyone's problem. By presenting statistics that impact on daily life he created a feeling of "I need to know."

As the Administrator of the Drug Enforcement Administration I face the drug problem every day. It is my problem. It is your problem, too. It is our problem. If you are a student, if you are a teacher, if you are a businessman, if you are a community leader, if you work for the government. Or, if you are a parent, drugs are your problem too. The drug problem is our problem. A problem for all of us.

We are the most drug abusing nation in the history of the industrialized world. We consume three tons of aspirins a day. Each year over 120 million prescriptions are written for psychoactive drugs in this country. Thirty million of us take sedatives. Twenty million of us take stimulants. Eight million of our citizens are chronic abusers of tranquilizers. . . . It is imperative for each of us to understand the scope of the drug abuse problem in this country and recognize that we—you and I—are all a part of the solution.[3]

In order to maintain the interest of the audience, the speaker must provide information that will satisfy the need focused on in the introduction. If the body of the speech provides that information, the listener will maintain attention through the conclusion. In many introductions, the same statement that directs initial attention also evokes the *interest* needed to maintain active listening. However, even if you have directed listener attention and interest, you still need more—trust in you as a source.

TRUST A speaker must gain the trust of listeners. Each listener needs confidence in what a speaker has to say. This sense of trust in a speaker's statements is called *speaker credibility*. Credibility results primarily from a combination of the speaker's perceived competence and trustworthiness, and in some circumstances from dynamism. These aspects of perceived credibility will be discussed at greater length in Chapter 15. Here we briefly define each component of credibility to assist you in planning introductions.

Skilled public speakers realize they must evoke trust from their listeners.

Competence refers to the listener's perception that the speaker is an expert on the topic or at least has sufficient knowledge to justify listening well. Skills in verbal and nonverbal expression, especially fluency and eye contact, add to the impression that a speaker is competent.

Trustworthiness is based on the perception that a speaker is fair and honest and has the best interests of the audience in mind. Statements from a person perceived to be speaking for selfish gain at the expense of the audience will be viewed with extreme skepticism.

Dynamism results from the speaker's animation and concern for what is being presented. The audience needs to feel that the speaker is sincere and personally committed to the topic. Often called *charisma* or *sincerity*, this perception is largely a response to the nonverbal manner of the speaker, including energetic gestures, vocal emphasis, and direct eye contact.

When the audience is familiar with the speaker's previous actions and/or reputation, some level of trust has been established prior to the speech. Trust can be increased by the speaker during the introduction. As you begin a speech, you and the audience are engaged in a type of bonding. If a positive emotional and intellectual climate is established, the speaker will have an advantage during the rest of the speech. A speaker who is not perceived positively by the end of the introduction will have a difficult time keeping the interest of the listeners and probably will not achieve his or her desired response.

The introduction is usually a speaker's first opportunity to establish a positive image in the minds of listeners. As one popular television commercial

171

warns us, "You never get a second chance to make a first impression." The speaker must be concerned with both verbal and nonverbal behaviors in the introduction. While delivering your introduction, you must focus your attention on the listeners and your message. Otherwise, your nonverbal signals will be interpreted as "She is not concerned," "He is not interested in us," "He is sneaky," "She is lying," "What is he hiding?" or "He just *says* this is important." You certainly want to avoid first impressions like those that follow. They were related to one of the authors by a student after observing speakers for a make-up assignment.

> Sue hurried to the front of the classroom, hunched over the lectern, and began reading her speech in soft muffled tones with only a glance at the audience. It was obvious that she was far more concerned with her fear than with her message or how we responded.

> Joe looked out the window, then down at the floor, then at the wall above his classmates. The last thing he seemed concerned about was establishing a relationship with us. His eyes kept shifting rapidly. He stumbled over simple phrases. Trust him? Are you kidding?

In contrast, Charlotte overcame her nervousness and established a positive first impression:

> It was obvious Charlotte was nervous from the slight tremor in her voice, but she looked right at us as she began to speak: "Last week my father embalmed three of my high school classmates. They paid in full for driving while drunk. We are about to go home for Christmas vacation. I hope none of you ends up in the hands of a mortician before classes resume in January." Her eyes, her posture, her hands, her voice all said "I care about you. I care enough to be sure of my facts. You can trust me." And we did!

FOCUS   In the last part of the introduction the speaker attempts to focus listener attention on the schema of points in the body of the speech. The speaker emphasizes the key ideas as landmarks that will help the listener perceive the speech as a whole and recall information. Unless this function of the introduction is done well, the listener is likely to lose track of the speaker's central idea and main points.

Many speakers focus attention by using a *preview summary* that forecasts the main points. As the old adage goes, "Tell 'em what you're gonna tell 'em." Because this technique is effective in focusing listeners' attention, you should always preview your main points whenever you speak.

The following example demonstrates the preview summary technique:

> . . . I'm here today to discuss personal computers. . . . To accomplish this I'd like to cover some history, talk about the present, and try to outline the future for you in "Is there life after the PC?"[4]

Jennifer Adams used this preview to focus her classmates' attention:

> When looking at the problem of teenage pregnancy, there are two main issues that need to be considered. Number one is the quality of education about reproduction, and number two is the question of whether or not teenagers are informed about methods of birth control.

Mike Bruening prepared listeners to follow his main points with this preview:

> There are three off-season programs that better the chances of a team having a winning football season. They are winter conditioning, spring practice, and summer conditioning. I'll describe the purpose of each and what is done to achieve that purpose.

▶ Functions of the Introduction

1. Direct listeners' attention to the topic of the speech.
2. Interest the listeners in the topic, purpose, and issues of the speech.
3. Establish trust in the speaker as a credible source of information on the subject of the speech.
4. Focus attention on the sequence of ideas or issues.

Length

How long should an introduction be? There is no simple answer to that question—long enough to perform the needed functions well and no more. One rule of thumb is that the introduction should not exceed 10 to 20 percent of the entire speech. Thus for a five-minute classroom speech, the introduction would generally last from 30 seconds to a little over a minute. For a 25-minute report the introduction might last as long as three to five minutes. When the audience knows the speaker well or a moderator has introduced the speaker, the introduction might be much shorter. When facing a strange or hostile audience, a very large proportion of the speaker's total speaking time may be needed to win the trust of the listeners.

Introductions should be carefully thought out. It is not an exaggeration to say that the first 15 to 45 seconds of your speech are the most important. Some student speakers begin with little more than an announcement of the topic of the speech; others talk about their interests, but not how the topic matters to the audience. Even more self-defeating, some students plunge head-on into a complex topic before giving the listeners any indication of where the speech is going or what issues will be addressed. The following introduction accomplishes all four functions of an effective introduction. It also prepares listeners for the body of the speech, in which three major causes are the main points, by giving them a background on the extent and nature of the problem.

COMMENTARY

Attention function: Speaker replies to moderator who introduced him and announces the topic that is of vital importance to the audience as part of society.

Interest function: Topic is vital to existence of businesses that listeners represent; their companies could be destroyed.

Interest function: Audience is prepared to understand the problem and be concerned about its causes.

Trust function: Speaker associates himself with a highly credible source on the issue, the chief justice of the Supreme Court, and also demonstrates a thorough grasp of the problem with statistics, examples, and expressions of concern and well-being for businesses and the United States.

Extended concrete examples used to arouse interest and convince listeners of the seriousness of the problem and need for a change.

INTRODUCTION

Thank you, Phil, I am delighted to have this opportunity to share with you a concern that is uppermost in my mind—namely, the destructive and rapidly escalating trend toward liability litigation in this country and the implications that this trend portends not only for industry but for society as a whole.

It is a trend that is costing the American public billions of dollars each year, it is undermining the competitiveness of U.S. industry, and it is threatening the very existence of some businesses in this country. Yet it is a trend that the vast majority of the American people has either failed to understand or has predominantly chosen to ignore.

The disturbing truth is that America has become the most litigious society in the world. Last year one out of 15 Americans filed a private lawsuit of some kind. In all, over 13 million private civil law suits were filed in state and federal courts.

No less than the highest court in the land is appalled at the situation. As Chief Justice Warren Burger lamented in a recent speech, our society today has an almost irrational focus—virtually a mania—on litigation as the way to solve all problems.

In some instances, the grounds for resorting to litigation strain credulity. Let me cite just a few examples—examples that sound more like stories out of Ripley's *Believe It or Not* than responsible examples of American jurisprudence.

Item: Two Maryland men decided to dry their hot air balloon in a commercial laundry dryer. The dryer exploded, injuring them. They sued the manufacturer of the dryer and ended winning nearly $900,000 in damages.

Item: An overweight man with a history of coronary disease suffered a heart attack while trying to start a Sears lawn mower. He sued Sears, charging that too much force was re-

COMMENTARY	INTRODUCTION
	quired to yank the mower's pull rope. A jury in Pennsylvania awarded him one million dollars, plus another $500,000 in pre-judgment interest. . . .
Here the speaker adds to the interest and competence functions by relating to more types of businesses and professions and using current court cases.	If you think these are isolated cases of absurdly generous liability awards, you are wrong. Last year, awards of a million dollars or more were given to more than 360 personal injury suits—an incredible 13 times the number ten years ago. The list of those afflicted by liability litigation runs the full spectrum of American business—including product manufacturers, retail stores, doctors, architects, and stockbrokers to name a few. Even ministers are being sued for malpractice. In cases currently pending before state courts, ministers are being accused of seduction, breaching confidentiality, failing to recommend professional help, and offering incorrect advise. In the wake of these claims, some 40,000 ministers have bought malpractice insurance—while others have become reluctant to counsel members of their congregation and are sending them to psychiatrists instead.
Attention function: Speaker makes use of two rhetorical questions to involve the audience. *Focus function:* A preview of three main causes that will be developed in detail in the body of the speech. Note the use of a rhetorical question as a transition into the speaker's preview.	Where will this end? Is no group sacrosanct in our litigation prone society? . . . What is causing the problem? I attribute the current situation to the following: first, the ambiguity of current laws; second, an increasing acceptance of the concept of victims' entitlement to compensation; and third, the contingency system for compensating the legal profession.
Transition between the introduction and the beginning of the body of the speech.	Let me discuss each of these in detail.[5]

With a rough outline of the introduction in hand, you are ready to plan the conclusion. Your introduction has been designed to accomplish the functions of directing listener attention on your topic, motivating listening, establishing your credibility with the listeners, and indicating what the major points or issues will be so listeners can focus on and recall them.

▶ Planning a Conclusion

Like the introduction, a conclusion must be planned carefully in order to perform certain specific functions. A variety of techniques can be used to perform these functions.

Functions of the Conclusion

The *conclusion* of a speech must accomplish three functions:

1. Provide a sense of psychological closure.
2. Reemphasize the main points of the speech.
3. Ask listeners to apply the central idea.

Usually the outline of the conclusion will require only two points to perform all three of these functions:

1. A **summary** of the main points or central idea.
2. A **suggested application,** or **appeal** for agreement or action.

CLOSURE   *Closure* is important to a sense of psychological balance. A speech without an adequate conclusion is like a puzzle with one piece missing or a joke without a punch line. The listeners feel dissatisfied; something is needed to complete the speech. One of our students sat down in what seemed to be the middle of her speech. When a classmate asked her if she was ill, she replied, "No, I'm finished." She had not provided her listeners with the satisfying sense of closure a conclusion should produce, so they were expecting something more.

A sense of closure can be achieved by referring back to the material used to direct attention in the introduction, reemphasizing the central idea, summarizing the main points, or asking listeners to act in some appropriate way in response to the speech. A combination of these techniques in the conclusion provides the sense of "the end" that both speakers and listeners need for psychological balance.

A speaker often signals that the speech will end soon by using a special transition signpost to alert the audience that closure is about to occur: "Let's review the main points of my speech . . .," "Let's see what this all adds up to . . .," "In my closing remarks . . .," "Finally, . . .," "In closing, . . ." Avoid using such phrases until just before you conclude. If you prepare an audience psychologically for a conclusion and then continue speaking for several more minutes, you will create a sense of psychological imbalance like that which results from a failure to provide closure. When the conclusion has been signaled it must come quickly.

REEMPHASIS Reemphasis means that the listeners' thoughts are directed back to the central idea. The listener is helped to view as a unified whole what was expressed point by point in the body. Such a concluding summary should be more than a hurried recitation of the topics of the speech. A complete restatement of the main points of the body is usually helpful, especially for instructional speeches. Carole used such a summary to reemphasize the main points in her speech so listeners would be able to remember the main steps in wallpapering and view the procedure as a whole.

> You now know from this simple demonstration that hanging wallpaper is not a difficult task, but one that does take planning. You can do much to update your home for a minimum of cost if you wallpaper yourself. Remember the four basic steps we have discussed today and join in the experience of interior decorating.
>
> Let's review those four basic steps. First, premeasure the room before buying the paper. Second, prepare the surface for the paper. Third, measure and plan paper placement in order to minimize waste and match seams. Fourth, take the time to do finishing touches that make the difference between an amateur and a professional papering job.
>
> Begin with a simple project and you will be encouraged by the success you achieve. The sense of accomplishment and the feeling of home-owner pride is worth the time and effort it takes to learn the simple skills of wallpapering.

Sometimes a story can be used to summarize and reemphasize the central idea, but be sure that the main points of the body of the speech stand out in the story. The following conclusion used a story to do just that:

> I will end my speech today by sharing one of my favorite stories with you. There was a young boy and an old man fishing in a boat on a large lake. As the old man looked into the water and watched the fish and surveyed the plant life, he turned to the boy and asked: "What do you know of biology and botany?" The young boy answered: "I haven't ever felt the need to learn much about that stuff." The old man nodded his head and said "Son, you have lost 25 percent of the value of your life."
>
> As time went on the sun started to set and the stars began to appear across the sky. The old man looked at the boy and asked: "Son, what do you know of astronomy and astrology?" The young boy replied: "Sir I haven't felt the need to learn that stuff and I never took the time." The old man rebuked the boy with "Son, you have lost 50 percent of the value of your life."
>
> After fishing in silence for quite some time the old man once more addressed the boy: "Son what do you know of philosophy and philosophers?" The boy, almost in a whisper, shook his head in shame and

replied: "Old man I never felt the need to learn about that stuff. I never took the time to study it." The old man in disgust mumbled: "Son, you have lost 75 percent of the value of your life."

Just then the boat sprung a leak and was sinking fast when the boy yelled out to the old man. "You can swim, can't you?" The old man, gasping for breath replied: "No, I never felt the need to learn that in my life. I never took the time to learn to swim." "Old man, you have lost 100 percent of the value of your life," said the boy.

Education is a life-long experience. We cannot afford to be pompously satisfied with our achievements, diplomas, or degrees. To know, is to know there is much more to learn. I am looking forward to a good year and many well-attended self-improvement classes. We will all be there—the swimmers and the philosophers.

Reemphasis is also essential in a speech to persuade. The audience can be reminded of all the main points to see that your central idea is logically inescapable. In concluding his speech on "Trade Conflicts," Ichiro Hattori (CEO of Sony Corporation) reemphasized his central idea and the arguments supporting it:

> Finally, to conclude my talk, I would like to touch once more on a point I made earlier, which is that Americans must understand that to expand the world economy in real terms, we must have more people participate in consumption. There is a limit to the expansion of the consumer population in North America, Europe, and Japan.
>
> Increased consumption in the remainder of the world, however, cannot occur with war and violence. To expand the consumer population, a continuing peace in larger areas of the world is and will always be the vital factor. I am afraid, however, that peaceful countries and the number of their people are today less than ten years ago. Countries like Cambodia, Vietnam, Iran, Afghanistan and Lebanon have been lost as consumer markets as a result of war or other violence. The markets for consumer products in Latin American and many African countries have been diminished in size for one reason or another. We have a shrinking world in terms of the size of the consumer market. How we can turn this situation around and expand the size of the world consumer market is the crux of the problem which we all face today.
>
> To address this problem is a mission truly worthy of the United States, the superpower of the Western World, and perhaps of Japan, also. Japan bashing and creating protective barriers may satisfy the emotion of the moment, but is neither a lasting nor a meaningful solution.[6]

APPLICATION   The final function of the conclusion is to apply what the speaker has explained or argued to some aspect of the listener's life. Audience members may listen to information and/or argument without seeing any application for what they have just heard. In the introduction the speaker should have stressed how the subject of the speech is relevant to the audience. That importance now needs to be stated in very specific terms. For instance, when ending a speech to inform, the speaker might say "So the next time you read about someone dying of cyanide poisoning you'll understand how cyanide destroys living cells," or "You can enjoy watching baseball games more now that you know the principles that make a pitch curve."

The application should be a request for agreement if the desired response is agreement with a controversial central idea. For instance, one student said this: "I trust you now agree with me that the university should eliminate all nonacademic scholarships." Another ended this way: "The evidence I've presented leads to the inescapable conclusion that the United States should press forward with the Strategic Defense Initiative."

An appeal for definite action concludes many persuasive speeches. For example, "Please sign up for your blood donation on the schedule cards I will now pass around." One student made an appeal for action this way:

> How can you help? Well, of course, we can use your financial donations, and I will gladly provide you with pledge cards at the conclusion of this program. But even more than your generous financial contributions, we are asking you to donate that most important quantity—the one we cannot buy at any cost. We need your time. We need people who are willing to spend two hours a week with a child. We need men and women who are willing to share their lives with a child who is waiting for a friend. We need Big Brothers and Big Sisters who care enough to love a child. Won't you please be a part of our program? I guarantee you that you will never regret it. I guarantee you a child will never forget it. I know I'm asking for a big commitment, but isn't the future of a child worth it?

▷ **Functions of the Conclusion**

1. Provide a sense of psychological closure.
2. Reemphasize the main points of the speech.
3. Ask listeners to apply the central idea.

Length

The conclusion should never include a new idea, new argument, or information the speaker forgot to include in the body. The conclusion should be brief, usually not more than 5 or 10 percent of the total speech. That means that in a typical five-minute classroom speech you would conclude in about 15 to 30 seconds. To accomplish so much in so few words means you must plan your conclusion very carefully.

▶ Summary

By the end of the introduction the speaker needs to have accomplished four functions to prepare audience members for listening well: directed their attention to the topic of the speech, aroused a strong interest in listening to and understanding the body of the speech, created a sense of trust in the speaker as a source of information on the topic, and focused attention on the main points or issues to be developed. These functions can be accomplished in a variety of ways.

Conclusions should be planned to accomplish three important functions: establish psychological closure for the speech; reemphasize the central idea and main points developed in the speech; and make some application or appeal for direct or indirect action as a result of the speech.

▶ Learning Activities

1. Each of the following introductions by beginning speakers fails to accomplish
• one or more of the major functions of an introduction. First, state what is missing from the introduction. Second, write an addition to perform the absent function(s).

Since the invention of the laser in 1960, thousands of uses have been discovered for it, ranging from entertainment to delicate eye surgery. Today I will explain the three basic characteristics of laser-generated light beams: single frequency, coherency, and intensity.

Do you have fears in elevators? Are you afraid when you're on a ladder that if you look up or down you are going to fall? Do you fear the day you're going to be standing in my position and going to have to speak to the class? I have these types of fears; I know everybody has fears like those. I did some research on how to combat my fears and found a really helpful book in the library by John T. Wood, *What Are You Afraid Of?*

I suffer from asthma, so have studied it intensively for years. Asthma can strike anyone—young or old, male or female, of any ethnic background— so some of you may have asthma now or develop it in the future. Today

I'll explain what happens during an asthma attack, then what causes such an attack.

2. Listed below are several speech topics. Write what you might say in the introduction to a speech on each topic to arouse the sustained interest of your classmates by either linking the topic to their lives and concerns or arousing a need to know.

   Corruption in collegiate athletics.
   Compulsive gambling.
   A new "miracle" fabric.
   Individual Retirement Accounts.

3. For each of the following sets of main points write a brief summary suitable for the conclusion of a five-minute speech, then a suggested use or appeal statement.

   I. Rape has been stimulated by pornography.
   II. Incest has been stimulated by pornography.
   III. Murder has been stimulated by pornography.

   I. A heart attack begins with a blockage of a coronary artery.
   II. The blockage is followed by a lack of oxygen to body and brain.

   I. A successful student relates each class to real-life situations.
   II. A successful student adjusts to personal limitations.
   III. A successful student organizes time.

4. After listening to a classmate's speech, write down what you believe to be the central idea of the speaker. Read your central idea statement to the entire class. If there are considerably different perceptions of the speaker's central idea:
   a. In the introduction did the speaker fail to focus attention on the central idea and main points? How might this have been done or done more effectively?
   b. How adequate was the refocussing and synthesis in the conclusion? Was a more complete summary needed? Can you formulate such a summary?

Notes

1. Ronald Reagan, "First Inaugural Address," *Public Papers of the President of the United States* (Washington, DC: Office of the Public Registrar, National Archives and Records Service, 1982), p. 1.
2. William L. Kissick, "Health Care in the 80's," *Vital Speeches of the Day* 52 (January 15, 1986):213.

3. John C. Lawn, "Drugs in America," *Vital Speeches of the Day* 52 (March 15, 1986): 322.

4. Eugene Manno, "Is There Life After the P.C.?" *Vital Speeches of the Day* 52 (March 15, 1986):342.

5. R. H. Malott, "America's Liability Explosion," *Vital Speeches of the Day* 52 (January 1, 1986):180–181.

6. Ichiro Hattori, "Trade Conflicts," *Vital Speeches of the Day* 52 (January 15, 1986): 220–221.

Writing Speech Outlines

Questions to Guide Reading and Review

1. How does a speech preparation outline resemble a blueprint for a building in both design and purpose?
2. What are the major parts of a preparation outline? In what order are they arranged?
3. What is the standard alphanumeric symbol and indentation system for speech outlines?
4. What are the outline rules of *coordination, subordination,* and *the rule of twos?*
5. Why is it important to follow each of four major principles when composing main or subpoint sentences?
6. What are the purposes, locations where needed, and components of transitions?
7. On a preparation outline, how and where do you indicate developmental materials, visual aids, transitions, and references?
8. How is a rehearsal/delivery outline similar to and yet different from a preparation outline? How do you prepare and use such an outline?

Key Terms

Alphanumeric symbol
Connective
Internal preview
Internal summary

Parallel sentences
Preparation outline
Rehearsal/delivery out-
  line

Signpost
Subordinate
Transition

A speech *preparation outline* is the visible product of all the organizing and planning of the body, introduction, and conclusion we described in Chapters 8 and 9. The outline is like a "working blueprint" that may need to undergo additions, deletions, and substitutions as speaking practice proceeds. When you are satisfied that your outline is a plan adequate to achieve your desired response, you can then write it into a final clean copy. Many instructors require that a preparation outline be submitted to them when you speak. Others will require the outline a class meeting or more before the speech is to be given. You may also want to make an abridged version of your preparation outline to use during rehearsals and your presentation to the audience.

Writing an outline is quite different from writing a manuscript. Some students write such extensive and detailed outlines that they are virtual manuscripts in outline format. This defeats the purpose of outlining before composing the speech, of planning *before* constructing. Changes are easier to make in an outline than in a manuscript. Freedom from the exact wording of a manuscript gives an extemporaneous speaker flexibility to adapt to listener reactions.

By now you have polished your central idea as the "whole," or thesis, of your speech and your desired response statement. You have decided on a schema of main points and possibly schemas for subpoints under some main points, selected development materials appropriate for each point, and drafted a sequence of statements to accomplish the functions of the introduction and conclusion. Your organizing has mostly been done, but there are still a number of things to do before your preparation outline is a complete and adequate plan for speaking. You need to be sure you can express main points and subpoints clearly and forcefully, plan transitions between main points, indicate where visual and other aids will be used, and add a bibliography of references used in the speech. You may need to compose a title and to write an abridged speaking outline.

▶ Completing the Preparation Outline

A preparation outline serves several purposes: It helps the speaker express main points precisely and clearly; it helps the speaker test and clarify relationships among ideas and supporting materials; and it serves as an aid to memory for both speaker and listeners. It can only do these things if it is prepared according to some basic principles and conventions. Planning your preparation outline according to the guidelines we suggest will result in a more effective speech.

Conventions of Speech Outlines

There are six rules about writing speech outlines that, if followed, will help you to achieve simplicity, clarity, emphasis, and unity in your public speeches. Just as you would need to adhere to the conventions for writing research papers, memoranda, or company business letters, so conventions of speech outlining should be followed until they become habits.

▷ **Conventions of Speech Outlines**

1. Include all major parts.
2. Begin the numbering in introduction, body, and conclusion with Roman numeral I.
3. Use conventional symbols and indentations to show the levels of abstraction and subordination in your outline.
4. Follow the rules of subordination and abstraction.
5. Coordinate items at the same symbol level in each section of the outline.
6. If you divide a point, it must have two or more subpoints.

(1) **Include all major parts.** A complete preparation outline contains all of the first six parts listed below and sometimes needs the seventh part in the list.

> Title.
> Central idea.
> Desired response.
> Introduction.
> Body.
> Conclusion.
> Reference list (bibliography).

You can see where all these parts belong in the completed preparation outline in Figure 10.1, which shows the outline for a classroom speech by Linda Worman. You can use this outline as a model. Linda indicated where each verbal and visual component of the speech would be located and how it related to other components of the speech.

(2) **Begin the numbering in introduction, body, and conclusion with Roman Numeral I.** Even though there may be several parts (functions) in the

Day Care—More than Just "Mom's Problem"

Central idea: Employers should take an active role in solving the child-care problems faced by their employees.

Desired response: I want the listeners to agree that employers should take an active role in solving child-care problems faced by their employees.

INTRODUCTION

I. Jennifer is in a need-to-work, need-for-child-care bind.
II. The need for day care is great and growing.
   A. Statistics on working mothers (chart 1).
   B. Projections of future needs.
   C. Quotation, B. Kantrowitz.
III. This will affect us all in the near future, if not already as it now affects me.
   A. It will affect us as employees, parents, employers, and citizens.
   B. It affects my child and my studies.
IV. I will discuss the growing problem, some employer efforts, and benefits of such programs.

(Transition: First, we will examine the need for day-care programs.)

BODY

I. Quality day care is a growing problem for working parents.
   A. Future needs can be projected.
      1. Ten million children by the end of the decade (Kantrowitz).
      2. 1984, 47 percent under 5 cared for by nonrelative.
         a. Less than 10 percent of these are licensed facilities.
   B. Most day care is very expensive for hourly employees.
      1. Variable costs (chart 2).
      2. Up to 30 percent of family income.

(Transition: Now that we've seen the growing problem of day-care needs, the question arises what can be done to solve it?)

II. A few companies and government agencies have shown that there are workable solutions.
   A. A few companies have solved the problem for their employees.
      1. Examples (chart 3).
   B. Several government agencies have helped with laws.
      1. San Francisco developers must set aside space in new office buildings.
      2. Massachusetts has low-interest loans for companies.
      3. U.S. tax law has deductions for companies.

(Transition: We've seen that a few companies and government agencies have provided workable solutions. But are these worth the cost?)

Figure 10.1 The preparation outline for a classroom speech.

(continued)

III. Day-care programs benefit both employee and employer.
   A. The benefits to employee and family are less expense, better quality, and greater convenience.
      1. Comparative statistics (chart 4).
      2. Standards.
      3. Convenience in travel.
   B. The benefits to employers are less absenteeism and turnover and better recruiting.
      1. Control Data decreased to half of industry absentee rate.
      2. Lower turnover of trained personnel for Neuville Industries.
         a. Cost offset by tax savings.
      3. Enhances recruitment of talent.
         a. Hoffman-La Roche Pharmaceutical, men.

(Transition: Let's review the current day-care situation for American employees and companies).

CONCLUSION

I. Availability of quality day care is a rapidly growing problem for parent employees, but a few companies and government agencies have shown that it can be solved to the benefit of both company and employees.

II. I hope you agree with me that in the United States we should greatly expand these programs so they are available to all employees in need of quality day care.

REFERENCES

English, Carey W., and Maureen Walsh, "Tot Care Brings a Bundle of Benefits for Employees," *U.S. News and World Report* 25 (November 1985):86.

Kantrowitz, Barbara, "Changes in the Workplace—Child Care Is Now an Item on the National Agenda," *Newsweek* 31 (March 1986):57.

Kantrowitz, Barbara, "Day Care: Bridging the Generation Gap," *Newsweek* 116 (July 16, 1990):52.

Konrad, Walencia, "Corporate Day Care Attracts Top Male Employees, Too," *Working Woman* (November 1985):31.

Marshall, S., "In Pursuit of Good Child Care," *National Review* 42 (April 16, 1990):18.

Shell, Adam, "Firms Starting to Grapple with Child Care Issues," *Public Relations Journal* 46 (March 1990):12.

Statistical Abstract of the U.S. for 1990, 110th ed.

Figure 10.1

introduction, use I again as the *alphanumeric symbol* (numbers and letters) before the first main point in the body. Also, begin with I for the first part of the conclusion. Why? Because introduction, body, and conclusion are distinct divisions of the speech plan, each with a very different function to perform in the process of communicating with an audience.

(3) **Use conventional symbols and indentations to show the levels of abstraction and subordination in your outline.** Alphanumeric symbols and indentations are used to show which statements are equivalent in importance and which are logically *subordinate* and less abstract than those that precede them. The most generally accepted pattern of symbols and indentations for outlines is the one following. This sequence is used in word processor programs for outlining as well as in public-speaking textbooks.

I. Main point (idea) of body or function of introduction or conclusion.
   A. Subpoint of I or developmental material if no subpoints.
   B. Subpoint of I or developmental material.
      1. Developmental material to B, such as examples, comparisons, statistic, or testimony.
      2. Developmental material to B.
         a. Detail of 2.
         b. Detail of 2.
II. Main point.
   A. Subpoint of II.
      1. Developmental material to A.
      2. Developmental material to A.
   B. Subpoint of II.
      1. Developmental material to B.
      2. Developmental material to B.

In addition to the sequence of Roman numerals, capital letters, Arabic numerals, and lowercase letters, still lower levels of detail or abstractness can be indicated by Arabic numerals in parentheses, such as (1), followed by lowercase letters in parentheses (a).

Each *type* of symbol is used with statements at the same level of generality in a section of the outline. Thus I, II, and III are the most important statements in the outline of the body of the speech and of approximately equal importance (main points). A, B, C, and so on under each main point are either all subpoints (subdivisions subordinate to the main point and narrower in scope) or specific materials used to develop the main point. Items indicated by Arabic numerals (1, 2, 3, and so on) are either materials developing the subpoint they follow or specific details of a developmental item, such as an extended example or analogy. In the outlines of the introduction and conclusion, Roman numerals indicate statements to perform each function, such as focusing attention on the topic, providing the perspective of a brief history of a problem, previewing or reviewing the main points in the body, or making an appeal for an action, such as voting "Yes."

You should use the sequence of alphanumeric symbols consistently and keep indentations aligned on the outline. Some students fail to do this, resulting in an outline that does not clearly reflect relationships among components of the speech. Sloppy use of symbols or indentations reflects sloppy thinking about what is relatively major and minor, what is a key point and what is a supporting statement to that point, or the logic of an argument. The outline helps you test your thinking and analyze the organization of your speech.

(4) **Follow the rules of subordination and abstraction.** All items in an outline must directly support the next higher level of statement as shown by symbol and indentation. As we explained in Chapter 8, the main points in the body of a speech must all relate to the central idea. Each subpoint must relate to the main point above it. Developmental materials must be logical clarification or supporting evidence for the point under which they are located. To avoid confusing your listeners, check your rough outline again to be sure you have not made some error in level of abstraction/subordination.

(5) **Coordinate items at the same symbol level in each section of the outline.** The rule of *coordination* is that all points at the same level in a specific section of the outline should be of equal value or abstraction, related, but not overlapping. At any one symbolic level there is no subordination. Thus B is not subordinate to A; they are related as coequal points or developmental materials. This principle of separate and equal applies to all levels of the outline. If you find a point that does not seem to be equal in importance to others at the same level of symbolization and indentation, it may be a subpoint rather than a main point like the others or a sub-subpoint. Any subpoint irrelevant to the central idea should be removed from the outline. Consider the following example of a violation of the rule of coordination:

Central idea: Appetite suppressant pills, fasting, and one-food diets are ineffective and dangerous ways to lose weight.

BODY

I. Appetite suppressant pills are an ineffective and dangerous way to lose weight.
II. Fasting is an ineffective and dangerous way to lose weight.
III. Eating only one food is an ineffective and dangerous way to lose weight.
IV. Diet foods are expensive.

The first three points in this outline follow the rules of subordination and coordination; all are subdivisions of the central idea that are equal in importance. Main point IV does not fit with them. It is not about an ineffective and dangerous type of fad diet, but about the cost of food used in fad diets. It should either be deleted or the central idea of the speech would have to be completely changed to something like "Fad diets are ineffective, costly, and dangerous."

(6) **If you divide a point, it must have two or more subpoints.** This rule is called the *rule of twos*. If A under I is a subpoint, there must also be a subpoint B. If 1 under A is a sub-subpoint, there must also be a sub-subpoint 2. Of course there might also be subpoints C and D, or sub-subpoints 3 and 4. The more general rule is this: You cannot divide something into one part!

Rule 6 does not apply to developmental materials such as examples and statistics. If A is an example developing I, and the only supporting material you plan to use to explain I, then there would not have to be an item B in this part of the outline. A in this case is not a subdivision of I, but an illustration or evidence developing it. In some cases one diagram, extended example, statistical trend, or item of testimony is all you need to explain or convince adequately.

Completing the Outline of the Body

With the conventions of outline writing in hand, you are now ready to put the polishing touches on your speech preparation outline. For all practical purposes, you have completed the outlines of the introduction and conclusion when you have applied the above rules to them. However, you will still have to polish the wording of main points, add transitions, and indicate all aids and supplements to your speaking before the outline of the body is complete.

PHRASING MAIN POINTS AND SUBPOINTS Main points need to be worded carefully so that listeners will find them clear and memorable. Taken together, they are the central message of your speech. It may not matter much if listeners forget who supplied them with new ideas, nor if they forget details of fact, testimony, and comparison used to develop the ideas. What matters is that they remember—and possibly act upon—the main points of your message. How main points are worded is a critical factor in how well they are understood and recalled. Think of the guidelines you follow in making decisions. You probably recall these as very simple, short sentences or even phrases. We recall best ideas stated in vivid language, having rhythmic or parallel wording. The point is this: *Sentences that are main points in the body of a speech should be revised until you are confident that they are likely to be understood quickly and remembered easily* by both you and audience members. Depending on your present skill in expressing ideas, you may be able to plan statements of main points quickly or have to make several revisions. By the time you are satisfied with the wording of a set of main points you will be able to state them clearly while speaking without having to depend on word-for-word memorization.

Apply four key principles when phrasing your main points:

1. State each main point as a complete sentence.
2. Present only one idea about the subject in each main point.
3. State each main point in a clear, concise style.
4. State each main point in a form parallel to that of the other main points.

(1) **State each main point as a complete sentence.** You want to make a point about a topic, not just announce the topic. What is the idea about this topic that you want listeners to understand and remember? State it as clearly as possible. You will remember that an idea is expressed as a complete sentence,

with both a *subject* (topic), and *predicate* (point about the topic). Key words, phrases, and signposts can only announce, not state ideas. Also, to be clear, the point must be a declarative sentence, not a question. The following examples illustrate differences between topic announcements and main point sentences.

Topics: (incorrectly presented as if they were main points)
I. Heel. **(A key-word topic, saying nothing about the topic.)**

I. Next we will consider the heel of a boot. **(A preview sentence announcing the topic but saying nothing about it; part of a transition.)**

I. The design of the heel in a cowboy boot. **(A noun phrase that limits the topic, but still says nothing about it as a main point.)**

I. What should you look for in the heel of a cowboy boot? **(A question that could be part of a transition used to call attention to the new topic in the body of a speech; it makes no point about the new topic.)**

I. Should match the intended use. **(A verb phrase stating the point, but failing to state the topic about which the point is being made.)**

Main points: (correctly stated as full sentences in which a point is made about the topic)
I. The design of the heel should match the intended use of a boot.

I. Choose a heel style to match the intended use of the boot.

(2) **Present only one idea about the subject in each main point.** Main points should not be complex sentences presenting two ideas about the subject of the speech. Correctly worded main points present one idea each, and these ideas are of approximately equal importance in developing the central idea of the speech. What follows is a rough draft of main points violating this principle, followed by a corrected revision of the main points.

Central idea: Four C scales are used to determine a diamond's worth.

INCORRECT
I. A diamond's value depends on its weight in carats.
II. A diamond's value depends on its clarity and color.
III. A diamond's value depends on its cut.
(Clarity and color are not the same characteristic. They should be treated in two different main points, of equal importance.)

CORRECT
I. A diamond's value depends on its weight in carats.
II. A diamond's value depends on its clarity.

III. A diamond's value depends on its color.
IV. A diamond's value depends on its cut.

(3) **State each main point in a clear, concise style.** Long, rambling sentences are difficult for listeners to understand. They are impossible to remember. They lack the punch of short, crisp sentences. The easiest sentences to recall are short in length and use concrete words. Compare the following pairs of contrasting sentences that illustrate this principle:

> If the front end of a car is not properly aligned the tires will wear out rapidly (**rambling**).

> Improper alignment wears out tires (**concise**).

> The connections must all be checked carefully with a soap solution to prevent loss of gas and danger of explosion (**wordy**).

> For safety, check all connections for leaks (**concise**).

> Books are extremely effective weapons in the war to win supporters to our democratic ideals (**vague**).

> "Books are bullets in the battle for mens' minds" (F.D. Roosevelt) (**emphatic**).

(4) **State each main point in a form parallel to that of the other main points.** This means that you try to write all main point sentences in the same format, although this may not always be possible. *Parallel* wording helps both speaker and audience recall key sentences. Notice the increased emphasis and clarity when the following main points were revised into parallel form.

NOT PARALLEL

I. The 55 MPH speed limit greatly reduced the loss of life on American highways.
II. Limited natural resources are conserved due to the 55 MPH limit on automobile speed on our highways.
III. Our balance of trade improved as a result of using less imported oil after reducing the speed limit to 55 MPH.

PARALLEL

I. The 55 MPH speed limit saves lives.
II. The 55 MPH speed limit saves limited resources.
III. The 55 MPH speed limit improves our balance of trade.

INDICATING DEVELOPMENTAL MATERIALS All materials that develop ideas must be indicated on the preparation outline—examples, statistics, testimony, comparisons, and descriptions. A quick examination of an outline will indicate if any idea has not been developed for clarity or logical support. Developmental materials should not be written in detail on the outline; to do so would make it a virtual essay or manuscript of the speech. Use a key word or brief phrase to indicate where each developmental material or detail fits into the speech. For example:

I. Chocolate is a high-energy food.
  A. Athletes and soldiers use chocolate for extra energy when under stress.
    1. Examples of runners and football players.
    2. In C rations of WWII.
    3. Operation Deepfreeze.
  B. Explorers use chocolate on long journeys to keep down weight.
    1. Admiral Perry.
    2. Sir Edmund Hillary.
    3. Space flights.
II. Chocolate is nutritious.
  A. Quotations from *The World of Chocolate*.
  B. Protein content.
  C. Minerals—calcium, phosphorus, potassium.
  D. Vitamins.

Put references to visual aids in parentheses following the line of the outline where they will be presented to the audience. The sample preparation outline shown in Figure 10.1 (pp. 187–188) indicates how this can be done.

Completing the Outlines of the Introduction and Conclusion

Outlines of the introduction and conclusion are included in the total preparation outline as separate divisions from the body of the speech. Begin numbering each with the Roman numeral I, then continue with the alphanumeric symbols in the same order of subordination as explained for the body of the speech. Label each major division of the speech just above it on the preparation outline: introduction, body, and conclusion. By separating these major portions of the total speech, you can better ensure that you have given sufficient attention to each.

Planning Transitions

A *transition* is a word or phrase used to keep listeners oriented when the speaker shifts from one topic to another. Transitions are not part of the logical structure of a speech, so they are usually indicated in parentheses at the point where each fits in the speech outline. No alphanumeric symbol or indentation is used. Your instructor may have some specific form in which these are to be written; if so, follow that direction. If not, put transitions in parentheses between the parts of the speech they connect and label them.

Jamie Colinwood illustrated the need for transitions. She switched abruptly from one main point to another. What she said was:

> Senators are elected by popular vote in November. For example, Senator Johnson, representing the district in which we are now sitting, was re-elected last year by a vote of 26,923 to 17,384 for his challenger, Karl Harl. The legislature created the laws by which our state is governed during its annual sessions that begin in January. . . .

Few listeners realized she had changed from discussing *how* the legislature is formed to *what it does*. A transition between the two main points could have helped emphasize both of them and kept listeners from becoming lost and confused.

Some type of transition is needed each time you move from one main point to another in the body of a speech. A transition is usually needed between the introduction and body and between the last point in the body and the conclusion. Some people use *markers* such as *okay* or *got that?* between main points. Markers do not express the relationship between two or more ideas.

A listener's focus of attention may shift from what the speaker is describing to a personal problem or other topic, then back to the speaker. Such shifts of focus may occur in a matter of seconds, temporarily "tuning out" the speaker. Transitions help to reorient listeners who have made such shifts. Even the most conscientious active listener needs transitions to help keep perspective on where the speaker has been and is going next.

There are four major types of transitional devices used by speakers and writers. Transitions between two points often contain two or more of these devices.

CONNECTIVES   A *connective* is a single word or short phrase that connects words or groups of words. These devices warn us that something new and different is coming next. They also indicate the logical relationship between the two items being discussed. The simplest connectives are words such as *and, also, besides, next,* and *additionally*. Of greater help to listeners are connective phrases such as *in addition to, the next point, this brings me to, this is followed by,* and *another important consideration*. Especially helpful to listeners are connectives used between phrases or clauses representing the ideas being connected. These phrases are in boldface print in the following examples:

> Walking is not only good for the legs; **it also** strengthens the heart.

> Now that the freon has been compressed, **it is ready for the next step in the air-conditioning cycle,** heat absorption.

> So much for the plants in a pond. **We are now ready to consider** the animals that live among these plants.

Books not only spread the English language, **they also** spread American political ideas.

Connectives are frequently used in combination with emphasis devices known as *signposts.*

SIGNPOSTS *Signposts* are words or phrases used to emphasize sentences or call attention to the next statement. They are often spoken with vocal emphasis, such as increased loudness and higher pitch. As signs along a highway point out intersections and features of special interest, so signposts in a speech point to landmark ideas the speaker wants the listeners to focus on and remember. Signposts may be numbers, words, phrases, or even sentences. In the following examples the signposts are in boldface.

> The **first step** in tiling your bathroom is to lay out the walls.

> **This next** procedure must be done perfectly, so listen carefully. I repeat again, ...

> **Never, but never,** has a worse fiend . . . .

> **Be extra careful** while draining the gasoline.

> **Whatever you do,** be sure the marks are aligned before reassembling. . . .

> We have examined the problem of shoplifting; **next,** we will examine the solution for that problem.

You probably noticed that in the last example the speaker referred to the previous main point, then to the forthcoming one. Frequently transitions include both internal summaries and previews of the next main point.

INTERNAL SUMMARIES Internal summaries restate a main point with a review of its subpoints before proceeding to a new point. An internal summary reminds listeners what the developmental materials just presented mean. By stressing the structure of a speech, they help to keep attention focused on ideas instead of details. While listening to extensive developmental material, it is easy to lose sight of the point. If there are several subpoints under a main point, an *internal summary* shows how they all fit together. Here are a few examples:

> Now we've got the body of Santa Claus formed by cutting, furling, gluing, and painting the pages of a copy of *Reader's Digest.* Next, ...

> In review, the engine's problems have been diagnosed by a combination of listening, test driving, and scoping. With the diagnosis in hand, the mechanic is ready to . . . .

In summary, rotation of the ball creates uneven air pressure against the sides of the ball. This will lead to . . . .

INTERNAL PREVIEWS   Previews contained in the body of a speech tell listeners what the next point will be about. An *internal preview* is often a list of subpoints under the main point. Like signposts, previews call attention to the next idea as important, warning the listener to focus attention and remember the major subpoints rather than just the developmental materials. It is important to preview a main point when it has two or more subpoints. For example:

> The third step is to cut and set the tile. I'll explain how to place the tiles and how to measure and cut tiles that are less than full size.

> Next I will compare three aircraft that we have evaluated to determine the one most suitable as an executive vehicle: the Piper Comanche, the Lear Execjet, and the Cessna 2000.

> When you have all your equipment together, you will then need to advertise for customers for your fledgling lawn service. I'll explain how to use newspapers and pamphlets, then how to write copy.

Such previews help the listener follow the development of a main point, just as an internal summary reemphasizes the subpoints of a previous main point.

The following is an example of an internal summary of the four types of components used in creating transitions. "We've considered four components of transitions: connective words and phrases, which link items in a series; signposts, which verbally underline main points; internal summaries, which reemphasize previous points and subpoints; and internal previews, which forecast subdivisions of a main point in the body of a speech." These transitional devices can be used in any combination that you think will help keep listeners oriented and their attention focused. Plan them carefully. Without them, the body of your speech is likely to lack the important qualities of unity, cohesion, and emphasis.

Reference List

You should include a list of all references from which you obtained ideas and materials used in the speech. These would be books, articles, pamphlets, and interviews, films, videos, and other nonprint sources. The list of references must include bibliographic data for all developmental materials referred to in the speech: statistics, testimony, and examples used as evidence. You will not present the reference list as part of your speech. However, you may need to refer to it if anyone asks questions about your sources of information during a question–answer period following your speech. It is common for instructors to assign a minimum number of references for certain speech assignments. A few types of speeches may not require any references.

▶ Writing a Rehearsal/Delivery Outline

Although a complete sentence outline is essential for thorough analysis and planning, it is not wise to use one during the actual speech. Most speakers find a complete-sentence outline too detailed to follow while maintaining eye contact and a fluent conversational style. Such an outline, taken to the lectern, becomes more of a handicap than an aid.

A brief outline of phrases and single words to represent main and subpoints is much more useful to the speaker during oral rehearsals and the presentation of the speech. A *rehearsal/delivery outline* can be referred to with a brief glance while continuing to speak. Usually a rehearsal/delivery outline does not include references to developmental materials. However, you may want to indicate on it where sensory aids, such as transparencies or charts, would be used. Figure 10.2 is a rehearsal/delivery outline prepared from the preparation outline shown in Figure 10.1.

Some instructors recommend the use of such speaking outlines while addressing the class, some prefer students to use note cards with outline portions on them, whereas others insist that no notes other than a direct quotation, lists of statistics, or visual aids be used for short in-class speeches. We have used all three methods at various times in our classes. We believe strongly that the most important criterion is that *the use of notes must not produce a psychological or physical barrier between speaker and audience. Notes should not call attention to themselves or the speaker's handling of them.*

There are many techniques that a speaker can use to avoid dependence on notes. Visual aids can provide the speaker with notes while at the same time focusing listener attention and aiding memory. Flip charts are used by many speakers who need to remember lists of details or a lot of supporting evidence. Instructors often use prepared transparencies that outline their lectures. While the transparency is helping students understand and follow the lecture, it also provides teachers with an outline from which to speak. It assures the speaker of not getting confused or omitting some important idea or developmental detail. As you do more public speaking, you will develop ways to use notes so they do not distract or break the bond of communication established by direct eye contact. Until then we offer several suggestions for preparing and using speaking outlines.

(1) Use the same symbols and indentation pattern that you used for the preparation outline. This will help keep you organized and eliminate the chance of accidentally leaving out an important point. You will remember better, because all main points will have been labeled consistently throughout your preparation and delivery. If your speech has been carefully organized and is simple enough for your audience to remember, you will see the key word outline in your "mind's eye."

(2) Make your outline as clear and readable as possible. A speaking outline should be a final copy, not a scribbled mess. If you write by hand, use black ink or a felt tip pen. Write or print in large, clear letters. Leave enough

Day Care

INTRODUCTION

I. Jennifer's bind.
II. Need is growing.
    A. Statistics (chart 1).
    B. Kantrowitz.
III. Affects us all.
IV. Problem, employer efforts, benefits.

BODY

I. A growing problem.
    A. Future needs.
    B. Expensive for employees.
        1. Costs (chart 2).
        2. 30 percent.
II. Company and gov't agency solutions.
    A. Companies (chart 3).
    B. Gov't agencies.
III. Benefits to employee and employer.
    A. To employees (chart 4).
    B. For companies.

CONCLUSION

I. Summary.
II. I hope you agree that. . . .

Figure 10.2 A rehearsal/delivery outline for a classroom speech.

white space so you can quickly locate specific items at a glance. If you type, use capitals, triple space, and leave wide margins. Large-type typewriters and word processors with variable font sizes are ideal for making speaking outlines.

(3) Write on only one side of the paper. It is distracting to listeners to see notes on the back of a paper, and it is very easy to lose your place if notes are written on both sides of cards or sheets of paper. Flipping cards over to find a note on the back side is also distracting for some listeners.

Unless your instructor gives you specific directions, the type of paper you use for a delivery outline is a matter of personal preference. Some people like note cards, whereas others prefer 8.5 × 11-inch paper. Small note cards have the advantage of being easy to hold in one hand, but you may need more than one for a delivery outline. If so, it is easy to get them shuffled or upside down or drop one on the floor. If you use note cards, use the largest size and limit yourself to no more than two to prevent such problems. Thin paper is never advisable for a delivery outline or quotations. It is almost impossible to hold up while reading.

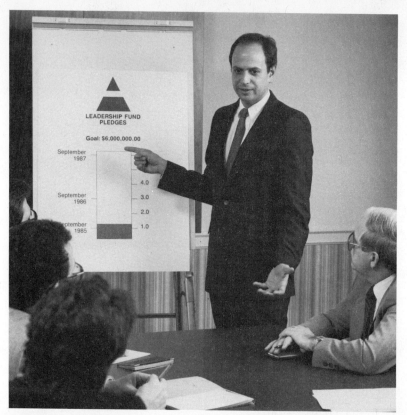

An outline on a flip chart serves as a reminder to the speaker and the listeners.

(4) If you are going to use a speaking outline, practice with the same one you will use when speaking to your audience. It is important to be extremely familiar with the outline so you can find something with one glance. A new version of a speaking outline may cause you to lose your place or get confused.

▶ Composing a Title

Often a title will be requested by a group to whom you are going to speak. The program coordinator may want to include the title in a printed program or promotional material. Because of the frequent demand for titles, many public-speaking instructors require students to title their speeches as part of the total speech preparation procedure. Although this may seem like a minor task, you may find the assignment to be more difficult than anticipated.

The title of a speech should entice audience members to listen, if only out of curiosity. The title should indicate the content of the speech. A title can be a simple direct statement of what the speech is about (e.g., "How New Tax Laws Will Affect Your IRAs") or may be an indirect "hooker" designed to stimulate interest. For example, advertisements for an upcoming speaker sponsored by Campus Crusade for Christ were posted all over campus, with the title "MAXIMUM SEX" in bold letters. As you would imagine, the lecture hall was packed with students eagerly awaiting to find out how to maximize their sex lives. The speaker held his audience in close attention while explaining that the way to maximum joy in sex was to engage in a loving, sexual relationship in a marriage sanctioned by God. The speaker was able to attract a much larger audience than if he had advertised with a direct, less intriguing title such as "The Importance of Marriage to Sexual Satisfaction."

When composing a title, *be creative*. Avoid trite phrases. In many cases the title makes your first impression on the audience. Make that first impression positive. The following examples illustrate what we mean:

What the Mafia Does for You (impact of Mafia on typical citizen).
Dragon Hunting (about the game "Dungeons and Dragons").
Think Strawberries (selling, especially strawberry desserts).
The Sounds of Silence (shyness, fear of speaking).
Sending Degrees to the Dogs (diploma mills).
Getting the Lead Out (of gasoline).
The Thickening Fog (Alzheimer's disease).

▶ Summary

A full-sentence preparation outline serves three purposes: it helps the speaker organize and define relationships among ideas; it helps the speaker determine what supporting materials belong where; and it serves as a memory aid to both speaker and audience. A preparation outline must have full sentences for all main points and subpoints. In addition to outlines of introduction, body, and conclusion, it must include the central idea and desired response statements, transitions, references to all supporting materials and visuals, references used in the speech, and a title.

A rehearsal/delivery outline can be prepared for use during oral practice of the speech and may be used while actually speaking as a reminder to the speaker. It should have the same symbol–indentation scheme as the preparation outline, but is greatly abridged. Key words or phrases are used to represent main points and subpoints, without most details of developmental material. If used in speaking, it should be looked at only occasionally to prevent interfering with eye contact.

▶ Learning Activities

1. Among the statements that follow are main points, subpoints, and developmental materials. Arrange these in outline form as part of the body of a speech. Be sure to conform to the rules of coordination and subordination as you use appropriate alphanumeric symbols. For convenience, just use the letter identifying each statement following the appropriate outline symbol instead of copying the entire statement.
   a. Use protective clothing.
   b. Three examples of stupid stunts of daredevils.
   c. Long pants and shirt or jacket.
   d. "Invisible man" for alertness.
   e. Joe, cracked helmet.
   f. Boots or leather shoes.
   g. Don't be a daredevil driver.
   h. Rich's accident when showing off.
   i. Brain damage for Jim.
   j. Use caution in driving.
   k. Cover as much of your body as possible.
   l. Drive defensively.
   m. Always wear a helmet.
   n. Kevin's injury when inattentive.

2. What's wrong in the wording of each of the following main point statements? How might you revise each to conform to the guidelines for stating main points in a preparation outline presented in this chapter?

   I. What is cystic fibrosis?
   II. Treatment of cystic fibrosis.

   I. Drunk drivers and the problems they cause.
   II. By applying three suggestions you can do a lot to reduce the damage resulting from drunk driving to your friends and to yourself.

3. For your next assigned speech, present both a preparation outline and a practice/delivery outline to your instructor for evaluation and advice.

4. Arrange to listen to a public speech with two or more classmates. Write the best and most complete preparation outline you can to represent what the speaker said. Compare your outline with the outlines prepared by your classmates. Then discuss the questions below with them. One person should keep a record of agreements you reach in answering these questions and either give an oral report of your conclusions to the class or a written report to your instructor.
   a. What difficulties did you encounter in trying to outline the speech?
   b. What may have caused these difficulties for you?
   c. What advice would you give the speaker about how to outline and/or prepare to speak?

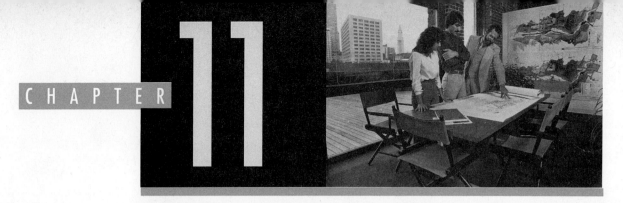

Selecting, Creating, and Using Sensory Aids

Questions to Guide Reading and Review

1. What four advantages can be gained by using sensory aids effectively?
2. Why is a model sometimes more useful to a speaker than the original object? Give examples of instances where models would be preferable to objects as speaking aids.
3. What are some difficulties a speaker should consider before deciding to use photographs or other types of pictures as visual aids? How might these problems be overcome?
4. What are the advantages and disadvantages of transparencies shown with an overhead projector?
5. What are the characteristics and uses of each of the major types of graphs: line, circle, and bar? Give an example of when each type might be used to illustrate statistics developing a speaker's point.
6. What are the main advantages and disadvantages to using the chalkboard as a visual aid? If used, what can you do to ensure its effectiveness?
7. Why and how might you create aids to involve the senses of hearing, smell, taste, and touch?
8. What are eight guidelines to follow when planning and using sensory aids?

Key Terms

Bar graph	Line graph	Sensory aid
Circle graph	Pie chart	Visual aid
Flip chart		

Ed walked to the front of the room, unrolled a large poster of *Playboy's* Playmate of the Month, and taped it to the chalkboard. He turned around, took his place behind the lectern, and smiled at the audience. "Now that I have your attention I would like to talk to you about the major causes of house fires."

Not only is this a poor introduction for a speech, but the example illustrates an ineffective use of a *visual aid* to direct the attention of the audience. The speaker gained attention, but the results were counterproductive to the purpose of Ed's speech. A few members of the audience were stimulated by the photograph, but did not transfer their attention from the visual to the topic when the speech began. More importantly, most members of the audience were offended by the speaker's use of a visual aid that denegrated women. Even if the topic had been one that dealt with the nude photograph (nudity, pornography, or sexism), this visual would have been a mistake. It was certainly a mistake to keep it in view of the audience throughout the speech.

▶ Why Use Sensory Aids?

When used appropriately, *sensory aids* can give listeners a firsthand experience with the topic or at least an experience based on more than words. They can heighten attention, enhance understanding, reinforce main points, and increase recall. The combination of a visual and oral message increases both immediate and long term recall over either type of message alone. About 70 percent of an oral message can be recalled immediately, but after three days only 10 percent of the message is recalled. Visual messages result in immediate recall of 72 percent, with 35 percent recall three days later. The combination of oral and visual messages results in 85 percent immediate recall and 65 percent recall after three days. This represents an improvement of 550 percent in recall after three days with combined oral and visual messages over speech alone![1]

Visuals can also be highly persuasive. For example, Otis wanted to convince his colleagues of the need for a uniform marketing logo. He knew the main objection he would face was that everyone saw their own department as a separate entity. Department members didn't want their separate images to be lost in a company logo. Otis knew it would take a dramatic visual to make his point. The day of his presentation, he brought a large grocery bag to the

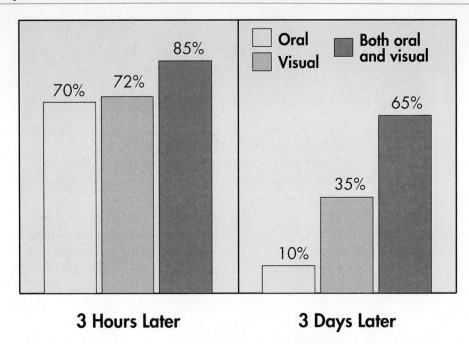

Figure 11.1   Visual messages can greatly increase the amount of recall.

front of the room. As he spoke, he slowly placed box after box of cereal on the table.

> All these products are different. No one mistakes Rice Krispies for Corn Flakes or finds it difficult to distinguish the Sugar Pops from the Raisin Bran, but all these cereals have one thing in common. They are all Kellogg products. Look at each box. As much as they are different—different names, different pictures, different print styles—they are also remarkably the same. Is it difficult to see the Kellogg logo? No, it appears on every box in exactly the same print style and in the same place. Even the colors used are similar. Each box uses a combination of the same shades of red, blue, yellow, and white. The ingredients can be found in the same place on each package, and they even open in exactly the same way.
>
> Kellogg pays millions of dollars a year to have this same/different image. Why? Because nobody can mistake their products for those of Post, General Mills, or Nabisco. That's also why they employ lawyers to protect the packaging logo and image.
>
> It is about time that we take advantage of the knowledge of successful companies and create uniform packaging for all our communications and marketing tools. Today, I will show you a plan to incorporate a company image without losing departmental identity.[2]

Otis used visuals to illustrate a point that might have been lost without such reinforcement.

▶ Types of Aids

Although in this chapter we will deal mainly with the preparation and use of visual aids, speakers may also employ sound recordings, scents, textures, tastes, and other sensory aids to clarify and enliven speeches. Because visuals are used most often, we devote more space to the creation and use of visual aids, but you should not limit your thinking about how to supplement your words to visuals alone. Think of how you might use *sensory* aids to communicate effectively while you prepare to speak.

Visual

There are many types of visuals you might use to help listeners understand and recall. The type of visual you select will be determined by the subject of the speech, time available for preparing the visual, materials available, and suitability to the audience and setting.

OBJECTS   A speaker demonstrating the correct way to pack a backpack for an audience of hikers would be foolish to try to do so without a backpack and contents. The speaker discussing the benefits of one style of ski boot over another would lose attention or confuse unless both pairs of boots were seen while the differences were pointed out. Nor would you be convinced to spend more money for one cassette recorder over another unless you heard the difference in quality and saw the advantage in size. In each of the preceding examples, the subject dictated the use of specific objects as sensory aids. Sometimes objects are too large to bring into a room, too small for viewers to see, too cumbersome to use, too dangerous, or too complicated for the speaker's limited subject and objective.

MODELS   Models can be used as substitutes for objects when the object is unsuitable or impossible to use as an aid. You have been exposed to the use of models throughout your education. Science instructors use larger-than-life models to explain the parts of an atom, cell reproduction, the functions of the inner ear, and many other things that would otherwise be too small or impossible to observe. They also use smaller-than-life models to teach students about the movement of the earth around the sun, the makeup of the solar system, the stages of a rocket ship, the anatomy of a dinosaur, and numerous other things that cannot be brought into the classroom. Architects use models to explain and sell their designs. Engineers use models to demonstrate the inner workings of machines. Life-sized models can allow one to practice on nonliving objects. You are probably familiar with life-sized models such as the dummy called *Resusci Annie* used for the practice of CPR, breakaway pieces of furniture that show the process or materials of construction, and a set of teeth used to demonstrate the correct procedure for brushing.

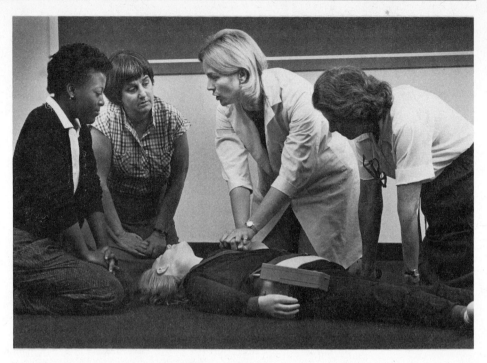

A model makes it easier to demonstrate CPR.

PICTURES   Pictures may or may not be worth a 1000 words; before you use pictures as a sensory aid you must estimate their relative value. For example, because of their small size, ordinary photographs are usually a liability rather than an aid when speaking to more than three listeners. Passing them around distracts listeners. While a picture is being passed from one person to the next, one listener is examining the photo, a couple of others are craning their heads to see it, and the speaker is continuing with another point in the speech to which they are not listening. As the photographs are handed from person to person, verbal exchanges often take place creating even further noise. By the time the last person in the room receives the photographs, their relationship to the main point has probably been forgotten.

If you are fortunate enough to have greatly enlarged photographs, consider how you will display them. Drymounting protects them from being torn or bent, but the process is costly. The pictures should be placed on a neutral background and displayed so that all members of the audience can see them simultaneously. An easel or clips on a blackboard are useful for displaying enlarged photographs. Avoid holding them, as this does not allow you to move or gesture freely. A photograph that is moved around by a gesturing speaker is distracting and blurred. Such a visual is not an aid, but a handicap.

Slides are less costly than enlargements and are easier to see, but may require darkening the room. Unless several slides are used, the inconvenience of setting up, turning lights off and back on, noise from the projector, and movements required to operate it offset any advantage. There is always a danger of a bulb burning out, making it impossible to show your slides. Weigh the value of slides against the dangers and disadvantages before deciding to use them.

Films and videotapes are most often used by speakers who are making much longer presentations than those you will be making in your speech class. Films and tapes are usually quite expensive. Unless they are of high quality, they may detract more from the speaker's message than they add. Equipment needed is costly, complex, and subject to a host of technical problems. It can be difficult to handle.

However, if you have special skills in shooting and editing, you may want to create a special videotape or short film to present a sequence of steps such as in the building of a bookcase, painting a room, or scoring a wrestling match. You might videotape features of a state park or other scenes to which you cannot take listeners. We recommend such visuals only if you have inexpensive access to the recording equipment and have special training so that your images do not have a distracting homemade quality.

One of the most popular ways to present pictures, drawings, and graphs is on transparencies shown with an overhead projector. Unlike films and videotapes, they are inexpensive, simple to make and use, relatively trouble free, and readily available on most campuses. The projected image can be seen by members of a large audience, the transparencies are easy to carry, and they can be shown with room lights on. You can make your own transparencies on acetate film with a special marking pen or have them made in an audiovisual center. Transparencies can be made from photos, print, typescript, drawings, graphs, charts, and other visual forms. When using the projector, turn it off if you will not immediately replace one transparency with another; listeners are inclined to focus on the lighted screen even when there is no image on it.

Two types of transparencies are used frequently by speakers: single sheets and continuous roll. Most college audiovisual departments have both types of equipment and can supply students with inexpensive materials for creating transparencies. A continuous roll of film is used like an endless chalkboard on which you can write as you talk, rolling used visuals out of the way as you make new ones. Because single-sheet transparencies are the most common and most versatile, we explain several techniques for preparing and using them to illustrate your speeches.

Single-sheet transparencies can be produced either by drawing and writing directly on acetate film with a special pencil or pen or by creating the visual on a piece of paper and then producing the transparency in a photocopying machine. An advantage of drawing directly on the acetate film is that it can be done quickly, either in advance or during a speech. You need not go to a special copy center. One disadvantage is that it is easy to smear the drawing and writing. Transparencies made using a copy machine are permanent and almost smudge proof. Another advantage is that the copy machine can reproduce any printed page on film, allowing you to reproduce computer-generated or professionally created graphics.

An additional advantage of using single transparency sheets is that they make possible the creation of overlays. By placing one transparency on top of another it is possible to show steps in a process, how functioning parts relate to each other, or add different colors to highlight an illustration or chart. Overhead projectors allow a speaker to add information as a speech progresses, eliminating the problem of interference when information is revealed before the speaker is ready to use it to support an idea.

GRAPHS, CHARTS, AND DIAGRAMS   An inexpensive way to illustrate a speech visually is with speaker-drawn graphs, charts, and diagrams made on poster board or plain newsprint with felt tip pens. Many speakers choose to make their own simple drawings, charts, graphs, and diagrams because they do not require any special equipment or room setup. Although you do not need to be an artist to produce effective drawings and diagrams, you should be sure they are neat, large, and dark enough to be seen easily by all listeners and not cluttered with unnecessary details. If made of stiff poster board, the finished chart or diagram can be placed on an easel, tacked to a corkboard, taped to a chalkboard or wall with masking tape, or held up by special clips provided above some chalkboards.

Many types of visuals can be created on card or paper: lists of key points, simple outlines, flow diagrams of procedures, floor plans, diagrams of operating systems such as a welding rig or air conditioner, metabolic processes, organization charts, and so forth. Statistics and statistical trends can be presented more effectively in graphic form than in any other way. You may have access to a personal computer and software that can make excellent graphs, charts, tables, and diagrams. Your audiovisual or educational media center may have a special machine that can project images from a computer disk or tape on a large screen.

With graphs you can present trends, proportions, comparisons, contrasts, and changes. The three most commonly used types are circle, line, and bar graphs.

Circle graphs, or *pie charts*, are most often used to illustrate relative sizes of parts to a whole. A media salesperson speaking to a group of restaurant owners might use a pie chart like the one in Figure 11.2 to explain the percentage of each dollar spent on various services. The visual comparison would impress the listeners with how small advertising costs were in relation to monies spent elsewhere.

Many types of proportions, breakdowns, and distributions can be clarified with pie charts, such as proportions of funds spent on various university operations, distributions of voters by party, relative amounts of different types of meats consumed, sources of government funding, and proportions of expenditures going into major categories. The number of slices in a pie chart should be kept relatively small, usually from two to five and never over eight, if the chart is to do its job of emphasizing relative sizes.[3]

A *line graph* is most commonly used to illustrate patterns or trends through time. A businessperson might use a line graph like the one shown in Figure

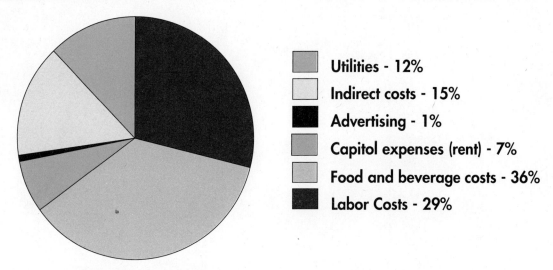

Figure 11.2   This pie chart shows restaurant owners how little they spend on advertising.

11.3 to emphasize the problem created by a drop in sales the company has suffered over the past three years. A speaker could use a line graph for explaining changing population growth rates, the acceleration in the growth of our national debt during the past 20 years, changes in the numbers of bank failures, or any statistical trend. The vertical dimension of the graph always represents the relative amount or size of the statistic, whereas the horizontal dimension of the graph represents time. Marginal labels on the graph indicate these dimensions. The line rises and falls in direct proportion to changes for each time period.

Comparisons of two or more similar items on one characteristic are best illustrated with a *bar graph*. Bar graphs are easy to construct and easily understood. The bar graph shown in Figure 11.4 represents revenues of a community college. By using this graph the president of the college could be fairly certain that an audience of taxpayers would understand the sources of funds and the major expenditures of the college.

In creating a bar graph, all bars are kept the same width, but they vary in length proportionate to the size of the number each represents. The bars can be either horizontal or vertical. Each bar can be separated if only one characteristic is being compared, such as the size of the armies of various nations. Sets of up to four bars can be grouped if two to four organizations are being compared on several characteristics, such as a comparison of how much consumer income was spent on food, shelter, medicine, and transportation in the United States, USSR, and Japan.

When a speaker needs to communicate more statistical information or more details than can be illustrated on a graph, a *chart* may be needed. Charts, including flowcharts, outlines, and tables are most useful when the speaker needs to present detailed information, a lot of numbers, step-by-step proce-

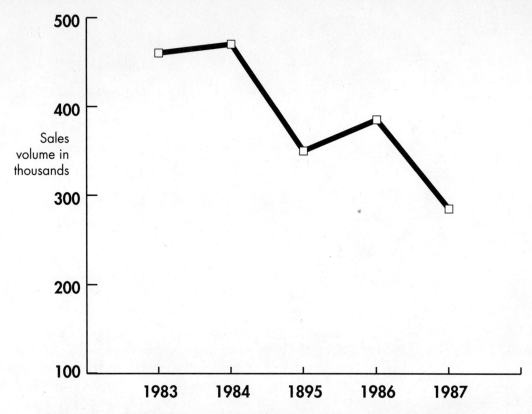

Figure 11.3   A line graph illustrates a dramatic decline in sales during the previous three years.

dures, or outlines of points. Charts are often used to provide specific information that some listeners may wish to copy. Some examples of charts are provided in Figures 11.5, 11.6, and 11.7.

Instead of using a speaking outline, many speakers put a brief version of the outline (usually key words or phrases for main points and possibly some subpoints) on a chart or charts. The audience and speaker can then follow the speech easily by glancing at the charted outline.

Flip charts are often used by speakers when several graphs, charts, diagrams, pictures, words, or other visuals will be needed during a speech. The flip chart arrangement allows the speaker to control the pace by turning to the next chart only when ready to refer to it. Flip charts also keep all the visuals in sequential order without the need for constantly putting up large poster boards or papers while taking others down. Unless designed to sit by itself on a table, a set of flip charts is best hung on an easel. Many salespeople use professionally made flip charts in sales presentations. Students construct their own flip charts by fastening several cards or sheets of paper together near the upper corners with rings, wires, or pieces of string. A computer version of flip charts may be available if you have a graphics package.

Revenues & Expenditures

1985–1986

Revenue

Tuition and fees	3,025,627
Local support	1,014,676
State support	4,821,071
Federal support	975,966
Sales and services	347,285
Other support	363,863
Fund balance	(57,168)
Total Revenues	$10,605,656

Expenditures

Arts and Science	1,556,547
Vocational-Technical	3,967,415
Community services	843,264
Support services	2,551,177
Physical plant	1,686,753
Total Expenditures	$10,605,656

	Other support 7%			Community services 8%
	Federal 9%			Arts and Science 15%
	Local support 9%			Physical plant 16%
	Tuition 29%			Support services 24%
	State support 46%			Vocational-Technical 37%

Figure 11.4 A bar graph used by the president of a community college to explain revenues and expenditures. (**Source:** Iowa Western Community College, "1985 Annual Report.")

CHALKBOARD Sometimes you may want to create an impromptu visual in response to a question or when speaking impromptu. For this purpose the chalkboard is ideal. Although many student speakers consider the chalkboard a convenient and easy-to-use visual, it should be used only after careful consideration. The main disadvantage of the chalkboard is that it is hard to keep eye contact and speak while writing or drawing. While using the board, many speakers turn their backs to the audience and have long silences while drawing or writing. While the speaker is silent, listener attention wanders off. A lot of speakers do not write sufficiently large or legibly for listeners to read what they wrote. Frequently the speaker may stand between the chalkboard visual and part of the audience, blocking sight lines. It is extremely difficult for most people to write or draw while thinking/feeling about the idea being expressed, so the voice may go very flat and monotonous even if the speaker keeps talking. Only if you are willing to practice a lot to overcome all the problems inherent in chalkboard use should you consider it as a visual aid.

However, if used well, the chalkboard can be an effective and convenient

The Principal Determinants of Organizational Climate

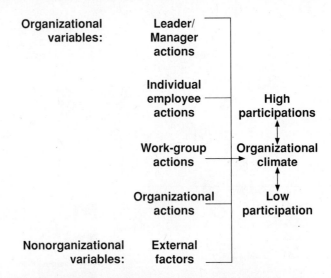

Figure 11.5 A flow chart showing actions producing an organizational climate. (**Source:** James M. Higgins, *Instructor's Manual for Human Relations: Concepts and Skills.* New York: Random House, 1982.)

visual tool, and its use may be essential for some impromptu speaking. For extemporaneous speaking, plan carefully what you will draw and/or write and practice until you can do it well without losing listener contact. Then you can use the chalkboard to advantage for several purposes. You can keep adding steps in a diagram explaining a process or procedure while speaking about those steps (a flow chart). You can write key words that are new to listeners so they can both see and hear them. You can use the chalkboard to finish what

Type Z Management

A. Long term employment

B. Slow evaluation and promotion

C. Moderate career specialization

D. Consensual decision making

E. Individual responsibility

F. Informal, implicit control—with explicit measures available

G. Holistic concern for employees and the family

Figure 11.6 An outline of characteristics of Type Z management. (**Source:** James M. Higgins, *Instructor's Manual for Human Relations: Concepts and Skills.* New York: Random House, 1982.)

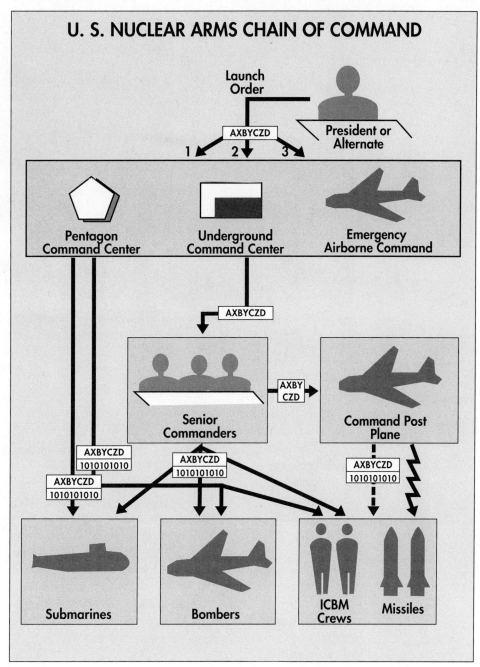

Figure 11.7 Pictures can be used to increase the impact of a chart. (**Source:** original by author, based on article by Bruce G. Blair and Henry W. Kendall, "Accidental Nuclear War," *Scientific American* 263 (December, 1990): 53–58.)

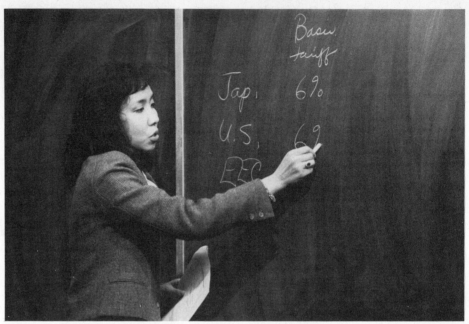

If used well, the chalkboard can be of great assistance to a speaker.

were intentionally incomplete diagrams, drawings, graphs, or charts prepared on the board before you begin to speak. In general, use the chalkboard sparingly, when some more completely prepared visual seems impossible, and only after careful planning and practice.

When you practice with or use the chalkboard, try to adhere to the guidelines shown in the following box, organized as "Dos" and "Don'ts."

Newsprint chart pads and overhead projectors with rolls of plain acetate film can be used as an alternative to the chalkboard. The chart pad allows the speaker to add to or highlight premade materials. Many speakers pencil in lightly before the speech and merely trace with felt marker during the presentation. This gives the effect of spontaneity while allowing the speaker the advantage of not referring to notes to add information to charts. This also gives confidence to the nonartist who wants to create an illustration or model during the speech. The chart pad is also effective when the speaker uses audience input in creating the visual. The overhead has the added advantage of allowing the speaker to remain facing the audience while writing on or pointing to parts of the visual.

DEMONSTRATION   A gymnast who had won an Olympic gold medal delivered part of his speech while standing on his head on a chemistry table in front of the classroom. As he spoke, he demonstrated how points are lost or won by allowing his legs, back, and arms to shift position. This unorthodox posture was not only attention getting—it was highly instructive to the listeners, who were curious about how gymnastics was scored.

▶ **Do**

Do use the chalkboard if you are skilled at drawing and talking at the same time.

Do practice using a chalkboard. Have a friend stand back and let you know how well it can be viewed from all parts of the room, or leave the lectern to check how visible and clear your writing and drawing may be.

Do put drawings and charts on the board before your speech (when feasible to do so), then cover with a screen or paper until ready to uncover and use them.

Do use the chalkboard for quick views of statistics, dates, spellings, or terms that will be referred to repeatedly during your speech.

Do use a chalkboard to summarize or list audience responses when you ask for them.

Do use a chalkboard when no other option for visual assistance is available as a result of time or circumstance, such as when answering questions.

Do use the chalkboard to explain in more detail when you notice that your audience members do not understand an important idea.

▶ **Don't**

Don't talk with your back to the audience! Stand to one side of the chalkboard, facing toward the audience, writing with your dominant hand. Turn your head toward the board just enough to see what you are writing. Keep glancing from board to audience as you draw or write.

Don't allow periods of silence while you draw or write.

Don't write in normal script size—write and draw *big*.

Don't squeal the chalk. Practice to find an angle that prevents this irritating noise.

Don't try to be a detail artist. Quick, simple drawings work best.

Don't leave the board a mess for the next speaker. Erase your work before sitting down so the next person has a clear board to use.

Don't leave previous information on the board when you go to use it. Remove all writing and drawings from a board before you begin to speak. This is noise that competes with you for attention.

For many purposes, the best visual is the speaker, sometimes aided by an assistant. For instance, you might want to demonstrate some skill, style of dress, makeup, or nonverbal signals. A hurdler demonstrated to novice runners how to get in and out of the starting blocks and how to cross the hurdles. A jogging enthusiast used himself to show how to find a pulse and calculate one's base heart rate. In five minutes, one woman taught her entire class to do the basic polka step. Another student, with the assistance of a friend, demonstrated various wrestling holds and their scoring to classmates who were occasional spectators at meets. Numerous student speakers have demonstrated tennis grips, golf swings, and other sport skills to classmates. One of the most impressive speakers explained the impact of hair color on perceptions while she changed from brunette to blonde before our eyes. Often your best visual aid will be your body performing a demonstration.

Other Senses

Many kinds of direct sensory experiences have been created by speakers to help listeners understand the nonverbal phenomena to which the words referred. Through imaginative planning you can often create cost-effective aids using the senses of hearing, smell, taste, and touch.

SOUND   Sound messages are often used to help listeners perceive, interpret, enjoy, and choose. Many of our students have played excerpts of music to illustrate characteristics of musical genres, to help listeners distinguish among the sounds of different instruments in an orchestra, or to recognize bird and animal calls. For a group of classmates at a campus almost surrounded by forests occupied by wild turkeys, one student used a turkey call to explain how to recognize turkey "talk." Another speaker used recordings he made on a canoe trip to prepare a group of scouts for sounds of wolves, grouse, loons, and other fauna they would probably hear while on a forthcoming canoe trip to the boundary waters of Minnesota. A student who tuned racing cars demonstrated the sounds of an engine with different timing settings so her backyard-mechanic classmates could do a better job of timing their own engines. Hearing a sound is much more effective in creating listener awareness than is hearing *about* the sound.

SCENT   If you want listeners to be able to perceive or distinguish among scents, they will need to experience them directly. Unfortunately, there is no way to record smells. If your desired response is that listeners can identify the aromas of different herbs, distinguish the smell of a toxic chemical, or recognize some common woods, you will need to have them smell the objects. One student speaker gave each classmate a treated card that, when scratched, released the smell of the chemical added to natural gas. Another used both an expensive original perfume and an inexpensive copy as evidence for her argument that the original was worth the additional cost. Still another had arranged for three classmates to distribute samples of wild mushrooms to help his biology club listeners distinguish between the smell of an edible mushroom and a poisonous species that is similar in appearance.

TASTE   If you have visited a winery, you probably observed a speaker using small samples to help listeners select among the vintages available. Usually an assistant pours and passes small samples around while the speaker describes the wine. A food-science major contrasted a new soft drink that is part fruit juice with a competing drink that had no juice in it. You have observed a demonstrator using samples of two different colas to sharpen listeners' perceptions of the differences in the tastes of the beverages. One amateur chef used samples of scrambled eggs with and without a garnish of basil to demonstrate the effect of this herb on the flavor of eggs. We have tasted samples of many different recipes explained by student speakers advocating that classmates make the food to entertain family or friends. A taste experience through a small sample can be useful as motivating evidence as well as to help listeners understand. When using samples, arrange for assistants to distribute the samples as quickly and unobtrusively as possible, or use them as part of your conclusion.

TOUCH   What something feels like can sometimes be illustrated by a verbal comparison to a different, but more familiar thing. Generally, however, the sense of touch needs to be used directly to communicate an idea about a texture, degree of hardness, or pressure. For example, a textile major wanted us to believe that a polyester–wool blend would both look and feel superior to a pure polyester fabric. To accomplish this, she gave a small swatch of each type of fabric to each audience member. A classmate distributed the paired swatches while the speaker described them. A student who was a skilled woodworker brought enough small pieces of oak for each classmate to hold one at the same time. He had them feel the different textures of two different types of finishes on opposing sides of the pieces of wood. When textures like these are important characteristics for listeners to be able to choose with discrimination, you may be able to create a sensory aid that provides listeners with a direct touch experience.

▶ Guidelines for Creating and Using Sensory Aids

No matter what type of sensory aids you decide to use, there are eight guidelines to follow that will increase their effectiveness in achieving your objective as a speaker:

1. Plan the aid carefully.
2. Be sure it can be seen (heard, etc.) clearly by all listeners simultaneously.

3. Keep the aid simple.
4. Coordinate the sensory aid and speech.
5. Use only cost-effective aids.
6. Avoid sensory aids that might injure your listeners.
7. Rehearse with all aids.
8. Tell the audience what to see or hear.

Plan Carefully

Sensory aids should be planned carefully, not created as an afterthought while speaking. Consider what types of sensory aids will serve your purpose best, then plan them in detail. Color or black and white, exactly when and how to use the aid, how it will be displayed, how much detail and information to include on one visual, and what materials to use are a few of the questions the speaker will have to consider while planning aids. In some cases you may need to order and check out equipment. Determine where outlets and switches are located; you may need an extension cord. If you need to have lights turned on and off, you may need to arrange with someone to do this for you. Such decisions should be made long in advance of the actual speech. Leave no detail to chance. As has been said of many human ventures, "To fail to plan is to plan to fail."

Be Sure the Aid Can Be Perceived by All Listeners

One of the most common mistakes is creating a visual that is not easily seen by some members of the audience. Many student speakers have spent hours producing detailed visuals with labels or print too small to read from the back of a room. If it cannot be seen easily, it will not be an aid. When using photographs or other pictures, be sure they are large enough to be seen simultaneously in detail by all listeners. Likewise, sound must be loud enough, or a chemical aroma potent enough to be smelled by everyone. You may need to prepare a large number of small samples of a food or beverage to be distributed rapidly to everyone in the audience.

You will want to be sure the lines on charts or graphs are dark and heavy and that print is dark, large, and legible. Avoid pastels and light colors for lines and letters; they are almost impossible to see clearly from a distance. Black letters on a white background are the most legible. Block lettering is more legible than line lettering. Sightlines must be unobstructed for any visual material. Heads of listeners may be in the line of sight for people in back rows. Speakers often get between a visual and some listeners. If time and circumstances permit, it is best to set up the visuals in the room where you will speak, then check for visibility, or plug in your sound equipment and adjust the volume level so it is clearly audible in all parts of the room without being too loud.

Keep the Aid Simple

Keep visuals simple so the viewer does not get lost in detail. When creating a visual, decide what information is most important, then limit your visual to this. Do not overload the visual with excess words, many colors, or artwork that calls attention to itself. Figure 11.8 shows a visual that would not be effective in a speech, but might be suitable for a poster that could be studied at some length. If you fail to observe this guideline, the same thing that happened to the following student could happen to you!

David taped a 5 by 8-foot drawing of a longitudinal section of a tractor on the wall. This diagram had over 10,000 parts represented in 40 different

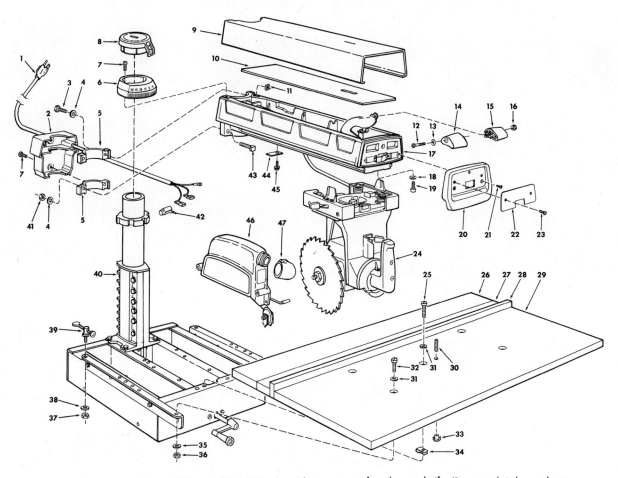

Figure 11.8 A cluttered visual can do more to confuse than to clarify. (**Source:** technical manual, not copyrighted, for Craftsman radial arm saw.)

colors. While David explained one small section of the tractor, the torque converter, his listeners were distracted by all the other parts. Almost no one was listening to David's explanation of how the converter worked.

Remember, the aid should complement the speech and not be cluttered with unexplained details, which will distract from the verbal message.

Coordinate the Sensory Aid and Speech

When to use an aid is almost as important as what to use. Some speakers create a distraction by presenting aids before they are ready to point them out and talk about them. A sound recording turned on before listeners are told what to listen for will divert attention from the idea it illustrates. A pleasant aroma may take attention away from what you are saying if released before you are ready to explain it. A visual displayed before you are ready to refer to it may no longer hold interest when you finally begin to explain it. By then listeners have drawn their own conclusions from the visual, probably not the desired ones. Keep your sensory aid out of sight until you are ready to refer to it. This can be done by placing a blank piece of poster board over your visual(s), leaving them turned over on the easel or board, or leaving them face down on a table until you are ready to use them. Then produce them quickly, without pausing in speaking or groping around. Remove every sensory aid when you are finished making the point it develops so it will not take attention away from your next point.

Use Only Cost-Effective Aids

It might be cost-effective for an architect to construct a $1000 model of a multimillion dollar complex on which he or she is making a bid, but it may not be cost-effective for a student speaker to spend $10 and three hours constructing an impressive model for a five-minute classroom speech. Many beginning speakers spend more time and energy on preparing sensory aids than they do on preparing the main ideas and delivery of the speech. Keep in mind that the sensory aid must *supplement* the verbal message. *No* sensory aid should compete with or detract from the idea it supports. Calculate carefully the benefits of any type of aid before investing time and money in its creation.

There are many ways you can produce simple and effective aids at little cost in time and dollars. Simple charts on poster board can be as effective as a multicolor overhead transparency. One speaker spent about $25 for small plants, pots, and soil at a floral shop before trying to teach us how to repot a houseplant. He could have done as well with two sizes of paper cups, some weeds he had previously put in the smaller cups, and garden dirt. A felt pen drawing will represent aerodynamic forces as well as an expensive professionally drawn diagram. Time spent on sensory aids should never interfere with time needed for research, audience analysis, outlining, and rehearsal.

Avoid Sensory Aids that Might Injure Your Listeners

The use of certain sensory aids can potentially result in physical or psychological injury of your audience. As a public speaker, you have an ethical responsibility to never intentionally subject your audience to such risks. Consider the following examples:

> Karen, an ROTC student, was giving an informative speech on the various weapons used by the infantry. In the middle of her speech she removed a grenade from her pocket and began explaining how the weapon was used. At the close of her speech Karen informed the audience that the grenade was ''live''!

> Hank, a biology major, was giving an informative speech on the medical uses of snake venom. He began his speech by removing a live rattlesnake from a burlap bag he had concealed under his chair. A student sitting in the front row, who was terrified of poisonous snakes, began screaming uncontrollably and ran from the classroom!

In both cases, these speakers carelessly exposed themselves and the members of their audiences to potential risks. Karen never considered what could have happened if something went wrong and her live grenade exploded! Hank never considered the possibility that someone in his audience might be terrified of snakes. While preparing, you should carefully plan how to safely demonstrate a potentially dangerous sensory aid and warn listeners in advance if the sensory aid poses a potential risk. Many speakers have safely demonstrated how to use power tools, knives, and even guns. In general, if there is any doubt whether or not a particular sensory aid you intend to use is a potential risk to your audience, consult your instructor. Your instructor can advise you properly and inform you of any rules that regulate what you can or cannot bring onto campus and into a classroom.

Rehearse with All Aids

Only by practicing using an aid while actually speaking can you discover difficulties in handling objects, operating equipment, and demonstrating what you might encounter while speaking to the audience. If these problems are identified during a rehearsal, you can then make adjustments so they will not disrupt you while facing the audience. On many occasions we have seen speakers fumble trying to get a videocassette recorder (VCR) or projector working, focusing an overhead projector, or locating some object in a bag full of visuals. Without practice, you may not be able to fasten charts to a chalkboard while you continue discussing those charts. To discover that the chart clips above a chalkboard are so bent that they will not hold up your diagram while you are trying to explain the diagram will disrupt the flow of your speech and distract the listeners. During your speech is no time to fix broken models, locate a switch, or coach an assistant. Listeners properly resent such signs of inadequate preparation. Furthermore, the stress of speaking will make it difficult to think of how to handle difficult sensory aids, unless you have already practiced such handling and solved any problems encountered while rehearsing.

Tell the Audience What to See or Hear

The childhood game of "show and tell" can be a guide for using visuals in your speech. When you show something to the audience, also tell the listeners what to look at and how it is related to what you are saying. A good sensory aid should never stand alone. It should be explained. Many beginning speakers simply hold up a chart or photograph and expect listeners to see what the speaker has seen or play a recording and expect listeners to be able to hear a rhythm, instrument, lyric, or other characteristic. Some members of the audience may focus attention on different details of an aid than what you intend unless you guide their attention and perceptions. Some will be confused or bored from not knowing what to do. Some may receive messages that are contrary to the speaker's intentions. In such cases the visual has been a hindrance rather than an aid. No matter what type of aid used, the show-and-tell principle applies to it.

▶ Eight Guidelines for Creating and Using Sensory Aids

1. Plan the aid carefully.
2. Be sure it can be seen (heard, etc.) clearly by all listeners simultaneously.
3. Keep the aid simple.
4. Coordinate the sensory aid and speech.
5. Use only cost-effective aids.
6. Avoid sensory aids that might injure listeners.
7. Rehearse with all aids.
8. Tell the audience what to see or hear.

▶ Summary

Sensory aids can greatly increase the effectiveness of speaking if proper attention is given to their planning, creation, and use. Complex processes and procedures, mountain scenes, historical trends, musical styles, color combinations, dress designs, aromas, tastes, and textures are among the many sensory experiences that cannot be explained adequately with words alone. They need to be sensed directly or through the use of diagrams, photos, charts, models, recordings, and demonstrations. Useful as they can be, sensory aids can also be counterproductive to achieving desired responses if they are used inappropriately and distract your listeners. The most common visual aids are objects, models, pictures, graphs, charts, diagrams, chalkboard, and demonstration. Other frequently used aids include sound recordings, videotapes, scents, textures, and multisensory participation. By following eight guidelines a speaker can use sensory aids with confidence in their effectiveness: plan carefully, be sure it can be seen or heard, keep it simple, coordinate with the verbal message, be sure it is cost-effective, rehearse, carefully point out what the sensory aid illustrates, involve listeners as directly as possible, and avoid sensory aids that might injure your listeners. Better attention, less misunderstanding, more acceptance, and enhanced recall of ideas will be the benefits.

▶ Learning Activities

1. Arrange a tour of the audiovisual center on your campus or a briefing by some member of its staff. Ask for a demonstration of the equipment and production facilities available to students for supplementing speeches. A videotape of such a presentation may be available for viewing by your class.

2. In a small group discuss several ways that you might use visual or other sensory aids to illustrate effectively each of the following.
   a. Fire safety in the home.
   b. The importance of aerobic exercise.
   c. Smart investments for the 1990s.
   d. Basic canoeing techniques.
   e. What's happening to social security?
   f. Differences between light, acid, and heavy metal rock.
   g. The anatomy of a foot.
   h. Making chocolate chip cookies.

3. While planning how to develop your next speech, brainstorm a list of ways to illustrate your main points visually or with other sensory aids. Following the eight guidelines explained in this chapter, determine which of your ideas should be used. Actually use at least three of your ideas in making your speech.

   Ask your classmates for reactions to your visual and other aids. Try to find out what they think was the effect on their attention and interest, understanding, and recall.

   How did using the visuals affect your feelings while speaking?

Notes

1. Conwell Carson, "Best Memory by Eye and Ear," *The Kansas City Times* (April 12, 1987):13A.

2. Otis Elkin, Speech delivered to Iowa Western Community College faculty and staff, November 1984.

3. Robert Lefferts, *Elements of Graphics: How to Prepare Charts and Graphs for Effective Reporting* (New York: Harper & Row, 1981), p. 65.

12

Wording a Speech

Questions to Guide Reading and Review

1. How can a person increase his or her functional speaking and listening codes?
2. What are two reasons for being as concrete as possible when speaking? Why might a speaker choose excessively abstract language?
3. How can you increase the specificity and sensory appeal of your verbal imagery?
4. What produces verbal "clutter" when speaking, and how can you reduce it in your speaking?
5. How can phrasing be used to increase the likelihood of central ideas and main points being remembered?

Key Terms

Alliteration   Connotative meaning   Language
Antithesis   Denotative meaning   Meaning
Clutter   Functional code   Symbol
Code   Imagery

The book of Genesis says that all people spoke the same language, and they began to build a great tower reaching unto heaven.

> And the Lord said, "Behold, they are one people, and they have all one language; and this is only the beginning of what they will do; and nothing that they propose to do will be impossible for them. Come, let us go down, and there confuse their language, that they may not understand one another's speech." (Genesis 11:6–8)

As this biblical story indicates, it is extremely difficult for people to work together if they do not share a common *language*. In order to choose words that will evoke intended meanings in listeners, a speaker needs an understanding of the nature and functions of language. This understanding gives a person more flexibility in adapting to different language communities. In this chapter, we explain the major components of language and provide some guidelines for using language to increase listener understanding and recall.

▶ Language in Public Speaking

Communication is possible only to the extent that people have similar vocabularies and experiences associated with those vocabularies. Public speaking requires using a vocabulary shared with listeners and expanding the vocabulary of listeners when necessary. For example, a speaker is almost certain to have a more extensive vocabulary than listeners who know less about the topic. In such cases, audience-centered adaptation is required.

The effective public speaker needs a basic understanding of *linguistics*, the study of language. Language is symbolic in nature, consisting of a *code* of symbols and *rules* for using the code.

Symbols

The response of a listener to a signal is the listener's *meaning* for that signal. Of course, the speaker may have intended something very different, but the listener's reaction is that person's meaning for the words received. Because symbols are subject to different interpretations, we strive for sharing similarity in meanings. The greater the similarity between meanings of a speaker and a listener, the greater the success of their communication (see Figure 12.1).

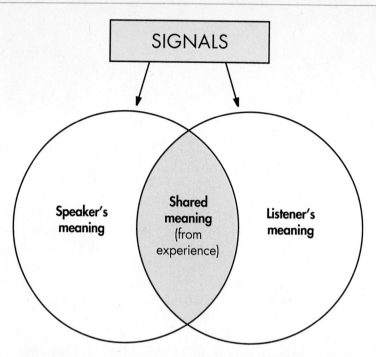

Figure 12.1 The greater the meaning shared by speaker and listener for the words, the more effective the speech.

All words are *symbols*. The same object can be referred to by the symbols *chair, silla, stuhl* or any other symbol you or other people choose to represent that object. With symbols we can evoke responses to objects and experiences without needing pictures and/or bulky objects to communicate about them.

Denotative and Connotative Meanings

Word associations have two major dimensions called *denotative* and *connotative meanings. Denotative meaning* refers to the object or concept indicated by a word. We sometimes refer to denotative meanings as dictionary definitions. *Connotative meaning* refers to personal associations, especially the "feeling or emotional aspects of a word meaning."[1] In response to a word or sentence, a person forms an image of some aspect of the world other than words. The person also has personal experiences and feelings associated with that image. The denotative response to words like *democracy, communism,* and *evolution* may be neutral, but the emotional response may be as extreme as those we call *fear* or *hatred*. In contrast, the denotative response to the words *sunset* and *friend* may also be neutral, but it is likely to be associated with a feeling of relaxation and pleasing images.

It is a *practical* matter to search for the words and word combinations most likely to evoke the meanings you desire from as many listeners as possible. This process is called *rhetorical sensitivity*, the conscious searching for the best way to evoke a desired response instead of saying what one thinks in the first words that pop into mind.[2] Language choices of a rhetorically sensitive public speaker are listener centered rather than self-centered.

▶ Using Language to Evoke Desired Responses

Developing skills in language choice and arrangement is a lifelong process. It never stops in part because languages undergo constant change as new terms are added, symbolic meanings are revised, and grammatical rules are slowly modified. College provides special opportunities to develop skill in using language to evoke desired responses, especially in courses such as public speaking, composition, public relations, and creative writing. We could compile a hopelessly long catalog of rules to follow for using language in public speaking. Instead, we have selected ten major guidelines that will be the most helpful in evoking desired responses from listeners.

Expand Your Functional Oral Codes

A *code* is a set of symbols used to think and communicate. The entire English language is a code of approximately 500,000 words. Each person has different

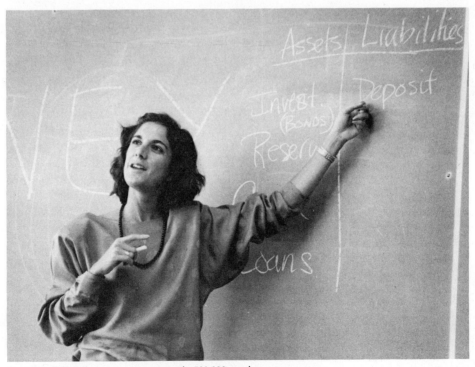

The code of English contains approximately 500,000 words.

functional codes for reading, listening, writing, and speaking. A person also has somewhat different speaking codes, or dialects, for different roles, such as engineer, council member, and parent. When speaking in public, evoking desired responses depends on using words that are part of the listening code of audience members and with which the listeners associate the referents intended by the speaker.

If you are perceived to be using codes that are inappropriate to your position in life or profession, your credibility will be lowered. For example, listeners would respond skeptically to a physician who referred to anatomy in slang terms. Mastering the verbal and nonverbal codes of the community of educated people in your profession and geographic region will be worth the effort. Your speaking codes must appear natural, not phony or put on. For that to happen you may need a lot of practice until appropriate speaking codes become habits.

By making a conscious effort to do so, you can expand your verbal codes of English in a manner analogous to how you learn a new language. Most college courses offer many new terms to add to your written and spoken codes. Reading extensively helps. Using language tools like an unabridged dictionary and thesaurus helps. Be sure to check the standard pronunciation of new terms before using them in speech. Use the new words in thinking, writing, conversations, rehearsals, and finally in public speaking to make them functional.

Select Language from a Code Shared with Listeners

While writing your preparation outline and during oral rehearsals, choose words likely to be used symbolically in the same way by you and your listeners. Only if the denotative referents are the same or similar can the image evoked be what you intended. Estevan said the response he desired from his classmates was that they could evaluate three major components of used cars. However, many of his most important words were not in the functional codes of his listeners. He urged them to do a compression check on each cylinder; look for signs of improper caster, camber, and toe-in; then look for body cancer in floorpan and rocker panels. More than half the listeners said they had no idea what he meant.

When Necessary, Expand Listener Codes

Sometimes a key term has no semantic equivalent in the code of listeners. In that case, if the concept referred to is vital in your speech, you will need to define the term before using it repeatedly. For example, you would need to define *byte* in a speech about how computers store information if your listeners were not computer literate. A word can be defined by giving examples of what it refers to, description, comparison and contrasts with familiar items, or using visuals to explain the concept. You should allow listeners to see as well as hear the new word. Put it on a chalkboard, chart, transparency, or other visual aid at the same time you introduce it in your speech. Then remind listeners by a brief internal summary or restatement of the definition when you use the term a second time. That way anyone who wasn't listening closely when you first mentioned the word will be able to understand, and anyone who forgot it will be able to remember and understand.

Select Concrete, Graphic Words

Language is used at different levels of abstractness, from very *concrete* to very *abstract*. If a verbal utterance properly refers to only one observable item or experience, it would be completely concrete. If speaker and listeners were all acquainted with this referent, there would not be any denotative misunderstanding. Your social security number is such a verbal unit. It applies to one and only one person. A dog registered with the American Kennel Club is given an alphanumeric symbol, unique to it alone. We rarely use such absolutely concrete language.

Usually, with even a relatively concrete term, we refer to a class of items or behaviors considered to be synonymous, such as "a cold," "a pound of table salt," or "a glass of water." People familiar with how a symbol is used in their society will share very similar referents when a speaker uses a term, although the connotations aroused may be very different. One person may begin to salivate in response to the word *sushi*, whereas another experiences mild nausea, but both think of raw fish.

At the other extreme are very abstract words, those used to refer to a wide variety of types of objects, categories of experiences, relationships, and patterns (see Table 12.1). Many referents of abstract words are *not* in any sense observable, for example, *democracy, lover of freedom, Christian, God, black, white, energy, institutional integration,* and *prejudice*. Extremely abstract sentences have been used to symbolize important sentiments: "all men are created equal," "variety is the spice of life," "I stand for the basic rights of animals, and urge you to do likewise," and "Higher education is the road to a better life."

One social scientist found that highly abstract utterances tended to slow the progress of groups trying to reach agreement. Signs of confusion, annoyance, conflict, and disorientation followed highly abstract statements much more frequently than relatively concrete statements.[3] As a speaker you want to evoke equivalent or very similar referents from listeners. This means choosing terms that will have as few referents as possible among your listeners. Numerous concrete examples and sensory descriptions can achieve this objective.

We certainly recognize that you often need abstract terms to represent general concepts. However, to the degree possible, use concrete words. If you are referring to a *baseball bat*, call it that instead of a *weapon*. A weapon could be a 2×4, a knife, an AK-47 assault rifle, a pistol, an army tank, an Exocet missile, or a brick.

Table 12.1
Words Vary from Abstract to Concrete

ABSTRACT	INTERMEDIATE	CONCRETE
Democracy	Representative government	Canadian government
Illegal	Cocaine	Crack
Road	Highway	I-80
Press	News magazine	*Time*; May 2, 1991
Person	Friend	Andy Vogt
Animal	Predator	Arctic fox
Politician	Senator	John Glenn
Ethical standard	Fair play	Social reciprocity
Goal	Specific purpose	Behavioral objective

Use Imagery to Hold Attention

Imagery is concrete language that describes specific details perceived by the senses of sight, hearing, touch, smell, body movement, temperature, and pain. Imagery focuses attention and evokes sharp images in the minds of listeners. Ideas associated with vivid sensory experiences are recalled better than those not related to vivid sensations. Amy Salem used imagery when she sought attention to her speech about how to travel to Europe at low cost:

> Imagine you're racing madly up a staircase trying to make it on time for a production of Agatha Christie's "Mousetrap," the longest running play in theatre history. Or maybe you'd rather be strolling down the Champs d'Elysses watching people go by, window shopping for Parisian fashions. Or how about you standing by the Fountain of Trevi in Rome?

Richard Chan described a camping breakfast this way:

> As you waken, the gentle rustle of leaves outside your tent soothes your nerves, not jangling them like traffic noises. Then your nose tingles with the smell of frying bacon and bubbling coffee. What an appetite you have! Food never tasted so good.

Martin Luther King described Mississippi in 1963 as "a state sweltering with the heat of injustice." One student speaker described the pain that can result from not stretching before and after strenuous exercise with words the audience could feel:

Your muscles seem to burn, then contract with spasms of pain shooting through your legs like burning needles.

Frank described what he saw in the aftermath of a huge tornado:

What had been the framework of a tall building now looked like a tangle of giant pretzels made from steel girders. Next to it where rows of neat houses had stood was now a flat field strewn with shattered boards, tangles of limbs, and crumpled cars.

It may take a good bit of practice and revising to create effective imagery. In describing her home area, Jennie first said this:

It's really beautiful, with lots of nice outdoor spots and rivers and things to do. The mountains are beautiful, and you see lots of animals.

The class listened politely, but no one could describe what she was visualizing to her satisfaction. When asked to describe more specifically, she came back the next class meeting with:

There are forests everywhere. And you see lots of wildlife. And there are cold, clear streams everywhere with good fishing. There are lots of high places, and nice little meadows where cattle graze, and deer come out to feed.

One listener said, "Sounds like the Ozark Mountains around here." Another said, "Sounds like where I come from in North Carolina." "No, no," said Jennie, "I'm talking about the Rocky Mountains—the Great Teton range!" Next time she was more specific still, selecting terms that were more concrete to create her image:

The mountains to the east of my home rise a mile above the plateau where I live. They are so steep that to look at the top almost makes my neck ache. You can see snow and ice on the peaks all year. Below the snow grow pine, spruce, and fir trees, which appear dark green to almost black. Then come aspens with white scaly bark, whose leaves are pale green in spring, then turn gold in fall. Clear, cold rocky streams filled with cutthroat and rainbow trout wind along the base of the mountains and into the meadows of our ranch. Bare rock sticks out in the highest places, in varying shades of gray. Like people around here, we see deer in the meadows, but we also see elk, an occasional black bear, and even a rare mountain lion.

In a sense such concrete imagery as Jennie finally created to describe her experience simplifies things for the listener. Mental images become sharper and leave us with more confidence in our understanding. Simple constructions also help accomplish such a desirable response.

Use Simple Sentences

Short, simple sentences are easier for listeners to interpret than are long, complex ones. They are much more likely to be recalled. This is more important when speaking than writing because the listener must retain all the phrases in a long, complex sentence in short-term memory in order to interpret the first part of the sentence with confidence (as with this sentence). If necessary, a reader can go over the sentence repeatedly. You cannot do that when listening. As you practice, try tape recording, then listen for long, complicated sentences. Try restating these sentences in two or more shorter sentences. When abstract language is used in long, complex sentences, the result is likely to be boredom and confusion. Imagine you are listening to the following excerpt from a talk given at a 1986 convention of communication teachers. How would you react?

> All of the talks this afternoon seem to hold in common a kind of implicitly egalitarian impulse toward the teaching of communication. My paper this evening is directed toward an articulation of a writing philosophy because I find it difficult to describe or recommend a pedagogical practice without recognizing the implicit philosophical and institutional directives that underlie the tasks that we assign to students. Even the structure of our classrooms, whether lecture, tutorial, or teacher-facilitated discussion, imply historically derived prescriptions about the nature of learning, prescriptions which exemplify and shape social perspectives. This view applies also to the communication technologies we value.

Simpler sentences and fewer, more concrete words might help us listen. For example, this might be done to simplify the statement:

> I'll explain my beliefs about what we should teach about writing, how to teach it, and why. Tasks we assign to students reflect how we feel about them and what we think about how learning occurs. How we teach and the technology we use show the same values and beliefs.

This is still abstract, but shortening and simplifying helped! So does removal of *clutter*.

Weed Out Clutter

You have seen radar maps of weather fronts on television and noticed how "ground clutter" confuses the image around major cities. Visualize a chest of drawers on which sits a trophy, four different framed photographs, a camera, two books, three dried flowers in a vase, some loose change, a crumpled facial tissue, a pack of chewing gum, and a portable AM–FM radio with earphones piled on top. The impression is one of disarray with nothing standing out; no emphasis on trophy, photo, or anything!

Language *clutter* can make a public speech just as vague, unfocused, and confusing as that chest scene or the radar image contaminated by ground clutter. If you wanted people to pay attention to the trophy and photo of your cat that won it, you'd remove everything else from the top of the chest or leave only a few items related to the cat. These would be organized to focus the eye on the trophy and photo. Visitors would notice the trophy, and most would remember it. The result is the same in public speaking. Cluttered language reduces the impact of words. Ideas are not noticed, or they are forgotten.

A cluttered verbal style has become epidemic in the United States among many academics, sportscasters, politicians, and other public speakers. Many students clutter their public speeches with "verbal garbage." They use a phrase when a word would evoke a clearer image. They talk around and about a point instead of stating it as simply as possible. They throw in words and phrases such as *okay, ya know?, n things like that.* Here are a few examples of cluttered speech and how each might be revised for greater clarity.

"In the course of my humble efforts to publicize the hallowed ideals of this great university . . ."

"When I tell people what the university stands for . . . ."

"Music is such a beautiful, lovely, wonderful way to relax and forget the cares of a trying day."

"Music relaxes us."

"He was humongous, y'know, a really tall guy."

"He was very tall," or **"He was 7′6″."**

"Platte River Park has lots of things for everyone to do, something for everybody, outdoor things, y'know? There are trail rides on horses for people who like that, hiking on nature trails or just through the woods, classes where you can learn lots of neat stuff, like about turkeys and mushrooms and things, bird watching for all sorts of our feathered friends—I even saw an eagle there once—campfire dinners with lots of outdoor goodies like barbecued buffalo, swimming, and lots of other fun things."

"Platte River Park provides a variety of outdoor activities, including trail riding, hiking, nature classes, bird watching, campfire dinners, and swimming."

Clutter is more common in the language of beginning speakers than experienced ones. It occurs most often when speaking impromptu or when a student does not practice aloud often enough to be confident and fluent. Most student speakers seem unaware of how much clutter they sprinkle among useful words. Reducing clutter on a desk or dresser is much easier than in speaking. However, with awareness of the problem and intentional practice, a speaker can reduce clutter.

First, you must be aware of the clutter before you can weed it out. To sensitize yourself, listen for clutter in others' speeches such as classroom lectures, sermons, reports, and briefings by work supervisors and at public meetings. However, *do not* do this when you need to focus on the content of the speech.

For practice, record a description of how to get to your house from the school you attend or explain your belief on some self-involving issue, such as school prayer. Describe the most recent book you read for pleasure, a TV show, or film. Then listen for clutter in the recording. Did you use unnecessary words that added nothing? Did you string adjectives together? Express ideas directly and concisely or talk around them? Were such *oral pauses* or interjections as *okay?, y' know, n things like that, now,* and *and* used repeatedly?

Next, record a rehearsal of a future speech. Try editing your speech to weed out clutter. Stop the recording each time you are aware of clutter and restate the passage without cluttering it up. You may find it helpful to transcribe two or three minutes of the speech, then using a red or blue pencil cross out all unnecessary words. Replace phrases with words, especially when you notice a cliché. The following is an excerpt from one student's edited transcript.

Many students ~~today~~ are under a great ~~deal of~~ stress. Stress can cause a

breakdown of our natural defense~~s~~ system. ~~And this breakdown of our~~

MAKING
~~natural defenses~~ makes us more vulnerable to diseases such as colds and

flu. Mom tells me to take ~~my~~ vitamin C in the morning so I won't get a

cold. I'm sure all of you have heard "Drink your orange juice!" I have

a
~~natural~~ deficiency of calcium. I drink a lot of milk, but for some reason

the calcium doesn't get into my bones. ~~So~~ I take cod liver oil so that the

calcium will get to them.

After extensive experience in speaking extemporaneously, we authors still struggle to eliminate clutter. We know that we have improved greatly. So will you, if you work at reducing clutter as we have suggested.

Choose Appropriate Words

Clutter words are not the only ones that can distract listeners from focusing attention on your central idea and main points. Language that violates listener expectations and standards is also distracting. Audience and situation analyses should have made the speaker aware of expectations about the language of a speech. Violating listener norms for language can distract, reduce credibility, or alienate listeners completely. Your words must not only be in the listener's code; they must also be perceived by the listener as appropriate to the speaking situation. The language a patron accepts from a comedian in a night club would shock the same person if spoken from a pulpit. The slang and careless grammar of casual conversation will not be accepted by many listeners to a public speaker.

The words you use and how you arrange them must also be appropriate to the subject. You would not use figurative language when explaining how to modify an editing program. Such language may be appropriate during a keynote address or when offering a toast during a banquet.

Be extremely careful with slang or profanity. Listeners may be embarrassed or shocked by words used in a speech even if they would use them in personal conversation. In the films *Platoon* and *Born on the Fourth of July*, the language was realistic, appropriate, and not shocking to most viewers, although it contained most of the English taboo words. A student speaker used a rhyming couplet with several of these taboo words to "get attention." She then said, "Did you notice the effect of the beat and rhyme in what I just said? As an English major, I've studied poetry extensively and come to appreciate how meter and rhyme affect us. So today I'm going to talk about. . . ." None of the other students were listening to what she said after the couplet. They were shocked by the words she used. Many looked around to see if others were reacting like them. Unless there is a very good reason to use profane words, our advice is *do not* do it. Be practical—choose language not to shock, but to enlighten and win support.

Create Memorable Phrases for Major Ideas

The form of a sentence can affect how well the idea expressed is remembered. Great speakers have always known this, and, for their most important ideas, worked to create phrasing that would stick in the minds of listeners. Consider Daniel Webster, spokesman for keeping the United States a united nation in the middle nineteenth century: "Union and liberty, now and forever, one and inseparable." Franklin D. Roosevelt: "I see one third of a nation ill housed; I see one third of a nation ill fed; I see one third of a nation ill clothed." Winston Churchill: "Never in the course of human history was so much owed by so many to so few." Abraham Lincoln: ". . . that government of the people, by the people, and for the people shall not perish from the earth." Such rhythmic, concise, and balanced phrasing helps create the images that bind us together as people.

An excellent example of how memorable phrasing can be used by a speaker with great effect is the 1988 presidential election. Think back on George Bush's campaign. Do any memorable phrases come to mind? How about "a thousand points of light," "Bush bashing," or "Read my lips. No more taxes!" Although you may never speak on occasions as momentous as the ones that produced the preceding phrases, the principle they manifest is a practical one for any speaker. Memorable phrases make your ideas memorable to an audience.

Advertisers work hard and spend millions of dollars to create phrases that will be easy to associate with their products. How about "Pepsi, the choice of a new generation," "Have you driven a Ford lately?" "This Bud's for you," or "Sometimes you gotta break the rules."

One technique for increasing recall is to create a slogan to represent the central idea of the speech. The slogan is used in the title, in main ideas or transitions, at other times throughout the speech, and repeated in the concluding sentence. For example, in a speech entitled "The Welfare Hydra," Pam Goldin repeatedly used "Hydra" (a mythical multiheaded snake that regenerated two heads for each one Hercules cut off) to give emphasis and unity to the speech: "The United States is like a Hercules facing a three-headed Hydra in programs to help the poor. One part of the Hydra is social insurance." ". . . the last major head of the Hydra. . . ." ". . . an effort must be made to replace this huge Hydra holding America. . . ." ". . . if we only act to defeat this American Hydra." Pam ended with "America can also defeat its Hydra by putting a halt to the many-headed problems of our poor by adopting a Guaranteed Income Supplement."[4]

Balanced phrases can help emphasize ideas, whether contrasting or cumulative. President John F. Kennedy frequently used *antithesis*, a sentence with two contrasting ideas phrased in parallel form. His most famous use of antithesis was "Ask not what your country can do for you; rather, ask what you can do for your country." Chris, a successful sales representative, used antithesis to stress his central idea: "Don't just do things right; do the right things." At the conclusion of his talk, audience members could state his theme because of the emphatic balanced phrasing. Wording your main points in parallel fashion takes advantage of the memory aid of balanced phrasing.

Occasional *alliteration* may help dramatize an idea. In alliteration the first sound in a series of words is the same. For example, one student kept referring to "deadly drunk drivers." Stephanie Pomonis Seyer said that "the value of a diamond is determined by its color, cut, clarity, and carat weight." These four C's became the topics of the main points of her speech.

With a little extra effort you can create a slogan, unifying theme, antithesis, alliteration, parallel wording, or other balanced phrasing to make your central idea memorable. The extra effort can have a dramatic effect on your listener's ability to recall your central idea.

Avoid Prejudicial Language

Just as a lack of oral literacy will prevent many people from listening attentively, so will words and syntax that reveal a rejection or denigration of people whom a listener believes deserve fairer treatment. Sexism, racism, religious prejudice, economic rigidity, and sundry other prejudices are often reflected in word choices. Consider a few examples of sexist language:

"The gals will . . . . The men will . . . ."
"Any policeman who knows his job . . . ."
"A cute chick in the audience may draw attention away from your speech."
"The history of mankind is replete with . . . ."

"Guys" or "boys" should balance "gals" or "girls," and "women" are the equal of "men." Since when are police officers only males? A woman is not a young chicken and will resent the putdown of being called such. Isn't history also about women? Or just *man*kind? Women were supporters, aids, helpmates, servants, and legal property of men until quite recently in the traditions of the Western world. Much of our language still reflects these outdated and offensive values. More and more women and educated men resent second-class linguistic and social treatment of women.

It can be difficult to recognize our prejudices or our prejudicial language. We recommend you listen to yourself and others to become aware of biases against classes of people in language. Use words and word combinations that are bias-free without the grammatical errors of "A person . . . they . . . ." in which singular and plural are mixed. One safe tactic is to use a plural for the noun, and "they" when you are not speaking of a specific individual. For example, "When a pilot wants to land, he must . . ." can become "When pilots want to land, they must. . . ." In the second version, subject and predicate numbers agree, yet there is no suggestion that a pilot is or should be a male.

If either your word choices or syntax now manifest violations of societal norms, it is a practical matter to change them if you want to be listened to and given high credibility. You *can* change these habits. Doing so will not be easy, but well worth the effort. You may need to ask other people to help you by pointing out your mistakes.

▶ Ten Guidelines for Using Language to Evoke Desired Responses

1. Expand your functional oral codes.
2. Select language from a code shared with listeners.
3. When necessary, expand listener codes.

4. Select concrete, graphic words.
5. Use imagery to hold attention.
6. Use simple sentences.
7. Weed out clutter.
8. Choose appropriate words.
9. Create memorable phrases for major ideas.
10. Avoid prejudicial language.

▶ Summary

Communication depends on our ability to create and employ symbols. Although symbols are extremely useful, they are also the source of much misunderstanding. For every symbol we have both denotative and connotative responses. These may vary greatly from person to person. Communicating effectively depends on similarity in referents of speaker and listeners.

Using language precisely for speaking requires precise thinking. College provides wonderful opportunities for expanding functional oral codes and developing a concise, concrete, graphic verbal style when speaking. Through careful observation and selection of concrete descriptive words, you can evoke vivid sensations in listeners. You can learn to speak primarily in simple, direct, uncluttered sentences. You can choose language appropriate to occasion and audience, and free of prejudicial implications. Finally, you can create memorable phrasing for important ideas.

▶ Learning Activities

1. *Surveying connotative reactions.* Either using the list provided below or using your own word list, poll your class to determine emotional responses to each of the words. Use the following scale to measure the responses:

Strongly negative	Mildly negative	Neutral	Mildly positive	Strongly positive
5	4	3	2	1

a. Unions
b. Computers
c. Shakespeare
d. Sweetheart
e. Foreigner
f. Texas

g. Credit card
h. Homosexual
i. Body building
j. Retirement
k. Pit bull terrier
l. Lover

m. Racist
n. Whore
o. Sexy
p. Student
q. Feces
r. Communism

Were you surprised by any of the reactions classmates had to words you felt very differently about? What does this suggest for you when speaking in public? If you have the opportunity, poll different groups of people, and see if there are any patterns of responses that seem to be related to such demographic variables as age, sex, education, occupation, etc.

2. Using speech manuscripts from such sources as the *Congressionl Record* and *Vital Speeches of the Day*, find at least two examples each of
   a. Trite phrasing.
   b. Meaningless clutter.
   c. Unnecessary abstractness.
   d. Inappropriate word selection.

3. For two days keep a diary noting all signs you can observe of oral illiteracy, such as mispronunciations, violations of grammatical rules, and limited vocabulary. Compare your findings with those of your classmates. Also discuss how you reacted to the people who seemed illiterate in oral English.

4. Prepare a three-minute speech in which you describe a feeling, a favorite place, a valued friend, or an unusual experience. Use the most graphic, concrete words you can to describe your sensory experiences. Ask your listeners to describe the images they formed while listening to you.

5. Make a list of phrases you can recall from famous speeches. In class discuss what seems to make these memorable.

6. Tape-record a rehearsal of an assigned speech. Now use the pause button while you listen to help you locate all clutter, violations of grammatical rules, inappropriate word choices, and other deviations from the most effective possible verbal style. Try working out revisions of your verbal encoding in writing. Then do so orally in another practice. Keep doing this until you are satisfied with the outcome, but do not memorize the speech word-for-word.

Notes

1. Joseph A. DeVito, *The Communication Handbook: A Dictionary* (New York: Harper & Row, 1986), p. 76.
2. Roderick P. Hart, Robert E. Carlson, and William F. Eadie, "Attitudes toward Communication and the Assessment of Rhetorical Sensitivity," *Communication Monographs* 47 (1980):2.
3. Dale G. Leathers, "Process Disruption and Measurement in Small Group Communication," *Quarterly Journal of Speech* 55 (1969):288–298.
4. Pam Goldin, "The Welfare Hydra," in *Winning Orations* (Mankato, MN: Interstate Oratorical Association, 1983), pp. 76–79.

13

Rehearsing and Presenting Your Speech

Questions to Guide Reading and Review

1. What can a speaker do to prepare physically and psychologically before beginning to speak?
2. What difference will audience-centered and self-centered delivery make in a speaker's perceived message?
3. What should be the focus of your attention as you progress from early through middle to final rehearsals?
4. How can new-to-you physical skills of voice and body be made a part of your natural, spontaneous repertoire of speaking skills?
5. How might a speaker discover and identify nonverbal signals that are contradictory to or distracting from verbal statements?
6. What are the important dimensions and desirable characteristics of nonverbal vocal and visual signals?

Key Terms

Articulation	Paralinguistics	Tone
Delivery	Pitch	Visual signals
Eye contact	Pronunciation	Volume
Gesture	Rate	

The week before she was to present her speech in class, Connie found it difficult to concentrate on anything. During school and while she was at work, she was distracted by thoughts of possible disaster. Connie replayed scenarios of dropping her visuals, forgetting everything she was going to say, and the audience laughing at her attempts to recover. Her nervousness was the center of most of her conversations with family and friends, so it did not surprise her when she couldn't eat or sleep the night before the speech. Even her rehearsals were centered on her delivery, not on her audience or her central idea. She asked several friends to listen to her speech and then asked them how she looked and sounded and if her gestures were smooth.

On the day she was to speak, Connie only half-listened to the speeches of her classmates. She thought about what she would do with her hands while speaking. Connie was almost in a trance when the instructor called her name. She proceeded to the front of the classroom to begin her speech.

As she began to speak, her voice was weak and choppy. She depended heavily on her notes and even dropped a notecard that contained one of her main points. Her attempts at eye contact were brief, so she didn't perceive the listeners' responses to her message. Audience members responded by sharing her feelings of anxiety and stress.

The experience was negatively reinforcing for Connie. She thought public speaking would be awful, and her failure proved to her that she was right. Connie could not understand why she did so poorly; after all, she had thought of little else except the speech for the last week. It had consumed her life, but she had still done poorly.

Norm had some anxiety about public speaking. His advisor told him a speech course would help him in his engineering career. He remembered the self-conscious feeling he had experienced in high school when he had to present a report to his history class, and he was not anxious to relive that experience.

Norm remembered discussing stage fright in class and recalled the instructor saying it was normal and helpful to feel some tension. His classmates described feeling self-conscious, uncomfortable, and nervous as well. He felt confident that his classmates wanted him to succeed and would overlook minor flaws in his presentation style.

Norm was convinced that his classmates could benefit from the information he had gathered about energy conservation. The speech assignment had become an opportunity for him to share something he believed was important. Norm spent a great deal of his rehearsal time revising developmental materials and working on the wording of his ideas. He asked two friends to listen to a rehearsal, and he asked questions to see if they understood and recalled his central idea and main points. He asked if he had used unfamiliar terms and asked for suggestions on how to make his points better. One friend suggested that he use a visual to emphasize the cost-effectiveness of energy conservation. Norm adopted this suggestion and practiced again, using the new visual to illustrate his point.

The day of the speech finally arrived. Norm was obviously nervous. On the way to school, he told a classmate about his topic. He admitted being nervous, but talked about the importance of his topic and how he hoped to get his classmates to conserve energy.

As his classmates began delivering their speeches, Norm couldn't help but think about his forthcoming speech, but he was able to focus most of his attention on the ideas of his classmates. When it was Norm's turn to speak, he felt eager to share *his* special knowledge with his classmates. He made two references to previous speakers who had developed ideas that were related to his topic. When he finished, Norm felt confident that he had accomplished his purpose. While answering questions following his speech, he thought of a topic for his next speech.

Both Connie and Norm experienced anxiety before speaking, but they handled this nervousness in different ways. Connie centered her attention during rehearsal and presentation on the mechanics of speaking, thus increasing her self-centeredness and anxiety. Though equally concerned about delivery, Norm's attention was audience-centered. During rehearsals, Norm paid a lot of attention to how he could make his message as clear as possible for his listeners. The different outcomes of self-centered and audience-centered rehearsals were obvious.

Although delivery is an important component of speaking effectiveness, the purpose is communication of an idea, not demonstration of personal speaking skills. A well-organized, audience-centered message can survive defects of delivery, but the most polished, fluent delivery will not make a competent public speaker out of a self-centered person who has not adequately focused on the audience during message planning and speaking.

In this chapter, we present guidelines for verbal and nonverbal activity in all public speaking and a rehearsal procedure to follow before you speak extemporaneously. The procedure presented here is ideal for the beginner. You may need to shorten it somewhat if time is short or you have considerable prior training and experience in public speaking.

▶ Voice in Public Speaking

Your voice does far more than merely transmit words in which you encode your message. It can become a fine-tuned communication instrument that enhances your verbal message. Except for the production of sounds that are combined into words, vocal signals are nonverbal, collectively called *paralinguistics*. Voice signals can do a great deal to clarify your meaning of otherwise ambiguous words. Most of us can recall listening to a dramatic, dynamic speaker whose voice seemed to stir the very depths of our feelings and aroused far more vivid mental images than any words alone could do. We also have listened when a speaker lacking vocal variety communicated disinterest and insincerity while speaking in a monotone. Some people are blessed with exceptional vocal qualities, but it is not necessary to have the skills of Ronald Reagan, Jesse Jackson, Martin Luther King, or John Kennedy to communicate well in the practical speaking situations you are likely to face.

In fact, it is important that your voice not *interfere* with the communication of your ideas. Charles Van Riper, famed speech therapist and theorist, says that "Speech is defective when it deviates so far from the speech of other people that it calls attention to itself. . . ."[1] If your voice sounds like that of a child, is so soft you can barely be heard, or is so precisely articulated that listeners pay more attention to pronunciation than to what you are saying, it is distracting. If the words are enunciated clearly and forcefully enough to be heard in a large room, and changes in pitch, rate, force and tone reflect your thinking and feeling, your voice skills will enhance the verbal message.

As models you might listen to network announcers, deejays on major radio stations, and local and national news anchors. All these people have been selected for their speaking skills. Notice the variety in pitch, rate, and force as they speak. If you listen closely, almost no two words in sequence will be at exactly the same pitch. The relationships among pitch, rate, and force reflect the relationships among the words in expressing images, ideas, and feelings. You may find it profitable to listen closely to your favorite television announcers. Notice how they pronounce words distinctly and how constant variation in voice reflects their thinking–feeling. Yet their voices do not stand out unless you specifically focus attention on vocal characteristics.

Articulation and Pronunciation

Words must be articulated and pronounced conventionally and correctly to maximize comprehension. Acceptable *pronunciation* is never distracting to listeners. If you are a native of New York, Indianapolis, Hanoi, Mexico City, Paris, Tokyo, or Dublin, your English pronunciation may vary considerably, as may stress and pitch patterns. However, as long as your pronunciation is intelligible, your credibility with reasonable listeners will probably be unaffected. However, mispronunciations will cause an audience to perceive you negatively and detract from your credibility as a speaker.

Acceptable pronunciation of certain words may vary from one region to another. As a speaker, you should make yourself familiar with locally accepted pronunciations of names of cities, personal names, or other entities so your pronunciation does not call attention to itself. For example, *bury* and *berry* are pronounced the same or differently, depending on where you are from. *Creek* is pronounced "kreek" in some regions, "krik" in others. *Root* may be pronounced "rooot" or "rut." In the Boston area, many speakers pronounce *Harvard, tomato,* and *aunt* quite differently from speakers in the Midwest. Likewise, vocational and professional groups develop pronunciations of important terms that may differ from pronunciations of other people. For instance, carpenters and builders do not say "two by four," but a "two buh four." The objective is to keep attention on your ideas, not your pronunciation.

Poor articulation is more often the reason for unconventional pronunciation than not knowing the standard way to say a word. This is especially true among beginning college students. Inadequate articulation of the sounds of words comes from sloppy or improper movements of tongue, lips, jaw, and other speech organs. Listeners then cannot be sure of the words spoken and may be unable to understand the ideas. *Articulation* precise enough to produce easily distinguishable words is important to effective public speaking. Some speakers habitually slur words, run sounds together, leave off parts of words, add sounds that do not belong, substitute one sound for another, or mumble many sounds so that no one can tell what words were intended. Sloppy speech sounds, just like sloppy handwriting, cannot be understood with any degree of confidence.

Poor articulation is *never* acceptable in public speaking. If you have such habits, a lot of hard work may lie between you and becoming an articulate public speaker. In Table 13.1 we have listed a few of the words most commonly misarticulated or improperly stressed by public speakers we have known. Do *you* have problems with any of these words? If you found that the second column represented your pronunciation of most of these words, chances are you usually articulate precisely when speaking in public. If the substandard pronunciation in the third column seemed natural to you, you need ·to give attention and practice to articulation in order to become clear and nondistracting as a speaker.

What may have been adequate in conversation with teenage peers may not be distinct enough to overcome noise and distortion common when speaking to an audience of 10, 20, or more people. The "mushmouth" articulator runs words into a slur without uttering consonants precisely, so listeners cannot be sure what was said. If "What did you say?" is a request you have heard often, you probably have been articulating sloppily. The person requesting a clarification is letting you know that he or she needs help to understand you. Repeated drills will enable you to respond automatically with precise articulation.

Public-speaking teachers often have their students participate in vocal drills to help them perceive the difference between correct and incorrect articulation. Practicing tongue twisters, drills of commonly mispronounced

Table 13.1
Some Words Commonly Misarticulated, Resulting in Substandard Pronunciation

WORD OR PHRASE	ACCEPTED	SUBSTANDARD
Have to	hav to	hafta
Going to	go-ing to	gonna
Because	be caz	cuz
Library	lie bra ry	lie berry, lie bury
Fraternity	fra ter ni ty	fut ter nu ty
Theatre	the uh ter	the a ter
Athlete	ath leet	ath uh leet
Government	guv urn ment	guv munt
Twenty	twen ty	tweny
First	furst	firs
Water	wat er	wader
Just	just, jus	jist
Larynx	lar inks	lar nix
Elm	lm	el um
Nuclear	*nu* clee er	nu cue ler
Genuine	gen u un	gen u wine
February	Feb ru ary	Feb u ary
Them	them	um
Didn't	did nt	Dint
What do you	what due ewe	Whaddaya

words, and reading aloud are a few ways articulation can be improved. If you have a habit of substituting one vowel or consonant for another, you may need to practice the correct sound in a variety of positions in different words. A very common substandard substitution is "n" for "ng" as in "workin," "fishin," and "thinkin."

A good way to improve your articulation is to record your speech, then listen to how you pronounce words. Any that are substandard can then be articulated correctly. Both ear and tongue must be retrained if you are to speak in a standard fashion when under the pressure of the public speaker's position.

In addition to articulating clearly, the sound of your voice also reflects your enthusiasm, sincerity, and interest in the listeners. In order to communicate these messages, the speaker must have a conversational *delivery* with considerable animation. The same person who is vocally animated with a friend often appears stiff, dull, and bored while in front of a class because the voice lacks variety and emphasis in pitch, tone, rate, and force.

Pitch

By varying the pitch of the voice, a speaker can avoid the dull monotone delivery characteristic of a novice speaker who reads notes unenthusiastically.

Pitch refers to the position of a sound on a musical scale. The animated, involved speaker's voice covers about one to one and one-half octaves. Major shifts in pitch occur when the speaker expresses key words or changes moods. This pitch variety is natural. Anything less is likely to be interpreted by listeners as disinterest on the part of the speaker.

Speakers who vary their pitch are more persuasive than those who do not.[2] Have you ever had a teacher who did not vary his or her pitch while lecturing? Can you recall how hard it was to listen, concentrate, and recall what the lectures were about? The most interesting materials can be made to sound boring when given no animation by the speaker.

Volume

The speaker can also communicate emphasis by changing *volume*. The loudness or softness placed on words affects their meaning and importance. Be careful not to overuse either extreme of volume. A speaker who shouts at the audience throughout the speech loses any impact that occasional increases in volume can provide. Likewise, a speaker who speaks constantly in quiet tones loses the potential to stress key words and statements.

Tone

The tone of your voice can be used to reflect changing feelings. *Tone* refers to changes in sound produced by the level of muscular tension while speaking and the degree to which various cavity resonators influence the sound. These resonators are the mouth, throat, and chest. Tone is the difference in voice of a mother when she says "baby" to soothe her upset child and "*baby*" to scold the child. Tone communicates the apparent levels of sincerity, conviction, and self-involvement the speaker has with the subject. Tone helps listeners to empathize with the speaker's feelings.

Tone can completely change the listener's interpretation of a message. Depending on the tone, "you devil" can be a curse or an endearment. Along with other vocal characteristics, practice varying your tone to notice what difference it can make in the total message. Use tone to express genuine emotions. Many listeners can detect coldness and insincerity. Listeners may not always know what physical cues they are reacting to, but most can detect someone who is not sincere.[3]

Rate

Rate refers to both the number of words per minute (wpm) and variations in the time allotted to speech sounds and silences (pauses). The average rate for public speakers is around 140 wpm, varying from as low as 90 to over 200 wpm. If articulation is sufficiently distinct and precise, listeners can easily keep up with a speaking rate of 200 or more wpm. However, complex ideas, reasoned arguments, and statements with a lot of new information may need to be spoken at a fairly slow rate to allow listeners time to interpret them. Think of a lecturer explaining the derivation of a statistical formula at 200 wpm or a geologist explaining the formation of a theory about earth's age at the fastest intelligible rate. You would have to give up as a listener unless you already knew the subject matter. On the other hand, telling a story or explaining a simple procedure should proceed at a rapid rate so listeners will have enough information to keep them stimulated and attentive. In a large room with hard walls, ceiling, and floor, you may have to speak more slowly and distinctly than in a small, comfortable conference room. Otherwise, echoes will interfere with the sounds being uttered and confuse listeners. You certainly can't speak to the crowd at a football game at 200 wpm, even with a good amplification system.

Intentional pauses can be used to emphasize words, phrases, or sentences that follow the pause. This is often called the *dramatic pause*. The effect is analogous to underlining, *italics*, or **boldface** in type. Paul Harvey's "Rest of the Story" series on radio illustrates the use of dramatic pauses to create suspense and emphasis. As with all emphasis devices, be careful not to overuse the pause.

Variations in average words per minute should occur naturally and frequently while you speak. An excited, positive mood is indicated by a relatively fast rate. A sad, depressed, worried, or concerned mood is naturally reflected by slowing down. You might want to practice pronouncing slogans or other key phrases, main points, and important examples or statistics very slowly after a pause. The combination of rate changes and pauses will help emphasize your words. All of us make use of rate changes and pauses naturally in our daily conversation. Just be sure you allow yourself to bring such vocal emphasis to public speaking.

In summary, vocal characteristics—not what you say, but how you use your voice—are a vital part of the nonverbal cues you send listeners. Considerable research evidence indicates that a conversational manner, with animated changes in pitch, volume, rate, and tone, enhances attention, understanding, and speaker credibility. Monotonous or hyper delivery detracts from attention and speaker credibility. Articulation and tone are best when they call attention to ideas and not to the voice or pronunciation. If you have problems in this area of encoding, you will need to learn how to act differently, then practice until the new ways become habits that will enhance your public speaking.

▶ Visual Signals in Public Speaking

Before you even begin to speak, you are sending nonverbal messages to your audience. Your appearance, bodily actions, posture, and facial expressions all send visual messages before you position yourself behind the lectern. As you begin to speak, visual messages continue to be part of your total communication, often affecting listeners more powerfully than the words you articulate. We judge a person's level of confidence, competence, and sincerity from nonverbal clues. As a speaker, you need to be aware of nonverbal *visual signals* you are sending your audience, always remembering that nonverbal signals should supplement your verbal message rather than contradict or distract from it. Visual signals that require a speaker's attention include personal appearance, bodily activity, facial expression, and eye contact.

Personal Appearance

The general appearance of a speaker can positively or negatively influence a listener's perception of competence and trustworthiness[4] and seriously affect how much people understand and recall. Although we could complain about the injustice of this basis for judgment, many studies confirm that audiences make initial judgments about a speaker based on appearance. John Malloy, author of *Dress for Success*,[5] has made an excellent living telling people how to dress and groom in order to get the most out of any type of situation. You should not underestimate the power of your personal appearance to influence others. The extent and kind of influence your personal appearance will have on an audience is largely within your control.

Speakers should try to present themselves in the most positive manner possible. Dress should be neat, appropriate to the speaker's position and speech occasion, and unobtrusive, unless special dress is worn to announce a position or demonstrate a skill. As a general rule, a speaker who is addressing a luncheon of business people should not appear in blue jeans and a T-shirt. On the other hand, a speaker who is addressing a group of construction workers on a job site would probably not need to wear a "power" business suit. In fact, dressing in such a way might have a negative impact on the audience. The way you dress is an important clue to how you perceive the group and yourself. Four guidelines will help you make decisions about dress when speaking.

(1) Dress so that your appearance does not call attention to itself. Plunging necklines, flashing jewelry, bold patterns, and high fashion are usually inappropriate. Grubbies, scruffies, cutoffs, wrinkles, dirt, and shirts with printed or pictorial messages may also be distracting to many listeners.

(2) Your dress should communicate that the audience and occasion are important to you. If you look as if this is just one more day in your life, audience members may not be interested in what you have to say. In a college class, a speech might be an occasion to dress more formally than usual.

(3) Dressing appropriately for the speaking occasion also means dressing comfortably. If you get nervous when speaking, tight clothing, sweaters, wool, or a shirt and tie may convey a positive image, but also make you more uncomfortable.

(4) Do not underestimate the confidence you can gain by dressing appropriately. When you look good, you feel good. Each of us has in our closet

A speaker's dress and grooming should be neat, appropriate to the situation, and unobtrusive.

articles of clothing that have special meaning: a favorite tie, a blouse your mother gave you, an outfit that makes you look and feel great. Take advantage of these items when dressing for your speech.

Bodily Activity

Posture, gestures, and entire body movements can supplement or contradict a speaker's verbal message. A student speaker once explained the benefits of exercise while leaning on the lectern; he looked tired and out of shape. Another presented shocking statistics about the increase in teen suicide while smiling at her listeners as if these facts were amusing. Still another tried to persuade classmates to support a local bond issue while hopping from foot to foot in such a way that the audience was fearful of her losing balance and falling. In each of these examples, the bodily activity of the speaker made it difficult for the listeners to focus on the intended message or believe the speaker was sincere.

A speaker should be sure that visual nonverbal signals do not call attention to themselves or counteract the verbal message. Mannerisms such as jiggling, swaying, fidgeting with pencils, twisting a strand of hair, rattling objects in pockets, and shifting weight from foot to foot are primarily stress responses that will decrease with experience, practice, and increased confidence. Other behaviors are personal habits that might go unnoticed in conversation, but become distracting in public speaking. Idiosyncratic movements like twisting a ring, pulling on an ear, buttoning and unbuttoning a coat, repeatedly pushing up eyeglasses, or finger tapping can be reduced by becoming aware of the behavior and substituting gestures and movements appropriate to what you are saying.

We certainly do not recommend trying to stay still! That is unnatural and will compound the problem. Be active, physically responding to ideas and feelings as you speak, just as you do in animated conversation with a friend. As a collegiate debater, Bonnie had a habit of clicking her ballpoint pen while delivering her arguments. She found it difficult to break this habit despite repeated comments from judges and her coach. After losing a debate by one point in delivery, her colleague took all her pens and replaced them with pencils. The problem was solved. Now, 20 years later, Bonnie refuses to use clicking ballpoint pens and is grateful for felt-tip pens! If you have a distracting habit like this, one way to change it may be to remove the offending article.

A public speaker's posture should be poised and relaxed, not sloppy or stiff. We have all seen speakers lean or drape themselves over a lectern, appearing more interested in resting than in communicating with us. At the other extreme are speakers who dash around the front of a room. Some speakers are so still and formal that they appear to be standing at attention. Ideal posture allows a speaker to take a step in any direction, lean forward or backward, or shift posture when responding to an idea or feeling. The entire body, from feet to face, should be free to respond. A basic stance allowing such freedom is like that used when coasting on skates, poised but not stiff or rigid.

When you want a very casual atmosphere or a sense of personal intimacy with listeners, sitting on a desk or stool may be appropriate. Generally, though, this reduces your ability to move, shift posture, and change distance from listeners, so be very careful when adopting this posture. At certain points, sitting for a few moments may be highly appropriate.

The question we hear most often about bodily movements is "What do I do with my hands?" Each of us, in our daily conversations with others, gestures naturally. Some people are more expressive than others. Hand and arm *gestures*, which are emphatic, descriptive, spontaneous, and almost constant while the person is engaged in a lively conversation, seem to cause many novice public speakers concern. Some seize the lectern with white knuckles, clasp their hands behind their backs as if in handcuffs, shove hands deep into pockets, or let their hands hang limply at their sides. The key to effective bodily activity in public speaking is to use the same amount and kind of gestures you would use if you were having a normal conversation. As you gain confidence in your speaking abilities and acquire more experience, you will begin to relax and gesture naturally. Manipulating and pointing to sensory aids often helps speakers to relax. The "What do I do with my hands?" question is a function of nervousness, not ability.

A few students try to preplan gestures, rehearsing them as one would dance steps. The problem with this "solution" is that the gestures are usually mistimed, resulting in a comic effect. Preplanned gestures usually look mechanical, because they are no longer spontaneous responses to feelings. Extemporaneous changes in wording or adjustments to listener responses are more difficult if gestures are memorized. Rehearsal of *types* of gestures is an excellent idea in order to expand one's repertoire of natural moves, just as skilled athletes practice serves, batting stances, twisting away from tacklers, dribbling, and feinting when passing a basketball. But these movements are not preplanned for a game; they become natural responses in appropriate situations. As natural spontaneous responses, gestures add emphasis and supplement verbal imagery. A shift in posture or a step often reflects a transition between ideas. Experience in public speaking should result in more natural gestures. Videotaping yourself while speaking will help you identify personal behaviors that you can concentrate on reducing during rehearsals. The most important point to remember is that gestures are natural, desirable ways of expressing thinking and feeling in both conversation and public speaking.

Facial Expression

Facial expressions communicate a variety of emotions such as excitement, fear, anger, sorrow, concern, appreciation, and enthusiasm.[6] Because most of the listener's visual attention will be focused on your face, facial expression can do much to reinforce verbal messages. Inappropriate expressions such as smiling when discussing a serious issue, biting your lip, wrinkling your nose in reaction to a nonverbal signal from a listener, or pursing your lips while trying to remember the next point can confuse and distract listeners. A videotape of a speech or use of a mirror can help you become aware of confusing facial expressions.

Make a conscious effort to eliminate facial expressions that seem distracting. You may find that some facial expressions are so much a habit that a friend can tell you that you use them in everyday conversations. One student stuck her tongue out every time she was trying to think of what to say next. When she saw herself doing this on videotape, she was surprised to find out it was a habit and quickly eliminated the expression. Another speaker rolled her eyes when she was annoyed at something, an expression that most listeners found distracting.

As in the case of bodily movement, the key to effective facial expression is being yourself. Facial animation is something we do naturally. It will occur

Facial expressions should indicate the speaker's feelings about the topic.

naturally as you gain experience as a public speaker if you are concerned enough about your topic and keenly aware of your listeners.

Eye Contact

Direct *eye contact* signals interest in the listeners' responses, whereas looking at notes, out windows, at chalkboards or other visual aids, or at walls—anywhere other than at listeners—signals that a speaker wants to avoid them or didn't really want to speak at all. Speakers with poor eye contact are not persuasive and are perceived as nervous, deceptive, disinterested, and/or incompetent.[7]

We do not advocate that you stare at listeners, but that you shift eye contact among the listeners as if you were having a conversation with all of them. Briefly looking at your notes or reading short quotations will not reduce your eye contact appreciably nor adversely affect listeners' perceptions of your responsiveness to them. However, your eyes must *always* return to focus on individual listeners, one at a time, until you are keenly aware of each as a person. Survey the entire audience, if possible, one member at a time. Look at one person until you are aware of him or her, then another, and so on. Use a pattern of left to right or front to back, being sure you do not omit any part of the room. As you do this, avoid the appearance of scanning the room mechanically without responding to listener reactions. *Really see and react to people* so you can smile if someone is laughing, comment on a facial expression you notice, reexplain a point if some listeners seem confused, and so on. If you do not adjust to the responses from an audience, you lose the primary benefit of establishing good eye contact in the first place.

▶ Rehearsing the Speech

Rehearsal as a step in preparation for an important event is not unique to public speakers. Scrimmages used by athletes, simulations used by astronauts, and role-playing sessions used by counselors are all forms of rehearsal. The main goals of any form of rehearsal should be to identify ineffective behavior, develop and polish new skills, and develop the ability to respond by using them naturally under pressure.

There are a variety of ways to rehearse before a public speech. The procedure outlined in this chapter has helped countless students prepare to speak extemporaneously. If you follow this procedure, you will avoid both the trap of memorizing your speech verbatim and the discomfort and distraction of getting lost or searching for words. This rehearsal procedure will help you focus attention on listeners and adapt to their responses. As you become more experienced, you will be able to shorten the entire procedure and make personal adaptations.

Early Rehearsals

As soon as you have completed a preparation outline, you are ready to begin rehearsing. The first step is to go over the outline, silently or aloud, until you are sure you can verbalize the main points and subpoints well and make smooth transitions between them. Be certain that you can express key ideas clearly and concisely before taking any further steps in rehearsing. You may need to revise the wording of some main points. You may even find it necessary to change the sequence of main points to create a more logical or smoother flow that you and your listeners can remember more easily.

You will sometimes find that ideas sound very different when spoken. Experiment with the wording of main points until they state your ideas as well as possible. Then try running through the introduction and conclusion until you are sure you can perform all needed functions of each concisely and emphatically.

Now practice reading aloud any quotations, short stories, excerpts of poetry, or other material you will read aloud as part of the speech. While reading, practice holding your book, paper, or notecard high enough that your voice is not muffled and you can look at the audience as much as at the paper.

Be sure you can easily shift your gaze from written material you are reading to your listeners and then back to your notes without getting lost or stumbling.

Middle Rehearsals

The next step in rehearsing is to put the preparation outline aside and practice the entire speech with the rehearsal outline. Write down the time when you begin and when you end so you can make adjustments if needed to conform to assigned or expected time limits. Imagine you are in your classroom with all your classmates looking at you. Make the mental picture as vivid as possible; visualize the listeners responding with nods, smiles, looks of puzzlement, or even dozing or looking bored. Now begin to speak. If you stumble over words or leave something out, keep going. This is a private run through during which you should avoid the temptation to look at your rehearsal outline unless you get completely stuck. Rehearse with any visuals you plan to use.

Continue rehearsing until you develop poise and confidence and can stay within time limits without having to glance at a watch. Except for main points, wording should vary with each rehearsal; at least you should not consciously commit the speech to memory! Now is the time to begin practicing with more and more gestures and movements, perhaps taking a step between main points, moving forward when you want to get more intimate, stepping backward as you feel revulsion for an example or statistic developing the problem, pointing or making a hand stroke to emphasize an idea, and so on. Practice oral skills of enunciation and articulation, pausing to emphasize or getting more variety in pitch and tone as your feelings and mood change. All of these vocal and bodily actions must be sincere reactions to what you are thinking and feeling about the subject of the speech, even if they are new kinds of encoding behavior for you.

If you have a tape recorder or video camcorder, you may want to record yourself delivering the speech in a practice run-through. If you do so, don't focus on just your appearance, movement, and voice. As you watch or listen to a recording of a rehearsal, give at least as much attention to words and ideas as you do to delivery skills. At this stage in your development as a public speaker, concentrate on one specific part of the speech or type of skill at a time.

Practice again, trying out any changes you think are needed until you are confident and comfortable with them. Again, do not memorize anything word-for-word except main ideas or very short quotations.

Final Rehearsals

During the final rehearsal of a short speech (such as you will be giving early in your public-speaking class), you should be able to do without the rehearsal outline. For longer speeches, you may need it. If it is feasible, now is the time to get reactions from some trusted person, such as a close friend, roommate(s), family member, or public-speaking classmate. Ask the person to listen and advise you about the clarity of your ideas. Ask specific questions about main points and supporting materials rather than general questions such as "What do you think?" Only *after* you have thoroughly discussed questions about the substance of your speech and its adaptation to the anticipated audience should you ask if you made any movements, had any posture habits, or used any words that distracted the listener.

Make revisions you might need, then practice again as often as you think necessary. The more practice you allow yourself, the more confidence you are likely to feel when your turn comes to speak in class.

During the final rehearsal(s), it is important to simulate the actual speaking situation as closely as possible. You may be able to practice in your classroom or one like it. If not, as you stand to practice speaking, try to imagine every detail about the room where you will speak. If you are going to dress in a special way, use props or visual aids, or even wear a suit jacket to which you are not accustomed, practice in these garments with the props or other sensory supplements you plan to use. Practice such details as focusing a projector, turning lights off and on, and disassembling and reassembling models you will use while speaking. If another person will assist you during the speech, that person should participate in the final practice(s).

▶ Final Preparations

Make sure you get a good night's sleep before a speech. When you are very tired, your ability to think on your feet is greatly reduced, and you will put less energy and enthusiasm into speaking. Allow time for usual morning routines, including breakfast. The more you treat this day like other days, the better off you will be.

On the day you are scheduled to speak, arrive a few minutes before class time so you can prepare yourself physically and psychologically. Physically, be sure all aids and props are ready for use so you won't have trouble handling them. If you will use an easel, be sure it is set up where all listeners can see it clearly and you can face the audience while referring to items on it. If you plan to hang charts from chalkboard clips, be sure the clips are in place and will hold your chart(s). If you will need to pull down a projection screen, be sure you can reach it or ask someone who can to do so for you at the right time. If you plan to fasten charts or diagrams to a wall with masking tape, now is a good time to tear off some small strips and place them on the corner of a desk ready to use. If you plan to use a projector, see that it is plugged in, focused, loaded, and ready to roll. Put tacks, tape, or other fasteners where you can get them unobtrusively when needed to fasten up graphs or diagrams. Finally, check to see that all books, magazines, or cards from which you want to read are arranged in the order you will use them. Number note cards if using more than one. This simple step would have saved many speakers the embarrassment of losing their place after accidentally dropping cards.

Prepare psychologically just before you speak by giving yourself positive self-messages. Tell yourself one more time how important what you have to say is to both you and the listeners and that you are as ready to speak as you need to be: "I know my subject well, I'm confident I can express my ideas clearly, and I will remember the main points." You know that from the way you rehearsed.

Just before you rise to speak, consciously take a deep breath and exhale. This will help to relax any undue tension in your muscles. Walk confidently to the front of the classroom, arrange any materials you will need, then face the audience and greet them nonverbally with eyes and facial expression *before* you utter the opening sentence of your introduction. If you were introduced by someone, respond briefly and launch into your introduction. By now you should be in a state of heightened awareness of your listeners and eager to share your ideas. Physically you should be "up," neither completely relaxed nor overly tense. Focus on the audience and proceed. Research and experience shows you will find that the initial tension will begin to fade to a more comfortable level quite soon. Remember, the audience wants you to succeed! So keep your focus on them and react to their response signals. Responses will mostly be supportive, but you will only get their encouragement if you keep in contact with the listeners. Let them know that you care that they understand your message and that you will adjust your explanations in order to help them get the most complete understanding possible. Being positive about yourself, listeners, and your subject will result in positive support from listeners.

▶ Summary

Purposeful practice and experience will help a speaker improve delivery skills to achieve predetermined purposes while reducing distracting effects of personal stress. A speaker who keeps attention focused on the message and the audience will be less likely to have debilitating anxiety problems than one who is focused on self while speaking.

Audio or video recordings can be used to observe both verbal and nonverbal expression. If contradictory or distracting nonverbal behaviors appear, the speaker can now experiment with a variety of more appropriate vocal and visual behaviors, then practice until chosen behaviors become natural responses. Personal appearance, bodily activity, eye contact, articulation, pronunciation, and vocal patterns should all be given attention. The goal is for all nonverbals to amplify, reinforce, or supplement the verbal message and never to contradict or detract attention from it.

The speaker should aim for a conversational manner that is spontaneous and responsive to reactions from an audience. By beginning with a sincere desire to communicate some idea, keeping this always in mind, and focusing on listener responses to the message, a student speaker will be able to overcome any self-conscious delivery.

For inexperienced speakers, rehearsals will need to be numerous, following a sequence from review of the preparation outline to a full dress rehearsal. During this time, feedback from self and others may result in revisions and reorganization. Later rehearsals should be as close to the conditions of the forthcoming public-speaking situation as possible. If notes, sensory aids, or other props are going to be used, they should be used during these rehearsals.

▶ Learning Activities

1. Prepare a two-column rehearsal schedule:
   Schedule   Accomplishments

   At the extreme left, number the rehearsals, then for each write out a brief statement of what you hope to accomplish during the rehearsal. After finishing each rehearsal, in the "Accomplishments" column record what you think you actually did accomplish.

2. Ask at least three classmates to write down all noticeable mispronunciations of words, words they find difficult to understand, and distracting vocal signals during your next speech. Then write out a plan to improve on each of these. Apply that plan.

3. Have a video recording made of a late rehearsal or the presentation in class of your next assigned speech. Ask the camera operator to occasionally focus on your audience. As you watch the playback, make a list of any distracting mannerisms, appearance distractors, movements, gestures, facial expressions, or eye contact that you want to improve upon. Make a second list of what you consider to be your strengths of visual expression in this rehearsal or speech.

   Do the playback a second time, this time noting evidence of your attention and adjustments to listener responses. Finally, write out a plan for improvements you want to accomplish.

   Repeat this exercise again after making at least two additional speeches, and note what changes you have already accomplished.

4. Practice reading each of the following tongue twisters aloud. First, pronounce each very slowly and distinctly to be sure you are not making any sound substitutions, omissions, or additions. Second, repeat each, gradually increasing the rate until it approaches 200 wpm. What do you discover about your articulation and pronunciation of speech sounds? This sort of practice is done extensively by announcers.

   A big black bug bit a big black bear.
   Amidst the mists and fiercest frosts, with barest wrists and stoutest boasts, he thrusts his fists against the posts and still insists he sees the ghosts.

Mable muddled madly amidst the massive mess.

Whatever, whichever, whenever work comes crashing crazily into my life, I will still instill thrill in toil.

Never in the course of human history was so much owed by so many to so few.

Traumatic tragedies triumph over tenacious temerity.

Three gray geese in the green grass grazing.

Six slippery snakes slithering in the slime.

Finagling financiers fudge fiscal fidelity in an infinitely fantastic fiasco.

5. Select a favorite passage from a poem expressing strong feelings or an important item of faith to you or a short scene from a favorite play. Practice reading this aloud until a tape recording of it seems as animated, vivid, and dramatic as if it has been done by some famous actor. While you practice, exaggerate changes in pitch, volume, rate (including dramatic pauses), and tone. No one else is listening—let loose! Express all your feelings. Your instructor may ask each person to read a very brief part of this practice passage in class. Let this expressiveness become a part of your extemporaneous speaking.

6. Observe two speakers, one whom you think is exceptionally communicative nonverbally and one whose behavior you find dull, monotonous, and boring. Write out a detailed list of differences in their audible (voice) and visual encoding behaviors. Compare your findings with those of classmates. You may want to compile a class list of "Dos and Don'ts for Public Speaking Delivery."

Notes

1. Charles Van Riper, *Speech Correction*, 6th ed. (Englewood Cliffs, NJ: Prentice–Hall, 1978), p. 29.
2. Judith A. Hall, "Voice Tone and Persuasion," *Journal of Personality and Social Psychology* 38 (1980):924–934. Kathy D. Taylor, "Ratings of Source Credibility in Relation to Level of Vocal Activity, Sex of the Source and Sex of the Receiver," MA thesis, University of Nebraska at Omaha, 1984.
3. James B. Stiff and Gerald R. Miller, " 'Come to Think of It . . .': Interrogative Probes, Deceptive Communication and Deception Detection," *Human Communication Research* 12 (1986):339–357.
4. Shelly Chiken, "Communication of Physical Attractiveness and Persuasion," *Journal of Personality and Social Psychology* 37 (1979):1387–1397.
5. John T. Malloy, *Dress for Success* (New York: Warner, 1975).
6. P. Eckman, P. Ellsworth, and W.V. Friesen, *Emotion in the Human Face* (New York: Pergamon Press, 1971).
7. Judee K. Burgoon, Valerie Manuson, Paul Minco et al., "Effects of Eye Gaze on Hiring Credibility Attraction and Relational Message Interpretation," *Journal of Abnormal Behavior* 9 (1985):133–146.

PART IV

Common Types of
Speech Situations

14

Speaking to Inform

Questions to Guide Reading and Review

1. Why would you be called on to make more speeches to inform as your knowledge and skills become more specialized?
2. How should you describe the objective of a speech to inform?
3. What can you do in a speech to inform to adapt to wide variations in the amount of knowledge listeners have about your subject?
4. What are three ways in which you can get listeners actively involved while you speak?
5. Why are familiar schemas so important for long-term memory of listeners?
6. What types of mnemonic devices can you create to help listeners store your main points in long-term memory and retrieve them when needed?
7. What advice would you give a speaker who is preparing to describe verbally some object, experience, or idea?
8. When creating a comparison as an instructional device, what is the most important principle to follow?
9. What are three techniques for defining new-to-listener words in such a way that the listener can relate them to prior experiences?

Key Terms

Acronym	Briefing	Mnemonic
Acrostic	Instructing	Reporting

Speaking to inform is common in our professional and personal lives. A coach instructs a team in the winning strategy for a homecoming game. A doctor explains the results of some recent tests to a patient. A club treasurer describes the income, expenditures, and assets of a student organization. A medical researcher reports recent findings about AIDS to practicing physicians during a convention. An economist explains the crisis facing the savings and loan industry to a congressional subcommittee. Your teacher lectures about organizing information for a public speech. You give a visitor directions to the library. You explain to the person who sits next to you in your public-speaking class what happened on a day that he missed. These are a few examples of informative speeches being given every day. You can think of many instances where you have benefited from the skilled expression of knowledge by persons speaking to inform, live or via television. In turn, as you become more knowledgeable and specialized, you will find yourself in need of specific skills for speaking to inform so that you can share your knowledge.

The more in-depth our knowledge, the more we need to know and apply principles that produce effective informative speaking. If we don't know the practical art of informative speaking, we are likely to be sources of confusion and frustration despite our knowledge. Members of the clergy often confuse laypeople by using the language of theology. Engineers leave nonengineers puzzled about plans for flood control. Computer specialists who think they are explaining how a program functions too often leave their listeners in hopeless puzzlement. Some chemists might as well speak Swahili when they try to explain to nonchemists how a herbicide destroys certain types of plants and not others.

Nonspecialists such as voters, political leaders, and executives need a general perspective on many issues in order to make appropriate decisions. All of us need to make decisions about many things on which we are not specialists. The more specialized and compartmentalized your knowledge becomes, the more need you have for special skills in speaking to inform people not knowledgeable in the area of your specialization. That's what this chapter is about—sharing your specialized information with people who lack it, yet who need to understand in general what you know in detail. This applies to you whether you speak because you are a welder, an accountant, a radiologic technologist, a nurse, an orthopedist, an umpire, a cattle feeder, a chef, a dentist, a quilt maker, or a computer technician.

► The Objective

Throughout this book we have argued for an audience-centered approach. The effective speaker takes into account the needs, background, and information-processing abilities of listeners. As we wrote in Chapter 4, the distinction between speaking to inform and speaking to persuade is not based primarily on the content of the speech, nor can a speaker control how a particular listener will respond to a particular message. Differences in the speeches themselves are more a matter of degree than of kind. To some extent all speeches can be persuasive, meaning they may produce new beliefs or actions on the part of listeners. Likewise, all speeches can be informative to the extent that they produce a grasp of new information by listeners. Guidelines in this chapter are intended to help you inform, but they are also applicable when your general purpose is to persuade. Listeners need to understand what they believe, and understandings are the basis of beliefs and actions taken by critical thinkers.

To Inform or to Persuade?

The most important criterion for classifying a speech as either informative or persuasive is the intention of the speaker. A speaker often has more than one purpose, such as to have listeners understand how a turbocharger can increase engine horsepower and, secondarily, to have them patronize his shop for auto repairs. However, it is on the primary desired response that the classification "to inform" or "to persuade" is made. To decide, ask yourself, "Is my primary objective to have listeners demonstrate an understanding of my message by what they do, agree with my idea, or take some definite action in response to it?" Whenever a speaker wants listeners to express agreement with a controversial idea or to take action, the intention is to persuade. On the other hand, if the desired response to the same idea is that listeners explain it to the satisfaction of the speaker, the purpose is to inform. For instance, a political scientist's objective might be that students explain the major premises and arguments in the political philosophy of Karl Marx, but neither agree nor disagree with it.

Amount of Information

As a general rule, informative speeches tend to convey far more information than do persuasive speeches. To illustrate, consider the difference between a typical lecture and a pep talk of the same length before a game or membership drive; the lecture provides new information, whereas the pep talk motivates by repeating familiar concepts. Functionally, a speech is informative to the extent that listeners acquire information that is new to them. The "new" may be a new way of interpreting previously held information or a clarification of something only partially understood. A speaker may correct a misunderstanding or replace misinformation with valid information. Occasionally the content of a speech is about a subject totally new to listeners. The guidelines in Chapter 5 are particularly useful for determining whether or not information will, in fact, be new to listeners. Regardless of intent of the speaker, a speech is informative only to the extent that it adds to the amount of information listeners can recall and apply.

A Noncontroversial Central Idea

Information refers to statements that are not controversial among persons informed on a subject. By information we mean statements limited to descriptions of what was actually observed by a competent observer. There may be much controversy revolving around the topic or issue dealt with by a speaker, but the central idea of an informative speech is a *noncontroversial statement* on which all persons well informed on the subject would agree. If reasonable, knowledgeable people disagree about the central idea, the speaker's primary general purpose is to persuade. The following examples of central ideas for speeches planned to inform and to persuade on the same subjects will remind you of the difference.

TO INFORM	TO PERSUADE
ORIGIN OF SPECIES	
Creationists believe that the Genesis account of creation explains the diversity of species found on earth.	The major forms of life were created by God in the form we find them today.
FOREIGN LANGUAGE STUDY	
International corporations need employees fluent in foreign languages.	Every business college graduate should be fluent in at least two languages.
RUNNING AS EXERCISE	
Persons who run regularly have lower heart rates, lower blood pressures, and greater lung capacities than comparable nonrunners.	Running is an excellent form of exercise for almost everyone.

Remember, whether or not a particular central idea is controversial is ultimately determined by audience member beliefs, not the speaker. The informative speaker makes the best possible assessment of the degree of controversy about a central idea based on a careful and thorough analysis of his or her audience.

Clarifying the Desired Response

When you have been assigned or have decided to speak to inform, the objective of the speech must be phrased as a specific listener behavior that you can observe. The observing might be done by asking a question and seeing how the listener responds, assigning the listener to do some job and seeing how he or she performs the task, or by some form of testing. Some words and phrases used to describe listener responses are too vague; words such as *know, understand, appreciate*, and *grasp* will be interpreted differently by different people. Such slippery words are used frequently in everyday conversation, where they may serve adequately to communicate. However, if a speaker uses such terms to phrase the desired response, it will be open to a variety of misinterpretations, and the speaker may not have a clear image of what to observe in order to evaluate how well the objective of speaking has been achieved. Active verbs such as *write, list, identify, build, construct, make, play*, and *follow*, however, describe specific desired responses.

In short, a specific desired response statement describes what a listener can *do* as a response if the objective for speaking has been achieved. You cannot see into a person's brain to observe what he or she knows, thinks, or feels. You can only observe what the person *does*, a performance of some sort. Your job, in writing the desired response statement, is to specify the performance of an act a listener can or will take if you succeed.

Objectives for instructing have been classified into a hierarchy of types, ranging from less to more difficult types of behaviors to achieve.[1] For example, cognition, or thinking, is classified in six levels, shown below with some specific verbs used to describe listener responses:

1. *Knowledge.* Define, describe, label, list, match, name, reproduce.
2. *Comprehension.* Explain, distinguish, give examples of, paraphrase, predict, summarize.
3. *Application.* Compute, demonstrate, make, construct, operate, prepare, produce, solve, find.
4. *Analysis.* Break down, differentiate between, classify into, infer, relate, subdivide.
5. *Synthesis.* Combine, compose, create, design, generate, organize, plan, write.
6. *Evaluation.* Appraise, compare, contrast, critique, judge, justify, pick, prioritize.

Although you will not classify the response you desire into a specific level, you should always describe specific behaviors you will be looking for as evidence that you have a clear objective in speaking.

▶ Types of Speaking to Inform

In this chapter we emphasize three common types of informative speaking: instructing, briefing, and reporting. You will probably do all three as part of your professional and personal life.

Instructing

Instructing is done by everyone who wants someone else to be able to do something new, such as teachers, nurses, supervisors, park rangers, mechanics, museum guides, doctors, and coaches. Instructing includes informative speeches commonly called *lectures*. A biologist might describe mitosis, the process by which a cell divides, so that the listeners would be able to explain

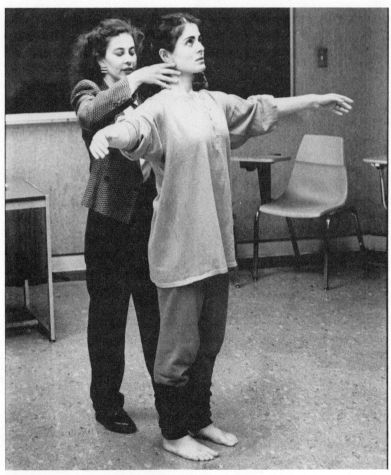

Instructing occurs in a variety of situations.

273

the sequence of stages through which cells grow and reproduce themselves. A historian might want listeners to be able to explain a theory of how economic forces contributed to the American Civil War. A jump instructor would want aspiring skydivers to be able to perform all steps in a jump in the correct sequence.

Speeches designed to instruct others are the most common type of informative speaking. In fact, all speaking to inform involves instructing. Visual demonstrations, listener actions, videos of processes and procedures, sound recordings, pictures, and summary charts listing steps are very commonly used as sensory aids when instructing.

Reporting

Reporting refers to sharing a special investigation of a subject or problem or relating information based on observations. A report usually includes much more detail about the topic than does the next type of speech to inform, a briefing, but otherwise they are quite similar. Also, reporters usually intend no specific use of the information they share, whereas instructors usually want listeners to be able to make a specific application of the information. For instance, consider a scientist who investigated an hypothesis about a particular form of cancer. When reporting this research to other specialists working on similar problems, the scientist would likely summarize prior research related to the problem, explain the purpose of the study, describe how it was done, give a rather complete account of all data gathered, describe the findings in detail, suggest what they mean for theories about cancer, and suggest some further research. A computer specialist in an engineering department who was assigned to investigate the merits of competing brands of computers would report criteria for evaluating competing products and how each computer measured up to these criteria. Unless the speaker was attempting to persuade the listeners to chose a specific computer, he or she would not recommend which to purchase. Committee chairpersons regularly report what their groups have learned to general membership meetings. Task forces give lengthy reports to the organizations that create them. Graphs, pictorials, and charts of data are likely to be used when reporting.

BRIEFING   *Briefing* refers to making a *condensed* report about some large body of information, often to help listeners make a decision or carry out an assignment. A briefing contains condensed, up-to-the-minute information such as pilots need about weather conditions before takeoff or an executive board of a corporation would need before deciding which of several sites to choose for a sales conference.

Usually the briefer and listeners are knowledgeable about the general topic and share a code for talking about it. Highlights and conclusions are reported with only a few details essential to the performance of the listeners. Most briefers are specialists who have studied a topic extensively for the benefit of the listeners who need the outcomes of such study, but do not have the time and/or skills needed to do the study. For example, senators have staffs of specialists to help them understand bills on which they must make decisions. A department manager may need to brief other department managers about changes in operations that will affect how departments relate to each other. Police officers are briefed at roll call. Generals are briefed by lower-ranking field officers and staff investigators. Briefing is very much a part of the practical world of work.

Instructing, reporting, and briefing are major types of functions performed by informative speakers. If you can do the preparation and planning required for these three types, you will be able to handle any speech to inform.

▶ Applying Your Audience Analysis

For your speech to be informative to your listeners, it is essential that you first determine what the listeners already know about the topic. Adapting to listeners' knowledge means you must quickly supply sufficient background information for the least knowledgeable to be able to understand your central idea without boring the highly informed.

Adapting to Different Backgrounds

Adapting to listeners with varying backgrounds may call for a lot of ingenuity while planning to speak. Television miniseries use an excellent means of doing this. After the first night, each new episode begins with a brief summary of preceding episodes so that viewers who missed the previous show(s) can still understand and enjoy the new episode. These summaries are often helpful reminders even for viewers who watched on previous nights. As a speaker, you can adapt this technique. Plan a brief summary of what the less informed listeners will need in order to follow you without overtaxing the patience and goodwill of the more informed. For instance, you might say "I'll review briefly the bernoulli effect so we can all understand why the faster a plane flies, the smaller its wings can be." A firefighter who wants to explain how to fight home electrical or chemical fires might "remind" listeners about the triangle of oxygen, fuel, and heat necessary for combustion.

Adapting to Listener Perspectives

You should always speak from the *listener's* perspective or relationship to the topic. All too often an informative speaker is "I" centered, speaking as if every listener had the speaker's relationship to the subject. Rick, a quarterback, spoke this way to a group of people who would never be more than spectators at games: "*You* must hold the ball. . . . *You* aim the pass. . . ." as if the listeners were quarterback trainees. What he had to say might help spectators appreciate a football game, but addressing them as if they were quarterbacks was inappropriate. The point is this: Be sure to think through how most of your listeners are or will be relating to your topic, then speak in terms of that relationship. Most listeners are not devoted enthusiasts like the speaker. It may help to recall how you perceived the topic *before* you became personally involved with it, then focus on what got you interested. Imagine yourself disinterested and not knowledgeable about your subject. What could a speaker do and say that would be most likely to arouse your interest and get you involved?

Adapting to Existing Knowledge

When analyzing what your listeners already know about your subject, you will need to consider what they may have studied, learned through television, and experienced firsthand. For example, if your subject was the life cycle of artificial lakes, you would need to consider what sorts and sizes of lakes listeners had probably seen, whether or not they had observed the same lake over a period of years during which it was beginning to change visibly, or if lakes were something they had never observed more closely than is possible from a plane, speeding boat, or passing auto. If your subject were quality circles, you might want to learn if any listeners had participated in such a group as well as what they might have read or heard about them from secondary sources. Remember, a speech is only informative to the extent that listeners acquire information that is new to them. Assessing an audience's existing knowledge enables you to successfully meet this criterion.

Involving Audience Members

Listeners must choose to be active participants in the process of communication for you to achieve a desired response. For that reason they must have a feeling of *need* for your information before you start into the body of your speech. Several motives can evoke active involvement of audience members.

REWARDS   As noted in Chapter 9, the introduction must demonstrate that there will be a reward for making the effort to listen and recall. The reward might be some practical application of new information such as saving money or time or a satisfaction of the human need to understand what is happening around one's self. Think of informative speaking as supplying answers to questions in the minds of listeners. You can use these questions to motivate listening.

CURIOSITY   In a public-speaking class or work situation, listeners may have little choice but to be present. Sometimes you can arouse curiosity about the answer to a question. Curiosity is the feeling of need for an answer to a question, an explanation that makes sense or completes a story. Radio commentator Paul Harvey graphically describes part of a story to arouse curiosity, then breaks for a commercial. Few people turn the dial before hearing "the rest of the story." Like Harvey, you need listeners who want to hear the rest of your story.

PARTICIPATION   Occasionally you can get active listening by having an audience participate with you in some activity. Lori had her listeners create paper jumping frogs while she demonstrated. Joel asked his classmates, most of whom had attended a nearby race track, to choose a horse on which to bet. He then explained how to interpret information about the horse provided in a daily racing form. After explaining the intent and structure of the Japanese poetic form called *haiku*, Peggy had each classmate create a personal haiku. Several then volunteered to read their haikus aloud to the rest of the class.

Informative speakers frequently involve listeners by asking them to think of personal examples or stories they have heard as support for the speaker's idea. This gets the listener to relate an abstract statement to a personal experience. For instance, Mike asked his classmates to recall how they felt while watching a boxing match, then developed his report about the pros and cons of boxing as a sport by using the experiences his listeners described. His audience analysis had discovered that all of his listeners had watched at least one boxing match and that most had strong opinions about the merits of boxing as a sport.

▶ Organizing Informative Speeches

Regardless of the type of informative speech you are preparing for and how well you have planned to get listeners involved during the introduction, you must select one of the schemas we described in Chapter 8 as the main framework for all your information. Only organized information can be recalled well.

Organizing and outlining begin from central idea and desired response statements from which you generate a sequence of main points for the body of the speech. If it is to be recalled effectively by the listeners, the body of a speech must be organized around one of the schemas embedded in the minds of listeners, such as chronological, problem solving, spatial, causal, or other arrangement for which there is a logical relationship among main points. Furthermore, the body should contain not more than four main points.

Transitional and focusing devices are very beneficial to recall. As educational psychologists have pointed out, a well-organized presentation tells students what to expect, keeps each point or topic in focus with reminders, and uses both internal and final summaries to remind students of information they have received.[2]

Special memory aids, called *mnemonics*, can be used to enable listeners

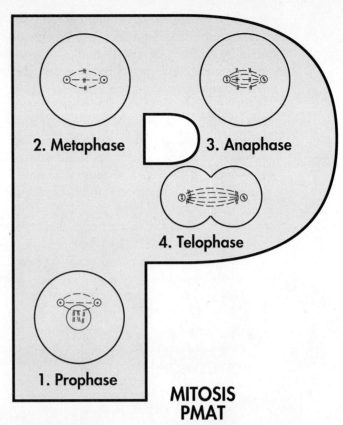

Figure 14.1   The PMAT diagram.

to remember more effectively and efficiently. Rhyming is a widely used mnemonic device. You probably remember which months have 30 days with the aid of a rhyme: "Thirty days hath September, April, June, and November. . . ." In what year did Christopher Columbus discover America? Do you recall, "In 1492, Columbus sailed the ocean blue"? Perhaps you can find a rhyme scheme for the key terms in the main points or even in their wording.

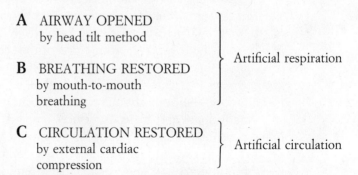

Figure 14.2   The ABC acronym representing the steps in cardiopulmonary resuscitation. (**Source:** The American National Red Cross, "Cardiopulmonary Resuscitation," 1974, p. 8.)

For instance, four phrases in a group's development were called "forming, storming, norming, and performing" to make them easier to recall.

Acronyms are letter cues that help us recall complex material. The acronym, "Roy G. Biv," helps us to remember the correct order of the colors of the visible spectrum: *r*ed, *o*range, *y*ellow, *g*reen, *b*lue, *i*ndigo, and *v*iolet. An acronym formed from the first letter of the key word in a set of main points can be used to enhance recall. By associating the acronym PMAT with a P-shaped floormat on which four large cells were placed, Lisa helped her classmates recall both the sequence of the four stages of cell division and what happens at each stage: *p*rophase, *m*etaphase, *a*naphase, and *t*elophase. A widely used mnemonic acronym is the ABC's of cardiopulmonary resuscitation:

*A*irway is cleared.
*B*reathing is restored.
*C*irculation is restored.

In all the preceding examples, you can imagine how hard the creators of some acronyms worked to find a way to state main points so that the acronyms they formed would be a word or familiar sequence of letters such as ABC. It may take many trials with different key words before you can create an acronym such as MADD, NOW, ERA, or NATO. If it is important that listeners remember a sequence of steps in correct order, the effort will be worthwhile.

Acrostics are mnemonic devices that use sentences formed from the first letter of each word that represents a specific item of information to be recalled by a listener. "Men very easily make jugs serve useful nocturnal purposes" helps us to recall the planets in order from the sun: *M*ercury, *V*enus, *E*arth, *M*ars, *J*upiter, *S*aturn, *U*ranus, *N*eptune, and *P*luto. Generations of students of anatomy have found it possible to remember the names of the pairs of cranial nerves in order from front to back by associating the first letter of the name of each nerve with the first letter in a rhymed acrostic: "On old Olympus towering top, a Finn and German brewed some hops."

When you create an acronym or other mnemonic device, use it to stress the structure of your speech. Present it in the preview of the introduction, preferably on a chart or chalkboard. Repeat it in transitions. Use the key letters in stating main points during the body of the speech. Reemphasize the acronym in the final summary of the conclusion. Ask listeners to visualize it. These letters will be the memory landmarks listeners will use to organize and recall your ideas long after they have forgotten what less well-structured speakers talked about.[3]

▶ Developing the Main Points

All four major types of developmental materials explained in Chapter 7 will at times be used to develop main points in informative speeches. In this section, we elaborate further guidelines and techniques to apply when selecting and wording supporting materials.

Describing

Describing means that you use words to evoke sensory-like experiences from listeners. The words used to describe must be associated by the listeners with things they have previously seen, smelled, touched, and so on. The purposes of describing include helping listeners do four things:

1. Identify the class to which some object belongs, such as "Is this the highly prized morel mushroom or the poisonous false morel?" "Is what I smell just an unpleasant odor or a deadly gas?"
2. Recognize specific objects, such as "Is that the face I saw on the most-wanted list?" or "Is this the lane into which I am supposed to turn?"
3. Imagine in detail a sensory/perceptual experience they have not experienced directly, such as the pain of a ruptured spinal disc or heart attack or the call of a male horned owl.
4. Follow or explain a procedure, such as the one by which a gene is spliced or the way in which a cell nucleus divides.

When describing, it is important to focus on unique, defining details. The object, concept, process, or sensation experienced must first be observed by the speaker with utmost attention to details, examining unique characteristics that distinguish it from all others of its type. Such observing is different from the casual, vague awareness that characterizes most experience. Examine the subject you'll describe in great depth, from many angles, in many ways. Try studying it in various conditions with varying backgrounds. Consciously shift the focus of your attention from one characteristic to another until you can think of no more characteristics to observe. The following questions and guidelines will help increase your sensory awareness.

COLOR   What colors do you notice? How do these compare to colors of objects familiar to both you and listeners? What words do you associate with the colors? How do the various hues and shades contrast and blend? Try looking at the colors in different light and at different angles. Now what do you see? What stands out? What might both you and listeners associate these colors with that you might use to evoke a sensory response in the listeners, such as lemon yellow, Granny Smith apple green, or cardinal red?

SIZE   Can you measure precisely? To what does the size compare that is familiar to listeners, such as how does the area of a national park compare with the size of the city in which you are speaking? How does the area of a building compare to the local football field? A nerve fiber to the diameter of a blade of human hair?

FORM   What shapes do you notice? What are the names you give to these various shapes? Are listeners familiar with these names? Is it straight, curved, wavy? Are the lines vertical, horizontal, or at a slant? How do they relate to each other? What are the angles like? Is the shape like that of some familiar object, such as a pear, egg, or grain of sugar?

TEXTURE   How does the surface appear? How does it feel to touch? Do you and the listeners share any names for this texture, such as "sandpaper" or "glassy"? What other surface does it resemble? For instance, does it feel like the silky hair of a collie or the spongy mass of fibers on a scouring pad? Does it have the resilient bounce of a fine plush carpet or the harshness of denim?

LIGHT AND SHADOW   What highlights do you notice? How are the shadows related to the highlights? What is producing them? What feelings do you have as you examine the light–shadow relationships?

WEIGHT   Can you express the weight in familiar units such as pounds or kilograms? What is the relative weight per unit of volume compared to that of water? How does the weight compare to that of more familiar objects, such as a quart carton of milk, a brick, or a postage stamp? One inventive speaker had us imagine the density of a black hole by asking us to imagine the mass and weight of the sun compressed into the volume of a book of matches. Another described a Saint Bernard dog as weighing about what she did.

SOUND   Sounds are usually best presented by a recording or an imitation. When you need to describe a sound you cannot reproduce or when you want listeners to perceive certain features of a sound, words are needed to represent the unique qualities of the sound. As with other sensory descriptions, comparisons to sounds with which listeners are familiar may help, such as whinnying wail, bleating, screaming, rattling, roaring, popping, sizzling, and crunching. Most of the preceding names for sounds have the characteristic called *onomatopoeia*, meaning that the word imitates the sound it represents. *Grunt, cough, wheeze,* and *moo* are all onomatopoeic. Select such words to evoke auditory sensory experiences from your listeners.

TASTE   What familiar foods does this taste resemble? What else might it be like? Reference to familiar items is most likely to be helpful, provided the listeners are familiar with the taste of the item used for comparison. For example, when someone asks what rattlesnake meat tastes like, it is usually described by comparison to chicken or frog legs. Comparison is a major technique used to share our knowledge of tastes. We have some unique names for tastes, such as *dry* for wines that are low in sugar and the primary taste sensations of bitter, sour, sweet, and salty. Combinations of these can describe many tastes. Names of common flavors are useful, such as chocolate, vanilla, pumpkin, and lemon.

Comparing

In Chapter 7, we described how to illustrate ideas with both literal and figurative comparisons in the form of metaphors, similes, analogies, fables, and parables. Careful audience analysis and adaptation is needed before you can apply the principle that "the new is learned best by comparison with the familiar." Finding or inventing comparisons often takes vivid imagining. While analyzing the audience, you should ask frequently, "What do my listeners know that is similar to, related to, or in sharp contrast with what I want them to describe, be able to explain, or do?" Try associating freely with the idea you want listeners to understand. Then select items likely to have been part of previous experiences of audience members and develop them into metaphors, analogies, and other forms of comparison that will help listeners understand and recall. One speaker compared the back brace used for spinal curvatures to a straight jacket and a corset. She compared the body cast worn after surgery for this disorder to the shell of a turtle. These comparisons were effective because the speaker related new concepts to something familiar to the audience. The American government used to be compared to a three-legged milking stool, a useful comparison when most Americans had used or seen a stool. However, today that is a useless comparison because few Americans have seen a cow being milked by a person sitting on a three-legged stool.

In addition to commonly used metaphors, similes, and analogies, you can also use parables, fables, and contrasts for explaining through comparison. These devices are explained in Chapter 7.

Defining

Sometimes you may decide that listeners need to be able to use a new word or phrase. The new term may help listeners to perceive or think more concretely, help reduce undesirable connotations, or represent some entirely new concept. A major part of learning any new subject is becoming familiar with its special terms and concepts. For instance, medical, computer science, psychology, and engineering students must master thousands of new terms before they are competent professionals. When you speak as a specialist to listeners who are novices in your field, you will invariably have to define some terms and use synonyms for others. We will explain how to decide whether to define a term or use a synonym for it and explain several ways to define new terms that are important for achieving listener responses.

First, try to identify each key term you might use that is not familiar to your listeners. Then decide if the term will be necessary to the listeners in the future. If not, search for and use approximate synonyms already in the vocabulary of listeners. In doing so you will be translating from your specialist's dialect to the nonspecialist dialect of listeners. For example, you would use *vomiting* instead of *emesis* with parents of a sick child, *explanation* instead of *exegesis* to laymembers of your church, or *temporary information storage* instead of *RAM* to people who do not need to use the specialist's name for sections of a computer. However, when the specialist's term can be used to save time in communicating, increase precision, or serve as a memory landmark, you will need to define the new term. There are three major ways to define terms so that they are grounded in sensory experiences.

(1) **Classification and differentiation.** The term defined is related to some broader concept, then distinguished on one or more characteristics from other subclasses of the broad concept. For example, "A gimlet is a type of drill (broad concept) that has an attached handle and screw shank (differentiating it from drill bits, augers, post drills, spade bits, etc.)." This is the type of definition used to identify plants and animals.

(2) **Examples.** A list of examples can indicate the type and characteristics of items referred to by the term being defined. For example, a speaker said, "By 'flora' I am referring to all plant life in the swamp, such as moss, algae, weeds, grasses, trees, and fungi." Another student said, "When I say 'Big Ten,' I am referring to any or all of the schools in the Big Ten conference: Northwestern, Iowa, Ohio State, Wisconsin, ..." Another said, "Rodents are gnawing animals, including rats, porcupines, mice, squirrels, beavers, gerbils, and others with large front teeth." The examples must, of course, be familiar to the listeners.

(3) **Describing operations.** This method of defining yields what are called *operational definitions*. An operational definition of a cake is its recipe: Follow these steps and you will have a cake. A concept is defined operationally by describing steps to be taken in a procedure, the outcome of which defines the term. For example, "By GPA I mean the average grade arrived at by converting letter grades to numbers with $A=4$, $B=3$, $C=2$, and $D=1$, then adding these numbers and dividing the sum by the number of grades entered into the sum. The quotient thus derived is the GPA." "By 'inflated,' I mean that a reading of from 50 to 60 pounds per square inch has been registered on a standard tire gauge." Operational definitions are most often used in explaining mathematical and statistical concepts, measurements, and procedures or processes. They are common in research reports.

Visual Aids

In Chapter 11 we explained the importance, principles, and types of visual and other sensory aids to use while speaking to an audience. Visuals are often essential if listeners are to be able to respond with some demonstration of understanding. Describing is usually much easier when both speaker and listeners are looking at an example of the object, a chart of the procedure, a graph of the statistics, and so on. Visual comparisons help listeners form the images and associations used for recall from long-term memory. An acronym or other mnemonic technique can be written on a chart or chalkboard and used throughout the speech. Comparisons and contrasts represented visually are more vividly perceived and recalled than those received only through the ears. Steps in an operational definition can be listed on a chart or handout. The point is this: Speaking to inform means planning ways to enhance images for your listeners. When the images are shown as well as described verbally, recall is more certain than when communicating is limited to verbal symbols.[4]

▶ Examples of Speeches to Inform

A Preparation Outline for a Speech to Inform

Following is an outline prepared by Stephanie Pomonis-Seyer for a group of 20 classmates enrolled in a basic public-speaking course. Unlike her, most of her audience members were unmarried, and none knew how to appraise a diamond. Notice the following characteristics of the plan Stephanie created to guide her while speaking extemporaneously:

1. A descriptive title related to the listener's perspective as customer.
2. The central idea is a simple declarative sentence indicating a schema focusing on characteristics as the topics of main points in the body of the speech.
3. The desired response statement describes behavior that Stephanie could observe as a basis for judging how well she had accomplished her purpose in speaking. For instance, she could ask people to name and explain the four characteristics and what to look for about each of them.
4. All four functions of an introduction are indicated.
5. Concise declarative sentences have been formulated to express each main point clearly. Also notice that these sentences use the mnemonic device of alliteration (same beginning letter for key words) and that they are worded in parallel so that each begins with a topic, followed by a verb and distinguishing feature.
6. Developmental materials are indicated for all main points and/or subpoints. Visuals with developmental details are indicated in parentheses.
7. Transitions are carefully planned and indicated in parentheses. These not only link ideas but also emphasize them.

8. The conclusion has a plan to reemphasize the central idea and main points with a detailed summary. The application (II) refers back to the opening example to provide a sense of closure.

Buying a Diamond with Confidence

Central idea: The four most important characteristics to evaluate when purchasing a diamond are its cut, color, clarity, and carat weight.

Desired response: I want my listeners to be able to explain how each of the four "C" characteristics of diamonds is related to the value of a diamond.

INTRODUCTION

I. Todd and Jane were cheated when buying an engagement ring.
II. Many of you will purchase some type of diamond.
III. I'm a diamond specialist in jewelry department at Brandeis Department Store.
IV. The "four C's" to examine when purchasing a diamond are its cut, color, clarity, and carat weight.

(Transition: The first characteristic to examine is the cut.)

BODY

I. The cut of a diamond affects its brilliance.
   A. For maximum brilliance, a diamond must be cut by experts.
      1. Cuts are based on scientifically determined angles or facets.
         a. Like a prism.
         b. The more brilliance, the more value it has.
      2. Most diamonds are cut with 58 facets.
   B. Diamonds can be cut into different shapes.
      1. Six basic shapes (chart 1).
      2. A matter of preference, not brilliance.

(Transition: The second characteristic to examine is color.)

II. The color of a diamond affects its sparkle.
   A. A colorless diamond acts best as a prism.
      1. Color affects reflected light.
      2. Examples (chart 2).
   B. Color is graded on the Gemological Institute of America scale from colorless to yellow.
      1. Differences in color are subtle.
      2. Each color grade is assigned a letter.
         a. Examples (chart 3).
         b. Letters on a merchandise label.

(Transition: The third characteristic to examine is clarity.)

285

III. The clarity of a diamond affects its reflectivity.
   A. A diamond free of inclusions is highest in reflectivity and value.
      1. An inclusion is an internal or external flaw in the diamond.
      2. Flaws interfere with the passage of light.
      3. Minute flaws do not affect durability, just clarity.
   B. Clarity is determined under 10-power magnification.

(Transition: The fourth characteristic to examine is carat weight.)

IV. The carat weight of a diamond directly determines its value.
   A. The size of a diamond is measured in carats.
      1. About 1/140 ounce.
      2. Divided into 100 "points."
   B. Value is determined by carat weight when the other three characteristics are unchanged.
      1. Two diamonds of the same size may be unequal in value (chart 4).
      2. Bigger is not necessarily better.

CONCLUSION

I. I have shown you the four characteristics to look for when purchasing a diamond: cut, color, clarity, and carat weight.
II. Remember what to look for on each of these characteristics and you will not find yourselves in Todd and Jane's place.

REFERENCES

1. *Transformation: A Guide to Gemstones* (Chelsa, MA: Town and Country Jewelry Manufacturing Corporation, 1983).
2. *The Four C's* (National Gemological Institute, 1984).

An Example of Speaking to Inform

Wendy Meyer presented this speech to inform her instructor and 23 classmates. Wendy chose her subject well. She had studied arthritis extensively during 13 years of suffering from the disease. A questionnaire had indicated very little knowledge and a lot of misinformation about arthritis existing in the minds of her listeners.

As you read the transcript, try to visualize a dark-haired woman in her late twenties approaching a lectern in front of a typical lecture classroom with four rows of fixed seats fastened on curving platforms, each of which is about a foot higher than the row immediately closer to the lectern. To one side of the lectern, Wendy placed an easel on which sat a large plain white card covering two charts she had prepared. One visual was a diagram of a hip joint with labels to all the parts mentioned in the speech. The other was a list of symptoms labeled "Warning Signs." These visuals are reproduced in Figures 14.3 and 14.4.

CHAPTER 14** Speaking to Inform

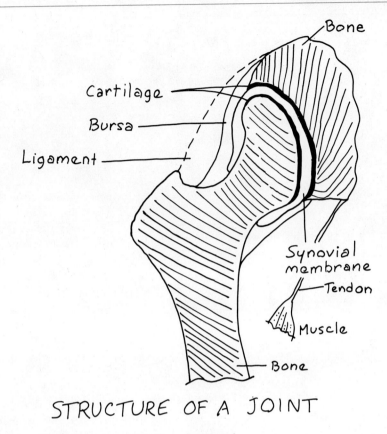

STRUCTURE OF A JOINT

Figure 14.3 Wendy's diagram; magic marker on poster card.

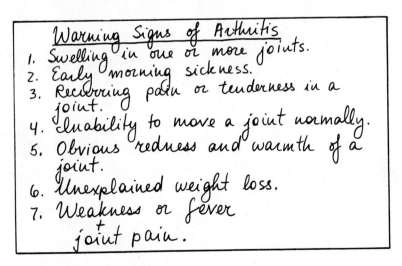

Figure 14.4 Wendy's chart listing symptoms.

COMMENTARY

Suspense is used to direct attention. Relates topic to all listeners.

Demonstrates importance with statistical evidence.

Personal competence.

Identifies with belief of many listeners.

Testimony of importance to all—motivation to listen.

Preview of main points in body of speech, focusing attention.

Rhetorical question used as transition.

Statement of first main point.

Subpoint A. Here she uncovered first chart, with diagram and labels, pointing to each label as she named each part of the joint. Note the extensive use of comparisons as she describes.

Simile.

Simile.

Simile.

Simile.

Internal summary by pointing to parts on chart.

Subpoint B.

Contrast (comparison). Analogy to defensive army.

ARTHRITIS

IT does not discriminate over whether you are a man, woman, or a child. IT is a painful part of the lives of over 36 million people in the United States, 250,000 of whom are children. IT is arthritis. I have had arthritis for over 13 years and suffered needlessly the first few years because I thought I was too young to have arthritis. Old people get arthritis; my grandmother had arthritis. Not me.

Jane Brody, author of the *New York Times Guide to Personal Health*, says that virtually all of us, if we live long enough, will develop arthritis in one or more of our joints. Today I am going to tell you what arthritis is, how it can be diagnosed, and what treatment is available.

Exactly what is this truly universal illness? Arthritis can be described as an inflammation of the joints. To understand arthritis, you must first know the basic structure of a joint.

A joint is where two bones meet; it acts as a hinge mechanism to help move the various parts of our bodies. Cartilage is on one end of the bones. It is a spongelike substance that keeps the bones from rubbing each other raw. The cartilage is nourished by the synovial fluid. This fluid is an oil-like substance secreted from the synovial membrane. This membrane looks much like plastic food wrap. Just outside the joint are ligaments, tendons, and muscles. The ligaments and the tendons are very much alike in that they are both cord-like structures. The ligament is what connects the two bones to each other. The bursa is a fluid-filled sac. This lubricates the muscle and the tendons that hold them in next to the bone. The combination of all these various body parts is what helps keep the joint strong and stable.

However, when the joint is inflamed it is not strong, and it is not stable. Inflammation is the normal reaction of the body's defense system. In a healthy body, the immune system—the body's defense system—rushes to the injured area and eventually heals the area. However, in an arthritic body the immune system becomes confused and it starts attacking healthy tissue.

COMMENTARY

Testimony.

Simile to Christianity.

Definition.

Transition to second main point.

Second main point, parallel in form to first. Subpoint A. She uncovers chart listing warning signs for self-diagnosis and points to each to reinforce her verbal message.

Brief examples.

Subpoint B.

Brief examples.

Transition to third main point; note how it links two main points.

Third main point, parallel to previous two.

Subpoint A.

Example.

Subpoint B. Comparison (balance).
Explanation.

Subpoint C.

Contrast between treatment and quackery, "cures."

ARTHRITIS

The Arthritis Foundation says that arthritis refers to more than 100 different diseases. You might compare this to the Christian religion. There is one Christian religion, but a variety of denominations. The various types of arthritis are part of a larger group called *rheumatic diseases*. In rheumatic diseases, the joint is inflamed and also the surrounding tissue.

Well, now that we know what arthritis involves, how can we tell if we have it?

Arthritis can be diagnosed by you and your doctor. You can make a preliminary identification by being aware of the warning signs: swelling in one or more joints; early morning sickness; recurring pain or tenderness in any joint; inability to move a joint normally; obvious redness and warmth in a joint; or unexplained weight loss, weakness, or fever combined with joint pain. If you have any of these symptoms for over two weeks, it is wise to see your doctor. Your doctor may run a series of tests: blood, urine, and X ray. He or she may test fluid from your joints and examine small samples of joint tissue. Your family doctor may refer you to a rheumatologist who is a specialist in this area.

Although there is no cure, people who are diagnosed as having arthritis need not despair. An arthritis victim is not doomed to eternal pain.

Arthritis can be treated. Treatment works best when it is started early. Most treatment programs include some combination of medication, rest, and exercise. Aspirin is still the most widely prescribed medication because it has both an anti-inflammatory agent and a pain killer.

It is important to find the best balance between rest and exercise. You do not want to fatigue your joints, and yet you want to keep them moving freely.

Now all this takes time, and you must follow your doctor's orders. Some people become impatient, and they get caught up in arthritis quackery. There is no miracle cure. If it sounds

(continued)

COMMENTARY	ARTHRITIS
Testimony, citing sources concisely.	too good to be true, it is. Author Jane Brody and the Arthritis Foundation both concur on a 1-to-25 ratio. That is, for every $1 spent on legitimate arthritis treatment, there are $25 spent in arthritis quackery. People spend $1 billion each year on quack devices and remedies.
Statistics show importance of the contrast.	
Conclusion. Application of this knowledge to lives of listeners. Note reference back to introduction for sense of closure.	IT is arthritis, a disease that will at some point affect everyone who lives long enough. IT can affect your daily life in a simple move, like going up and down stairs or kneeling down and trying to get back up again. Many people suffer needlessly from the pain of arthritis.
Application combined with a summary of the main points in body.	If you have wondered if you or someone you know has arthritis, you now know how it is diagnosed. You are familiar with the major symptoms. You know it can be diagnosed positively. You also know there is a treatment available to give relief, but that only a quack promises a cure.

▶ Summary

Sharing information through verbal signals is the most human of all social activities. To become skilled in informative public speaking requires knowledge of basic principles of rhetoric, attention, and memory. *Information* refers to descriptions of direct experiences and noncontroversial generalizations. Only the speaker can decide if the primary general purpose will be to inform or persuade. If knowledgeable people disagree with your central idea, your speech would be classified as one to persuade. Because knowledge is expanding and professional people are becoming more specialized, skills in speaking to inform are vital to every educated person. We described three major types of informative speaking situations: instructing, reporting, and briefing.

Public speaking requires careful audience analysis as the basis for specific adaptations. After discovering what listeners know related to what you want them to understand, you can invent ways to motivate them to listen. The more listeners are actively involved with your speech, the more information they are likely to retain.

Informative speeches should be organized by one of the basic schemas for main points: chronological, spatial, causal, problem solving, or other sequence of interrelated topics. Informative speeches need a preview of main points, restatements of them during the speech, and a final summary of them in the conclusion. These restatements help focus attention on main points and encourage the mental review by listeners necessary for long-term memory. Transitions also serve this purpose.

Informative speakers can consciously create mnemonic devices to help listeners recall the structure of main points in a speech. Visual schemas using spatial positions in mental images or visual associations can be invented. Acronyms and acrostics in which first letters of key words are used to create a new word or sentence are helpful for remembering lists of concepts. Rhyme schemes can be invented to make main points easier to recall in correct sequence. Any such mnemonic device must be stressed until it is embedded in long-term memory of listeners.

How you develop main points can also make a significant difference in the amount of listener understanding and recall. Visual description based on detailed observation by the speaker helps listeners to have vicarious sensory experience, thus effectively inputting information through more than one sensory channel. Color, size, form, texture, light, weight, sound, and taste can all be described in words shared by listeners and speaker, thus evoking similar sensory experiences. Comparison is a major method for explaining new ideas, especially abstract concepts and beliefs. However, comparison is effective only if the new object or concept is compared to past experiences of the listener.

New words listeners will need to understand should be defined by classification and differentiation, use of examples, or describing operations to which they refer. If specialist jargon will not be important to the listeners, translate the jargon into synonyms with which they are acquainted.

Finally, development of ideas should include visual and other sensory supplements that are likely to be effective in achieving the desired response from listeners.

▶ Learning Activities

1. Create two opposing central ideas about each of two different issues, concepts, or topics, such as security versus freedom or academic versus athletic excellence in universities.
2. Observe a leaf, ball, or other simple object for five or six minutes, shifting the focus of your attention repeatedly from characteristic to characteristic. Then describe this object to a small group of classmates who will next try to pick the object from a small pile of objects of that type.
3. Imagine you are settled into your career and are going to brief a group of people who need a general understanding of a subject in your area of specialization. Prepare to present this briefing to your classmates. As an alternative, brief a group of classmates in preparation for a tour of your hometown, place of work, or a public building.

4. Prepare for and present a four- to six-minute speech, the purpose of which is for the listeners to be able to perform some procedure or explain some process involving from two to four major steps. Plan, create, and use appropriate sensory aids when you speak to your class.

5. Plan and present a one-minute (or shorter) definition of some abstract concept, such as "educated," "brotherhood," "prejudiced," "freedom," or "rule of law" using one or more of the techniques for defining explained in Chapter 13.

6. Below are four topics for public speeches. For each, write a desired response statement for a speech to inform and for a speech to persuade (eight statements in all). Compare your statements with those created by three or four classmates. See if you can all agree about which statements are clearly informative and those that are clearly persuasive in intent.

> The Bill of Rights.
> The college or university you attend.
> Soap operas.
> The cost of medical care.

Notes

1. Benjamin S. Bloom (ed.), *Taxonomy of Educational Objectives: Handbook I, Cognitive Domain* (New York: David McKay Co., 1956); Norman E. Gronlund, *Stating Objectives for Classroom Instruction*, 2d ed. (New York: Macmillan, 1978), Ch. 3.

2. Steven V. Owen, H. Parker Blount, and Henry Moscow, *Educational Psychology: An Introduction* (Boston: Little, Brown, 1978), p. 200.

3. J. Ross and K. A. Lawrence, "Some Observations on Memory Artifice," *Psychonomic Science* 13 (1968):107–108; G. H. Bower, "Analysis of a Mnemonic Device," *American Scientist* 58 (1970):496–510.

4. J. R. Levin, "Educational Applications of Mnemonic Pictures: Possibilities Beyond Your Wildest Imagination," in A. A. Sheikh (ed.), *Imagery in the Educational Process* (Farmingdale, NY: Baywood, 1985).

15

Speaking to Persuade

Questions to Guide Reading and Review

1. What is a *target audience?* How and why are target audiences selected by speakers?

2. What can cognitive balance and dissonance theories contribute to the strategy of a persuasive speech?

3. How is a listener's level of ego involvement with an issue related to changes in his or her belief?

4. What are the minimum components of any complete argument? What is the function of each component?

5. How do inductive, deductive, causal, and analogous reasoning differ in the way a speaker develops them as arguments?

6. How should a speaker select evidence to support arguments? Why is it essential to use "new" evidence?

7. What are the five major types of motives in Maslow's theory? Can you provide several examples of each type that might be effective with different types of listeners?

8. What are the five major steps in the motivated sequence? What does the speaker do during each step? When is this sequence appropriate?

Key Terms

Analogous reasoning
Argument
Balance theory
Causal reasoning
Cognitive dissonance theory
Competence
Deductive reasoning
Dynamism
Esteem needs

Emotional appeal
Evidence
Inductive reasoning
Inoculation theory
Motivated sequence
Persuasion
Physiological needs
Primacy–recency principle

Reasoning
Reasons-why schema
Security needs
Self-actualization needs
Sleeper effect
Social needs
Social judgment theory
Stock issues
Two-sided approach

Every day we are bombarded by messages aimed at influencing our opinions, attitudes, and behaviors. Similarly, we attempt to influence the opinions, attitudes, and behaviors of other people. Understanding how persuasion occurs is vital. As individuals and as citizens we need to discriminate between would-be persuaders who are competent, honest, and concerned for the common good and those who are incompetent, dishonest, and concerned only with personal wealth and power. Knowledge of persuasion can help us decide what to support and what to oppose and how to influence others to do likewise.

In previous chapters, while developing other aspects of public speaking, we presented many principles and techniques that are involved in persuasive speaking. In this chapter, we review some of these, elaborate on others, and include additional principles and techniques to apply in your efforts to influence beliefs and actions. First, we define the concept *persuasion*, then describe the major sources of persuasive influence and how to include them in a speech to persuade. Finally, we focus on how to organize speeches to persuade.

▶ Persuasion of a Target Audience

Since the ancient Greek rhetoricians, persuasion has been studied as a means of influencing others. The term *persuasion* refers to both a process and a result. It is impossible to separate these two major factors when defining persuasion in a way useful to public speakers. By *persuasion* we mean a conscious attempt by a speaker to influence the beliefs, attitudes, or actions of listeners that produces some specific desired response. This definition includes both a conscious attempt on the part of the speaker to persuade and the accomplishment of the desired response. A speaker who fails to evoke the desired response from listeners has not persuaded them successfully.

A practical speaker aspires to an achievable goal. Members of an audience vary in level of commitment to existing beliefs, their perceptions of the speaker as a credible source, and their receptiveness to new information and ideas. Successful persuasive speakers take these factors into account when they decide on a *target audience. Target* refers to that part of the total audience the speaker has decided it is realistic to attempt to influence through the speech. This means giving up on trying to convince or convert the other listeners because the chances of doing so are remote.

In a typical public-speaking class, a student speaker might have determined that some people in the class are absolutely opposed to a central idea, because it is clearly contradictory to their core beliefs. They have publicly demonstrated their opposition to the idea and defined themselves in terms of its opposite. For instance, a speaker might advocate laws permitting any woman to select an abortion up to a certain time in pregnancy, but three classmates have previously identified themselves as active participants in "right to life" efforts. At best, the speaker can hope that one or two of these people may remember a piece of evidence that will evoke mild uncertainty. The speaker might also have determined that four other students are already active supporters of the position. At most the speaker might reinforce a belief of one or two of these people. The other 15 students in the class have relatively little knowledge of, involvement in, or strong feelings on the topic of abortion. Any beliefs they hold about it are incidental, subject to change on the basis of new evidence and reasoning. These 15 students are the target audience at which the speaker will direct the speech. The practical speaker will focus on the needs, values, and beliefs of this target group when preparing evidence and arguments to support the central idea.

▶ Sources of Persuasive Influence

What are the forces that combine to produce the effects we call persuasion? In one sense they are innumerable, a combination of all that has brought a person to the present and all that is acting at the moment to produce change. Understanding these forces can be made simpler by classifying them into a few categories. Aristotle, a Greek scholar who lived from 384 to 325 B.C., was the first to write that persuasion was effected by a combination of three types of forces: the perceived credibility of the speaker, *ethos*; evidence and reasoning accepted by an audience as valid, *logos*; and emotional appeals, *pathos*.[1] Effective persuaders seek to coordinate all three types of forces that influence beliefs and action.

Persuasion is not in the signals that a speaker sends, but occurs in listeners, who are motivated by needs, influenced by what they accept as truth, and want to follow people they find attractive. All persuasive influences are perceptual responses of listeners to messages. Credibility is not a quality of a speaker but a perception a listener has of a speaker. Evidence is not functional until accepted as truth by a listener, nor is reasoning meaningful unless perceived as valid by that same listener. Appeals are not emotional or motivating; they may evoke emotional responses and motives of listeners. The task of the persuasive speaker is to work with all three of these sources of persuasion, attempting to balance them in a way that will evoke the desired response from an audience.

Speaker Credibility

You learned in Chapter 9 that before starting into the body of a speech, a speaker must gain the trust of his or her listeners as a credible source of information on the subject. In the absence of perceived credibility, securing a desired response is virtually impossible. Credibility is a perception listeners have of you as a speaker on a particular subject. You are only as credible as your listeners perceive you to be. In this section we briefly elaborate on the components of credibility and discuss several strategies you can use to evoke a favorable perception by listeners.

BASES OF CREDIBILITY   Many attempts have been made to determine what causes listeners to perceive speakers as credible. Most experts agree that competence and trustworthiness are the two most basic components of speaker credibility.[2] At a minimum, speakers need to be concerned about the image they have with listeners in each of these areas. In addition, in many combinations of topic and situation, dynamism and other perceived traits may be important to the speaker's perceived credibility.[3]

Competence refers to listener perceptions of a public speaker's expertise in relation to the subject matter of the speech. A speaker perceived competent to discuss financial planning because of extensive experience as a successful financial consultant may not be perceived as competent to make predictions about college football standings. The perception of a speaker's competence is always subject specific.

Trustworthiness is based on the perception that a speaker will tell the truth. The trustworthy speaker is perceived as being sincere and willing to place the interests of his or her listeners above self-interest (often called *goodwill*). For example, a tobacco company spokesperson, advocating smoking for the benefits of stress reduction and relaxation, would be perceived by thoughtful listeners as speaking only out of self-interest, and be attributed low credibility. Studies have shown that listeners tend to rate a speaker higher in trustworthiness when the speaker is perceived to be speaking against his or her own personal interest.[4] To illustrate, a student on an athletic scholarship advocating that all students must meet the same high academic admissions standards would likely be perceived as more credible than would an honor student advocating the same position.

Dynamism was found to be an important characteristic in a number of studies of credibility. *Dynamism* refers to spontaneous but controlled enthusiasm, indicated by energetic delivery. Dynamism requires that verbal and nonverbal behavior be complementary. Sometimes the word *charismatic* is used to describe speakers who are dynamic. Speakers high in dynamism seem to captivate listeners with their physical animation.

Perceptions of a speaker's credibility are subject to constant change. The audience may have a preconceived notion of the speaker that can be reinforced, weakened, or even destroyed during a speech. A speaker needs to be aware of the difference between prior and acquired credibility and take necessary steps to enhance credibility while speaking to an audience. Prior credibility is the perception listeners have of you prior to speaking. Most student speakers have little prior credibility with listeners. Acquired credibility is the perception listeners have of you as a direct result of what you say and do during your speech. There are several strategies you can utilize to gain credibility.

ACQUIRING CREDIBILITY   Listeners judge a speaker in the first few moments, and these judgments are hard to change. As advertisers tell us, "You never get a second chance to make a first impression." In order to strengthen the potential for persuasion, the speaker should emphasize identification with the listeners. Identification involves establishing a sense of association and common ground with the audience members. You want a positive relationship, so never attack or blame an audience.

Listeners can readily identify with the speaker whom they perceive to be the kind of person they like and admire.[5] The speaker can increase the chance of this occurring by associating him or her self with people admired by listeners. This can be done by using quotations from sources deemed highly credible by the audience, mentioning personal links to respected leaders, and speaking positively about people respected by the listeners. Identification may be increased by expressing shared values, beliefs, and interests. The goal is to have the audience silently think "yes": "Yes, I like this person"; "Yes, the speaker is a lot like me"; "Yes, I want to be associated with the speaker and the speaker's values, ideas, beliefs, and plans."

Speakers who are perceived as being competent in advance begin speaking with a tremendous advantage. When a person who will introduce you as a speaker is unacquainted with you and your work, provide that individual with a data sheet outlining your background, experience, accomplishments, awards, and so on related to your subject. Even a few minutes of quiet conversation with an emcee will allow that person to find common ground with you personally. For example, notice how your perception of Don Ross is influenced by the following introductory remarks:

> As members of Ducks Unlimited, we have been very interested in preserving local refuge areas and in increasing their use by migrating birds. Don Ross, professor of ornithology at our college, has just completed an extensive study of changes in flight patterns of several species of waterfowl over the past decade. He believes this information will help us in our effort to stimulate legislators to spend more money in support of our project at DeSoto Bend Wildlife Refuge.

In some cases, such as your first speech in class, listeners have no perception of you as a source of information. All credibility at the end of the speech will have been acquired while speaking. From the initial seconds when you approach the rostrum, everything you do may affect credibility, including your appearance, gestures, evidence, reasoning, and organization. Describing your competence relevant to the topic can enhance credibility, so be sure that the plan for your introduction includes a description of your experience, study, or other ways in which you became knowledgeable about your topic.[6] For example, in her introduction, Patty said this to her public speaking classmates:

> After my brother committed suicide, I was driven to learn everything I could about why teenagers kill themselves and if there was anything I could do to prevent that from happening. I wrote a term paper in a psychology course about teenage suicides. I don't think there is any research on the subject I haven't seen.

A speaker may increase perceived credibility throughout the speech by continued expressions of good will, organization that is easily followed, and other signs of thorough preparation. Dramatic wording, meaningful comparisons, and citations of sources are signs of such preparation. An abundance of evidence contributes greatly to the perception of credibility, as well as producing the basis for long-lasting conviction and *inoculation* against countermessages.[7] You can also work to increase listeners' perceptions of you as a dynamic speaker. Many of the suggestions offered in Chapter 13 concerning delivery will help you speak with fluency, energy, and sincerity. In short, by improving delivery skills, you can enhance perceived dynamism.

Important as perceived credibility is to the persuasive speaker, it alone will not produce a lasting change in beliefs of critical listeners unless combined with *logos*, the persuasive impact of evidence and reasoning.

Evidence and Reasoning

Long-lasting changes of belief require evidence and reasoning perceived as valid by listeners. *Evidence* refers to all the information you use to support an argument or conclusion, such as examples, statistics, testimony, and comparisons. *Reasoning* is the procedure by which you draw inferences or conclusions from the evidence. Adequate planning for speaking persuasively includes determining what listeners already believe with regard to the speaker's central idea, how much these beliefs matter to them, and what evidence would contradict existing beliefs while supporting the ones you want listeners to accept. You should sort through the information you have available to select the evidence and reasoning patterns most likely to influence listeners to agree with your position on a controversial issue.

THEORIES ABOUT CHANGES IN BELIEF Theories about cognitive balance and dissonance, the sleeper effect, inoculation, and ego involvement with beliefs will help you accomplish the tasks of analysis, selection of evidence, and planning arguments.

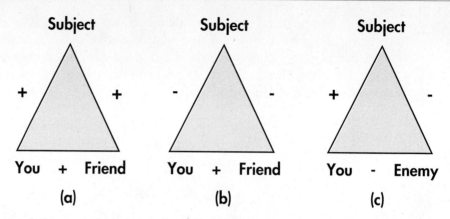

Figure 15.1 Types of balanced relationships. If you and a person you like (+) have opinions that are both positive (a) or both negative (b) toward a subject, cognitive balance exists. If you have a negative feeling toward another person and you disagree on an issue, balance also exists (c).

Cognitive Dissonance Theory   The theory of cognitive dissonance was developed as a refinement of *balance theory*, which was originated and developed by two psychologists, Fritz Heider and Theodore Newcomb. According to balance theory, we humans seek a sense of balance or harmony among our ideas and personal relationships (see Figure 15.1).[8] To create a balance between our feelings and beliefs, we want people whom we like to agree with us and people whom we dislike to disagree with us on important issues. That creates a balance between our feelings and our beliefs. If you and a close friend agree that tuition is too high, the local city government has abused taxation rights, and that the Republican party is losing ground, a balance exists. However, if your friend thinks tuition is too low, that city taxes are reasonable, or that the Republican party is improving its influence, you will feel some degree of psychological imbalance or dissonance. The amount of imbalance will depend on how important each of these issues is to your self-concept. There is also balance when someone you do not respect disagrees with you on a vital belief. If a neighbor you dislike supports a politician you think is unqualified, you feel balance.

Although balance theory addresses the need for consistency among beliefs, feelings toward people, and their beliefs on the issue being discussed, it does not deal with levels of commitment to either beliefs or people. Leon Festinger, another influential psychologist, developed a more elaborate balance theory that he called *cognitive dissonance theory* to include the degree of commitment people have to both beliefs and other people.[9] Festinger predicts that when two beliefs are contradictory (idea imbalance), we will experience psychological tension called *dissonance*, which we feel compelled to reduce. Dissonance results from an inconsistency between an existing belief and new information that contradicts that belief. According to cognitive dissonance theory, there are several ways in which we can attempt to reestablish cognitive balance:

1.   Decrease our degree of commitment to original beliefs.

2. Change our perception of the source of new contradictory information.

3. Discredit the new information by calling it misleading, distorted, or untrue.

4. Limit our exposure to additional new contradictory information.

5. Forget the discomforting information.

6. Seek out information that reinforces our existing belief.

In practice, the individual who experiences cognitive dissonance usually relies on a combination of these strategies to restore balance.

Let's look at an example. John just bought a new Honda Accord. He invested time and money in the purchase and is satisfied that he made a good investment. A few months after John bought his car, a friend, Tim, who owns an auto parts store, asks him why he bought a Honda Accord. Tim gives John some pamphlets that he says will prove that Hondas are not nearly so good as the advertisements claim. Tim scolds John for not asking his opinion before buying and tells John to see him before buying another new car. John feels dissonance! His beliefs that he made an excellent choice and that his friend Tim really knows cars are not congruent. John needs to reduce dissonance and restore cognitive balance. John can do this in several ways:

1. He can tell himself that his decision wasn't very important. After all, he changes cars every two years; he will buy a different make next time. "I took a chance on a foreign car. If it doesn't work out, next time I'll buy American like Tim says I should and like I always have in the past." **John decreases his degree of commitment to the original belief.**

2. He can tell himself Tim would be critical of any car he bought, because he wasn't consulted: "Tim thinks he knows everything about cars." His liking for Tim goes down some. **John changes his perception of the source.**

3. He can tell himself that the pamphlets Tim gave him were put out by American auto manufacturers: "Of course they are going to put down Honda and support their own cars." **John discredits the new information.**

4. He can throw the literature away without reading it: "Who wants to read such propaganda!" **John limits his exposure to information.**

5. He can only half listen to Tim. **John forgets the information.**

6. He can reread the materials he originally used to support his decision to buy a Honda and talk with satisfied Honda owners, who all agree, "We are smart." **John seeks out additional confirming information.**

From this example you can see how important maintaining your credibility and using incontrovertible, memorable evidence is to achieving persuasive responses.

The Sleeper Effect   In rare instances, contradictory evidence that has been presented so dramatically that listeners do not forget or ignore it has a *sleeper effect*. The dissonance felt between the evidence and an existing belief cannot be suppressed. To remove this dissonance, days or even weeks after hearing the speech the listener modifies the belief to be more congruent with the remembered evidence.[10] This sleeper effect often occurs after the source of the information has been forgotten. Vivid examples or statistics often result in the sleeper effect.

Inoculation Theory   In addition to choosing evidence, another decision you face in planning how to use evidence and reasoning is whether to take a one-sided or two-sided approach to a controversial issue. For example, if you favor a required period of military training or public service for all American youths, should you only give arguments and evidence supporting that position or also discuss some arguments for other positions on the issue? If members of a target audience believe strongly that there should be an all-volunteer military force, they cannot accept your central idea without first becoming dissonant toward their present beliefs. Usually you will be more effective with critical thinkers if you present reasonable arguments in favor of each position, showing how your proposed policy would do more good for both the individuals involved and the nation as a whole. You will certainly need good evidence to support the arguments you use to refute the idea of an all-volunteer force. As dissonance theory indicates, you must refute that idea before the listeners can seriously consider the idea of a universal draft.[11]

If listeners are neutral on the issue, it still may be more persuasive in the long run for you to spend some time giving the main arguments for positions that contradict the policy you propose and refuting them. You can then show the comparative superiority of your policy to listener-held beliefs with evidence and reasoning. This *inoculates* the listeners against counterarguments to your central idea by giving them evidence and arguments to contradict such arguments when they hear them at some later date. *Inoculation theory* is now being applied extensively in advertisements. Research demonstrates that inoculation can be an effective strategy.[12]

Inoculation theory has implications for organization, also. Usually you need some sort of problem-solving schema for main points, such as the applied criteria or comparative advantages sequences, which allow you to directly compare proposals for solving the problem about which you are speaking.

Social Judgment Theory   How people will evaluate messages that contradict their present beliefs depends on how far the new idea deviates from their present position. If the new idea deviates too far, the result is likely to be immediate rejection of the message. However, if the new idea deviates only slightly, the listener might accept the new information and alter previous beliefs to avoid dissonance. *Social judgment theory* explains that the greater a person's ego involvement with a position or idea the less likely the person is to be persuaded by new information dissonant with the idea. *Ego involvement* is a measure of how important an idea is to a person's self-concept. The amount of ego involvement is affected by how long the belief has been held; how the belief was acquired; whether or not the belief was publicly expressed; and how much time, effort, and money were invested in the belief. Some people are so ego involved with some beliefs that they label themselves with a position: "I'm a feminist," "I'm a Democrat," or "I'm an environmentalist." It is very difficult to modify the belief of a person who is that ego involved with a belief. To include such persons in a target audience may be impractical. Only repeated exposure over time to the new idea can have any effect on such a person's belief.

As illustrated in Figure 15.2, our beliefs fall into three levels of ego involvement: incidental, secondary, and core beliefs. *Incidental beliefs* are those in which we have little ego investment. A change in an incidental belief involves little or no change in self-concept. For example, whether asphalt or portland cement concrete is superior for highway building is incidental to most of us. Your favorite movie, restaurant, and color are probably all incidental to your self-concept. These beliefs are temporary and can be changed easily by providing new information that contradicts them.

Secondary beliefs are developed through interpersonal contacts as well as from information received from mass media, political, and religious leaders. The strength of a secondary belief is related to our judgment of people we

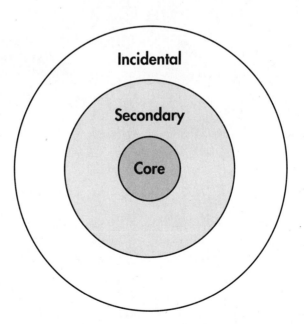

Figure 15.2 Three levels of ego involvement: The closer a belief is to our core, the more difficult it is to change.

associate with the belief. Secondary beliefs are more resistant to change than incidental beliefs because the speaker must discredit an existing authority or replace that authority with a more credible one. Ego involvement is much stronger than with incidental beliefs. For example, Norm may be a Democrat because his parents were Democrats. He reads publications that support the Democratic party and participates in state party activities. His ego involvement will be quite high with a candidate running on the Democratic ticket. To convince him that the Republican candidate is superior would be extremely difficult for he is highly ego involved with the Democratic candidate and party.

Core beliefs are the most ego involving. They are a direct result of personal experiences. Many are formed early in childhood; others develop as we interact with significant other people through life. Social values, parenting techniques, and religious beliefs are examples of core beliefs. They are very difficult to change, because they involve the greatest degree of self-concept for the listener. It is extremely unlikely that one speech would seriously influence a listener who held an opposing core belief. Repeated exposure to countermessages and credible people who hold the new belief are typically required to produce change in a core belief, and many such beliefs cannot be changed.

When planning for persuasive speaking, you should determine what listeners believe in relation to your central idea, how much it matters to them, and what evidence might contradict their present belief and support the one you want them to accept. You must present information so forcefully that listeners cannot ignore it, will readily understand it, and will remember it to achieve the change of belief you desire. The strategies used to persuade should be based on the degree of listener ego involvement with the central idea, as well as on what is ethical. You cannot make anyone change a belief or practice. Listeners ultimately persuade themselves. You can, however, help listeners do so by providing them with sound arguments from memorable evidence.

ARGUMENTS   A valid *argument* consists of three components:

1. Evidence (**data**)
2. A demonstrated or accepted connection between the evidence and the conclusion you want to draw (**warrant**)
3. The conclusion itself (**claim**)

An entire argument is invalid if any one of its component parts is not sound. Philosopher Stephen Toulmin organizes the components of an argument as shown in Figure 15.3.[13] The speaker begins by making a claim (conclusion) based on data (evidence) that are presented in the speech. The connection between data and claim is called the *warrant*. Sometimes a speaker may fear that listeners will not believe the data or warrant. Then it is necessary to provide special support, such as describing the source of the data, providing a detailed explanation of the logic of the warrant, or giving expert testimony in behalf of the warrant (see Figure 15.4). Toulmin's model of an argument can

Figure 15.3 Primary elements in Toulmin's model of an argument. (**Source:** Stephen Toulmin, *The Uses of Argument.* New York: Cambridge University Press, 1944.)

also include a *qualifier*, which is a statement about the degree of probability of the claim and any reservations about it. Reservations include circumstances that would affect the conclusion arrived at through the argument.

While preparing, you can test arguments for logical validity by using the Toulmin model. If all three components are included, the data and warrant are supported, and the claim is valid, the argument is well grounded and should be used. Some speakers omit the warrant, assuming incorrectly that listeners will fill in the reasoning from data to claim. Others use faulty reasoning when presenting claims. For example, if your evidence states that Idaho reduced traffic fatalities by one third after initiating a mandatory seat belt law (data), and you claim that California can also reduce its traffic fatalities by one third by passing such a law, then your reasoning rests on the warrant that the seat belt law will have the same effect in California as it did in Idaho. However, the argument is invalid if you have no support to show that the drop in fatalities was not produced by something other than the seat belt law. Perhaps Idaho and California drivers are different in how they react to seat belt laws. In other words, the warrant is at best doubtful and possibly untrue, unless support for it can be presented.

Persuasion will not occur unless evidence and claim are accepted by the audience. In many speeches, you may need to provide several pieces of data to support one claim. A statistic may be effective for one audience member, but another may be swayed more by expert testimony. The warrant is stated

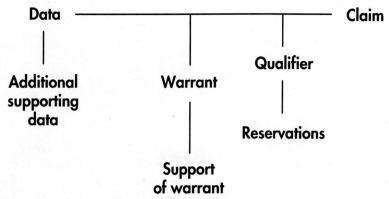

Figure 15.4 Diagram of a complete argument.

to let listeners understand how you arrived at your claim from the data. Four major types of reasoning used by speakers as warrants are inductive, deductive, causal, and analogous.

Inductive Reasoning We use *inductive reasoning* to reach a generalization about some class of phenomena from specific data such as examples. Inductive reasoning is used to test conclusions in scientific investigations, where observations form the basis for all conclusions. For instance, you notice that every apple you've eaten had seeds, then conclude inductively that all apples have seeds (see Figure 15.5). Because the conclusion is based on specific observa-

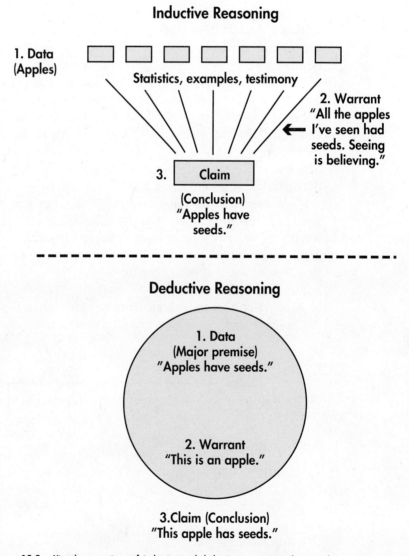

Figure 15.5 Visual comparison of inductive and deductive reasoning, showing three major components of each.

tions, which cannot include observations of all apples, the conclusion is said to be supported, not proven. The validity of a claim arrived at inductively depends on the number of cases used to support the claim, how well these cases represent all possible cases, the likelihood of significant exceptions, and whether the conclusion is supported by other facts and reasoning.

Deductive Reasoning   *Deductive reasoning* begins from a generalization and concludes with a prediction about some specific instance not yet observed or not observable. Formal deductive reasoning in structural forms called *syllogisms* is mostly used to test the logical validity of arguments; it is rarely stated in a speech. Instead, speakers use informal statements of deductive reasoning. In a syllogism, a generalization applicable to all items of some class is stated first, then the warrant is made that a given instance is a member of that class, and finally the generalization is applied to the instance being discussed. For example:

> Drunk drivers are dangerous to other drivers.
> Charles is a drunk driver.
> Therefore, Charles is dangerous to other drivers.

The first two statements, called *premises*, can be tested by observation to see if they are true. Are drunk drivers dangerous? Does Charles drink and then drive? Remember, though, that generalizations cannot be "proven" conclusively unless limited only to instances actually observed. So in one sense an "allness" statement is never true. Take the example we used earlier about apples: "All the apples I've eaten had seeds." If we change that to "All apples have seeds," we have a general premise for the deductive reasoning diagrammed in Figure 15.5:

> All apples have seeds.
> This piece of fruit is an apple.
> Therefore, this apple has seeds.

This conclusion may be false. Deductive reasoning predicts with some degree of probability, rather than the certainty stated in our syllogism. We should claim that "Since all apples I've eaten had seeds, it seems probable that this apple has seeds." A qualifier has now been included, *probable*. I can only say "The apple has seeds" in any scientific sense after opening it and observing. Indeed, it might be a mutant apple without seeds.

When speaking, you can use deductive arguments ethically if all your knowledge indicates the truthfulness of the major premise and if you qualify your claim: "This apple probably has seeds." Also, you will want to use only those generalizations that listeners will accept as true without any new evidence. Otherwise, to support the generalization you will first have to reason inductively. Only if you and all your target audience members believe that God hears prayers and acts in direct response to those prayers could you expect the following deductive argument to be convincing:

> We all believe God hears and sometimes does as we ask in our prayers. We all want our friend Bob, lying in a coma and declared brain dead by doctors, to recover. So let's all pray for him, asking God to make him whole again. It might happen!

As a practical matter, that would be a useless statement with listeners who did not accept your major premise about God; indeed, it might boomerang by leading them to suspect your competence.

The following deductive argument is typical of how speakers present arguments in less formal statements than syllogisms, without stating the major premises clearly.

> We should require that all farm and lumbering practices protect and preserve topsoil. The amount of life depends on the amount of topsoil. Erosion from land clearing and farming reduce the amount of topsoil at a far faster rate than it is being created. The earth will be able to sustain less life in the future if we don't change our farm and forest practices.

Could you detect the major premise in that argument? It was that the amount of life earth can sustain depends on the amount of topsoil. Deductive arguments can be used to persuade quite effectively, but only if the major premise (whether stated or not) is accepted as truth by listeners.

Causal Reasoning   You would use *causal reasoning* to claim that a specific type of relationship exists between two events. In simple terms, one event (A) is the cause of another (B), if B always follows A and B never occurs unless A precedes it. Actually, few events are produced by such a single preexistent cause. Most things that happen are the result of complex interaction among several causal factors. Likewise, the effect of some cause will most often be only partly predictable. For instance, what "causes" lung cancer? Smoking? Polluted air? Genes that produce susceptibility to certain agents called *carcinogens*? High levels of stress felt from day to day? Many such causal factors contribute to any single person developing lung cancer. Nonetheless, scientists search continuously for causal linkages, although they rarely expect to find them to be as simple and clear as the A–B relationship previously explained.

To use causal reasoning validly, the probability that one thing will contribute to the occurrence of another at some subsequent time must be demonstrated by the speaker. As a practical listener or speaker, you will be concerned with all the contributing causes that might be changed. You should not propose a particular solution to a problem unless you can demonstrate its causes. For instance, if you want to convince your listeners to support a program to solve the problem of teenage suicide, showing that certain factors occur only in the lives of teenagers who commit suicide would be necessary. You might urge that listeners take some action because it will almost certainly result in beneficial outcomes. For instance, you might produce evidence to warrant the claim that regular aerobic exercise often increases a person's productivity, disease resistance, and happiness. The key to valid causal reasoning is supporting data showing that one event almost inevitably leads to another, usually in the form of statistics based on numerous scientific observations of examples. We urge you *not* to claim a causal connection unless you provide such evidence.

Analogous Reasoning Sometimes an argument is based on a point-by-point comparison in which a speaker compares two situations, arguing that what happened in one situation is likely to happen in the other. This is called *analogous reasoning.* A causal relationship is presumed to exist between events in each of the two situations. For instance, Roseanne might argue that her city should not install a new landfill since the landfill at Point City polluted springs and wells in the region. For this to be a valid argument, however, she must show that conditions that are causative in the two situations are virtually the same: soil and rock types, sources and types of wastes, ground water flow, and so on. If you argue that members of your audience should support some action because it worked in another situation, you are obligated to demonstrate that conditions are practically the same in the two situations. Otherwise, your reasoning is faulty, and even though some listeners may believe you, you will lose credibility with more critical thinkers.

We have now considered two of the three major sources of persuasive influence, speaker credibility (ethos) and the use of evidence and reasoning (logos). Next we turn to the most important force for getting people to take specific actions: motivation.

Motivation and Emotional Appeals

To say that we experience *motivation* is the same as saying that behavior is purposeful. We act to satisfy some conscious or unconscious need. Persuaders must stimulate the needs of listeners to get them to perform some action. Evidence and reasoning may convince a listener, but still not provide enough stimulus to produce a sale, a vote, or other action. The speaker who requests listener action must demonstrate both that a need exists and that the best way to resolve the need is by acting in the way advocated by the speaker. In rhetoric, techniques used to stimulate motives are called *emotional appeals.* Emotional appeals are at the heart of every successful persuasive strategy that produces action. The motivating speaker uses tools of evidence and reasoning, organization, language, and delivery to arouse such powerful emotions as love, hate, fear, and guilt in connection with a need felt by the listener. The listener must respond by feeling the need and believing that it can be met by doing what the speaker asks. The more salient the feeling of need, the more likely the speaker is to evoke the desired action.

Fear appeals can be used to motivate listeners. Research demonstrates that there is a positive relationship between the level of fear in a message and attitude change only if the speaker can provide a means for removing the threat.[14] What matters is the fear induced in listeners rather than the content of what the speaker says. Grisly scenes in driver education films are an example of frequently ineffective fear appeals. Students can prevent cognitive dissonance without being persuaded to drive more cautiously by avoiding looking at and listening to the film, reacting negatively toward the source of the film, or minimizing the danger being described.[15] Successful life insurance salespersons rely on fear appeals to sell insurance. They arouse a fear of financial insecurity for surviving loved ones and then provide the means (insurance) for removing the threat. Research shows clearly that vivid examples are more likely to induce a high level of fear than are more abstract statistics.[16] An example of a friend dying of undetected breast cancer will be more motivating than statistics showing how many women have been saved by mammograms.

Effective motivation depends on understanding the existing or potential needs of the target audience. By understanding the general types of needs shared by people and adapting these to target audiences, you can plan how to motivate listeners to act on your message.

Numerous writers have attempted to categorize all motives, but no one classification scheme explains all motivation. One of the most useful classifications of human motives is the *hierarchy of needs* advanced by psychologist Abraham Maslow. This schema categorizes all motives into five broad categories in order of their potency.[17] Figure 15.6 illustrates this hierarchy. Maslow argues that a need emerges, is met for a period of time, subsides, and then reemerges. When a physiological or security need is actively motivating a person, one of the higher level needs is unlikely to be motivating at the same time. When the

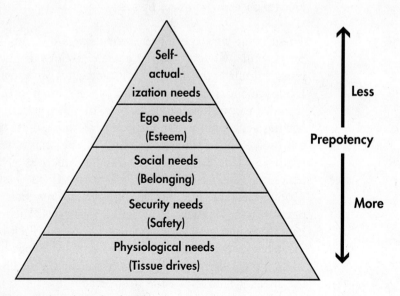

Figure 15.6   Maslow's hierarchy of needs.

lower level need has been temporarily satisfied, then higher level needs will emerge and be potent in producing action.

To illustrate the hierarchy of needs theory, imagine a drowning person. While fighting for air (physiological need), the drowning person will not be concerned about losing status by making a scene (esteem need). The physiological need is more potent at this moment than the need for esteem. Typically, the potency of these need types changes throughout life. In early childhood physiological and security needs dominate our behavior. As we mature and become confident that our physiological needs will be met, we seek fulfillment in areas of social, esteem, and self-actualization needs.

In Maslow's theory, the need is what motivates a person's behavior. We will next examine each of the five types of needs in Maslow's scheme and consider some ways you might evoke each.

PHYSIOLOGICAL NEEDS   *Physiological needs* refers to drives essential to continuance of life, such as the need for water, sleep, food, warmth, and sex. The sex drive is used extensively, though usually subtly, in advertising. The other tissue drives will rarely be appealed to in a speech, but when they are unmet, they preempt all other motive appeals. To illustrate, when you are hungry or need to eliminate, it is very difficult to pay attention to a speech or to think about some other person's needs. For starving Ethiopians or Kurds, appeals to esteem or self-actualization needs will be totally ineffective until their needs for food, shelter, clean water, and other necessities of life itself have been satisfied.

SECURITY NEEDS   Security needs motivate action when we perceive a threat, real or potential. Dangers from insane killers, toxic pollutants, drunken drivers, carcinogens, AIDS, and other threats to *security needs* prompt us to act if we have sufficient reason to think our lives will be endangered. Fear of the loss of necessary financial resources motivates us to buy insurance, join food cooperatives, and save.

To be effective in arousing security motives, you must overcome a listener's natural tendency to prevent dissonance by thinking "that only happens to other people." There is a tendency to avoid thinking about our mortality. The speaker must get the listener to *feel* the threat of an assault, a fatal accident, or lung cancer. For example, Ed wanted his classmates to enroll in a CPR class. He began with a vivid example to counteract the "that-only-happens-to-other-people" syndrome:

> I guess I have had at least a half dozen opportunities in my life to enroll in a CPR class, but despite the fact that in most cases there would have been no cost to me, I never felt it important enough to take the time to learn. I am here today to ask you not to make the same mistake I did by saying, "I'll never need to know how to do it." That's what I thought. I was wrong. Last summer my father and I were vacationing on a lake in Minnesota when he had a sudden heart attack. I had no idea what to do. He suddenly gasped for air, grabbed his chest, and stopped breathing. I

ran to the lodge for help and called an ambulance. Fortunately, another guest heard the commotion, rushed from the lodge to our cabin, and began to administer CPR to my father. When the ambulance arrived twenty minutes later, the driver told me that if it hadn't been for the CPR my father would be dead. The story has a happy ending. My father has recovered and is in good health. It was a scary way to learn, but I soon enrolled in a CPR class.

Ed appealed to social needs of his audience members by evoking emotions of love and guilt. He also appealed to self-esteem needs. The person who can supply CPR is a hero.

SOCIAL NEEDS Most of us will go to great effort to get favorable attention from others who matter to us. We have a need to be listened to, noticed, and treated as people who matter. If parents ignore them, children will even do things for which they are punished to gain attention. We attempt to meet our *social needs* for belonging and affection by buying expensive clothing and extravagant houses and paying for personal service in restaurants and even from therapists who listen with empathy.[18] Adolescents are especially motivated by needs for social acceptance. Teens pressure each other to "be like everyone else." Advertisers sell $100 athletic shoes and designer jeans by evoking symbolic social needs. Speakers assure us of the rewards of friendship, love, and acceptance into high-status circles if we do as they urge. Companies such as Hallmark Cards, AT&T, and McDonald's appeal to needs for love and acceptance by using traditions of family, home, holidays, and special transitions in life.

Speakers who want to arouse social needs often seek identification with the audience to create a sense of unity: "We must work together if we want to make our neighborhood a better place to raise children." "Because we understand the importance of . . ." "We're all in this together. . . ." The need for affiliation is powerful. Family and friendship groups are vital to our well-being. To feel cared about for what we are, to know that someone is interested in us and cares, is a great need. If you can show how doing what you request will help listeners meet this need, doing so may motivate them to act.

ESTEEM NEEDS Humans have a need for recognition, praise, the esteem of others, and self-esteem. To believe "I'm OK" and to have others indicate "You're OK" are powerful motivators. We want to be perceived as credible and intelligent people who accomplish worthwhile things. We want some level of recognition for what we contribute in our jobs, our neighborhoods, and organizations with which we affiliate. Everyone needs a role in which he or she can be recognized for making a useful contribution to the group. We often work very hard to win awards, praise, trophies, letters, and other signs of recognition. Fulfillment of esteem needs may take vastly different forms for different individuals. More money may enhance one person's esteem, but recognition by other members of a work team may be more motivating to other people. A title such as crew leader, sergeant, or department chair may be very motivating to some people, but not others.

Perhaps one of the worst mistakes made by public speakers is to fly in the face of self-esteem needs by insulting listeners. Some student speakers discredit classmates by acting as if they know nothing about a topic on which they have substantial knowledge. To be told "This is a knife, this a spoon, and this a dinner plate" before demonstrating how to arrange a place setting for a formal dinner is to deny the listeners' needs for self-esteem. To have a speaker suggest that audience members don't care enough about starving children, are selfish for not taking time to attend a home game, or stupid for not studying a foreign language will alienate them.

SELF-ACTUALIZATION NEEDS   Self-actualization needs include the desires for self-discovery and development. We need to create. For some people, this may mean developing craft skills of which there has been a great revival in recent years. For others, it may mean developing an athletic performance to a fine edge. Some people are driven to see how far they can develop their bodies. This is not a matter of competing with others, but of discovering how far you can go as a climber of mountains of your own choosing. Army recruiting ads have used this motivation extensively: "Be all that you can be in the Army." The speaker can often arouse such motives with statements like "Have you ever wanted to discover how far you could develop some talent, as Wilma Rudolph did by running, or Sir Edmund Hillary did in mountain climbing?"

Also included in self-actualization is a very human need to be able to explain the world we encounter. Superstitions and myths illustrate how people invent explanations for important phenomena in their lives when they do not really understand them. Thus they meet the psychological need for understanding. During audience analysis, you will sometimes be able to identify important events in the lives of listeners that they could easily be motivated to want to understand better, such as dreaming, a feeling of *deja vu*, or an illness.

The desire for new kinds of experience is a type of self-actualization need. Traveling to new places, trying new skills, or sampling new foods or any chance to try something new and challenging may be motivating for a secure person. What specifically will motivate a given individual depends on previous experiences and values. A variety of types of new experiences should be offered when the action you ask people to take warrants the offer. What appeals to one may not to another; to the degree possible offer a smorgasbord. For example, to motivate classmates to vacation at Chadron State Park, Bill described the riding, fishing, chuckwagon cookouts, summer theatre, swimming, rockhounding, and other types of activities one could try—something new for almost everyone.

MULTIPLE MOTIVES AND REWARDS   To become motivated, a listener must anticipate some reward from believing and acting as asked by the speaker. Usually this vision of a reward is not a product of one simple need, but the result of a complex set of intertwined motives at work: physiological needs, security needs, social needs, esteem needs, even self-actualization needs blended into immediate concerns of the person. A simple pleasure principle explanation does not adequately predict the agony people will go through to withdraw from chemical dependency or win a marathon. In almost all cases, change on the part of an audience member will take work, create discomfort, require new routines, cost time and money, threaten existing personal relationships, or endanger job security. The speaker must convince the listener that the benefits of the change will outweigh the costs. The more rewards anticipated by a listener, the more potent the motivation to act.

Determining what will reward is a prediction based on careful analysis of listeners. Then, evidence must be presented to convince the listeners of the probability of being rewarded. The speaker who dramatizes payoffs on many levels of need is most likely to succeed.

One effective technique in speeches to actuate is to visualize the listeners enjoying the benefits of acting as desired by the speaker just before making a final appeal. That is largely a matter of organizing, as we discuss next.

▶ Organizing Speeches to Persuade

You might at some time use any of the organizing schemas explained in Chapter 8, but several sequences of main points are particularly well suited for speeches to persuade. The sequence of points in the body of your speech will depend on such factors as the central idea, relevant knowledge and beliefs in the minds of listeners, situational norms, and whether your primary goal is to convince or to get some specific action as a response.

Speaking to Convince

If your primary goal is to convince listeners of a controversial proposition, it may be unwise to state the central idea or main points in your introduction. If some listeners have been inoculated against your central idea, stating it might arouse their defenses so they do not listen well. Instead, you can focus on the sequence of issues or questions you will discuss during the body of your speech. For example:

> There are three questions I think we need to consider while trying to decide whether or not to build more nuclear power plants. I'll present the scientific evidence needed to answer each in turn. First, how safe can nuclear plants be made in comparison with other types of power plants? Second, how much will they pollute our environment compared to fossil fuel plants? Third, how expensive will electricity from nuclear plants be in comparison to electricity from other sources?

If the speaker had said "Today I will show you that nuclear plants can be made safer than coal- or oil-fired plants, that they are far less polluting to the environment, and that they are far cheaper in the long run," chances are some members of the audience would have begun at once to argue mentally instead of continuing to listen.

The conclusion of a speech to convince will usually consist of a summary of the main points and an appeal for agreement. Consider this conclusion to the speech about nuclear power plants:

> The scientific evidence supporting a gradual and carefully regulated expansion of nuclear power plants is incontrovertible. Nuclear power plants can be built to be as safe, if not safer than conventional sources of power. Nuclear power plants pose a far less serious threat to our environment than fossil fuel plants. And nuclear power plants can produce abundant supplies of competitively priced electricity. The best scientific minds in our country support a gradual and carefully regulated expansion of nuclear power plants. The next time you turn on a light ask yourself, "Can I afford not to support the construction of nuclear power plants?"

Several schemas of main points may serve your purpose when seeking to convince. Two patterns of main points are particularly useful: *reasons why* and *stock issues*.

REASONS WHY For the speech about nuclear power plants the speaker chose the *reasons-why schema* for organizing main points in support of the central idea. When using this pattern, it is important to apply the *primacy–recency principle* for arranging arguments. People remember best the first and last of a series of words, topics, or items, other things being equal. If the target audience members are neutral or mildly in favor of your position, you will want to put the strongest or most important argument first and the second most important argument last. However, if the listeners are even mildly in disagreement with your position, put the least controversial reason first, proceeding to the most controversial argument last. In this way, you are likely to win gradual agreement with your central idea, with listeners saying to themselves, "Yes, that seems right," as you conclude each main point.

STOCK ISSUES When you want listeners to agree with some policy, usually you will organize the main points in one of the versions of the problem-solving sequence explained in Chapter 8. A variation of the problem-solving sequence widely used in speeches to convince is called the *stock issues* format, which consists of the following three topics:

1. Need.
2. Plan.
3. Practicality/benefits.

The first main point establishes a need for a change, the second proposes a plan to produce the change, and the third shows that the plan will work with more benefits than costs. This format is most appropriate with relatively neutral listeners. If more than one solution to the problem has been proposed, you can take a *two-sided approach* to inoculate your listeners against later contrary persuasive messages. Begin main point 3 with the solution(s) you believe to be inferior, then present the solution you think is most effective and beneficial just before your conclusion. Other variations on the problem-solving schema explained in Chapter 8 are often useful for speeches intended to convince, especially the applied criteria and comparative advantages sequences.

Speaking to Actuate

Any of the schemas of main ideas for a speech to convince might be used in a speech to actuate. In a speech to actuate, the speaker requests listeners to take some specific action in response to a problem. The conclusion should summarize the benefits of the requested action in vivid terms, ending with a specific appeal to act. A speech format we have not considered previously, called the *Motivated Sequence,* is well suited to speeches to actuate. Developed and popularized by the late Professor Alan H. Monroe, the motivated sequence places emphasis on motivating just before the final appeal.[19] Thousands of speakers have been taught this sequence over the past 50 years and have found it extremely effective when the desired response involves an immediate action such as contributing to a charity or joining an organization. The preparation outline can be in the conventional introduction–body–conclusion format, or you can have a five-section outline, with points in each section beginning with the Roman numeral I.

The five steps in the motivated sequence were based loosely on an analysis of how individuals solve problems when they think systematically (called *reflective thinking* by John Dewey, who developed this analysis), combined with the belief that people act on the basis of self-interest motivated by personal needs and desires.[20] The sequence is quite easy to understand and apply.

Step 1: *Attention*   At the very start, the speaker must direct attention to the topic and create a desire to listen. This means using some technique to capture attention and keep it on your topic. During the attention step, relate the topic to listener interests in some dramatic way, establish your credibility if needed, and let the listener know what issues or points to expect in the speech. The mental response you want to this introduction is "I want to hear this; go on."

Step 2: *Need*   In the second step, you present a problem, stressing its personal implications for the listeners. The response you seek in the listeners' minds is "I have a problem" or "We've got to do something about this." First, provide a factual description of the problem, then personalize it, tying it to the listeners'

▶ An Example of Speaking to Persuade

The speech that follows exemplifies skillful persuasive speaking. This speech won first place in the finals of the Interstate Oratorical Association in 1985. Trevor Giles was a student at Ripon College in Wisconsin when he presented this speech to an audience of speech coaches and fellow contestants.

SHEATHING THE SILENT KNIFE[21]

Trevor S. Giles

COMMENTARY	TEXT
Rhetorical question to gain attention based on the popular game of Trivial Pursuit.	Here's a trivia question for you. What do Julius Caesar, Shakespeare's MacDuff, and I, Trevor Giles, have in common? Not much, right? But we all started our lives in the same way. We were brought into this world by a cesarean section. Back in 1963, I was one of 4.5 babies out of a hundred born this way. But times have changed, and so has this statistic. According to *Health* magazine, in 1983 alone, 700,000 babies were brought into the world by this procedure, out of four million babies born. This means that, currently, one in five babies is brought into the world by a cesarean, an increase of over 300% in just 20 years. This increase is clearly not trivial, but the sign of a rising national epidemic, an epidemic that demands our attention. Such an analysis will be most effective if we look, first, at the reasons for this dramatic increase. Second, then, let us examine the many risks of a cesarean to both the mother and the child so as to, finally, suggest some steps that must be taken to bring this increase down and return the birth of children back to nature.
Speaker's personal involvement as a basis for competence. Use of statistics and citation of sources establish his competence and credibility.	
Cites credible source; statistics show importance of the subject.	
A problem exists that listeners must face.	
Preview of organization of the body of the speech. The speaker has adopted a problem–solution format in developing this topic.	
Speaker's first main point—causes of the problem.	In 1916, Dr. Edward B. Cragin uttered his now famous pronouncement, "Once a cesarean, always a cesarean." This policy is still in place in most hospitals nationwide, and the cesarean repeat rate in America today is almost 100%. But the sad fact is that 80% of these repeat surgeries are unnecessary, according to University of Cincinnati researchers. You see, medical
Establishes the extent of the problem with statistics. Note the citation of authoritative sources for data, which establishes the speaker's credibility along with the validity of his evidence. The data are used to	

(continued)

COMMENTARY

evoke dissonance with the idea that doctors always know what is best for patients.

Rhetorical question as transition to subpoint A, the first reason for the existence of the problem.

Subpoint A, the first reason why the problem continues.

Emphasis on shared values of morality, hence credibility.

Subpoint B, the second reason.

Testimony to refute reason B.

Notice the inductive organization. Speaker takes an indirect approach.

Subpoint C, the third reason.

Causal reasoning based on statistical correlation. The speaker argues that insurance coverage leads to an increase in the number of cesareans performed by physicians.

Credibility of speaker's claim is increased by the expectation that the AMA would defend its members.

Qualification of the argument supporting the third reason.

Authoritative testimony used to warrant the claim of unnecessary cesarean surgery.

TEXT

advances have simplified and changed the cesarean procedure, thus allowing most women who have had a cesarean to deliver safely and normally in subsequent pregnancies. But why have doctors stuck to this archaic policy? *The Journal of the American Medical Association,* in December of 1984, suggests that the primary reason is the convenience of the doctor. After all, it is easier to deliver a child by cesarean during working hours, rather than waiting around on weekends for the slower, natural birthing process, and many doctors use Dr. Cragin's philosophy as a justification for less work and easier, more convenient scheduling. But this blatant disregard of the medical truth makes this policy and its consequences both immoral and unacceptable. Other medical criteria include fetal monitoring to detect signs of fetal distress, breech babies, or babies whose descent is not head first, and low birth weight of the infant. But authors Nancy Cohen and Lois Estner, in their book, *Silent Knife: Cesarean Prevention and Vaginal Birth after Cesarean,* suggest that many of these criteria are often not accurate nor prudent and that many of the cesareans performed for these reasons are also unnecessary.

But the most shocking reason for the increase in cesareans nationwide is the clear economic incentive for the doctor. It is estimated that hospitals and doctors profit by $95 million from all of the unnecessary cesareans performed in just one year. This shocking reality is further enhanced by the correlation between cesarean delivery rates and the mother's ability to pay. *The Journal of the American Medical Association* notes that women with Blue Cross/Blue Shield insurance in 1981 had a cesarean delivery rate of 20%, while self-pay mothers had a rate of only 14% in the same year. What this means is that the assurance of reimbursement has replaced medical reasons as the deciding factor in many doctor's minds. To be fair, most doctors are concerned about their patients and are fairly careful about the decision to perform a cesarean; but far too many are not. Authors Cohen and Estner cite a study in their book that con-

COMMENTARY

Internal summary of point I.

Rhetorical question as transition to main point II.

Second main point. Notice that this point is an elaboration of the problem, detailing the harms or evil involved to arouse security and social needs.

Numerous brief examples to develop the risks, evoking security and social needs.

Statistical contrasts emphasizing the seriousness of the problem.

Description to motivate through security needs.

Dramatic example.

Another example of causal reasoning. The absence of federal regulations increases the risks to mothers and infants.

Second subpoint under II, risks to infants. Appeal to social need as good parents.

TEXT

cludes that 80% of all cesareans now performed are unnecessary surgical intervention, and the problem has reached staggering proportions.

But why should we worry? As one doctor put it, having a cesarean is as safe and easy as getting a haircut. Haircuts are not major abdominal surgery, cesareans are. While generally a safe operation, cesareans can still be dangerous, as can any surgery. But when 80% of that surgery is unnecessary, that danger acquires a brand new significance. In her study Madelaine Shearer identifies such potential complications from cesareans for the mother as gas, infections, hemorrhaging, transfusion complications, aspiration pneumonia, cardiac arrest, and death. This last one is the most shocking, and further studies have indicated that the chances of death for the mother are 26 times greater from a cesarean than from normal delivery. Morbidity, or disease rates, are even higher, with half of all cesarean mothers experiencing some form of postoperative complication. Instead of dealing with the real problem of unnecessary cesareans, doctors merely prescribe medication for pain, which in turn is a prescription for further complications. You see, what makes this situation unique is that two people are affected by the medication; the mother and the child. And as Joseph Heller would say, "we are left with a 'Catch 22.'" A woman can either take the medication and be too groggy and weak to hold her child, or she cannot take it and be in too much pain to care about her baby. As one cesarean mother put it, "My baby and I, we just lay there and cried together, he in his bed and I in mine. I couldn't even lean over to pick him up."

To make matters worse, nothing is being done by the people who can help. The Food and Drug Administration [FDA] has no regulations concerning obstetrical drugs, nor does it monitor the effect of these drugs upon the infant. As for the child, the risks are just as significant. Studies have shown that the chances for death of an infant are 3 to 7 times greater if delivered by a cesarean. Further complications

(continued)

COMMENTARY

Examples of risks to make problem more concrete.

Third subpoint under II; damage to mother–child bond.

Social need.

Restatement of the problem and a conclusion that follows from it.

Main point III: The solutions to stop the harms described in II are practical.

Subpoint A, first part of the solution.

Notice that the solution involves many groups of people and organizations involved in birth and health.

Subpoint B, the second part of the solution.
Subpoint C, the third part of the solution.

Subpoint D, the fourth part of the solution.

Subpoint E, the fifth part of the solution.

Appeal to self-actualization motives.

Subpoint F, the sixth part of the solution.

TEXT

include wet lung, lower blood levels, respiratory difficulties, and increased prematurity. Additionally, the separation of mother and child that occurs in the first few hours of life has a serious detrimental effect upon the natural bonding process that occurs at this time, thus erecting a psychological wall in their relationship. All of these problems, when combined, make this increase in unnecessary cesareans totally unacceptable. Clearly, something must be done!

While the problems associated with this increase in cesarean are not trivial, the solutions are really rather simple. On the part of the medical community, doctors must monitor their patients closer and for longer periods of time and should urge women who have had a cesarean to try vaginal delivery in subsequent pregnancies. *The Journal of the American Medical Association* also suggests that hospitals institute peer review of physicians with high cesarean delivery rates. If a doctor's percentage has risen too high, he or she should have to justify that increase. Further, medical insurance companies and the Federal government must realize that this increase in unnecessary cesareans costs them and the American people millions of dollars annually, and must exert pressure upon the medical community to bring this increase down. The FDA must also institute regulations of both operative and post-operative obstetrical cesarean drugs and measure the effect of these drugs on both the mother and the child.

As for would-be parents, education is the key. Pregnant women and their husbands must educate themselves about the entire birthing process and the medical indications that call for a cesarean section. They should never assume that their doctor knows everything, because when it comes down to the wire, when a decision must be made, it is better for all parties involved—both doctor and patients—to understand the costs and consequences of a cesarean. Prospective parents must also question their obstetrician about his or her cesarean delivery rate. If the doctor hesitates or is insulted, that

COMMENTARY	TEXT
Subpoint G, the seventh part of the solution.	should tell them something. Finally, would-be parents must never assume that once the mother has had a cesarean, that she can never deliver normally again or that cesareans are better for everyone, both mother and infant. The natural birthing process has worked well for thousands of years; why bypass it for the sake of myth or mere convenience? All of these steps, when taken by all of the parties involved will significantly reduce the number of unnecessary surgeries now performed on American women.
Notice the use of an internal summary as a transition.	
Visualization of the beneficial results of implementing the solutions proposed with strong motive appeals to security and social needs.	While I, obviously, will never undergo the pain and complications of an unneeded cesarean section, I, nonetheless, will feel the pain of my mother every time she relives this experience and the potential for pain for my future
Notice speaker's reference back to the opening material, providing a sense of closure.	wife and children. Our search for a solution to this problem is not a trivial pursuit, but, rather, the search for a cure to a national epidemic that, as one author put it, has a silent knife
Series of vivid metaphors; strong connotations.	slashing its way across the stomach of America, murdering our hopes and dreams for normal childbirth, stripping us of control, and leaving women wounded and vulnerable. Let's take that
Final appeal to agree in the connotative language of murder.	knife, cure these wounds, and restore hope by returning the birth of children back to where it belongs: with nature.

▶ Summary

Persuasion is the means to obtaining voluntary coordination of human behavior in a democratic society. We all need to understand the process by which it occurs and the techniques used in persuading. Persuasive influence is the result of a combination of forces exerted by the perceived credibility of the speaker, the impact of evidence and reasoning, and listener's needs. Persuasive speakers aim for achievable responses from a target audience. They understand that it will be extremely difficult to convince audience members whose core beliefs are contrary to the central idea.

Speakers who are judged to be credible before they speak have a distinct advantage over those about whom listeners have no preconception or a negative image. Skills in organizing, developing ideas, verbal and nonverbal encoding, and adaptation to listeners all enhance perceived credibility. Establishing a common ground of experience, values, and valued associates can also enhance acquired credibility. If credibility has not been previously established, a speaker can describe the basis for judging him or her to be competent on the issue being discussed, or have an emcee do so. Throughout the speech, expressions of goodwill, citations of sources, developmental materials, clear organization, and animated delivery will help.

Credibility alone will not persuade critical thinkers. In addition, the speaker needs sound evidence and valid reasoning adapted to the listeners' preexistent beliefs and degree of ego involvement. With evidence and arguments to create cognitive dissonance with previous beliefs, one can evoke agreement from listeners on both incidental and secondary beliefs. Vivid representative examples are especially effective as evidence.

At a minimum, persuasive arguments are composed of data on which to base a claim and a warrant connecting the data to a conclusion. Usually claims should be qualified instead of absolute. Arguments in support of claims may be inductive (specific cases used to support a general conclusion), deductive (an accepted generalization used to predict what will occur in a specific case), causal (reasoning that certain conditions led to some effect), or analogous (what happened in one situation will also occur in a similar situation). Combinations of these types of arguments are typical.

Behavior is not random; it is motivated by needs and desires. Speakers must adapt to the salient existing motives of listeners or make latent motives more salient, then show how taking the desired action will meet the salient needs. Five major categories of needs can be used to create emotional appeals to arouse listeners to act.

Skillful persuasive speakers organize their remarks in a sequence of main points that culminates in the response desired from a target audience. The main points may be stated very directly when listeners are neutral or favorable to the speaker's central idea or presented after evidence has suggested them if the audience opposes the speaker's central idea. For speeches to convince, the sequence of main points may be a list of reasons for adopting the speaker's belief, some variation of the problem-solving sequence such as the stock issues, or almost any schema presented in Chapter 8. Speaking to actuate may follow any of the above sequences followed by an appeal for immediate action, or the motivated sequence that is designed to get action. In this sequence, the speaker begins by directing attention, then establishes a need, satisfaction for the need, a visualization of the solution in action, and an action step in which a direct and specific appeal to act is made.

With the theory and techniques we have presented in this chapter, you should be able to listen critically to those who seek to persuade you and to influence the beliefs and actions of others in ways that are psychologically and ethically sound.

▶ Learning Activities

1. Make a list of at least five persuasive messages you are exposed to during the next three days. For each message on your list answer all of the following questions:
   a. What needs did the persuader try to evoke in an attempt to motivate you to change your belief or behavior?
   b. On a scale of 5 (high involvement) to 1 (low involvement), how strongly were you ego involved with your belief(s) and behavior(s) related to the message?
   c. What was your response to the persuasive message?
   In a small group, compare your answers with those of your classmates. Try to agree on two or three appropriate conclusions, then share them with the rest of the class.
2. For the following actions list at least three unfulfilled needs of classmates that might be used to motivate them to take the desired action:
   a. Donate organs in the event of untimely death.
   b. Contribute money for a drive to purchase Christmas gifts for poor children.
   c. Read a novel by your favorite author.
   d. Take riding, mountain climbing, or skiing lessons.
   e. Make a deep-dish apple pie as a surprise dessert for family or friends.
3. Analyze one of the speeches to persuade presented in the appendix.
   a. What is the overall organizational strategy? Does it seem to be the most effective for the speaker's purpose?
   b. What does the speaker do to enhance credibility? Does this seem to be effective? Might the speaker have done more to improve credibility? If so, what?
   c. What logical arguments does the speaker use? Are data, warrants, and claims appropriate and sufficient? Which had the most and least impact on you? What other arguments might the speaker have used?
   d. What emotional appeals does the speaker use to motivate? What other or different appeals might have been used?
   e. What changes would you recommend to the speaker?
4. List six topics or issues with which you are so ego involved that you have trouble being objective when responding to messages attempting to change beliefs or actions on these topics or issues. How did you establish each of these beliefs? What do you stand to risk losing or giving up in order to change any of these beliefs or activities?
5. Select three persuasive advertisements from newspapers or magazines that you judge to be especially effective or ineffective. Analyze each advertisement in terms of target audience, needs appealed to, probable effectiveness, and changes that might improve the persuasiveness of the ad.
6. Prepare a survey questionnaire to measure listener beliefs about your

tentative central idea for a forthcoming speech to persuade. Include at least one question to help you make inferences about your listeners' needs, values, and expectations regarding the topic of your speech. Discuss your questionnaire with at least one classmate before duplicating and administering it in order to get suggestions that might improve the questionnaire. Use the results of the completed survey in planning and adapting to your audience.

7. How might you establish common ground on two topics of your choice with listeners who are
   a. Lawyers, ages 28 to 50.
   b. Farmers, ages 45 to 70.
   c. High school students who work after school at least two days per week.

8. Using popular magazines, find one example of faulty and one example of valid reasoning of each of the following types: inductive, deductive, and causal. Then do the following:
   a. Explain how the claim exceeds the data in the faulty inductive argument and how it is appropriate in the valid one.
   b. Explain what is invalid about the faulty deduction and why you think the other is valid. Prepare a formal syllogism for each.
   c. Explain what is wrong in the faulty causal argument and why you think the other causal argument is valid.

9. Prepare yourself to speak extemporaneously to actuate your classmates or some target audience from among them. In your outline, after each main point, indicate in parentheses all the needs you expect to arouse with that point.

10. Using any controversial central idea for a speech you might deliver in class, explain what adaptation you would make if an audience analysis revealed each of the following conditions:
   a. Virtually everyone already agrees with your position.
   b. Virtually everyone strongly disagrees with your central idea, and it is a secondary or core belief for them. They also have high regard for you as a person.
   c. Virtually everyone has little or no prior knowledge on this topic, and is neutral toward your central idea, but some listeners have indicated that they are skeptical about you as a credible source.

Notes

1. Aristotle, "The Rhetoric," in *The Works of Aristotle,* trans. R. Robert (Oxford, England: Clarendon Press, 1924), section 1355b.

2. Daniel J. O'Keefe, *Persuasion: Theory and Research* (Newbury Park, CA: Sage, 1990), pp. 132–133.

3. Jo Liska, "Situational and Topical Variations in Credibility Criteria," *Communication Monographs* 45 (1978):85–92.

4. E. Walster, E. Aronson, and D. Abrahams, "On Increasing the Persuasiveness of a

Low Prestige Communicator," *Journal of Experimental Psychology* 2 (1964):325–342.

5. O'Keefe, *Persuasion,* pp. 145–151.

6. Lawrence R. Wheeless, "Effects of Explicit Credibility Statements by a More and a Less Credible Source," *Southern Speech Communication Journal* 39 (1973):33–39.

7. James C. McCroskey, "A Summary of Experimental Research on the Effects of Evidence in Persuasive Communication," *Quarterly Journal of Speech* 55 (1969):169–176; Rodney A. Reynolds and Michael Burgoon, "Belief Processing, Reasoning, and Evidence," in Robert N. Bostrom (ed.), *Communication Yearbook* 7 (Beverly Hills; CA: Sage, 1983), pp. 83–104.

8. Fritz Heider, "Attitudes and Cognitive Organization," *Journal of Psychology* 21 (1946):107–112; Theodore Newcomb, "An Approach to the Study of Communication Acts," *Psychological Review* 60 (1953):393–404.

9. Leon Festinger, *A Theory of Cognitive Dissonance* (Stanford, CA: Stanford Univ. Press, 1962).

10. Carl I. Hovland and Walter Weiss, "The Influence of Source Credibility on Communication Effectiveness," *Public Opinion Quarterly* 15 (1951):635–650; Mike Allen and J. Stiff, "Testing Three Models for the Sleeper Effect." Paper presented at the International Communication Association, New Orleans, LA, 1988.

11. Mike Allen and Raymond W. Preiss, "Using Meta-analyses to Evaluate Curriculum: An Examination of Selected College Textbooks," *Communication Education* 38 (April 1990):103–115.

12. William J. McGuire, "Inducing Resistance to Persuasion, Some Contemporary Approaches," in Leonard Berkowitz (ed.), *Advances in Experimental Social Psychology* (New York: Academic Press, 1984), Vol. I, pp. 191–229; Mary John Smith, *Persuasion and Human Action* (Belmont, CA: Wadsworth, 1982).

13. Stephen Toulmin, *The Uses of Argument* (New York: Cambridge Univ. Press, 1944).

14. S. Sutton, "Fear-Arousing Communications: A Critical Examination of Theory and Research," in J. Eiser (ed.), *Social Psychology and Behavioral Medicine* (New York: Wiley, 1982), pp. 303–337; F. Boster and P. Mongeau, "Fear-Arousing Persuasive Messages," in R. Bostrom (ed.), *Communication Yearbook 8* (Beverly Hills, CA: Sage, 1984), pp. 330–377.

15. O'Keefe, *Persuasion,* pp. 165–168.

16. O'Keefe, *Persuasion,* pp. 168–169.

17. Abraham Maslow, *Motivation and Personality* (New York: Harper & Row, 1970), pp. 35–47.

18. William C. Schutz, *FIRO: A Three-Dimensional Theory of Interpersonal Behavior* (New York: Rinehart, 1958); Charles Derber, *The Pursuit of Attention* (New York: Oxford Univ. Press, 1979).

19. Alan H. Monroe, *Principles and Types of Speech* (Chicago: Scott, Foresman, 1935).

20. Douglas Ehninger, Bruce E. Gronbeck, Ray E. McKerrow et al., *Principles and Types of Speech Communication,* 10th ed. (Glenview, IL: Scott, Foresman, 1986), pp. 152–153.

21. Trevor S. Giles, "Sheathing the Silent Knife." Reprinted with special permission of the Interstate Oratorical Association.

CHAPTER **16**

Speaking Impromptu

Questions to Guide Reading and Review

1. What are the types of public situations in which you are likely to need or want to speak impromptu?
2. How can a person be prepared to speak impromptu? When is one not justified in speaking impromptu? Why?
3. What does the speaker do during each of the four stages of speaking impromptu?
4. How should you respond to questions asked following a speech? What might you say if you don't know an answer to a question a listener suggests you should be able to answer?

Sally was asked by a classmate, "What's it like to work at McDonald's?" This was her reply:

Uh, working at McDonald's is lots of fun. You know what I mean? It's busy, and you can eat some good stuff for free. I really like all the people I met, but I had to work hard and they paid lousy. I'm glad I don't have to do all that stuff in my new job. Uh, maybe you'll enjoy a Big Mac soon with friends of mine.

During a workshop on employee retirement plans, a listener asked, "What is the difference in the way we can receive benefits from a regular retirement plan and a supplementary one?" Elissa, the briefer conducting the workshop, first confirmed her understanding of the questioner's intention by paraphrasing: "Is your question about the differences in how you receive your money from a supplementary retirement account and money from a regular retirement account?" The questioner answered "Yes." Elissa then responded:

This question may be of importance to many of you, including those who already have supplementary retirement accounts and those who still have enough years of service to begin one. First, I'll explain how you accumulate money in a tax-sheltered supplementary retirement fund, then two options for receiving your money not available for a regular retirement account.

Elissa then began a two-minute answer, organized around the two points mentioned in her preview.

Each of the above responses is an example of speaking impromptu. The contrast between the two speeches is a contrast between ineffective and effective, self-centered rambling and audience-centered, to-the-point speaking.

Whenever you are involved in a public gathering, you may need or want to speak in response to something that occurs during the meeting, even though you were not able to prepare in advance. Here are some typical examples of impromptu speaking situations:

After Christmas dinner, Grandma asks you to tell the family about your just-completed semester abroad at Heidelberg University.

Unexpectedly, your department manager calls on you at a meeting to describe your progress on a computer simulation of how wastewater flows in the manufacturing process.

During a quality circle meeting, you think of a way to solve a problem with a weak door hinge and want every member of the group to understand this idea.

After presenting your best arguments in favor of peer evaluation of teachers, a classmate raises an objection you hadn't dealt with in your speech and asks you to respond to it.

Impromptu speeches are frequently made during special ceremonies and other occasions that are part of organizational life. For example:

During a meeting of your fraternity you are given a special award, which is a complete surprise to you.

You are asked by the master of ceremonies to give an unexpected toast to a special guest or to offer an unplanned prayer.

In all these situations—and many others like them—people are called on to speak in public without any chance to go through the procedure for preparing to speak extemporaneously. They are obliged to speak on the spur of the moment, or *impromptu*. Any extemporaneous speaker who responds to questions after a prepared speech must speak impromptu. Developing skill and confidence in speaking impromptu is vital in the public and professional life of any person who wants to be influential. One cannot be an effective force in meetings without being a competent impromptu speaker.

All too often people who speak "off the cuff" do so ineffectively. They

People often speak impromptu during large group meetings.

wander from the subject. The point of their remarks is unclear to listeners. If it is clear, it is not supported with evidence and/or reasoning to make it compelling. The answer does not fit the question asked by the listener. Some listeners did not hear or understand the question, so the answer seems like a speech in a vacuum. Perhaps the speaker overelaborates, boring the listeners while seeming to enjoy reminiscing. Listeners are thinking "Get to the point" while the speaker rambles on an ego trip of "I", "I", and "I". Such ineptness when speaking impromptu is more common than efficient, listener-centered speaking. It need not be so in your case if you learn how to apply a compressed version of the procedure for preparing to speak extemporaneously. You can follow this procedure even when you have only seconds in which to prepare to speak.

▶ Preparing

You have an obligation both to yourself and to your listeners to be as well prepared for speaking as is reasonably possible. There is no excuse for speaking impromptu when it is possible to prepare to speak extemporaneously. In such a circumstance, a speaker's obvious lack of preparation communicates to the audience "You people didn't matter enough to me to bother preparing in advance." Understandably, the listeners will often reject the message of such a speaker.

To some degree you can prepare to answer questions that may be asked following a speech. Often it is possible to anticipate listener questions and think about how to answer them. This may require looking up information on the question; it may even entail outlining an answer. A well-prepared debater almost never encounters an opposing argument that was not anticipated, even though the specific wording and form of the argument may be novel and call for an impromptu rebuttal. Likewise, before a meeting of an organization you can often find out what other members or committees are likely to propose. This advance knowledge gives you an opportunity to locate evidence and plan arguments to support or oppose these recommendations for action.

Imagine you are participating in a campus campaign to get signatures on a petition calling for better funding of higher education in your state. If you speak repeatedly on the subject to different groups, you will discover that similar questions are posed after many of your presentations. You can then modify your speech outline to address these questions or at least have well-organized and supported answers when they are again asked. If you did not have an adequate answer the first time you heard the question, you should never again face that question unprepared to answer it.

If you do not know the answer, there are two ways to reply: (1) "I don't know" or (2) "I don't know the answer to your question, but I know how to find it. If you would like me to get you the answer, leave your name and address or phone number and I'll get back to you with an answer as soon as possible."

When speaking impromptu, you should never be totally unprepared to speak on the subject of discussion. The reason: If you do not have considerable knowledge on the topic, you have no right to speak impromptu on it in public. Meetings are not facilitated by the public speaking of ignorant participants, fabrication of evidence, or fervent assertion without substantiating evidence and reasoning. How do you feel when someone at a public meeting makes strong claims without evidence or tells transparent lies? Put upon? Angry? Certainly you do not place credibility in such a speaker; the net effect is to create distrust on the part of thoughtful, informed listeners. As a matter of personal ethics, we hope you never take a public stand on an issue unless you are confident of your knowledge about it and the issue is important to you.

On subjects about which your knowledge is extensive, your biggest problem will be to select from all that you know and believe about the topic. As with extemporaneous speaking, your goal when you speak impromptu is to achieve a desired response to a central idea. In order to avoid digressing from the topic, speaking in an ego-centered fashion, or forgetting to develop and adapt ideas to listeners, you can use a time-compressed version of the procedure for planning to speak extemporaneously when you speak on the spur of the moment.

▶ The Impromptu Procedure

There are four major stages in speaking impromptu:

1. Planning, done silently during the few seconds to minutes available for thinking before you must begin to speak.
2. Introducing your speech.
3. Developing your point(s).
4. Concluding your remarks.

We will explain what to do during each stage in order to avoid the common pitfalls of digression, self-centeredness, vagueness, and wordiness. We illustrate this procedure with examples from a variety of impromptu situations you are likely to face.

Planning

There are always at least a few seconds before you must say anything. During this time, you can go through a compressed version of the analyzing and organizing stages in preparing to speak. The occasion may involve special norms or listener expectations to which you will need to adapt.

The situation determines the topic, but you will need to decide quickly on a central idea about that topic and how you want listeners to respond to the idea. First and most important in guiding your thinking while rising to your feet, walking to a microphone, or pausing silently is to answer this question: What is the point I want listeners to understand, accept, or act upon? Second is to decide what you want listeners to do in response to that point. For instance, you may want listeners to be able to explain it, to use it in some activity, to agree with it, or to take some action such as voting "yes" or "no."

Often there is just one point to an impromptu speech, the central idea. However, if more than one main point is involved, the third step in stage 1 will be to decide on a simple pattern of organization and the main points in that pattern. The pattern of main points will be one of the schemas explained in Chapter 8: chronological, spatial, causal, problem solving, or other logical sequence of topics. The body of an impromptu speech should never have more than three main points, clearly related to each other, and implied by the wording of the central idea. If your central idea suggests a chronological relationship between main points, keep it simple and clear with numerical signposts such as "The first step is . . . The second step is . . ." If space is the relationship between main points, limit those points to a clear sequence such as inner and outer, east and west, or first floor and second floor. If you talk about solving some problem, stick to the simple sequence of problem and solution. If you explain a causal relationship, limit main points to cause and effect or effect and cause. If a different topical sequence is selected, there should only be two or three topics. For example, you might describe the two or three most important characteristics of the subject or the two or three most important reasons for a belief or action. Such simplicity of organization is illustrated in the following examples:

CHRONOLOGICAL
  I. Treat the oil stain with Spotout.
 II. Wash the Spotout from the sweater with laundry detergent.

  I. I greatly appreciate the honor you've given me tonight.
 II. Tomorrow I'll continue to give my best effort to build our Boys Club.

SPATIAL
  I. Below the timberline you will find common mammals such as deer and elk.
 II. Above the timberline you will likely encounter the rarer sheep and goats.

  I. Highlight the eyes with liner.
 II. Highlight the cheeks with blush.
III. Highlight the mouth with gloss.

CAUSAL
I. Lung cancer is now the most common cancer of women.
II. This epidemic was caused by the increase in smoking by women.

I. Repaving the drive to our sorority house would cost thousands of dollars.
II. Such a great expense would leave us unable to meet our mortgage payment.

PROBLEM SOLVING
I. A skid takes away your ability to control the direction of your car.
II. You can regain control by steering into the skid without braking.

I. Our fraternity cookout next weekend will produce a lot of mess.
II. We should appoint a committee to clean up before we leave the park.

OTHER TOPICAL SEQUENCES
I. The black widow spider has a red hourglass mark on its abdomen.
II. The brown recluse spider has an orange fiddle-shaped mark on its back.

I. This shredder has three different settings.
II. It can cut salad ingredients from fine to coarse.

SPEAKING IN REPLY While listening to another speaker to whom you may want to reply, you can make notes of that speaker's main points, evidence, and reasoning. These can provide a topical sequence for the points in your speech, which might be either a speech of *refutation*, in which you argue against the other person's ideas, or a speech to support those ideas. If you agree with the speaker's position, you can jot down a concise summary of what was said, then a brief list of two or three additional reasons for agreeing or supporting the proposed action. Under each additional reason you would make a brief note of evidence to support it. If you disagree, note weaknesses in the speaker's evidence or reasoning. Does the speaker overgeneralize from too little evidence? Are the examples atypical? Is the evidence out of date? Are sources biased? Does the speaker make assertions without supporting them? Is the reasoning fallacious? If so, these collective flaws can be the first main point of your impromptu speech, followed by reason(s) for doing the opposite of what the speaker has urged (e.g., vote "nay" instead of "yea"). Or you might be able to compare the relative advantages of the speaker's proposal with the advantages of a different course of action. In many cases your notes will be an outline of the body of an impromptu speech, looking somewhat like this:

I. The previous speaker's proposal is not sound.
   A. (Fallacies, inadequacies of evidence,
   B. Problems created by the proposed solution, etc.)
II. A different course of action is superior.
   A. (Comparisons showing the benefits of your proposal over the one you oppose.)

ANSWERING QUESTIONS Many impromptu speeches are responses to questions asked by listeners following a prepared speech. When someone asks you a question, be sure to listen well to discover the exact intention of the questioner. Paraphrase your understanding of the question in your own words, and then ask the questioner if you understood the question correctly. If you respond to a misunderstanding of the question, your credibility is likely to be lowered— "How can we trust a speaker who didn't understand? Is he dense, or is he trying to hide something by evading the question?" Also, some listeners may not have heard or understood the question, and your paraphrase will orient them. So play it safe—paraphrase *every* question and ask the questioner for confirmation. If you did not hear well enough to paraphrase or did not understand the question, say so and ask the questioner to repeat it or try to make it clearer to you: "I did not understand your question. Could you please restate it?" An added benefit of doing this is your credibility as a careful, precise, and honest person will probably be enhanced.

If a questioner appears to be making a statement rather than inquiring, simply point this out, and then ask if the person has a *question*. If not, you may want to refute the point briefly or ask if anyone else has a question.

Be sure you do not get into an extended debate with one audience member or allow one person to dominate a question–answer period. Each listener should have an equal chance to ask you a question. Many speakers allow no one to ask a second question so long as any listener still wants to ask a first question.

When you can't answer a question with confidence, say so—*never* bluff or lie! Your self-concept and your credibility are both at stake. When you can answer the question, but think it is so specific that almost no one other than the questioner would be interested in the lengthy answer, offer to answer the questioner personally after the meeting has ended, perhaps in an informal conference.

Whether answering a question or speaking of your own initiative, you have now decided on a limited central idea, a desired response to that idea, and, if needed, a simple pattern of main points in the body of your impromptu speech. You are ready to begin speaking. You can rely on the formula you learned for planning the introduction to a speech prepared extemporaneously: attention, interest, trust, and preview.

Introducing Your Speech

Unless you are responding to a question you have just paraphrased to the satisfaction of the questioner, you should usually begin an impromptu speech by stating to what you are responding. For example, "Jamil has just urged us to vote in favor of a boycott against companies doing business with dictatorships. I think we need to consider all the issues before deciding whether or not to take this action," or "We seem about to drop the issue of increased tuition altogether now that the motion to stay home next Wednesday has failed.

I think there is something else we might do that would be effective in expressing our opposition. I move . . . ." After relating to the stimulus that evoked your speech, you need to be sure its importance to the listeners is clear to them. Unless that has already been done by a previous speaker or questioner, state precisely why the matter you are about to discuss is important to listeners. Many impromptu speakers fail to do this, and they receive little attention. Doing so will also help you complete your audience analysis and adaptation when speaking under the severe time constraints of an impromptu situation. A few examples of what skilled impromptu speakers have said to relate their subjects to listeners will give you a further idea of how to do this.

> The answer to this question is important to every one of us as taxpayers, for it will affect how much property tax we must pay next year (**in response to a question**).

> Jake asked how to avoid diarrhea while on a trip to Mexico. Chances are that most of you will make at least one trip south of our nearby border, and you will be miserable most of the time from Montezuma's revenge unless you know what to do.

> The procedure I'll describe will almost always keep you safe from an audit by the Internal Revenue Service.

> If we do what Senator Brown has recommended, the student newspaper will crucify us and we are likely to lose credibility with the administration when we urge them to be more conservative fiscally. That could hurt every one of us. I'll explain why I think these things would happen (**speaking in response to a motion that a student senate purchase logo T-shirts for all senate members to wear on campus**).

Listeners now know what you are responding to and how it matters to them. You are ready to establish your competence on the subject *if* that is not well known, but do so concisely and descriptively, just as in the introduction to an extemporaneous speech. You might mention your study of the subject for a term paper, a course you took on the subject, personal experience, or special training. Here are a few examples from impromptu speeches made by our students and others:

> During the two years I worked at Burger King I learned all the details of how their foods are cooked.

> As a jewelry appraiser at Brandeis I was trained to appraise diamonds.

> I grew up in Chadron and worked one summer at the park, so I have a good idea of what you can do if you vacation at Chadron State Park.

> We made a special study of that very issue involving Russia last year in the Senate Foreign Relations Committee (**from the chair of that committee to a gathering of collegiate debaters**).

If there will be more than one main point, the final step in the introduction is to preview the structure of the body of the speech. If yours will be a one-point speech, you are ready to state that point clearly and concisely. Of course if listeners already knew what you would speak about, realized its importance to them, and knew your specific qualification, previewing the point(s) might be all you do in the introduction. One effect of a preview will be to help you keep from digressing; the other important effect will be to focus listeners' attention on the main points. Here are examples of previews for impromptu speeches:

> I'll explain two reasons I believe we should not enter into such a treaty: National security would be weakened by it, and the economy would be slowed down.

> There are three steps in removing old varnish from an antique: (1) applying a finish remover; (2) scraping the loosened varnish off; and (3) removing all traces of the finish remover.

> You can remove infected fescue from your lawn either by repeated tilling or with the herbicide Round-Up. I'll describe the procedure for each in turn.

Developing Your Point(s)

Just as soon as listeners know what to expect during the body of your impromptu speech, you should then state the first main point (or only point) and develop it. To develop a main point, you can select one or two items from long-term memory that are likely to be most clarifying or convincing to your listeners. This calls for "thinking on your feet." Be sure you develop main points. Some impromptu speakers state ideas without bothering to develop them, acting as if to state an idea were enough to make it meaningful or convincing.

Be sure to develop each point, but do not overdo the developing. Some impromptu speakers ramble on and on, telling personal anecdotes long after the point has been made. Be concise. Use no more developmental material than necessary for listeners to form a mental image akin to yours or accept your idea as valid. Then make a brief transition to the second point (if there is one), state it simply, and develop it. Because you are speaking on a subject about which you have considerable knowledge, you can think of sufficient material to develop ideas when you state them.

Concluding Your Remarks

You can wrap up your impromptu speech both quickly and effectively with a summary of the main point(s). Then suggest a final application or appeal for agreement or action—and sit down! This is no time to ramble, add second thoughts, tell one more story, or add some supporting materials you just remembered. Apply or appeal, and end. Many inexperienced speakers are inclined to ramble, add more information or digress to some vaguely related subject. They do not seem to know how to end cleanly when the time is right. However, you know how to do this. Remember, a conclusion should usually be only about 5 to 10 percent of the total length of a speech.

▶ **Speaking Impromptu**

1. Plan silently: central idea, desired response, and sequence of main points (if needed).
2. Introduce your speech.
3. Develop your point(s) as you follow your plan.
4. Conclude your speech.

▶ **Summary**

Most of us will speak impromptu in public situations more often than we will be able to prepare extemporaneously. If we do not have a method for doing so, we will likely add to the confusion, boredom, and frustration so common at public meetings. Developing skill at speaking impromptu is a highly practical art.

One should never speak impromptu in a meeting unless knowledgeable about the topic of discussion and personally concerned about it. You are prepared to speak impromptu to the degree that you are informed on the topic of discussion and can follow a time-compressed version of the procedure for preparing to speak extemporaneously.

In the few seconds before you speak (or while listening to a speaker to whom you will reply), you complete the first stage of a four-stage method of speaking impromptu: deciding on a central idea and listener response you desire to that idea, and then selecting a sequence of main points if more than one point is involved in the central idea.

The second stage is to begin your introduction with reference to whatever provoked you to speak, then proceed to complete the introduction with any of the following steps that are needed: Relate the topic to listeners' interests and lives, establish your credibility on the topic, and preview the main points of the body of your talk. In the body of your talk, state each point clearly and succinctly, then develop it from your recall of materials that are likely to make sense to your listeners. To conclude, summarize the main points or central idea, then end with a suggested application or an appeal. Do not ramble! Using this four-stage formula, you will be able to speak concisely, clearly, and forcefully in many situations where you need to speak without opportunity to prepare in advance.

▶ Learning Activities

1. Following your next assigned extemporaneous speech, answer two or three questions asked by listeners. Before attempting to answer, be sure to confirm your understanding of the question with a paraphrase or request for the questioner to clarify. Then apply the four-stage procedure for speaking impromptu.

2. Your instructor will give you two or three broad topics based on your areas of expressed interest and your background of experience, study, travel, and work. Immediately you should select one of these topics, then decide on a limited central idea and the response to it you want from your listeners. You will have from as little as 20 seconds to as long as a preceding impromptu speech for such planning. As you walk to the front of the room, you can decide on the sequence of two or three main points. Then proceed through the other three stages of the procedure for speaking impromptu as it was explained in this chapter.

3. For practice in answering questions, your class will be divided into small groups of from four to six persons each, seated in a circle. Persons in each circle will take turns answering each other's questions.
   a. When it is your turn, announce a topic that is important to you and about which you feel knowledgeable.
   b. Proceeding from your left, each group member should ask you one question. Answer each questioner in turn.
   c. After you have answered all questions following the guidance of this chapter, your classmates will briefly discuss how well you answered them (your instructor may provide a scale on which to evaluate the answers).
   d. Briefly present your judgments about the questions asked. Consider the clarity, degree of inquiry (rather than trying to make a point), and whether you thought the question was primarily aimed at making you uncomfortable.

4. Your instructor will present you with a list of special-occasion impromptu speaking situations, such as
   a. Person X is a visitor from a different school; you are to introduce him or her.
   b. You are person X; respond to your introduction.
   c. You have just been selected by vote of your classmates to represent them in a public-speaking contest open only to representatives of current public-speaking classes.

5. Turn your class into a forum to discuss a topic of current concern on your campus. Students should have several days to investigate the topic before the forum takes place. Each class member must speak once, impromptu, responding to the prior speech(es). Your instructor or an invited guest will make the opening speech.

   As a part of this activity, each participant may be required to write a brief evaluation of one or more speeches by classmates. If so, your instructor will assign who will evaluate whose speech.

17

Speaking in Special Situations

Questions to Guide Reading and Review

1. Why is it important for students to become proficient at communicating as members of small groups?
2. What is the source of the general procedural model for problem solving? What goes on during each of the five major stages in this procedure? How can following it benefit a small problem-solving group?
3. What is the best way to present a substantive statement during a problem-solving group discussion? Why?
4. What does *leadership* imply in a small task group? What is the leader's role in a task group?
5. Why is it so important that speeches given on special occasions be appropriate to the demands of the situation and expectations of listeners?
6. Why is it important to accomplish each of three functions during a speech of introduction?
7. What should you try to accomplish during a speech of welcome or farewell?
8. What should you include in a speech of nomination?
9. What should and should not be included in a speech presenting or accepting an award?
10. What guidelines should you follow if interviewed on television or radio?

Key Terms

Argumentation	Interdependent goal	Problem
Consensus	Leadership	Small group
GPMPS		

You will often speak in situations for which there are special circumstances and norms not previously covered in *Practical Public Speaking*. In fact, some of these situations are not what we normally think of as "public"; they may involve small groups in which the listeners are also the speakers, but, because of circumstances, make few if any prepared speeches. Others are special functions where the listeners have specific expectations of the speaker. Many of these special occasions involve important ceremonies and rituals. Because of the position you have in an organization, you may suddenly find yourself having to prepare for a special occasion speech. Every manager, political leader, or official is likely to face such speaking situations. Even if you do not have to make ceremonial or other special occasion public speeches, you are certain to be a member of many small groups that make up larger organizations, for example, committees, task forces, quality circles, and work teams. Such groups sometimes get a reputation for wasting time because members do not know how to speak as members of a problem-solving team.

On special public occasions, you will need the skills you have been developing as a public speaker, with adaptations to occasion-specific formalities and rituals. This chapter is devoted to planning for and participating in such specialized situations as group discussion, introducing another public speaker, welcoming and bidding farewell, nominations, award presentations, and interviews on public media.

▶ Speaking in Small Groups

More of the speaking you do will be as a member of a small group than in any other setting. Wherever you find people, you find small groups: families, hunting parties, work crews, teams, task forces, quality circles, neighborhood improvement groups, small clubs, committees, study groups, therapy groups, and self-help groups. Large numbers of small groups make up any organization.

The variety of groups indicates how important they are to human existence. Human beings need small groups to satisfy basic needs for belonging, love, and esteem; to accomplish work; and to do many other things we enjoy. Unfortunately, few individuals have had formal instruction in small-group participation and leadership. You may have had some excellent indirect instruction about small groups if you were blessed with a supportive and close family of if you were part of a successful scout group or cohesive athletic team. On the other hand, judging from the increase in family problems in our country and our relative lack of success in competing with some countries that stress teamwork, we Americans need to learn a lot more about how to participate in small groups.

In this short chapter we cannot develop a full-fledged description of small groups nor a complete study of small-group communication. Instead we provide background information needed to understand problem-solving groups—the most common kind—then focus attention on speaking as a member of such groups. Family and friendship groups call for additional attitudes and skills you could study in an interpersonal communication course.

Characteristics of Small Groups

A *small group* consists of several interdependent persons who coordinate their behavior in order to achieve some mutually accepted goal. The means to such coordination is communication. Through the exchange of signals members function as parts of a larger whole. *Interdependent* means that the members depend on one another to achieve some goal; success or failure is shared by everyone. The group is needed by its members just as the group would not exist without the roles performed by the members. For instance, to perform a complex surgical operation takes a team of specialized, interdependent professionals who depend on each other to do the job. People who accept membership in a task force to advise the president about illicit drug use need each other to accomplish such a complex job. It takes a committee to figure out all the capacities needed in a computer system to serve an insurance company.

Small groups range in size from 3 to 15 members; groups with more than 15 members usually become formal, lacking the qualities of a small group. When a new small group such as a committee or work team is forming, members do not have much of an impression of each other. Their first major task is to find out what each can do to help the group accomplish its purpose(s). If a person is to become a committed, dependable member, he or she must develop a role that contributes to the group. One person might be best at keeping meetings organized and coordinated. Another might excel at reducing tensions and conflicts. Another may be outstanding at doing research for the group. Still others will have other skills and knowledge. On these bases a division of labor develops.

Participating in Discussions

Communication relevant to the group's business is needed in small-group discussions if they are to be productive. For excellent solutions, members need to share all they know that is relevant to problems they discuss. Each needs to know where each other member stands on proposals and why. The assertive individual who is also sensitive to feelings and needs of other members is the ideal participant in group meetings. Detrimental to group discussions are people who: do not speak up when they have information or ideas; try to force their ideas without thorough evaluation of them by other members; monopolize the attention of others; are inflexible, ambiguous, or frequently switch topics; and do not listen to understand and recall what others say. Hopefully, all your small groups will have norms encouraging open, honest communication. If this is not the case, you can help the group by pointing out what you think is harmful about its norms and asking if the other members, like you, want to make a change.

LISTENING   Most of the time during a group meeting you should be listening to other members to determine how what they are saying is relevant to the group's goal achievement. As when listening to a questioner after a speech, your listening should be aimed at being able to paraphrase concisely what a prior speaker has said. When you are uncertain or confused, ask for examples, comparisons, or other clarification. "When you said . . . did you mean . . . ?" is an excellent formula to use. Before arguing, disagreeing, or adding to some other member's complex statement, paraphrasing and asking for confirmation will prevent a lot of wasted time that comes from misunderstanding and tension.

If you listen well, you will be able to give a running summary of the discussion up to the time you speak. In a sense the group members are together constructing a sort of essay or speech about some problem, concern, or subject they are exploring. It is easy for a discussion to become disjointed from frequent changes in subject. Members who have not listened well are likely to disorient the group with tangential remarks.

ORGANIZING AND DEVELOPING YOUR STATEMENTS   To help reduce the problem of disorganized discussions, use the following formula for organizing most of your impromptu comments during a problem-solving discussion:

1. Refer to what was previously said and to which you are responding.
2. State your point or idea, that might support the previous statement, disagree with it, or add a new perspective or information.
3. Provide the supporting evidence that led to your position.

For example, during a discussion of special urban bus fares for college students, Charlotte said she did not think students should have special rates different from those paid by low-income workers or old people. Charles checked his understanding by saying "I take it that you think college students are no more impoverished than many other bus riders, so they should pay the same fares as do those people." Charlotte nodded affirmatively, so Charles said:

> We were created as a committee of the Student Senate to determine what, if anything, might be done to reduce traffic congestion on campus. Some of us favor trying to get reduced bus tickets as a means of reducing the number of cars. Charlotte says that is not fair to other riders. I think

some kind of reduced fare for all persons could help get more students on buses. I know this is done in several other cities, such as Chicago and Des Moines. The Senate survey found that about one-fourth of drivers said they would take the bus if it could save them enough money. I think we should look into such a pass at a reduced rate.

You may recognize this format of (1) referring to what preceded, (2) stating the point, and (3) supplying evidence as a form of argument. *Argumentation* is needed in group problem-solving discussions to test ideas. Always argue about the merits of ideas and evidence, not about the intelligence, loyalty, or other personal characteristics of people with whom you disagree. Remember, you and that person are interdependent members of a problem-solving team, not enemies. You are arguing to help the group arrive at wise decisions, not to win a personal victory.

As a general rule, you should make only one point or express a single position or idea in any speech that is part of a problem-solving discussion. Discussions are not the place for major speeches of two to four main points, unless you are reporting on an investigation requested by the committee. Then you would speak as explained in Chapter 14. However, after the report you would be back to short one-point comments.

BEING ASSERTIVE The ideal group member is neither passive nor aggressive, but assertive. Passive members go along with the majority even when they disagree. They do not argue or protest when someone violates their basic rights as persons. Aggressive members put self-interest above the group's interests: they attack, control, dominate, and name call. Their behavior often violates the personal rights of other group members.

In contrast, assertive people speak up, but only when they have something to contribute to the discussion. You need to be informed on the subject of the meeting, then speak assertively when you have relevant information, an evaluation of information not previously voiced, an idea for a possible solution, or a question that needs to be answered before the group reaches a decision. Knowledge kept in your head is useless to the group. It must be asserted to benefit the group.

Groups that fail to encourage thorough evaluation of all information provided as evidence and of all proposed solutions frequently make poor decisions. The breakdown of critical thinking that leads to poor decisions is called *groupthink*. Some famous examples of groupthink decisions include the decision of personnel under President Reagan to bargain with Iran in a weapons-for-hostages deal and use the profits to support Nicaraguan rebels; the abortive invasion of Cuba at the Bay of Pigs early in the Kennedy administration; the Watergate burglary and coverup under President Nixon; and the decision by President Johnson to wage a full-scale war in Vietnam. Such disastrous decisions are produced in small groups where disagreement with high-status persons is stopped or minimized.[1] All evidence and reasoning should be evaluated rigorously if good decisions are the goal of a group.

Sometimes you will have a question that should be answered before moving forward in the discussion. For example, if you think the group needs information, say why and ask for it. If no one has an adequate answer, the group should then develop a procedure to get the needed information. If you are puzzled about how to proceed, ask. You may realize that the group needs to test an idea before making a final decision on a policy. If so, ask how the proposed solution could be tested before an expensive, irreversible step has been taken.

At times you will have a different interpretation of information from other members of the group. There is a tendency to keep quiet when one does not see things the same way as others. However, that is when your perceptions and interpretations are most needed by the group. If all members think alike, one person could do the thinking; a group is not needed. Speak up unless what you have to offer has previously been considered fully by the group and dismissed.

BEING PROVISIONAL   People who speak in a dogmatic "this-is-it-and-that's-all-there-is-to-it" way evoke defensiveness in others that impairs thinking and speaking.[2] The members of a small group need to begin discussion of a problem in a mood of *inquiry*, asking "What is the best answer or decision we can create or find?" Discussants should never start in the mood of certainty in which a person feels "I have the best possible answer; my job is to convince the rest of you to accept my idea!" If two or more members come to a discussion with their minds made up, a stalemate results unless one gives in. If members all come with information and *tentative* answers or ideas, then each is ready to convince and be convinced during the group discussion. The group can work out a consensus decision about what to report, recommend, or do. *Consensus* means that every member of the group believes in the action decided upon as the best action that everyone can support. There is no majority–minority split in a consensus.

BEING CONCRETE   Being concrete and specific by using examples, statistics, and descriptions is every bit as important in small-group discussions as in public speaking. Dale G. Leathers, who investigated the effects of different kinds of statements, found that vague statements produced confusion, tension, and disorganization in small groups.[3] When someone else utters a vague abstraction, you can help the group by asking for specifics or paraphrasing in concrete terms. Just as in public speaking, using statistics and citing concrete examples help clarify abstract statements.

Organizing Problem-Solving Discussions

Even though comments during a group discussion are stated clearly and with good support, the entire discussion can be disorganized and incoherent because comments are not related to each other in some systematic way. Keeping an entire discussion organized is not easy; it requires knowledge of problem-solving procedures and special leadership.

Small-group researchers have shown that coherent organization is important to discussions, much like it is in public speeches. When asked to evaluate the overall quality of problem-solving discussions, both participants and non-participating observers based their judgments more on how adequately the discussion was organized than on any other basis.[4] A whole line of research led to the general conclusion that almost any structured procedure for problem-solving discussion was superior to no procedure. In order to explain how to organize problem solving by a group, we first need to define what we mean by *problem*.

All writers agree that a *problem* includes a difference between a perceived situation and a desired situation. For example, your car may be running rough, wasting fuel, and lacking power. You want it to run efficiently, smoothly, and with enough power for passing or accelerating into fast-moving traffic. The difference between the way it is operating and what you desire is the problem you face. If at midterm you have a grade point average of 2.75, but need a 3.00 to retain a scholarship, your problem is how to increase your GPA by at least 0.25 before the end of the semester.

Obstacles to achieving the desired situation are part of every problem. A lack of cash, a lack of skills, and a lack of a credit rating could all be obstacles to achieving the desired operating condition of your car's engine. Causes of the unsatisfactory situation are among the obstacles to changing it. A combination of poor health, a broken romance, and a 40-hour work week may be causes contributing to your poorer-than-usual academic performance. Thus every problem has at least three major components:

1. An unsatisfactory condition.
2. Some contributing conditions and other obstacles to change.
3. A desired condition (goal).

Problem solving means moving from left to right in Figure 17.1.

We may begin problem solving with only a vague sense that something is unsatisfactory. Before proceeding further, we need as accurate a description of the problem as possible. Then we need to diagnose all causal conditions and decide what we can realistically hope to achieve before we talk about how to solve the problem.

THE GENERAL PROCEDURAL MODEL FOR PROBLEM SOLVING   The *general procedural model for problem solving* (GPMPS) is based on the method for investigating and solving problems we call *science*.[5] As the name indicates, it is a general model, one that can be modified to suit the nature of specific problems and groups. With some problems, such as people not wearing seat belts or drinking alcohol immoderately, how well the people affected will accept and follow a proposed policy will be a major criterion for evaluating possible solutions. In

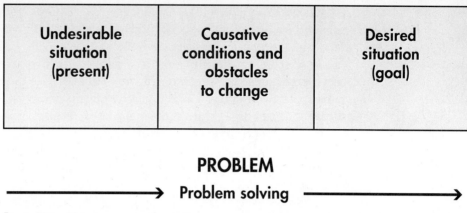

PROBLEM

Problem solving

Figure 17.1   Three components of a problem.

other problems, only technical details need to be considered (e.g., how to keep ceramic tiles from falling off a spacecraft). Some situations, such as design problems, call for a great deal of creativity, whereas others are limited to a few available options (e.g., how to get from home to school).

The GPMPS can be used to outline a procedure for a problem-solving discussion lasting from a few to many meetings, between which the members do investigative work. For instance, a presidential task force may need many meetings, several hearings, substantial library and field research, and a great deal of writing before it is ready to make its report. A group of engineers designing a space station may need years to complete their problem solving. On the other hand, a group of iron workers may decide in five minutes how to put a heavy beam in place. The actual sequence of questions to be taken up in discussion can be adapted to contingencies such as the type of problem and time available.

In the following version of the GPMPS, only general questions are included in order to emphasize the sequence of major issues to be taken up. A group should agree on the actual questions before going very far in the discussion of a problem. The words used to phrase those questions would come from the problem being discussed, using the sentence formulas shown in the model. After we present the model, we show examples of how it was used to provide a structure to guide the discussions of actual problem-solving small groups.

THE GENERAL PROCEDURAL MODEL FOR PROBLEM SOLVING

1.   *What are the characteristics of the problem we are discussing?* During this stage, most of the talking should be about the details of what is unsatisfactory, what may have caused this state of affairs and other obstacles to a solution, and the characteristics of the desired goal. Later, such characteristics may serve as criteria for judging possible solutions.

2. *What might be done to solve the problem we have described?* In this step, the focus is on discovering, inventing, and explaining possible courses of action to change the contributing causes, overcome any obstacles, and achieve the goal without creating new problems.

3. *What are the relative merits of the possible solutions?* The group may need to define and agree on criteria by which to evaluate possible solutions. Each and every proposed course of action should be evaluated against these criteria, the causative conditions, and evidence indicating new problems the solution might create.

4. *What solution can we all agree on as likely to succeed?* Often this will be a synthesis of two or more ideas. Ideally, all members of the group will believe they have created the best solution they can all support. The solution selected is the group's property, not some member's personal solution.

5. *What do we need to do to implement our solution?* Usually one or two members will write up and present a report to the person or large group that established a committee, or each member will agree to do some part of the necessary work.

After some introduction to their assignment, a problem-solving group should begin by agreeing on an outline of questions following the GPMPs. Often such an outline is prepared by the chairperson of the group, who then asks the members to comment, suggest changes, or accept the outlined procedure. Once adopted, this outline of questions is a general plan or "road map" for the group to follow for however many meetings are required to solve the problem. A group such as a standing committee may be working on several problems at the same time. For each problem, the group may be at some different stage of the problem-solving procedure. During a meeting, they will take up one problem and work on it until they need more information or other resources, then turn to a different problem.

The outline of questions to guide the group should be adapted to the characteristics of the specific problem. It might be very short or quite long and involved. The group may want to invent possible solutions in a procedure known as *brainstorming.*

Brainstorming is a procedure during which no critical comments or gestures are allowed. Innovative thinking is encouraged by asking repeatedly for more and unusual ideas, not for "good" ideas. Even wild ideas are encouraged and written down for later evaluation. When possible solutions are few, the group can begin evaluating them almost as soon as they are presented.

The following adaptation of the GPMPS to a specific problem is brief. It does not include a period of brainstorming because the options are relatively few.

I. What type of written final exam should we have for our public speaking class?

A. What is our understanding of the limits to our authority in planning an exam?
   1. We can only recommend.
   2. It must be worth 100 points.
   3. It must be comprehensive.
B. What facts and feelings should we take into account in planning the final written exam?
   1. Student concerns and choices?
   2. Our instructor's needs and desires?
   3. The textbook?
   4. The goals and practices in the course?
   5. Other facts?
C. What are our objectives or other criteria to guide us in proposing an exam?
   1. Learning objectives to be accomplished by the exam?
   2. Effect on final grades?
   3. Type of study needed?
   4. Fairness to all students?
   5. Other?
II. What kinds of written final exam might we consider?
III. What are the advantages and disadvantages of each type?
IV. What will we recommend to our instructor as the type of written final exam for our public-speaking course?

Next is an abridged version of an outline followed by an advisory group that was asked to help a student solve a problem involving a neighbor's dangerous dog.

I. What do you perceive to be John's problem with his neighbor and the neighbor's dog?
   A. What do we find unsatisfactory?
   B. What do we think is a realistic goal?
   C. Why does the difference exist?
II. What might we advise John to do about the dog? (Let's brainstorm without any evaluation.)
III. By what criteria shall we evaluate the ideas we have listed?
IV. How well does each idea measure up to our criteria?
V. What will we tell John we think he should do and how he might do it most effectively?

Following a procedural outline like the two above is not easy for some group members. Often groups jump back and forth among the steps and questions of the GPMPS. To help keep discussions organized and to see that no major question, issue, concern, or step is forgotten, small problem-solving groups such as committees, task forces, and quality circles usually have a designated discussion leader.

LEADING PROBLEM-SOLVING GROUPS In most small task groups such as committees and advisory councils, a special role is created so that one person is charged with seeing that jobs get done, decisions are made when needed, the group stays reasonably close to the procedural outline they have agreed on, and decisions are acted on. Such a person is usually given some leadership title, such as *chair, coordinator, facilitator,* or just *leader.* A committee leader is not a boss, dominator, controller, authority, or supervisor. Rather, the leader is a coordinator or a servant of the group. An appointed or elected chairperson serves the group by helping each member make a worthwhile contribution and by keeping the work organized and goal oriented. The leader should see that work agreed on by group members is done when promised rather than doing it him or herself. The leader does not make the major decisions for the group nor does more work to carry them out than other members do.

Following up on meetings is a part of everyone's responsibility, but coordination of such work is done by the chair. She or he may write up reports and make recommendations to the person or organization that created the group. If a motion is to be made at a meeting of the parent organization of a committee, the chair of the committee makes the motion and speaks first in its support.

A major responsibility of a chairperson is to coordinate the discussions: seeing that the group does not overlook some important issue or question in the problem-solving procedure, keeping members from changing the subject of discussion unless the entire group wants to make the change, seeing that everyone has equal opportunity to get the attention of others, and promoting good human relationships. A designated small-group leader should rarely propose a solution or take a stand early in a discussion. If you would like to know more about this role, we urge you to enroll in a small-group communication and leadership course.

▶ Preparing to Speak on Special Public Occasions

Throughout *Practical Public Speaking* we have emphasized relationships among speaker, audience, and message, with somewhat less emphasis on the situation in which a speech will be presented. Sometimes, however, a special public occasion demands special adaptations from the speaker in message content, style, organization, and even delivery. Audiences in such situations expect the speaker to conform to these specific norms. Your success will often depend on how well you understand the demands of a social ritual or ceremony of which your speech is a part.

Social rituals and ceremonies bind individuals to a group by reaffirming shared beliefs, values, and attitudes. Commencement speakers reinforce the value of education and challenge graduates to use their skills to better themselves and society. Speeches of tribute unify members of an organization by applauding shared values and achievements, whereas speeches of welcome extend special courtesies and good will. Occasions such as these require special adaptations to the social rules of the group and event. One key to succeeding is *appropriateness*. The speaker must plan a message appropriate to the situation. For example, it would be inappropriate for a university commencement speaker to extol his or her personal success by emphasizing how he or she learned from the "school of hard knocks," without mentioning the benefits of formal education. It would be equally inappropriate for the presenter of an award to tell a story embarrassing to the recipient, no matter how funny the story. A speech of introduction should focus the attention of the listeners on the main speaker and topic, not the introducer. Appropriateness is of the highest importance in ceremonial and traditional occasions. The following guidelines will help you create messages that conform to audience expectations in several types of special occasions common in the United States.

Speeches of Introduction

Many occasions require that a speaker be introduced by a member of the audience. In most such cases the speaker is not affiliated with the organization sponsoring the speech. For instance, many service organizations have speakers at breakfast, lunch, or dinner meetings. Doubtless you have had guest lecturers in classes or attended speeches sponsored by organizations on campus. Occasionally the speaker being introduced is a member of the organization holding the meeting who has been asked to share some special information or opinion. For example, a staff member may report a special investigation at an annual meeting of stockholders, or a campus administrator might report to the student body or the assembled faculty.

The job of a person introducing a speaker is to tell the audience three things: why this person is speaking; why on this topic; and why at this time. In other words, the speech of introduction should be planned to perform three functions:

1. Direct the attention of listeners to the subject.
2. Establish the competence of the speaker on the subject.
3. Stress the timeliness of the subject.

In addition, on behalf of the audience the introducer is expected to welcome a guest speaker. The speech of introduction should be short, yet concrete.

When you are asked to introduce someone, contact the speaker prior to the speech event in order to obtain the information you will need to enhance the speaker's credibility and stress the importance of the message to the audience. Now is the time to learn how to pronounce the speaker's name correctly; get specific facts about the speaker's study, experience, and background on the topic; and discover what values and beliefs the speaker and audience share. After you have obtained such information you can prepare an introduction to bring speaker and listeners together. If possible, tell the speaker what you are going to say in the introduction. Together you may plan some changes before it is too late.

A poor introduction can embarrass or handicap a speaker. Praise, especially if effusive, can embarrass many persons. Avoid trite phrases such as "It is my honor to present . . ." and "I know you will all join me in giving Mr. Jones an enthusiastic Tiger welcome." *Never* say that the person you are introducing is a great speaker. That is likely to focus attention on style and delivery instead of on ideas. Also, the speaker may not be so enthusiastic and energetic as you expect.

Brevity is a virtue in introductions. Speak only as long as it takes to give the audience sufficient information to appreciate the speaker and message. "Ladies and gentlemen, the president of the United States" is the epitome of brevity; no further detail is needed. For less well-known speakers, you will take more time, but never more than a few minutes.

Speeches of Welcome

The president of a university might give a welcome address to a convention of military engineers hosted by the engineering department. A plant manager might welcome a group visiting a factory for a few days to gain information about manufacturing techniques. An officer of a local chapter of a fraternity might welcome a delegation from a distant place. In each of these cases the norms of the occasion are similar: focus on the importance of the group of visitors; outline anticipated advantages of the visit to both visitors and hosts; call for cooperation during the visit; and set up a channel for future communication. A speech of welcome should be brief. It should leave the welcomed person(s) feeling positive about the host organization.

Speeches of Farewell

Often occasioned by retirement or a move, farewell speeches are expected to express gratitude for accomplishments of the departing person or persons. The person making a farewell address represents the audience or organization, which expects the speaker to applaud accomplishments made by the honoree as a member of the group.

A speech of farewell is usually organized around characteristics or contributions of the person departing. Sometimes interest and common ground are achieved with stories of events that happened while the honoree was associated with the group. Such a story should never be one that might embarrass the person departing. This is a time to emphasize the good, the pleasant, the shared. The conclusion is usually a restatement of the contributions of the honoree that will be remembered by those who remain and a wish for his or her future success and happiness. Brief information about what the departing person plans for the future can be included in the conclusion.

When a farewell speech is given on behalf of a group, the departing person should be given an opportunity to respond. Like the speech representing the organization, the response should be brief. A person honored by a farewell speech is expected to stress positive relationships with the organization and appreciation for its members, *not* enthusiasm about getting away. In the case of a farewell following a short visit, the visitor is expected to express appreciation for specific benefits of the visit. Again, the speech is usually organized around two or three topics, developed with concrete examples. The main caution is to avoid a saccharine speech filled with insincere praise.

A different type of farewell speech is the eulogy, most often given in a special service for a recently deceased colleague, friend, or relative. Sometimes a eulogy is part of a funeral service; other times it is part of a memorial following the funeral. The speaker should create a highly personal message expressing sentiments shared with the audience. Such a speech is expected to recall accomplishments and virtues of the deceased individual, leaving the listeners feeling good about their association with the departed. Not every accomplishment needs to be recalled, but brief highlights of the major attributes and contributions should be stressed as main points. Feelings of sadness and mourning should be uttered in the introduction or early in the body rather than in the conclusion. The ending should reiterate the upbeat, the blessing of having been an associate of the deceased, or what the life of the deceased means to the speaker and listeners.

Speeches of Nomination

When nominating a person for an office or award, the speaker is expected to present a tightly organized speech packed with information about the nominee's qualifications for the position or award. An applied criteria sequence is most often used in planning the body, emphasizing the nominee's experiences, personal attributes, and other qualifications *relevant to the office or award*. Evidence should be provided that the nominee meets or exceeds all these criteria. Mention the nominee's name often to ensure that it stays in the minds of listeners when the time comes to vote. The conclusion usually includes a brief summary, an appeal for support, and a forceful restatement of the nominee's name.

The person presenting a speech of nomination must have high credibility with the audience. The nominator must be perceived to be honest and sincere when praising the nominee. If you are not well known or accepted within the organization, someone else should speak in nomination.

Speeches to Present and Accept Awards

As an officer, manager, or administrator, you may discover that it is your responsibility to present awards. An award presenter should summarize the purpose of the award, then give a brief history of past recipients with whom it is an honor to be identified. The speaker is expected to express appreciation to the awardee for services and accomplishments for which the award is being given. Such awards are designed to highlight the values, ideals, and purposes of the organization, reminding members how they ought to behave. Thus the body of the speech is usually organized around criteria for the award. The conclusion should leave the listeners feeling that the award was appropriately given and that they, too, want to be worthy of it. The speaker usually concludes by handing the award to the recipient and saying something ceremonial, such as "Congratulations!"

When you receive an award or nomination to office, it is appropriate for you to respond to the presenter and audience. Sometimes a simple "Thank you" is sufficient, especially if the program is long and includes numerous awards. However, often you will be expected to make a speech of acceptance. When you feel that an acceptance speech is expected of you, there are several conventional topics to guide your planning. First, express your gratitude to the nominator, or if you have been given an award, thank the organization for honoring you. Express your appreciation for the good work of the organization. Then be sure to give credit to the many persons who helped you do the work for which you have just been honored: members of the audience, family, friends, mentor, and others. If appropriate, pledge your continued efforts for the organization. If you have been nominated, you might state the specific values and objectives you will work to accomplish if elected.

Avoid lengthy speeches of acceptance, false modesty, and a matter-of-fact manner. This is no time to go into detail about the organization, your reminisces, or your platform. Nor should you suggest the nominators were incompetent for having selected someone so undistinguished as you. Rather, express gratitude for having been recognized as a good servant and friend of the listeners. Equally in bad taste is to suggest arrogantly that "of course" you were nominated or given the award.

Television and Radio Interviews

Sometimes a speaker is asked to respond to a radio or television reporter or interviewer. If you have little experience in broadcasting, this can be an anxiety-provoking situation.

You can retain control during such an interview by taking time to think before speaking. Paraphrasing the question can give you a few seconds to collect your thoughts. Don't ever pretend or make false claims. Broadcasters can expose phonies dramatically. Be as straightforward as you would be in a conversation with a friend. Admit when you do not know. If you are making an important policy statement or reporting a decision of a group, it is usually best to read the statement from manuscript or teleprompter to avoid misrepresentation or omissions. Of course, you would practice the reading several times until you can do it fluently and confidently and with vocal variety.

If you are interviewed for television, remember that all gestures and vocal variations are magnified by the television medium. Be conservative in movements and vocal inflections, unlike when facing a live audience.

Other Special Occasions

Many other ceremonial occasions include speeches, commencements, anniversaries of historical events, pep rallies, ground breakings, official openings of buildings, and conventions. Each type of occasion has norms and expectations as guidelines for speakers. The values of the organization or society involved should be stressed in any kind of group renewal. The purpose of any special occasion provides guidance in choosing topics for the body of your remarks. Long speeches are never appreciated nor are speakers who talk at length about themselves and their personal accomplishments. The group for which the ceremony is held should be the focus of your central idea. In all special occasion speeches, evidence and reasoning are not called for so much as are concrete examples to illustrate and dramatize. A vivid conclusion calling forth shared sentiments related to the occasion is almost always appropriate.

▶ Summary

Membership in both small groups and large organizations means participating in numerous special kinds of situations as a speaker. In addition to the more general principles and skills you have developed for speaking in public, each type of special situation requires specific kinds of adaptations.

Much of your speaking will be as a participant in small groups. Members of task groups such as committees, work teams, and quality circles are unified around a shared objective. Each member must find a role in which he or she can contribute to the group—part of a division of labor that provides all the activities needed to accomplish the group goal. During discussions one needs to be both assertive and an active listener. Comments should be related to what preceded them, concise, usually limited to one point, and supported if any claim is advanced by the speaker. Argumentation is needed as an application of critical thought to information and ideas so that the group arrives at the best possible conclusion. Ideally, all major decisions are settled by consensus. Every participant in a problem-solving discussion needs to propose solutions tentatively, in a mood of inquiry, if consensus is to be achieved.

To achieve quality decisions efficiently, problem-solving discussions need to be organized around the basic procedure of scientific investigation. A model to follow for doing so is the General Procedural Model for Problem Solving, in which there are five major phases: (1) problem description and analysis; (2) discovery of possible solutions; (3) evaluation of the possible solutions; (4) deciding on a solution or policy; and (5) planning how to test or implement the decision. Leading problem-solving groups means coordinating the efforts of members, not dictating or deciding for the group.

In addition to being a member of small groups, participating in organizational life involves many special occasions on which public speeches are made. Visiting speakers are introduced, visitors are welcomed, farewell is bidden to associates, members are nominated for offices and awards, awards are given and accepted, and broadcast interviews are conducted. In all these specialized situations, appropriateness to the social norms and the purpose of the occasion should guide the speaker's planning. Brevity, sincerity, concrete examples, and emphasis on shared values and beliefs are important characteristics of all such speeches. A schema stressing characteristics or criteria is usually needed when there is more than one main point in the body of the speech. A sense of appreciation and sharing should permeate the speech, emphasizing the values and purposes of the organization. The organization, not the speaker, should be central in special occasion speeches.

▶ Learning Activities

1. Create a one-page outline of questions based on the general procedural model for problem solving (GPMPS) for a problem assigned by your instructor. Compare outlines in a class meeting of your small group, then create one outline as a guide for your subsequent problem-solving discussion.

    Arrange a time and place to meet outside of class for your problem-solving discussion. After the group has decided what to recommend or do, one person should write a report signed by all members of the group. Follow this format for your report:
    I. *Problem*: Description or question.
    II. *Findings*: Summary of facts and your interpretations of them concerning this problem.
    III. *Possible solutions*: A list of all proposals suggested and evaluated by the group members.
    IV. *Solution recommended by the group as a consensus decision*: Describe the solution your group decides on and your reasons for choosing it as best.

2. Your instructor will provide you with an outline for applying the GPMPS to some campus or area problem. Your class will be divided into task forces of approximately five people each.

   At the first meeting you will have approximately 20 minutes in which to clarify the problem as much as possible, including your goal as a group. You will need to make assignments (largely by deciding what needs to be done, then asking for volunteers to do these tasks) for investigative research into the problem.

   Your second meeting will be approximately two weeks later, allowing time to carry out investigative assignments. At this second meeting, lasting about 45 minutes, you will complete your discussion following the outline. A reporter should be selected by the group to report the group's recommendation and arguments for it, both in writing and orally to the class. Additionally, this report may be signed by all members and submitted to appropriate administrator(s) or other responsible persons with authority to act on it.

   At the close of your second meeting, conduct a brief discussion of the following questions:

   a. How well did we apply and follow the GPMPS?
   b. How do we feel about the GPMPS as a way for organizing group problem-solving work and discussions?
   c. How well did we follow the guidelines for communicating provided in this chapter?

3. Divide your class into five-person committees to plan and arrange an end-of-class celebration. Each committee will report its recommendations to the class for adoption, amendment, or rejection. Possible committees:

   Attendance: Who should be invited and permitted to attend?
   Entertainment.
   Food and beverage.
   Facilities: Site for the party.
   Program: Probably include two or three speeches selected as best of the semester in this class.
   Decorations.

   Each committee should select (or instructor appoint) a chairperson to co-ordinate discussion and report to the entire class for the committee. This report should include a formal motion:

   "The _____ committee moves that our class (do what?)."

   This motion should be followed by a brief speech supporting the committee's recommendation. Your instructor will serve as presiding officer, adhering to a simple version of *Robert's Rules of Order* for large group meetings.

4. Prepare to nominate one of your classmates for an office in student government or some other organization assigned by your instructor. Then present the speech to either a small group of classmates or the entire class.

5. On behalf of your class or school, plan and present a brief speech giving a humanitarian award to a well-known person.

6. Introduce a classmate (who will present a specialist's report to the class) or a guest speaker whom you know and respect (of course, the person will not be present).

7. On behalf of your institution, welcome a visiting delegation of students from a college or university in some other country. They have come to your campus for a two-week visit in order to compare student life at home and here.

8. Imagine that you are participating in a memorial service for a deceased person whom you admire as a great American hero (e.g., Lincoln, Washington, King, Malcolm X, Chief Joseph, Sacajawea). Prepare and present a three-minute speech of tribute to the memory of this person.

Notes

1. Steven M. Alderton and Lawrence R. Frey, "Argumentation in Small Group Decision-Making," in Randy Y. Hirokawa and Marshall Scott Poole (eds.), *Communication and Group Decision-Making* (Beverly Hills, CA: Sage, 1986), pp. 157–173, especially pp. 159–161.

2. Jack R. Gibb, "Defensive Communication," *Journal of Communication* 11 (1961):141–148.

3. Dale G. Leathers, "Process Disruption and Measurement in Small Group Communication," *Quarterly Journal of Speech* 55 (1969):288–298.

4. Dennis S. Gouran, Candace Brown, and David R. Henry, "Behavioral Correlates of Perceptions of Quality in Decision-Making Discussions," *Communication Monographs* 45 (1978):62; William E. Jurma, "Effects of Leader Structuring Style and Task-Orientation Characteristics of Group Members," *Communication Monographs* 46 (1979):282–295.

5. John K. Brilhart and Gloria J. Galanes, *Effective Group Discussion*, 7th ed. (Dubuque, IA: Wm. C. Brown, 1992), pp. 236–246.

Appendix
Speeches for Illustration and Analysis

Some of the speeches that follow are outstanding examples of excellence in planning and execution. Some contain common deficiencies. By careful analysis and evaluation of what the speakers have done well—and not so well—you can learn much about speaking effectively.

What Goes Up Must Come Down
Kelli Belshe

Speaking in order to instruct listeners to perform complex physical activities is quite common, such as teaching job skills, coaching, and so on. A speech of this type was presented by Kelli Belshe to her fellow students enrolled in a basic public-speaking class at Southwest Missouri State University in the fall semester of 1990. For the first extemporaneous speech, the instructor had assigned a speech to inform about a process or procedure; sensory aids were required.

Kelli had discovered that her classmates either wanted to learn to play tennis or knew how to play tennis at a beginner level and wanted to learn how to play better. She had taken tennis lessons for three years, played on a high school tennis team for two years, and given some lessons. Before beginning to speak, she had her classmates sit in a semicircle so all could see her demonstrations. Printed here is a slightly edited transcription of the recorded speech, with permission of Kelli Belshe.

When I first started playing tennis, there were a couple of times when the ball I tried to serve ended up in the middle of my racket instead of on the other side of the court. After three years of lessons and two years on a high school tennis team I learned to avoid such embarrassing errors. Most of you have indicated that you want to learn to play tennis or to play better. I hope to help you avoid embarrassment from such awkward strokes by showing you five steps to serve a tennis ball correctly. These steps are the placement of the ball, the grip of the racket, the stance, the ball toss, and the follow-through.

First, we will consider the placement of the ball. When serving you must first decide on the spot where you want the ball to go. Just as when a basketball player shoots to hit the basket, a tennis player also has to hit a certain spot on the court to make the serve good. As you can see in my diagram of a tennis court, the server must be behind the baseline in the shaded area of the lower left corner of the drawing. The ball must go over the net and hit the court in the area just across the net diagonally opposite the server. That is the larger shaded part of my drawing, right here. [At this point Kelli was pointing to her drawing, first the lower left shaded area, then the upper right shaded area shown in Figure A.1.] If you are serving from the other side of the court, you must stand in this area behind the baseline and the ball must go over the net and hit in this part of the court, here on my diagram. Now you know where to place the ball.

The second step is to grip the racket. When serving, you need to use a continental grip. The handle of the racket is octagon shaped with eight sides. You line up the V formed by the thumb and index finger of your dominant

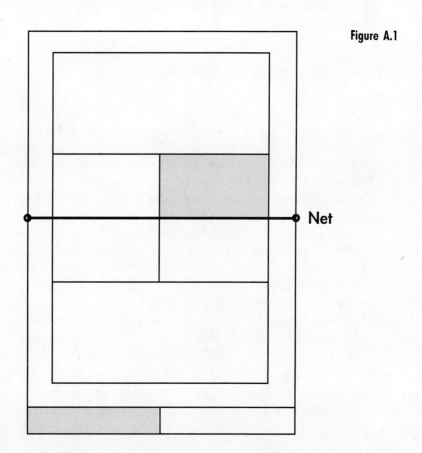

Figure A.1

Net

hand with this side of the racket. [Points to racket.] This continental grip is important for two reasons. It will give you better control of the racket than any other. Once you have begun serving you will find it gives you consistent ball placement.

The third step is to take the stance you will need to serve. When serving, your foot opposite your dominant hand should be slightly in front. I'm right handed, so my left foot will be slightly in front of my right foot, like this. You want to have your feet spread far enough apart so that you can easily sway back and forth on them, like this. You want to have your feet pointed toward the spot to which you are serving. If you are right-handed, your feet should be placed like this [here Kelli held two cutouts shaped like feet in position on the diagram], and like this if you are left-handed. Having determined where the ball is to go, gotten a good continental grip on the racket, and properly placed your feet, you are ready for the fourth step, the ball toss.

The reason my speech is entitled "What Goes Up Must Come Down" is that this is the most important part of your serve. When tossing the ball, you want to be sure your arm is shoulder high, your elbow is straight, but not locked, and you have the ball cupped loosely in your hand. When you toss the ball, you want it to go straight up and high. Then when your racket comes through, you can hit the ball without having to reach for it. The toss must be high enough so you do not have to bend your arm to hit it. A bent arm takes away from your power. Without a good ball toss, your serve will not be smooth and powerful. So if you make a bad toss, it is best just to catch the ball and start over instead of trying to serve it.

Once you have become familiar with the placement of the ball, the continental grip of the racket, the stance you need to be in for serving, and the high straight ball toss, then you are ready for the last step, the follow-through. That is basically swinging your racket, having it hit the ball, and continuing the swing. You start with the racket in one hand and the ball in the other. Bring your racket down across your body and back behind you, like this. Then it will come up behind your head in a motion sort of like when you are scratching your back or washing it with a back brush. Your arm comes up fully extended because you want to hit the ball forcefully, which you can't do if your arm is bent. Your arm must come totally to the opposite side of your body in the follow-through. This is really important, because if your arm just stops when you hit the ball, you will not have as much power as if your arm comes right on down in the follow-through. Also, if you stop the swing without a completed follow-through, the ball is going to stray out of the placement area; it will most likely go over the fence. [Here Kelli demonstrated the follow-through in both slow motion and at full speed.]

So in conclusion you now know the steps important to serving a tennis ball: the placement of the ball as your aim, the continental grip to give you control of the racket, the stance to aim your body and allow you to sway back and forth, the high straight ball toss, and the follow-through to give you power and accuracy. These steps will help you play a successful game of tennis without the embarrassment of a wild serve or a ball caught in the racket. If you don't play, now you can appreciate more fully what you see professional players do when serving during matches shown on television.

Puzzles

Lael Borchert

This speech to inform was presented by Lael Borchert in forensic competition during the 1984–1985 academic year. A student at Concordia College in Moorhead, Minnesota, she was coached by Professor John Bourhis.

Lael chose for her competition speech a topic in which she was personally interested and knowledgeable. Her listeners would be primarily forensic contestants and judges, people she knew could be readily interested in intellectual challenges. As you study the speech, notice the simple, clear language and specific examples she used to explain basic principles. She cited many sources, including both expert testimony and descriptive statistics to develop her ideas. The sequence of main points is also simple and clear. The functions of an introduction and conclusion are accomplished concisely. You may find it instructive to outline the speech. Lael won many awards for this speech at both regional and national tournaments. The copy that follows was slightly edited and reprinted with the permission of Lael Borchert.

Is it legal in South Dakota for a man to marry his widow's sister? Can a woman living in Aberdeen, South Dakota, be buried east of the Mississippi? If a plane crashes directly on the border between North and South Dakota, where are the survivors buried? No, this is not a speech about South Dakota. It is, however, a speech about a phenomenon that has been sweeping this country—puzzles.

Dr. James F. Fixx, in his book *More Games for the Super Intelligent*, says that there are two types of people in the world: those who love puzzles and those who can't stand them. Regardless of which type of person you are, puzzle books have become a staple of the American publishing industry. Dr. Martin Gardner's mathematical puzzles from past columns of *Scientific American* have been collected in ten different volumes, with total sales of more than a half million copies. James Fixx's books—*Solve It, Games for the Super Intelligent*, and *More Games for the Super Intelligent*—have collectively sold over a million copies. And, of course, there is the multimillion dollar industry that has been created by people's fascination with crossword puzzles.

Like you, I am one of those people who love puzzles, enough not only to do a lot of them, but also to read everything I can about their nature and creation. Today I will share with you some of what I have learned about the nature of puzzles and how they are used to entertain, as indicators of intelligence, and to help develop problem-solving techniques. First, I will examine what puzzles are.

Dr. Fixx defined a puzzle as a collection of symbols—such as words, numbers, letters, pictures, and/or geometric shapes—to form a problem that has a correct, but not obvious answer. Now, not all problems are puzzles. For instance, "What does two plus two equal?" is a problem, formed from symbols, that has one correct answer. However, it is not a puzzle because the answer is obvious. The solution requires only the mechanical application of a mathematical principle to arrive at the correct answer, four. Here is an example of a puzzle. [Points to chart, Figure A.2.] You have three distinct groupings of four numbers each. The puzzle is to determine into which grouping the numbers 15, 16, and 17 belong. The solution to this puzzle requires us to abandon traditional approaches to solving this sort of problem. Traditionally, we view numbers mathematically. We may attempt to solve this problem by adding, subtracting, dividing, and multiplying in an attempt to discover mathematical relationships that will help us answer the problem. Eventually we abandon this approach and begin looking for unconventional relationships. Are these ages? Dates? Bus numbers? Addresses? Or maybe shapes? The correct answer is, of course, that these numbers are grouped according to their shapes.

Now that we know that a puzzle is a problem formed from a group of symbols with a correct, but not obvious solution, we are ready to examine the uses of puzzles to entertain, to indicate intelligence, and to develop problem-solving techniques.

If you are one of the people who enjoys the challenge, for you a good puzzle can be a source of entertainment. Professor Bostock Hacket describes the thrill of mental exercise provided by puzzles. These aerobics for the mind can exercise our imaginations and wile away many an hour. Puzzles are great for taking on trips. Besides taking up lots of time and very little room, it says something to people around you when they see you reading books with titles like *More Games for the Super Intelligent* and the *Mensa Genius Quiz Book*. Puzzles can be fun and entertaining, especially for people who eventually figure out the correct answer.

Besides being an excellent source of entertainment, puzzles can be used to measure intelligence. Intelligence is an interesting phenomenon. All of us recognize it when we encounter it. We can quickly decide if someone has an

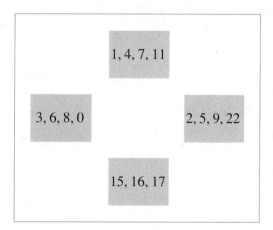

Figure A.2

abundance or deficiency of it, yet scholars have had a difficult time agreeing on the nature of intelligence. Scholars may not be exactly sure what intelligence is, but they have been measuring it since 1905, when Alfred Binet devised the first IQ test. IQ tests and measurements of intelligence have been devised and criticized ever since. In spite of the difficulty of measuring intelligence, scholars have created a variety of different measurements. One new method of measurement being examined is the puzzle. Many puzzles are short IQ tests.

Psychologists Robert Sternberg and Janet Davidson of Yale University conducted a study in 1982 examining the correlation between performance on certain insight puzzles and intelligence. First, individuals were given an intelligence test, the Henman–Nelson Test of Mental Ability, which includes questions of vocabulary, math, and reasoning. They also gave subjects a deductive reasoning test, followed by an inductive reasoning test. They found that performance on the insight puzzles requiring inductive reasoning closely correlated with scores on the traditional IQ tests.

Here is an example of the inductive reasoning puzzles used by Sternberg and Davidson. Water lilies double in area every 24 hours. At the beginning of summer there is one water lily on the lake. It takes 60 days for the lake to become completely covered with water lilies. On what day is the lake half covered? To find the correct answer, the subjects had to realize that the critical fact was that the lilies double in area every 24 hours. If the lake is to be completely covered on the sixtieth day, it has to be half-covered on the fifty-ninth day. In Sternberg and Davidson's study, this particular puzzle was the best predictor of IQ score.

An important caveat to make here is that not all puzzles involve inductive reasoning, and therefore not all puzzles are good indicators of intelligence. Puzzles like the next one, found in *More Games for the Super Intelligent*, are not reliable indicators of IQ. "You have 35 cents in two coins. One of them is not a quarter. What are the coins?" The answer to this puzzle requires detecting a trick in the wording of the question, involving the statement that one of the coins is not a quarter. The coin that is not a quarter is a dime—the other coin, of course, is a quarter.

In addition to serving as indicators of intelligence, puzzles can help us develop our day-to-day problem-solving abilities. Doctors Karen Billings and Alice Schwandt of Columbia University wrote in their article "New Techniques for Thinking Clearly" that problem-solving puzzles "involve the same sort of structuring and retrieval of information that many of life's problems do." Effective problem solving involves deciding what information is relevant and how it is relevant, fitting together seemingly unrelated bits of information, and comparing the problem we are working on to past problems. Puzzles can provide us with stress-free practice for improving these skills.

When attempting to solve a problem, much of the information we are given may not be relevant to the solution. Here is an example. If you have black socks and brown socks in your drawer, mixed in the ratio of 4 to 5, how many socks will you have to take out to make sure of having a pair of the same color? If we dwell on the ratio of 4:5, which is, in fact, useless information, we may miss the obvious. If there are only two colors of socks in the drawer, we will need to take out three socks to find two of the same color.

Another helpful skill in problem solving is the ability to relate seemingly unrelated pieces of information. Here is an example of a puzzle from Billings and Schwandt's article illustrating this technique. It's about a hunter tracking a bear. Here are your clues: the hunter follows the bear one kilometer south, then he goes one kilometer east, and finally he goes one kilometer north, only to find that he has returned to his starting point. What color is the bear? We have to fit together directional information that at first seems totally unrelated to what we need to know in order to determine the bear's color. To find the correct answer, we must realize that if the hunter only went in three directions and his ending point was the same as his starting point, the hunter must have followed a triangular path. Geographically, the only place this could happen would be the North Pole. Therefore the bear must be white, since only polar bears inhabit that part of the earth, and all of them are white. Thinking about puzzles like this one can aid us in solving our real-life problems by developing the skills of compiling information and drawing conclusions from it.

The third key in solving problems is comparing the problem we're working on to problems that we've encountered in the past. Look at this group of letters. [Points to chart that she has just put on easel, Figure A.3.] We see that the letters of the alphabet are grouped into three categories. We are asked to put the remaining letters in the proper categories. Now think about the problem we looked at in the introduction. There the numbers were categorized by shape; here the letters are also grouped according to shape. The first group contains letters that are formed by straight lines, the second group's letters are formed by straight and curved lines, and letters in the third group are formed by curved lines. By applying what we learned in the first problem we can solve this problem easily. In daily life, we often encounter problems that we can solve more readily if we think of them in light of what we've found true in other situations.

Solving puzzles is a growing pastime in our culture. However, puzzles have more implications for us than just passing the time and keeping us amused. Some of them can be used as measures of intelligence. In fact, some scholars suggest that puzzles be used to replace such traditional standardized tests as the SAT, GRE, LSAT, and MAT. Many of them can help us develop our problem-solving abilities such as sorting out useless information, organizing information that we are given, and applying past problem-solving experiences

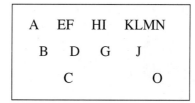

Figure A.3

to current problems. In psychiatry, puzzles are being used to diagnose and treat patients with severe mental disorders and even to retrain amnesiacs.

Now that you know what puzzles are, how they can be used, and how to solve them, you are ready to answer the initial questions I posed to you. "Is it legal in South Dakota for a man to marry his widow's sister?" It may be legal, but most dead men don't remarry. "Can a woman living in Aberdeen, South Dakota, be buried east of the Mississippi?" Of course it's possible, but we don't usually bury living persons. "If a plane crashes directly on the border between North and South Dakota, where are the survivors buried?" Now you know the answer.

Pigeons
Larry Perkins

This speech was first delivered by Larry Perkins to his public-speaking class at Southwest Missouri State University during the spring of 1990. His instructor, Vicki Stanton, had assigned an extemporaneous speech to persuade using emotional appeals. To fulfill the assignment, Larry chose to speak about homing pigeons, a topic with which he was deeply involved. He raised them, raced them, and had personally experienced the pain of having prize-winning birds wounded and killed by thoughtless shooters. Such personal involvement contributed to the amount of effort Larry made to prepare and the manner in which he spoke. We selected Larry's speech partly because of the vivid imagery he used to evoke an emotional response. Notice how he directed listener attention and interest with a graphic example involving suspense and courage, probably predisposing listeners to think well of pigeons. Is the comparison of his feelings about having a pigeon shot to your feelings if your pet dog or cat were shot effective motivation? Do the evidence and reasoning seem adequate to support his central idea, or is this an example of a speaker trying to arouse emotions when he lacks substance to support an idea? How well do you think he applied the motivated sequence pattern of organization? What do you think would have been your response as an audience member when Larry introduced Rommell just before his appeal for your agreement?

Larry decided to enter the Public Speaking Showcase sponsored by the Department of Communications for students enrolled in Basic Public Speaking and was awarded first place by the judges. His presentation during that contest was recorded and transcribed. It is reprinted here with the permission of Larry Perkins.

It was October 27, 1918, deep in the Argonne Forest of France. Major Charles Wittlesee, who was in command of a battalion attached to the 77th Division, found himself and his men surrounded by German forces, out of food, and being shelled by American artillery. By the end of the day one-third of the men in this "Lost Battalion" were dead, and no medic was left alive to care for the wounded.

A message with their plight and location was attached to the leg of their one remaining carrier pigeon, Cheramee. She was their last hope. Cheramee rose above the battalion and circled several times before being shot to the ground. Two more times she rose in the air, and twice again the Germans shot her down. Finally, Cheramee rose and cleared the trees. Twenty-five minutes later she was home at battalion headquarters. The message was received, and the Lost Battalion was saved.

Cheramee became the first homing pigeon decorated as an American war hero. During Cheramee's valiant effort to save the Lost Battalion, her breast bone was pierced by a bullet, and one eye and a leg were lost. The lifesaving message that she carried to battalion headquarters was held in place by ligaments of her missing leg.

During the two world wars thousands of lifesaving and battle-winning messages were carried by homing pigeons. Many of these stories are documented in Marion Kauthran's book, *A Fancy for Pigeons*. Because of their heroic deeds and abilities in helping maintain freedom, a special law was passed at the close of World War II making it illegal to maim or kill a homing pigeon.

In 1988 this law was repealed, based on arguments that it was costly to enforce and no longer needed. My purpose today is to convince you that this law is needed to protect the investment of modern-day pigeon raisers, to protect this unique form of communication, and, most importantly, to protect the life of a creature to whom our society owes a tremendous debt.

Today homing pigeons are used primarily for racing. In a pigeon race, the birds are taken hundreds of miles from their home and released. Then they fly at speeds up to 70 miles per hour to return home. I participate in this sport and have raised many winners. Some birds I own are worth thousands of dollars, which is not a large sum when you consider that pigeons participate in races where the payout can reach $1 million or more. As you can see, the investment and potential winnings of today's carrier pigeons can be great.

Unfortunately, each year thousands of birds are maimed or killed during these races, partly because there is no law that protects them. Beyond the investment in money that is lost when a pigeon is killed, we pigeon fanciers have an emotional investment as well. Imagine how you would feel if your dog or cat dragged its bleeding, gun-shot body to your doorstep and died at your feet. You would be devastated, just as many pigeon owners are when this happens, just as I have been. Luckily for you as pet owners, this rarely occurs because of protective laws. Homing pigeons deserve no less.

Since World War II, homing pigeons have been used very little as messengers. However, their unique ability always to find their way back home makes them a potentially valuable tool, even in today's high-tech society. The department of hematology in Plymouth, England, recently discovered the value of homing pigeons. The organization was spending $40,000 a year to get blood samples from local hospitals to their main lab. Because of heavy traffic, trips between hospitals and the lab often took as long as 45 minutes. Mrs. Hilary Sanders, a hospital employee, came up with the idea of transporting samples by homing pigeon to the main lab, where a rooftop loft was built. This unique idea is saving the hospital over $39,000 per year, and the samples are arriving in five to ten minutes. Sometimes low technology is best! With a protective pigeon law, innovative ideas like this one could be implemented here in the United States.

In opening my speech I told you the story of Cheramee. But there are many other pigeons that have saved lives and passed information that helped win battles. According to Wendell Levy in his book *The Pigeon*, over 10,000 successful missions were flown by homing pigeons in World War II alone. The timing of the retaking of Rome in the Second World War is directly related to information passed by a pigeon named "GI Joe."

The world wars helped to establish and maintain the freedoms we enjoy today. We owe a part of that freedom to homing pigeons. In return, we owe pigeons the right to fly free and protected. A law that would protect homing pigeons is not an outdated piece of legislation but a way to repay a debt we owe to these courageous and valuable birds.

In summary, I have shown you that homing pigeons represent a monetary and emotional investment for those who own them. I have shown you that homing pigeons can be a valuable resource even in our high-tech world. Finally, I have shown you that as a society we owe these birds a great debt of gratitude.

As I conclude, there is someone I would like you to meet. This is Rommell, a homing pigeon. Within him beats the heart of a champion. I hope that I have touched your heart today, your emotions, and your logic and convinced you that this bird deserves protection—this heart deserves to go on beating, and any person who silences it should be held accountable to the law.

Dream Turned Nightmare*
Shelley Schnathorst

This speech was delivered in the final round of the 113th annual contest of the Interstate Oratorical Association; Denver, Colorado, May 2–3, 1986. Shelley Schnathorst, then a student at the University of Northern Iowa coached by Mary Ann Renz, placed second with this speech. We chose it for your study because we think it is an excellent model of using evidence to support ideas, appropriate citation of a variety of credible sources, and clear organization in a problem-solving sequence.

Last fall, I had one of the most frightening experiences of my life. I wear soft contact lenses, and for some reason, my right lens began to irritate me. I blinked quickly and out popped half my contact lens. My contact had torn in two. The other half was still inside my eye, stuck to my eyeball. Everytime I blinked, it scratched. Luckily, my pain ended when I was finally able to remove the remaining portion of the contact. Other contact wearers aren't so lucky. They may be on their way to an even more frightening experience. They are the wearers of extended-wear contact lenses.

*Reprinted with permission from *Winning Orations, 1986*; Larry G. Schnoor, executive secretary; Interstate Oratorical Association; Department of Speech Communication; Mankato State University; Mankato, MN 56001.

In 1981, the Food and Drug Administration (or FDA) approved a lens which could be left in for longer and longer periods of time, called extended-wear lenses. Perhaps you have considered purchasing such a lens. Since *Consumer's Research* magazine noted in April of 1982 that one of every two Americans wears a corrective lens of some type, the chance is good that choosing a lens is a decision you have already faced or will face as your eyes change with age. According to the November 8, 1985, *Wall Street Journal*, over the past two years the sale of extended-wear contact lenses has grown faster than any other type of lens. About five million Americans wear these lenses. But just recently it has become apparent that these millions may be endangering the eyesight they had once hoped to improve.

To understand the problems they face, let's consider the construction of the lens, the problems it creates, and why these dangers continue. Then we will know how you and I can better protect our own vision and the vision of those we care about.

Extended-wear contacts are constructed from a specially developed plastic polymer that's strong enough to be shaped into a very thin lens about four hundredths of a millimeter thick. As with both hard and soft lenses, the extended-wear lenses are placed over the cornea. Dr. Jim Flaugher, a member of my state's optometric association, explained to me that the extended-wear lens contains a much higher water percentage, about 50–70%, whereas regular soft contact lenses contain about half that much. Since water carries oxygen, this characteristic is intended to allow oxygen to pass through the lens. As the Scripps Howard News Service tells us in October, 1985, the FDA approved 12 different lenses put out by 10 manufacturers for continuous, day and night wear up to 30 days at a time. Sounds like an answer to a contact wearer's dream, right? Wrong.

For some responsible and perhaps lucky people, these lenses pose no problems. But they can endanger the eyes in three ways. First, because of the high water content, the lenses tend to absorb the cleaning solution and release it into the eye, causing irritation. This irritation can lead to allergic reactions and possibly infections. And infections can be caused in a second way. Even if a lens is cleaned properly, it is inevitable that small particles will be left on the lens, trapped between the lens and the cornea. While the wearers are complacent, reassured by the FDA that their contacts are safe for 30-day wear, the bacteria are festering. According to Dr. Flaugher, the most serious type of infection can develop within 24 to 48 hours and can cause permanent vision loss within that time. The Madison *Capital Times*, on October 3rd, noted that the latest independent research indicates that anywhere from 3,000 to 6,000 wearers will suffer from these types of infections. *Time* magazine of January 27, 1986, writes that within two days after 30-year-old Carol MeElzer of LaGrange, Illinois, was bothered by her extended wear lenses, the infection they had caused scarred her cornea so badly that "she was virtually blind in her right eye."

The third problem is even worse. Wearing these contacts overnight for days at a time is extremely risky. Researchers have found that not nearly enough oxygen gets through to keep the cornea healthy when worn during sleep. Other parts of our bodies get oxygen through blood vessels. A normal cornea has no blood vessels and therefore relies on exposure to air. When a cornea is deprived of oxygen because the lenses are being worn day and night, the eye will compensate by forming new blood vessels, compromising the clarity of the cornea. In other cases, as the *Wall Street Journal* explains, when the surface of the cornea is deprived of oxygen, scraped or scarred, bacteria and pus pockets or corneal ulcers will form. If perforated, partial or total vision loss will occur. Dr. Frederick Brightball, a Clinical Professor at the University of Wisconsin Department of Ophthamology and Medical Director of the Wisconsin Eye Bank, has treated 20 to 25 cases of infected ulcers over the past two years which he attributes to extended-wear lenses. He states that corneal ulcers from extended-wear lenses have become "almost an epidemic on a national basis." And so the contact wearer's dream becomes a true nightmare—a nightmare from which not one of the five million people with extended-wear lenses is immune.

But why are these dangers allowed to continue? There are two basic answers. Dr. William Platt, President of the Contact Lens Manufacturers Association, is critical of the way extended-wear lenses are marketed. Many optical discount stores are simply businesses which use extended-wear lenses as a commodity—like a can of beans—to make a profit. Recently, some ophthamologists have begun to refuse to prescribe extended-wear lenses, but they are still available in discount stores. For example, we could go to an optical discount store or a hardware store—Sears Roebuck or Montgomery Wards—and pick up a pair of extended-wear lenses. Dr. Michael Lemp, Chairman of Ophthamology at Georgetown University, acknowledges that such high-volume, low-chair-time operations account for a significant percentage of the problem. While such a store may train clerks to carefully fit customers, they have not provided them with the professional judgment regarding the needs of patients months after the initial fitting. And we, lured by the promise of extended-wear and low-cost contacts, may be fitted by a store clerk with no optical license who may feel no obligation to warn us of the dangers of extended-wear lenses. When I called Sears, I was told that the qualifications of the person who would fit me with extended-wear lenses depended upon who was working that day. A scary thought, isn't it?

Perhaps even scarier is the fact that while we may learn from our sad experience, others can't learn from our mistake because doctors are not required to report injuries to the lens manufacturers. The Scripps Howard News Service in October, 1985, reported that manufacturers are required to report injuries caused by approved products. Doctors are encouraged, but not required, to report injuries to either the lens manufacturers or the FDA; apparently few have. Dr. William Platt of the Contact Lens Manufacturers Association was unaware of any cases of permanent vision loss from extended-wear lenses until contacted by a reporter from the *Capital Times* in Madison, Wisconsin. Dr. Platt says, "I started looking into it since I agree—it's a major problem . . . not a minor problem. . . . It's huge." Some of the ophthamologists, eye clinics, and hospitals he has contacted each have reported 20 to 30 cases of lens wearers who have suffered from corneal damage that was not reversible . . . except with a corneal transplant.

We must act now before this nightmare becomes a reality for even more people. First, we need to mandate that doctors report injuries from extended-wear lenses directly to the FDA. This will insure that others won't have to learn from their own mistakes. Second, we should adopt stricter rules on the dispensing of such a lens, including the licensing of optical store employees, mandatory follow-up care, and careful warnings to the public about possible complications. Wisconsin has already taken the lead in this area. Just two months after the *Capital Times* published a series of articles on the dangers of extended-wear lenses, Wisconsin adopted an emergency rule that requires all Wisconsin optometrists to warn buyers that extended-wear lenses can cause permanent eye damage. For any of us who live in other states, we can pressure the Department of Regulations and Licensing in our own state to adopt similar rulings. But we must not rely entirely upon investigative journalists or changing government regulations, but instead take this matter into our own hands. For any of us who do wear contact lenses, or our friends or relatives who do, it is our responsibility to request information about potential dangers, clean lenses properly, and wear them for only limited periods of time. At the first sign of trouble, we should remove our lenses and contact our doctor immediately. Red, uncomfortable eyes and blurred vision are not signs of adjustment, but rather warning signals that something is wrong. In the end, it is our responsibility to have our eyes cared for by a licensed ophthamologist or optometrist.

Because of my experiences, I know I would never do anything else. Like you, I am aware of the value of vision. I can never conceive of anyone endangering his or her own vision through simple carelessness. By improving the reporting regulations, dispensing standards, and our own behavior, we can better protect the vision of those who choose to wear extended-wear lenses. In our quest for convenience and comfort, we shouldn't have to sacrifice vision, for as Shakespeare wrote: "He that is strucketh blind can not forget the previous treasure of his eyesight lost."

I Have a Dream*
Martin Luther King, Jr.

Martin Luther King, Jr., was the universally acknowledged leader and spokesman of the civil rights movement in America in August 1963 when he made this speech from the steps of the Lincoln Memorial in Washington, D.C. He had founded and was leader of the Southern Christian Leadership Conference, which had organized the March on Washington to promote the civil rights of black Americans. In another year Dr. King would be awarded the Nobel Peace Prize for his emphasis on nonviolence while actively campaigning for equal rights for all American citizens. Even though he spoke forcefully about the

*Reprinted by permission of Joan Daves Agency. Copyright © 1963 by Martin Luther King, Jr.

shameful violation of the civil rights of black citizens, he appealed for under-standing and even love of their oppressors.

The audience, estimated to be well over 200,000, had assembled as part of the "People's March" on Washington in front of the Lincoln Memorial. Within this audience were both black and white supporters of the civil rights movement. Many were from the South, although civil rights activists from every part of the nation were present. Millions of other people heard the speech on television, among whom were racists, people who were uncertain of how they felt about the effort to win full citizenship for Negroes, and militant blacks who were already speaking out against Dr. King for being too patient and too pacifist. Leaders like Malcolm X and Stokley Carmichael were already speaking about a more violent route to freedom for blacks. Their followers were part of Dr. King's larger audience. As you read, notice what King did to adapt to these audiences.

We think the style of Dr. King's language merits your special attention. Notice how it is both clear and stylized, simple yet ornate. King chose words so that people with all levels of education and from all walks of life could understand and remember his major theme. As you read the speech, keep in mind that Dr. King was a fourth-generation Baptist minister whose listeners were mostly familiar with the language of the King James translation of the Bible. Notice his use of striking imagery, metaphors, figurative analogies, vivid contrasts, repetition and refrains, and varied sentence structures.

Credibility, reasoning, and emotional force were combined well in this address. Notice the motives to which King appeals and how he made those appeals. His arguments are mostly based on ideas on which the United States was founded, ideas with which most Americans (then and now) say they agree.

The organization, too, is worthy of study. Do you think he followed the motivated sequence when planning this speech? In typical King fashion he built to an emotional crescendo in the conclusion.

Since the March on Washington, uncountable people have heard and seen recordings of "I Have a Dream." This speech is now a classic of American public address. If you have not heard a recording of this address, we urge you to do so. Dr. King's voice added greatly to the power of his speech.

▶ I am happy to join with you today in what will go down in history as the greatest demonstration for freedom in the history of our nation.

Five score years ago, a great American, in whose symbolic shadow we stand today, signed the Emancipation Proclamation. This momentous decree came as a great beacon light of hope to millions of Negro slaves, who had been seared in the flames of withering injustice. It came as a joyous daybreak to end the long night of their captivity.

But one hundred years later, the Negro is still not free. One hundred years later, the life of the Negro is still sadly crippled by the manacles of segregation and the chains of discrimination. One hundred years later, the Negro lives on a lonely island of poverty in the midst of a vast ocean of material prosperity. One hundred years later, the Negro is still languished in the corners of American society and finds himself an exile in his own land. So we have come here today to dramatize a shameful condition.

In a sense we've come to our nation's Capital to cash a check. When the architects of our republic wrote the magnificent words of the Constitution and the Declaration of Independence, they were signing a promissory note to which every American was to fall heir. This note was a promise that all men—yes, black men as well as white men—would be guaranteed the unalienable rights of life, liberty, and the pursuit of happiness.

It is obvious today that America has defaulted on this promissory note insofar as her citizens of color are concerned. Instead of honoring this sacred obligation, America has given the Negro people a bad check; a check which has come back marked "insufficient funds." But we refuse to believe that the bank of justice is bankrupt. We refuse to believe that there are insufficient funds in the great vaults of opportunity of this nation. So we've come to cash this check—a check that will give us upon demand the riches of freedom and the security of justice. We have also come to this hallowed spot to remind America of the fierce urgency of *now*. This is no time to engage in the luxury of cooling off or to take the tranquilizing drug of gradualism. *Now is the time* to make real the promises of Democracy. *Now is the time* to rise from the dark and desolate valley of segregation to the sunlight of racial justice. *Now is the time* to lift our nation from the quicksands of racial injustice to the solid rock of brotherhood. *Now is the time* to make justice a reality for all of God's children.

It would be fatal for the nation to overlook the urgency of the moment. This sweltering summer of the Negro's legitimate discontent will not pass until there is an invigorating autumn of freedom and equality. Nineteen sixty-three is not an end, but a beginning. Those who hope that the Negro needed to blow off steam and will now be content will have a rude awakening if the nation returns to business as usual. There will be neither rest nor tranquility in America until the Negro is granted his citizenship rights. The whirlwinds of revolt will continue to shake the foundations of our nation until the bright day of justice emerges.

But there is something that I must say to my people who stand on the warm threshold which leads into the palace of justice. In the process of gaining our rightful place we must not be guilty of wrongful deeds. Let us not seek to satisfy our thirst for freedom by drinking from the cup of bitterness and hatred.

We must forever conduct our struggle on the high plane of dignity and discipline. We must not allow our creative protest to degenerate into physical violence. Again and again we must rise to the majestic heights of meeting physical force with soul force. The marvelous new militancy which has engulfed the Negro community must not lead us to distrust of all white people, for many of our white brothers, as evidenced by their presence here today, have come to realize that their destiny is tied up with our destiny. And they have come to realize that their freedom is inextricably bound to our freedom. We cannot walk alone.

And as we walk, we must make the pledge that we shall always march ahead. We cannot turn back. There are those who ask the devotees of civil rights, "When will you be satisfied?" We can never be satisfied as long as the Negro is the victim of the unspeakable horrors of police brutality. We can never be satisfied as long as our bodies, heavy with the fatigue of travel, cannot gain lodging in the motels of the highways and the hotels of the cities. We cannot be satisfied as long as the Negro's basic mobility is from a smaller ghetto to a larger one. We can never be satisfied as long as our children are stripped of their selfhood and robbed of their dignity by signs stating "For Whites Only." We cannot be satisfied as long as a Negro in Mississippi cannot vote and a Negro in New York believes he has nothing for which to vote. No, no, we are not satisfied, and we will not be satisfied until justice rolls down like waters and righteousness like a mighty stream.

I am not unmindful that some of you have come here out of great trials and tribulations. Some of you have come fresh from narrow jail cells. Some of you have come from areas where your quest for freedom left you battered by the storms of persecution and staggered by the winds of police brutality. You have been the veterans of creative suffering. Continue to work with the faith that unearned suffering is redemptive.

Go back to Mississippi, go back to Alabama, go back to South Carolina, go back to Georgia, go back to Louisiana, go back to the slums and ghettos of our northern cities knowing that somehow this situation can and will be changed. Let us not wallow in the valley of despair.

I say to you today, my friends, so even though we face the difficulties of today and tomorrow, I still have a dream. It is a dream deeply rooted in the American dream.

I have a dream that one day this nation will rise up and live out the true meaning of its creed: "We hold these truths to be self-evident; that all men are created equal."

I have a dream that one day on the red hills of Georgia the sons of former slaves and the sons of former slaveowners will be able to sit down together at the table of brotherhood; I have a dream—

That one day even the state of Mississippi, a state sweltering with the heat of injustice, sweltering with the heat of oppression, will be transformed into an oasis of freedom and justice; I have a dream—

That my four little children will one day live in a nation where they will not be judged by the color of their skin but by the content of their character; I have a dream today.

I have a dream that one day down in Alabama, with its vicious racists, with its governor having his lips dripping with the words of interposition and nullification, one day right there in Alabama little black boys and black girls will be able to join hands with little white boys and white girls as sisters and brothers; I have a dream today.

I have a dream that one day every valley shall be exalted, every hill and mountain shall be made low, and rough places will be made plane and crooked places will be made straight, and the glory of the Lord shall be revealed, and all flesh shall see it together.

This is our hope. This is the faith that I go back to the South with. With this faith we will be able to hew out of the mountain of despair a stone of hope. With this faith we will be able to transform the jangling discords of our nation into a beautiful symphony of brotherhood. With this faith we will be able to work together, to pray together, to struggle together, to go to jail together, to stand up for freedom together, knowing that we will be free one day.

This will be the day—this will be the day when all of God's children will be able to sing with new meaning "My country 'tis of thee, sweet land of liberty, of thee I sing. Land where my fathers died, land of the pilgrim's pride, from every mountainside, let freedom ring." And if America is to be a great nation, this must become true.

So let freedom ring from the prodigious hilltops of New Hampshire. Let freedom ring from the mighty mountains of New York. Let freedom ring from the heightening Alleghenies of Pennsylvania!

Let freedom ring from the snowcapped Rockies of Colorado!

Let freedom ring from the curvaceous slopes of California!

But not only that; let freedom ring from Stone Mountain of Georgia!

Let freedom ring from Lookout Mountain of Tennessee!

Let freedom ring from every hill and mole hill of Mississippi. From every mountainside let freedom ring.

And when this happens, when we allow freedom to ring—when we let it ring from every village and every hamlet, from every state and every city—we will be able to speed up that day when all of God's children, black men and white men, Jews and Gentiles, Protestants and Catholics, will be able to join hands and sing in the words of the old Negro spiritual, "Free at last! free at last! thank God almighty, we are free at last!"

Choices and Change: Your Success as a Family*
Barbara Bush

Speeches are a part of many special events. A speech is usually a part of a ceremony with which we are all familiar, the commencement. The address that follows was presented by First Lady Barbara Bush during the graduation ceremonies at Wellesley College on June 1, 1990. We chose this speech for inclusion here because we think it is a classic example of a commencement speech and because of the excellent adaptation Mrs. Bush made to the controversy surrounding the occasion. Her selection as commencement speaker had been openly opposed by many Wellesley students who thought she was an inappropriate role model. Her prominence had not come from accomplishments in a career field, but from her marriage to President George Bush. Feminists protested strongly that a woman who was only a mother and wife should not be honored as their commencement speaker. Mrs. Bush faced the difficult task of adapting to overt hostility from many audience members. We think she did so admirably, with good humor and humility. Tom Brokaw, NBC

*From *Vital Speeches of the Day* 55(18) (July 1, 1990); 549. Reprinted by special permission of *Vital Speeches of the Day*.

anchor, commented at the conclusion of her speech, "It is one of the best commencement speeches I've ever heard."

▶ Thank you. President Keohane, Mrs. Gorbachev, trustees, faculty, parents, Julie Porer, Christine Bicknell and the Class of 1990. I am thrilled to be with you today, and very excited, as I know you must all be, that Mrs. Gorbachev could join us.

More than ten years ago when I was invited here to talk about our experiences in the People's Republic of China, I was struck by both the natural beauty of your campus and the spirit of this place.

Wellesley, you see, is not just a place, but an idea, an experiment in excellence in which diversity is not just tolerated, but is embraced.

The essence of this spirit was captured in a moving speech about tolerance given last year by the student body president of one of your sister colleges. She related the story by Robert Fulghum about a young pastor who, finding himself in charge of some very energetic children, hit upon a game called "Giants, Wizards and Dwarfs." "You have to decide now," the pastor instructed the children, "Which you are . . . a giant, a wizard or a dwarf?" At that, a small girl tugging on his pants leg, asked, "But where do the mermaids stand?"

The pastor told her there are *no* mermaids. "Oh yes there are," she said. "I am a mermaid."

This little girl knew what she was and she was not about to give up on either her identity *or* the game. She intended to take her place wherever mermaids fit into the scheme of things. Where *do* the mermaids stand . . . all those who are different, those who do not fit the boxes and pigeonholes? "Answer that question," wrote Fulghum, "And you can build a school, a nation, or a whole world on it."

As that very wise young woman said . . . "Diversity, like anything worth having, requires *effort*." Effort to learn about and respect difference, to be compassionate with one another, and to cherish our own identity, and to accept unconditionally the same in all others.

You should all be very proud that this is the Wellesley spirit. Now I know your first choice for today was Alice Walker, known for *The Color Purple*. Instead you got me—known for the color of my hair! Of course, Alice Walker's book has a special resonance here. At Wellesley, each class is known by a special color, and for four years the class of '90 has worn the color purple. Today you meet on Severance Green to say goodbye to all that, to begin a new and very personal journey, a search for your own true colors.

In the world that awaits you beyond the shores of Lake Waban, no one can say what your true colors will be. But this I know: You have a first class education from a first class school. And so you need not, probably cannot, live a "paint-by-numbers" life. Decisions are not irrevocable. Choices do come back. As you set off from Wellesley, I hope that many of you will consider making three very special choices.

The first is to believe in something larger than yourself, to get involved in some of the big ideas of your time. I chose literacy because I honestly believe that if more people could read, write and comprehend, we would be that much closer to solving so many of the problems plaguing our society.

Early on I made another choice which I hope you will make as well. Whether you are talking about education, career or service, you are talking about life, and life must have joy. It's supposed to be fun!

One of the reasons I made the most important decision of my life, to marry George Bush, is because he made me laugh. It's true, sometimes we've laughed through our tears, but that shared laughter has been one of our strongest bonds. Find the joy in life, because as Ferris Bueller said on his day off

> Life moves pretty fast. Ya don't stop and look around once in a while, ya gonna miss it!

The third choice that must not be missed is to cherish your human connections: your relationships with friends and family. For several years, you've had impressed upon you the importance to your career of dedication and hard work. This is true, but as important as your obligations as a doctor, lawyer or business leader will be, you are a human being first and those human connections, with spouses, with children, with friends, are the most important investments you will ever make.

At the end of your life, you will never regret not having passed one more test, not winning one more verdict or not closing one more deal. You will regret time not spent with husband, a friend, a child or a parent.

We are in a transitional period right now, fascinating and exhilarating times, learning to adjust to the changes and the choices we, men and women, are facing. I remember what a friend said, on hearing her husband lament to his buddies that he had to babysit. Quickly setting him straight, my friend told her husband that when it's your own kids, it's not called babysitting!

Maybe we should adjust faster, maybe slower. But whatever the era, whatever the times, one thing will never change: fathers and mothers, if you have children, they must come first. Your success as a family, our success as a society, depends *not* on what happens at the White House, but on what happens inside your house.

For over 50 years, it was said that the winner of Wellesley's annual hoop race would be the first to get married. Now they say the winner will be the first to become a C.E.O. Both of these stereotypes show too little tolerance for those who want to know where the mermaids stand. So I offer you today a new legend: the winner of the hoop race will be the first to realize her dream, not society's dream, her personal dream. And who knows? Somewhere out in this audience may even be someone who will one day follow in my footsteps, and preside over the White House as the president's spouse. I wish him well!

The controversy ends here. But our conversation is only beginning. And a worthwhile conversation it is. So as you leave Wellesley today, take with you deep thanks for the courtesy and honor you have shared with Mrs. Gorbachev and me. Thank you. God bless you. And may your future be worthy of your dreams.

GLOSSARY

acquired credibility See *credibility*.

acronym A word formed from the first letters of a series of words that represent a sequence of main points, steps in a procedure, or a name that has several words, e.g., NATO (North Atlantic Treaty Organization).

acrostic A sentence in which the first letter of each word represents an item of information to be remembered. The sentence "Men very easily make jugs serve useful nocturnal purposes" helps recall the planets in order from the sun (*Mercury, Venus, Earth, Mars, Jupiter, Saturn, Uranus, Neptune,* and *Pluto*).

active listening Conscious effort by one person to comprehend another's message(s) as intended by that person, often involving a paraphrase of the other's ideas to determine how well the listener has understood.

adaptation Adjustment to a characteristic of listeners or speaking situation; adaptations are based on analysis of the thing(s) to which they are made.

alliteration A series of words beginning with the same sound, e.g., petty partisan politics.

alphanumeric Using both alphabetical and numerical symbols.

analogous reasoning A point-by-point comparison in which two similar situations are compared followed by a claim that what happened in one situation is likely to happen in another.

analogy A complex comparison in which several features of two or more things, situations, or other phenomena are compared.

anecdote A humorous imaginative story which uses comparisons to dramatize or clarify abstract ideas.

antithesis A sentence containing two contrary ideas that are presented in parallel, balanced phrasing, e.g., "Ask not what your country can do for you, but what you can do for your country."

argument A coherent series of reasons, statements, or facts intended to support or establish a particular view. A valid argument consists of evidence (*data*), a demonstrated or accepted connection between the evidence and the conclusion you want to draw (*warrant*), and the conclusion itself (*claim*).

argumentation Discussion involving the evaluation of reasoning and ideas by tests of evidence, standards of logic, and group judgment.

articulation   Production of the sounds of which words are formed by combining movements of tongue, teeth, lips, and other organs modifying the breath stream.

attention   Awareness focused on selected signals during which other signals being received are perceived only marginally, if at all, and not decoded nor responded to.

attitude   A general and enduring tendency to act in a positive or negative way toward some person, object, or issue or class of people, objects, or issues.

audience   A collection of people present during a public-speaking event who are potentially listeners and responders to the speaker. **voluntary**   People who have chosen to listen to a particular speaker or topic. **captive**   People who did not primarily assemble to listen to a particular speaker or topic.

audience analysis   Gathering and interpreting factual data about a prospective audience so that adaptations can be made while preparing to speak that will increase the probability of securing the desired response from listeners.

balance theory   A theory that argues that people seek a sense of balance or harmony among ideas and personal relationships. A speaker can persuade listeners by creating a sense of psychological imbalance among ideas and relationships and suggesting ways to restore balance. See *cognitive consistency*.

bar graph   A chart containing two or more bars of uniform width, but varying length proportionate to the size of numbers that the bars represent; it is used to represent the relative size of two or more comparable statistics.

behavioral objective   See *desired response*.

bibliography   A list of sources relevant to a particular subject from which a speaker or writer develops a general background of knowledge as well as specific references.

body of a speech   The central portion of a speech in which the central idea is analyzed and developed to make it clear and/or convincing to listeners.

brief example   An example which is named but not described in detail. See *example*.

briefing   A concise summary of an extensive body of information presented by a specialist for the benefit of listeners who need the information but lack time and/ or resources to acquire the information firsthand themselves.

bypassing   A misunderstanding resulting when two or more persons do not realize they have significantly different referents for the same symbols or are referring to the same referent with different symbols.

captive audience   See *audience*.

card catalog   A catalog on alphabetized file cards including all books held in a library; each book is listed by author name, subject heading, and title.

causal   Name of a schema of main points in the body of a speech emphasizing a cause–effect relationship among these points.

causal reasoning   One event (A) is the cause of another (B), if B always follows A and B never occurs unless A precedes it; claim that one event is the cause of or is caused by other event(s).

central idea   A declarative sentence that expresses the thesis, theme, or proposition of a unified speech; this sentence contains a subject (topic) and predicate affirming some generalization about the subject.

ceremonial speech A public speech for which the primary purpose is to reaffirm values or beliefs important to the organization or society conducting the ceremony.

channel Any medium in which signals are carried, such as air, light, and sound waves.

chronological A schema for main points in the body of a speech emphasizing a time relationship among the points, usually from first to last.

circle graph A sensory aid used to illustrate relative sizes of parts to each other and to the whole that they collectively form by dividing a circle into wedges with proportionate sizes.

claim A conclusion or interpretation of data. See also *argument*.

closure Remarks made by a speaker in the conclusion of a speech which provides listeners with a sense of completion.

clutter Unnecessary words that add little or nothing to the meaning evoked by a sentence, statement, or speech.

code A set of symbols and signs that make up the vocabulary of a language, dialect, or person.

cognitive consistency and **cognitive dissonance** *Cognitive consistency* refers to self-perceived agreement among beliefs and actions resulting in a state of ease or peace, opposite of the state of **cognitive dissonance,** which is characterized by the mental pain of being aware that one's beliefs and/or actions are not consistent with each other.

communication A process involving at a minimum the response of a person to perceived signals.

communication ethics The choices individuals make about what they ought to do when communicating with others in relation to values such as "justice," "goodness," and "truthfulness."

comparison To examine the relationship between persons, ideas, or things in order to estimate their similarities; developmental material used to explain a concept by reference to similar and familiar concepts.

competence Listener perceptions of a public speaker's expertise in relation to the subject matter of the speech.

conclusion of a speech Final remarks of a public speech designed to reemphasize the central idea and suggest or urge the response to that idea desired by the speaker.

connectives Words, phrases, or longer passages used to link two related ideas or parts of a speech.

connotative meaning Emotional component of a person's response to a symbolic message.

consensus Agreement by all group members that a decision is the best that can be supported by every member of the group; there may or may not be unanimity that this is the best possible decision.

correlation A statistic which indicates the degree to which two sets of measurements or scores are related.

credibility Listener perception of a speaker's degree of competence, trustworthiness, and dynamism. **prior credibility** The perception of a speaker's credibility held by listeners before he or she speaks. **acquired credibility** The perception of a speaker's credibility held by listeners that is a direct result of what a speaker says and does during a speech.

criterion A standard on which a judgment or decision may be based, a yardstick against which possible solutions can be measured.

data Evidence used to support a claim. See also *argument*.

deductive reasoning The process of reasoning from a generalization to a prediction about some specific instance not yet observed or not observable, e.g., reasoning from the general to the specific. Example: All apples have seeds, therefore this apple has seeds.

delivery The totality of verbal and nonverbal signals created by a speaker while communicating with listeners.

demographic data Information describing observable chracteristics of members of an audience, such as age, gender, occupation, education, and ethnic origin.

denotative meaning The referent meaning of the object, concept, idea, and so on referred to by a symbolic message. Denotative meaning is often associated with a dictionary definition.

desired response A declarative sentence describing observable behavior of listeners sought by a public speaker as a response to the speech; this behavior may be potential (latent) or manifest. The practical purpose of public speaking is to obtain such a response, not merely to express something. Synonym: behavioral objective.

developmental materials Materials used by a speaker to illustrate and support ideas (e.g., examples, statistics, testimony, comparisons, and contrasts).

Dewey decimal system The numerical system for classifying all books into nine broad categories that are further subdivided; named for inventor, Melvil Dewey.

dynamism Spontaneous, but controlled enthusiasm indicated by energetic delivery; the perception of speaker charisma.

egocentrism Behavior motivated by one's own apparent best interest; self-centeredness to the extent that one lacks concern for or cares about the needs, concerns, interests, and ideas of other persons.

emotional appeal Attempt to motivate an action or support an argument by arousing an emotion such as fear, love, or hatred.

entertaining speech A public speech for which the primary desired response is one of enjoyment characterized by vicarious sharing in some pleasure of the speaker or laughter.

esteem needs The desire for a stable, firmly based, high evaluation of oneself, e.g., self-respect, self-esteem, and the esteem of others.

ethics See *communication ethics*.

evaluating Making judgments about quality or merit of something; when listening, evaluating involves judging the merit of information and ideas of a speaker.

evidence Information used to support a claim (e.g., testimony, examples, comparisons, and statistics).

example A particular single item, fact, incident, or aspect that is typical or representative of a group or type.

extemporaneous speaking Speaking based on thorough analysis and planning (preparation outline), but without writing and reading or memorizing a manuscript.

extended example   An example which includes detailed description; a story used to evoke a particularly vivid image in the minds of listeners, evoke feelings, or dramatize an idea. See *example*.

eye contact   The use of vision to establish a relationship with listeners and to monitor their nonverbal response signals to a message.

fable   An imaginative story with a moral or point about human behavior involving miraculous powers or acts by animals (e.g., the fable of the tortoise and the hare).

feedback   Response signals and the process by which a speaker adjusts to such signals.

fixed-answer question   A question accompanied by two or more possible answers, asking the respondent to indicate one as his or her answer to the question, e.g., a multiple-choice question on a test.

flip chart   Several visuals, usually drawn and written on posterboard or paper, fastened together along the upper edge so that they can be flipped over like pages in a book without getting out of sequence as a speaker progresses from one to another during a presentation.

functional codes   Words and signs that a person can actually employ while communicating; speaking, listening, and reading codes are progressively larger, including more words.

General Procedural Model for Problem Solving (GPMPS)   A five-step procedural model for problem solving by individuals or groups based on scientific method that is sufficiently flexible to allow adaptations to any problem situation.

general purpose   The type of primary objective sought by a public speaker. Primary objectives include to inform, to persuade, to entertain, and to commemorate.

gesture   A movement of the body used to express and reinforce ideas.

grammar   Rules for using code units of language.

hearing   Mechanical reception of air waves by the ear and their conversion into signals in the auditory nerve.

hypothetical example   An example which contains details of typical or actual cases even though it is not a report of an actual event. See *example*.

idea   A thought or mental conception.

illustrate   To make clear or easily understood.

imagery   Descriptions using relatively concrete words that evoke vicarious sensations from listeners.

impromptu   Speaking without specific advance planning or on the spur of the moment in response to some unanticipated message or messages.

inductive reasoning   The process of reasoning from specific data to reach a generalization about some class of phenomena; reasoning from the specific to the general. (E.g., The last six apples I have eaten each had seeds; therefore, apples have seeds.)

information overload   A state of feeling overwhelmed and confused by the vast amount of signals/information being received.

informative speech   A public speech for which the central idea is generally accepted as true by persons knowledgeable about the topic; desired response behaviors would be described with active verbs such as be able to: build, list, name, describe, and identify.

inoculation theory   A theory for structuring arguments based on the assumption that people exposed to a weakened version of possible counterarguments will become more resistant to any such counterarguments.

instructing   Any effort by one individual to inform other people how to perform some task (whether mental, physical, or both) or explain some concept, phenomenon, process, relationship, and so on.

interdependent goal   Members of a group needing each other to accomplish some objective all perceive to be worthwhile.

internal preview   A sentence(s) which forecasts the subpoints under a new main point.

internal summary   A sentence(s) which restates a main point with a review of its subpoints before proceeding to a new point.

introduction   The opening remarks of a public speech designed to direct attention of listeners to the topic of the speech, interest listeners in the topic, establish trust in the speaker as a source of information on the topic, and focus attention on the sequence of ideas or issues in the speech.

landmark   A device used to help listeners recall specific details associated with main points and to create a pattern among the main points in a speech so they fit together as a psychological whole.

language   A socially created symbolic system for communication, including code units, rules for using code units, and a structure of assumptions about the nature of the world.

leadership   Member behaviors that help a group coordinate all member action toward clarification and achievement of an interdependent goal, such as helping to keep discussion organized, arranging for meetings, and following up on decisions with reports to the larger organization of which the small group is a part; special responsibility of an elected or appointed person designated as leader.

Library of Congress classification system (LC)   The alphanumeric scheme for classifying books into 21 broad subject categories developed by the Library of Congress.

line graph   A line formed by a series of points representing changing magnitudes of two numerical characteristics that vary together, such as height and weight or year and amount of exports in dollars; most often used to portray statistical trends through time or in relationship to each other.

listener   A person in an audience who is both receiving and responding to signals of a speaker.

listening   Sensing, interpreting, evaluating, and responding to auditory signals (messages) from one person to other(s).

main point   A point that is directly related to the central idea of a speech. A speech is usually divided into several main points which develop the speaker's central idea.

meaning   The total response or reaction of a person to a message, including symbols such as words, logos, phrases, and statements.

message   Any set of signals; the meaning given signals by a speaker or listener.

metaphor   A comparison in which the speaker calls something by the name of the item to which it is being compared (e.g., "My new car is a lemon").

mnemonic   A device or technique for assisting memory, such as a rhyme scheme or acronym.

motivated sequence A schema for organizing a persuasive speech that has as its desired response some specific action from listeners. Associated with Alan H. Monroe, the motivated sequence places emphasis on motivating just before the final appeal.

motive Inner drive or need that causes people to do something or act in a certain way.

noise Any signals that interfere with signals intentionally created by a speaker to evoke a desired listener response.

norm A rule that governs the behaviors of members in a particular group.

on-line data base A computerized index or set of indexes to works in print dealing with some broad category of interest during a defined period of time (e.g., medicine, psychology, or management). Topic headings are used to generate bibliographic (and in some cases reprints) from such data bases.

open-ended question A question about a topic or issue not accompanied by or suggesting any specific answer (e.g., "What do you like most about public speaking?")

parable An imaginative story with a moral or point which involves human actors.

parallel sentences Two or more sentences which are written in the same stylistic format.

paralinguistics Signals other than words produced while speaking (e.g., rate, pitch, tone, articulation, pronunciation, and volume).

paraphrase The restatement of another's point in one's own words, rather than the exact words of the original speaker.

passive listening Listening during which the listener is mentally and/or physically inactive.

periodical A publication issued at regular intervals of less than a year but more than one day, including general interest magazines, trade journals, and scholarly journals.

persuasion A conscious attempt by a speaker to influence the beliefs, attitudes, or actions of receivers that produces some specific desired response.

persuasive speech A public speech for which the desired response is some change in degree of agreement or action relative to a belief on which the listener has failed to act.

physiological needs The most basic needs necessary for human survival (e.g., food, water, air, and shelter). Physical needs are considered the lowest level of human needs in Abraham Maslow's hierarchy of needs.

pie chart See *circle graph*.

pitch That quality of a tone or sound determined by the frequency of vibration of the sound waves reaching the ear; the highness or lowness of a speaker's voice.

preparation outline A detailed outline of a public speech which includes: title, central idea statement, desired response statement, introduction, body, conclusion, and reference list.

preview summary A sentence or sentences in the introduction of a speech which forecasts the main points contained in the body.

primacy–recency principle A principle for organizing a speech based on the fact that listeners remember best the first and last of a series of words, topics, or items.

prior credibility See *credibility*.

problem Difference between an existing unsatisfactory situation and a desired condition (goal), including some causes and/or obstacles to change.

process Ongoing, interactive exchange among parts of a system in a specific situation.

pronunciation The act or manner of pronouncing words with reference to the production of sounds, the placing of stress, and intonation in an acceptable or standard manner.

pseudolistening Feigning attention to another's message in order to appear socially acceptable or be liked.

public speaking A social event in which a person (speaker) encodes in oral verbal symbols, usually in relatively continuous discourse, in order to produce perceptions, beliefs, and actions that are new to other persons involved (listeners). Most public speaking is face-to-face (though it may be electronically mediated) to an audience from a few to a very large number of listeners.

questionnaire A set of preplanned questions the answers to which are needed for understanding the knowledge, beliefs, and practices of respondents; may be administered either in writing or orally (interview).

rate The number of words per minute (wpm) and variations in the time allotted to speech sounds and silences (pauses).

reasons why schema A schema for organizing a persuasive speech based on providing the reasons why listeners should change their beliefs, attitudes, or actions.

rehearsal/delivery outline A brief outline of phrases and single words to represent main points and subpoints used during rehearsal and delivery of a public speech.

reporting A detailed description of an investigation and its outcome in much greater detail than a briefing and usually of a much narrower problem or subject; a report will usually include descriptions of the problem or issue investigated, procedures of the investigation, findings, and possible courses of action if some problem is involved.

response signal A signal which is a listener's response to a speaker's signal.

rhetoric Principles and techniques of speaking used to evoke specific desired responses from listeners.

rhetorical question A question posed by a speaker to which the speaker neither expects nor wants an overt response.

scale question A question asking respondents to indicate some degree of agreement, importance, or relative frequency of an action by indicating a position on a linear scale.

schema A logically structured sequence for organizing points in a speech (e.g., chronological, spatial, causal, or problem solving).

security needs Need for freedom from threats, violent attacks, or life-threatening events.

self-actualization needs The desire people have for self-discovery and development. Self-actualization needs are considered the highest level of human needs in Abraham Maslow's hierarchy.

sensory aid Any device or activity used by a speaker to present sensory signals to supplement a verbal message.

sign A signal that has a natural relationship as a part or product of whatever it represents to perceivers.

signal A stimulus that is perceivable by a listener.

signposts Words or phrases used to emphasize sentences or call attention to the next statement in a speech.

simile A simple one-point figurative comparison in which the comparison is stated with the word "like," "as," or "resembles" (e.g., "The speaker roared like a lion").

situation The entire context in which a speech event occurs and in which speaker and listeners are involved in the process of communication, including historical context, social context, reasons for assembling, and physical conditions of the immediate setting.

sleeper effect The process whereby a persuasive message may have greater delayed impact than initial impact on a listener's beliefs, attitudes, and actions, such as changing a belief several days after hearing a speech planned to secure that change.

small group Three or more persons (up to 15) who are aware of each other as unique individuals and as members of the same group, have some interdependent goal, and coordinate their efforts toward the accomplishment of that goal by communicating primarily through face-to-face speaking and listening.

social judgment theory A theory which suggests that the greater a person's ego involvement with a position or idea the less likely the person is to be persuaded by new information dissonant with the idea.

social needs The desire to feel a part of a group or to belong (e.g., belongingness, acceptance, and friendship).

social reciprocity A central guideline for ethical public speaking that states that a speaker should treat listeners as he or she would like other speakers to treat him or her.

solution A way of changing an unsatisfactory situation to a satisfactory one.

spatial A schema for organizing points in a speech in which there is a space relationship among the topics.

startling statement A device used to direct listener attention to the topic of a speech in which the speaker uses a statement that startles listeners.

startling statistic A device used to direct listener attention to the topic of a speech in which the speaker uses a statistic or statistics that startle listeners.

statistic A number used to develop or support ideas.

stock issues Three issues or topics which must be dealt with by a speaker advocating a solution or policy: (1) need; (2) a plan to meet the need; and (3) evidence that the plan will be both practical and beneficial.

subpoint A subordinate point which is directly related to and helps develop a main point.

summary A sentence or sentences in the conclusion of a speech in which a speaker reviews the main points in the body of the speech.

survey Tabulated responses by a selected sample of persons to some questionnaire administered in person, by telephone, or in writing, usually reported in statistical terms.

symbol A signal created by humans to represent something with which it has no inherent natural relationship; all words are symbols.

target audience That part of the total audience a speaker has decided it is realistic to attempt to influence through a speech.

testimony The use of opinion(s) as evidence to support an idea. ***Expert testimony*** refers to the opinion(s) of others who are experts on the speaker's topic. ***Personal testimony*** refers to the opinion(s) of a speaker who is an expert on the topic.

tone Changes in sound produced by the level of muscular tension while speaking and the degree to which various cavity resonators influence the sound.

topical A schema for organizing points in a speech in which there is a logical relationship among the topics (e.g., functions, characteristics, components, reasons, or effects).

transaction Ongoing exchange of energy and influence among speaker and listeners; simultaneous interchange with signals flowing in all directions among participants and being responded to on the basis of different perspectives of people involved.

transition A word or phrase used to keep listeners oriented when the speaker shifts from one topic or point to another.

two-sided approach In speaking to persuade, an organizational schema in which a speaker presents an argument(s) in favor of a central idea and refutes an argument(s) which oppose the central idea.

value A belief about the relative worth or quality of some object, individual, issue, concept, event, practice, or other phenomena.

visible signals Signals received by the eyes, including a speaker's personal appearance, bodily activity, facial expression, and eye contact.

visual aid A visible sensory aid such as object, model, chart, illustration, picture, drawing, or demonstration used by a speaker to enhance understanding of a verbal message.

volume The degree of loudness or intensity placed on words.

voluntary audience See *audience*.

warrant The logical connection between data and a claim or conclusion. See also *argument*.

PHOTO CREDITS

Unless otherwise acknowledged, all photographs are the property of Scott, Foresman.

Part I
1 Spencer Grant/Stock Boston.

Chapter 1
3 Lionel Delevingne/Stock Boston. **14** UPI/Bettmann.

Chapter 2
30 The Bettmann Archive. **37** Lionel Delevingne/Stock Boston.

Chapter 3
43 Susan Lapides/Design Conceptions. **54** Bob Daemmrich/The Image Works.

Part II
59 Alan Carey/The Image Works.

Chapter 4
61 Spencer Grant/Stock Boston. **65** Tony Freeman/Photo Edit.

Chapter 5
78 Beringer-Dratch/The Image Works. **80** Joel Gordon Photography.

Chapter 6
101 Ellis Herwig/Stock Boston. **113** Joseph Schuyler/Stock Boston.

Part III
123 Peter Vandermark/Stock Boston.

Chapter 7
125 Joel Gordon Photography.

Chapter 8
146 Joel Gordon Photography.

Chapter 9
164 Joel Gordon Photography. **171** Paul Conklin/Photo Edit.

Chapter 10
183 Bob Daemmrich/The Image Works. **200** Addison Geary/Stock Boston.

Chapter 11
203 Richard Pasley/Stock Boston. **208** Charles Gupton/Stock Boston. **216** Addison Geary/Stock Boston.

Chapter 12
227 Cary Wolinsky/Stock Boston. **231** Susan Lapides/Design Conceptions.

Chapter 13
244 Susan Lapides/Design Conceptions. **254** Bob Daemmrich/Stock Boston. **257** UPI/Bettmann.

Part IV
265 Joel Gordon Photography.

Chapter 14
267 Bob Daemmrich/Stock Boston. **273** Joel Gordon Photography.

Chapter 15
293 Bob Daemmrich/Stock Boston.

Chapter 16
328 Bob Daemmrich/Stock Boston. **331** Spencer Grant/Stock Boston.

Chapter 17
342 Rhoda Sidney/Stock Boston.

Appendix
363 Maurie Rosen/Black Star.

INDEX